Two
Control

HUMANITY'S SOLDIER

Contemporary France
General Editor: Jolyon Howorth, University of Bath

Volume 1
Humanity's Soldier: France and International Security, 1919–2001
David Chuter

Volume 2
The Road to War: France and Vietnam, 1944–1947
Martin Shipway

HUMANITY'S SOLDIER

France and International Security, 1919–2001

David Chuter

Berghahn Books
Providence • Oxford

DC
367
· C4

Published in 1996 by

Berghahn Books
Editorial offices:
165 Taber Avenue, Providence, RI 02906, USA
Bush House, Merewood Avenue, Oxford, OX3 8EF, UK

Library of Congress Cataloging-in-Publication Data
Chuter, David.
Humanity's soldier : France and international security, 1919–2001
/ David Chuter.
p.   cm. -- (Contemporary France : vol. 1.)
Includes bibliographical references and index.
ISBN 1-57181-893-6 (alk. paper)
1. France--Foreign relations--20th century. 2. France--Military
policy. 3. National characteristics, French. 4. Security, International.
5. Symbolism in politics. 6. Gaulle, Charles de, 1890–1970--Influence.
7. Europe--History, Military--20th century. I. Title. II. Series.
DC367.C53   1996
327.44--dc20   96-9584
                                                         CIP

British Library Cataloguing in Publication Data
A CIP catalogue record for this book is available from
the British Library.

Printed in the United States on acid-free paper

This book includes the results of research work carried out by the author as part of his official duties for the Ministry of Defence. The results of his research work are Crown copyright and have been reproduced with the permission of the controller of HMSO. The views expressed are those of the author and do not necessarily represent those of the Ministry of Defence, Her Majesty's Stationery Office or any other government department.

France, once the soldier of God, today the soldier of
Humanity, will always be the soldier of the Ideal.
George Clemenceau, announcing the Armistice
to the French parliament in 1918

The terrible misfortunes which have overwhelmed the
country are not the doing of chance but the result of
errors and mistakes ... it is not too late to attempt to
draw some lessons from the catastrophe of June 1940.
National Assembly Report, 1947

Who controls the past controls the future.
Who controls the present controls the past.
Slogan of the Party in George Orwell's *1984*

CONTENTS

PREFACE

This book is concerned with the historical, cultural and philosophical origins of French security policy as it exists now, and as it has been conceived and implemented since 1919. It explains how and why it has developed since that date, and provides an indication of whether and how it may change in the future. The point of departure is the defeat of 1940 and the many competing analyses of the reasons for it; but the book argues that the ultimate origins of current French policy lie considerably further back.

The book is not, primarily, a narrative history of the period: an attempt to write this would have produced something that was either much too long or hopelessly superficial. Rather, it is concerned with how a variety of themes in security and defence recurred and developed over the years. It demonstrates how French reactions to even quite recent events are heavily influenced by memories of events of the past, including some that are either scarcely known in Anglo-Saxon countries, or else interpreted very differently. It also shows how these reactions and these memories are associated with a whole mass of cultural and philosophical assumptions about the place of France in the world, with the attitudes of other nations and with a rich and varied collection of historical myths, symbolisms and articles of iconography that reach back into the distant past and are still current today.

This study is also written from the perspective of a career civil servant in the Ministry of Defence, who has had a certain amount to do with the French over the years, and played a minor role in some of the episodes towards the end of the book. Indeed, the origin of the book lay in the dissatisfaction I felt with my own ability to understand what the French were up to, and with the limited time that Whitehall had to ponder such problems. I have therefore tried to analyse much of the subject matter of this study from the perspective of a bureaucrat, used to looking for patterns and for the impact of practical politics on strategy and policy. The study sheds some light on the concepts and assumptions that animate French diplomats, civil servants, military officers, academics and even journalists and businessmen in the defence and security area, accepting that many of them are quite different from anything that might be found in Great Britain or the United States.

A book of this sort cannot avoid engaging with the impressive person of Charles de Gaulle, and, indeed, I do try to address the question of whether the security policy pursued by de Gaulle after 1958, and especially after 1966, was an aberration in terms of the objectives of previous governments, or not. My conclusion is that at the level of objectives, rather than tactics, there was little that was new, even although the form of expression changed somewhat. The book tries to put de Gaulle in perspective as a particularly effective exponent of traditional attitudes and aspirations that preceded him, and have survived him also.

This does not mean that de Gaulle's predecessors would have acted exactly as he did, although it does mean that they would have had much the same overall objectives. I will also suggest that the question of NATO integration can too easily become a touchstone: if de Gaulle had believed that he could have accomplished his objectives whilst remaining in the integrated military structure, he would have done so; his successors may do so again. But it is the assumptions and objectives that are important and that are more similar than the tactics actually employed, and I have explored those in this study.

For this reason, I have not limited myself to the 1966 decision, as though that were all there was to French security policy: indeed, that only comes in the last chapter of the book. I have attempted to describe the historical and other factors that brought about the defeat of 1940, and the overthrow of the Fourth Republic in 1958. I have tried to show why and how France accepted the way in which European defence and security was organised after 1945, how dissent rapidly set in, and what successive governments tried to do about it. I also deal with such questions as the organisation in Paris for discussing security questions, the position of the military, the organisation of arms procurement and French attitudes towards such subjects as nuclear policy, the Non-Proliferation Treaty and conventional arms control.

ACKNOWLEDGEMENTS

This book was researched and written during the year that I spent, from April 1993 to April 1994, as a Visiting Research Fellow at the Centre for Defence Studies, King's College, London University. My first and most pleasant duty is to thank the Executive Director of the Centre, Mr (now Professor) Michael Clarke, and his staff for welcoming me so warmly and involving me in all aspects of the Centre's work. The Centre has a very close relationship with the Department of War Studies, and I was also very hospitably received by Professor Lawrence Freedman and his colleagues.

I am especially grateful for the advice and help I have received regarding the subject matter of this book. At King's College, Michael Clarke read the whole of the text with great care and made a number of suggestions for its improvement, while also saving me from various academic solecisms. Professor Freedman kindly read the whole of the text also, and made numerous helpful comments. Dr Beatrice Heuser opened many doors for me, and was a constant source of help and encouragement as the scope of the book threatened to spiral out of control. Dr Brian Holden Reid read Chapters 3 and 4 with care, and saved me from many errors. Professor Jolyon Howorth of the University of Bath happily shared his vast erudition with me, as well as commenting helpfully on many parts of the text. I am grateful to Dr (now Professor) Martin Alexander, then at the University of Southampton, for giving up a whole day to discuss the issues covered in the book. A number of friends and colleagues in Whitehall, in both the Ministry of Defence and the Foreign and Commonwealth Office, also read some or all of the text, and I am grateful for many helpful suggestions. It need hardly be added that the views expressed herein are, nonetheless, entirely my own.

I am also grateful to a number of French scholars who kindly agreed to see me, and provided me with a whole range of useful insights, as well as tolerating my indifferent French: Professor Georges-Henri Soutou, Professor Jean Klein, Professor Samy Cohen, Admiral Marcel Duval, Frédéric Bozo. For the blemishes that remain I am, of course, totally responsible.

Finally, I must thank my family for their forbearance in allowing me to turn two successive houses into rubbish tips of books and papers for the best part of a year, and somehow managing to move house around me in the middle of everything.

INTRODUCTION

Political Truth and Symbolic Politics

This book ranges rather more widely among disciplines, including literature and philosophy, than is common in studies of defence and security. This is partly because – as anyone with experience inside politics and government will have noted – the influences that come to bear on government decision-making and the presentation of policy are by no means limited to official documents and correspondence, valuable (invaluable, indeed), as those may be to the researcher. Ministers, politicians, diplomats, civil servants and the military in every country all carry intellectual baggage of a very varied nature, and are called upon to respond to a public and to a media that often express concerns that have arisen on the basis of an amalgam of memories, prejudices and received wisdom. This amalgam typically consists of a jumble of somewhat simplified history, half-remembered statistics, TV programmes and cinema films, family memories, books read long ago and prejudices so deeply ingrained that the holder takes them to be simple common sense.

Because a government that is consistently ahead of or behind public opinion will face difficulties, there are inevitable practical limits on what governments can do. Very often, these public attitudes are uninformed, but they may be powerfully supported in the media and elsewhere, and they make up a significant part of the unspoken assumptions that experts themselves bring to their work. In the defence and security area, there is, beyond the strategy elaborated by experts, an unofficial meta-strategy elaborated by non-experts; a complex of ideas, memories and associations that sets the boundaries within which a government can work. Often, this meta-strategy is a vulgarised form of the official strategy, although often out of date, and highly schematised. Generally, this meta-strategy is not a coherent whole, or a fully worked-out theory; rather, it is a series of assumptions and judgements, each varying in intensity in different parts of the political spectrum, between them constituting an envelope outside of which governments will feel uncomfortable acting, and will attract general criticism if they do.

This is not intended to sound patronising: all of us tend to think in this way. But this dimension, because it is difficult to grasp properly, sometimes gets less attention than it deserves; which is a shame, because it is an important part of the way in which government operates. It is the more important because, in modern times – and certainly for most of the period covered here – national leaders and the bureaucracies that serve them have been exceptionally busy, and have been concerned mostly with the daily task of survival – rushing from one hole in a dike to another, with little opportunity for long-term thought. Governments wish to survive; they try to do things that are popular, and they try to avoid initiatives that will cause them difficulties with the public, with their parliaments, with the media, with their allies or with other interest groups that need to be appeased. There is often no objectively right answer; but even when there is, political reality can prevent its being implemented.

To take a simple example relevant to this study: in 1934, Lt.-Col. de Gaulle published a book that advocated the formation of a 100,000-strong professional tank force, assuming that only professionals would be able to handle these highly complex machines. The controversy it stirred up was only partly technical, and to criticise the French government and army for not implementing its ideas is to ignore the political and historical memories and prejudices that the idea aroused, and that made its implementation impossible. Many on the Left[1] feared that the proposal was really intended to lead to the formation of units for the repression of the civil population, and even to the organisation of a military coup. Some on the Right were attracted to the proposal precisely because of these possibilities. Each side saw the proposal through a haze of republican or anti-republican fervour, dubious history, political folklore and memories of atrocity and counter-atrocity. A book as

---

1. I have used 'Left' and 'Right' to designate organised political groups or tendencies of thought; otherwise I have used 'left' and 'right'.

long as de Gaulle's own would be required to provide a proper background. Even if de Gaulle's thesis had been right (and events proved it was wrong), and even had the money been available (it was not), there were not remotely enough votes in the National Assembly to implement it.

Governments and officials have to navigate these waters as best they can, often on the basis not of how things are, but how they are believed to be. Things that may appear clear to historians were perhaps not so clear at the time, or if clear, then impossible to take action on. This is not a simple argument against the use of hindsight, but rather a plea that the evaluative and the interpretative be kept apart. Later analysis and better knowledge may demonstrate that, on a particular issue, a government was wrong or misguided to act as it did. But that does not tell us very much. What is more interesting is to try to recapture the atmosphere in which the decision was taken, with all the confusion, ignorance and misunderstanding that might have accompanied it.

Political Truth

It follows that I am not particularly interested in the truth as such. Partly this is because the truth of an issue (the Dreyfus affair, to be returned to below, is an example), may not be particularly important to the contestants. Even if the truth is known, it may not be politically expedient to recognise it: to do so might undermine one's case. Partly it is because the truth may simply be unknown. It is interesting to see that the United States forces in France in the late 1940s were being put on standby to take action in the event of an expected Communist-led coup. No doubt the French government would have been perturbed about this had it known; but it did not know, and this episode is thus of no real importance to an understanding of how the French thought of the Americans at the time. On the other hand, I am very concerned with a number of things that did not happen. Myths of conspiracy and betrayal are an important element of this study, and they are not the less powerful for being untrue. Indeed, because myths of this nature do not require historical proof, but rather have to respect only literary concepts of truth and decorum, they are almost always more powerful than the truth. From a vast number, I would mention a few that will be met later in their full glory.

Before the First World War, many Frenchmen believed that the Dreyfus affair was a conspiracy by some or all of the Jews, the Freemasons and the Germans to undermine the French army and thus prevent the proper defence of the country in the next war. In 1936, many believed that tens of thousands of armed Communist activists were waiting to seize power on the orders of Moscow when the Popular Front government came into office. Before the fighting started in 1940, it was widely rumoured that anti-republican generals had destroyed defences opposing the Germans in their sector. At the same time, many believed that tens of thousands of armed Communist activists were waiting to seize power on the orders of Moscow when the Germans attacked, and even that Soviet troops would be fighting alongside the Germans. After the Second World War, many believed that the social legislation of the Popular Front of 1936–37 had so damaged production of defence equipment that the war had been lost. Others believed that the Generals – most notably Pétain – had been conspiring with the Germans for years, and had deliberately ensured that the Germans would win. Some believed that the Coca-Cola Company of the United States had used its political leverage on the Truman administration to pressurise France to spend scarce foreign exchange importing a drink known to be injurious to public health. Others in the 1940s believed that tens of thousands of armed Communist activists were waiting to seize power on the orders of Moscow when one hundred thousand Soviet paratroops landed. And as late as 1961, some Frenchmen believed that the United States was behind the military coup that nearly toppled de Gaulle.

From time to time a historian has uncovered a shard of truth in some of these accusations; but truth or falsehood is not really the issue. Many of these myths progressed to the status of political truths – that is, governments or other forces acted on them *as though* they were true, at which point the distinction between truth and falsehood ceases to have much utility. In theory, governments should not be influenced by myths, and should make their decisions on the basis of facts as they are known. But in practice this is impossible, for several reasons. Firstly, those involved in the formulation of policy bring certain assumptions to it that seem to them so obvious that they are scarcely conscious of holding them, and would refer to them, if at all, as 'common sense'. These are often cultural and historical assumptions, very widely shared, that condition the way policy-makers think before they actually start thinking. To some extent this is what is called 'ethnocentrism'; but it is not limited to that. In this book, I have tried to set out some of the myths that animated (and still animate) French policy-makers.

To take a simple example, the destruction of the French fleet by the Royal navy at Mers-el-Kébir in 1940 was universally deplored in France, as much among those who resisted as among those who collaborated. De Gaulle condemns the action in his memoirs, not as an isolated incident, but as another example of a consistent trend in British policy that would naturally lead the British to behave in such a way. And others, of all persuasions, made the same judgement, interpreting British behaviour in terms of the myths with which they were familiar. The British argument – that the fleet might fall into German hands – was dismissed as specious. Yet the British (who appear genuinely to have had no ulterior motive) themselves routinely dismiss such French complaints on the basis that, since French claims are factually incorrect, *therefore* they have no meaning and can be ignored. Yet if French perceptions on this issue, or any other, are as they are, and if French governments act on them as though they were the truth, they have the pragmatic effect of truth. The inability of the British (and others) to take French protestations seriously, and the consequences of this, is one of the themes of this study.

Secondly, the right information might not always be available. This is not simply a reflection of the difficulties of policy-making as outlined above; it is also a reflection of the transitory nature of bureaucracies. Although the structure may be permanent, individuals within a system move around. Any structure that relies upon recruiting individuals at the start of their careers, giving them exposure to a variety of jobs, and then rewarding them with occasional promotion, will have a high turnover of staff, even if those staff are a homogeneous cadre that does not serve outside this single structure. A standard tour length would be two to three years, if no special factors intervene. A division of ten people, for example, is unlikely to have more than two or three with two years' experience. Together with the furious production of paper, and the consequent need to send old papers to archives frequently, this often means a lack of proper bureaucratic memory. As a substitute, a kind of bureaucratic folklore develops, by which the main elements of problems that arose in the past are handed down in a truncated and simplified form, embellished with the prejudices of the organisation itself. I have seen this in action, for example, in the simple case of the relationship between France and NATO since 1966. And in any bureaucracy, there is too much current work to do to spare time and effort digging back through the archives to find the actual truth.

Finally, truth itself may be uncomfortable or irrelevant, and may interfere with a cherished myth. I shall have something to say about the reality of 1940; but rather more about the myths. In 1942 the Vichy government put its political enemies from the Third Republic on trial for losing the war. The intention of the Riom trials was to sanctify the Vichy interpretation of the defeat, and to settle political scores from the 1930s; yet often the trials ended in farce, because the facts refused to support the interpretation that the French government of the day placed upon them.

The Single Right Answer

By definition, this meta-strategy, in all its aspects as described above, is nowhere summarised. Some idea of the totality of factors that have operated on French governments, the practical limitations they have worked under, and the bureaucratic folklore of the Quai,[2] the Ministry of Defence and the Élysée can nonetheless be discovered. But it must be sought in pieces, and not in learned journals or in policy statements, but in schoolbooks, popular histories, the media, incidental statements by politicians, inscriptions on monuments and a dozen other places where the French are talking informally to themselves, often in shorthand with the nuances left out. It is for this reason that, in this study, I have gone somewhat beyond the dry recitation of facts and acts. I have cast my net wider, to include the media, such as the cinema, works of fiction and even works of philosophy, since they often illustrate, and even contribute to, the spirit of the times within which government has to work. I have likewise looked at books of popular history, including those used by schoolchildren. I shall give examples throughout the chapters that follow, and, at the end, some indications of what the limits of the informal meta-strategy appear to be now.

In France, there does seem to be a tendency for the meta-strategy to be more organised and coherent than in most other countries. There are two principal reasons for this. One is the amount of conscious organisation by government. The Republicans after 1870, Vichy after 1940, and de Gaulle after 1958 are particular

---

2. As the Ministry of Foreign Affairs is universally known, from its address at 37, Quai d'Orsay.

examples of this tendency; but the didactic function appears seldom to have been absent from official thinking during this time. Such was the disunity of the nation, it was felt that only a single truth, unencumbered by shades of meaning, was permissible. And there is a related tendency for French historical works to be far more didactic and partisan than is the case elsewhere: a judicious summing-up that tries to be fair to all points of view and reaches a nuanced conclusion is not common.

Partly, also, there is the cultural and philosophical heritage. There is reason to doubt how far the French have really been influenced by the detail (as opposed to the general outlines) of Descartes's work, and it often shows up only as a kind of desiccated formalism, and an attraction to surface elegance of organisation. But the idea that absolute truth can be deduced from theoretical postulates, whereas empirical evidence is a dangerous and unreliable guide, has left its footprints everywhere in modern French culture, not least in bureaucracy and administration. The idea that there is a single right answer to every question, to be expressed as clearly as possible, is inculcated into every French bureaucrat. Foreigners who have worked in French administration report that, far from the British habit of producing texts of studied ambiguity that can be interpreted differently as circumstances change, the French tradition is of the production of a text with a single, unambiguous meaning. This kind of approach is formally taught, in the kind of textbooks that every *Énarque* will have studied, for example. Among them are textbooks on 'Philosophical Methodology' – a concept that scarcely exists in Britain. One such book advertises philosophy as being 'method above all – thinking is also knowing how to think'.[3] This is the approach of the book itself, which works in great detail through a series of practical exercises, in which there is a right and wrong answer to every question, from the right way to take notes to the correct interpretation of a given text. The same approach is taken at ENA itself, where there is much emphasis on a standardised, three-stage interpretation of documents and analysis of problems. And such analysis will not be built up *from* the facts of the case, as British officials might be taught, but will rather be the application *to* the case of theoretical principles that others have elaborated, and that it is the officials' duty to implement everywhere.

3. Dominique Folscheid and Jean-Jacques Wunenburger, *Méthodologie philosophique*, Paris, Presses Universitaires de la France, 1992.

Such an orientation distrusts compromises and grey areas, and will naturally move from one violent extreme to another. The historical elements of this study will demonstrate a continued French preference for ideological coherence over practical utility – that is exactly what one would expect. As a result, much of French history since 1789 amounts to lurches between extremes, followed by over-correction, and by a reluctance, as after 1789 and 1945, to adopt compromise proposals. If a dialectical process of sorts has taken place, and France has moved, hesitantly, in one direction since 1789, then the various syntheses have been uncomfortable, and temporary; often no more than the uneasy coexistence of conflicting elements, as in the case of relations between the army and the Third Republic.

Truth and Consequences

If the influences on politics are so various, and the freedom of action of governments often constrained, does this imply that the ability of great men to influence history (taking de Gaulle as an example) is not so great as is sometimes suggested? It is certainly the case that no politician can command public support and remain in power without incarnating something that the majority of the population support, or at least do not actively oppose. Even dictators who behave otherwise have only a tenuous hold on power. The French turned to Pétain in July 1940 because he appeared to be a figure of national salvation; but many soon became disenchanted when he could not live up to the enormous symbolic demands placed on him. When de Gaulle first offered himself for the same role in the late 1940s, he was rebuffed, and only accepted, grudgingly by some, in a situation of extreme crisis in 1958. Even then, he was accepted more for what he symbolised than for his personal qualities, which for many Frenchmen were scarcely known. Likewise, de Gaulle's subsequent innovations in security policy would not have been accepted and would not have endured, unless they had responded to a felt need, often more on the emotional than on the rational level. In responding to this need, he was acting not only in conformity with his own view of history and of France, but with the views of many others, also.

This is one reason why the present study – whatever faults it doubtless has – at least does not fall into the trap of claiming to be a general work, whilst in fact being about de Gaulle. There are many books about de Gaulle – perhaps too many – and this is not one of them. Indeed, my argument is, not that de Gaulle is irrelevant – that would be silly – but that he has to be understood as a man who brought to culmination many things that had been planned, and even begun, by others. Finally, and on another note of negative recommendation, this is not a work of polemic. There is a polemical and irascible quality that easily infects Anglo-French relations in the security area, and risks turning studies of the problem into presentations of the case for the prosecution or the defence. I have tried as far as possible to eschew both advocacy and judgement: I have limited myself to trying to explain what happened, what various actors thought, why they thought it, and how it affected what they did.

PART I

WHY

1

THE UNIVERSAL MISSION

Jesus Christ is Emperor of France.

Fourteenth-century coin

*United, the French Nation has never been conquered ... there
is no miracle that cannot be accomplished by the genius of
the French when the National Independence is threatened.*

First Consul Napoleon Bonaparte, 1803

*France, once the soldier of God, today the soldier of Humanity,
will always be the soldier of the Ideal.*

Georges Clemenceau, 1919

*For every thinking patriot, the essential problem ... is the
maintenance of the unity of France and the restoration of
her grandeur.*

French Communist Party, 1944

Is there a nation that has not, at one time or another, overtly or
covertly, believed itself to be specially favoured by God or history, and to have a glorious destiny that it must fulfil? Few nations
have escaped this temptation at some stage in their history, and
France is not among them. Yet the quality of the French perception
of France's history and purpose, its role in the world and its civilising mission, is certainly unusual, and perhaps unique; and its
practical effects have been profound. The assumptions of the
French about themselves and the destiny of their country play a
powerfully determining role, even today, in the way in which decision-makers approach questions of the relations between states.
And much of recent French politics has, in turn, been determined

by the aching disequilibrium between the destiny of the nation and the means available to pursue it.

As good a place to start as any is the coronation of Louis XIV at Rheims, on 3 June 1654. The boy-king was greeted by the Bishop of Soissons, who addressed him as follows:

> Sire, the Lord's Anointed, son of the Most High, shepherd of the flock, protector of the Church, the first of all kings on earth, chosen and appointed by Heaven to carry the sceptre of the French, to extend far and wide the honour and renown of the Lily, whose glory outshines by far that of Solomon from pole to pole and sun to sun, making France a universe and the universe one France.[1]

Even by the demanding standards of royal sycophancy in the age of absolutism, this text contains rather extreme claims. Yet the idea that the king of France and his realm were the foremost in the world, and had a special status as the chosen instrument of God, had a history of centuries behind it. Two themes recur pervasively in earlier texts, almost always together: they are, the antiquity and continuity of the French nation compared to all others, and the special relationship of the French king with God. These assertions, which alter their outward appearance, but not their essential significance, after the Revolution, are the basis of the extraordinary claims that have been made over the centuries for the special and unique status of the nation.[2]

Magical History

Medieval French chroniclers, like their colleagues in Britain and elsewhere, had no difficulty in finding mythical and magical antecedents for their nation, although they faced a particular problem in deciding whether to trace this origin simply back to the Franks, or further back to the Gauls. Much ingenuity was expended in trying to reconcile the two origins, as political fashion changed, thus projecting continuous French history back to Classical times.

1. Mgr. Simon Le Gras, Bishop of Soissons, *Procès verbal du sacre du roy Louis* ..., Soissons 1694, cited by François Bluche, *Louis XIV*, trans. Mark Greengrass, Oxford, Basil Blackwell, 1990, p. 12.

2. Much the same was said even on the very eve of the Revolution itself. The record of the consecration and coronation of Louis XVI is as full of references to Charlemagne, Clovis and the special status of the French king as any for hundreds of years past. See *Le Sacre et couronnement de Louis XVI, Roi de France et Navarre*, Paris, 1775.

Earlier attempts tended to focus on the Franks alone, because the aristocratic and warlike image of the Franks was a more comforting point of departure in an aristocratic and warlike age. One theory was that they were of Trojan origin.[3] A chronicle of the seventh century describes Priam as the first king of the Franks. The (previously unsuspected) Francion, a relative of Priam, founds what was later to become the Frankish nation between the Rhine and the Danube.[4] Later writers elaborated this theme, adding in the original inhabitants of France – the Gauls – whom the Franks had, of course, replaced. In this version, the Franks are actually of Gaulish origin, since Troy itself was founded by a wandering Gaul, who thus indirectly spread Gaulish (for which read French) civilisation to Greece and Rome.[5]

By the sixteenth century it was being maintained that the Franks were, in fact, Gauls who had left their country after the Roman conquest, and had later returned to liberate it. Finally, in the impressive synthesis of Dom Jacques Martin, in the first half of the eighteenth century, the Gauls achieve their apotheosis. Directly descended from Adam and Eve, they colonised the whole of the Western world, and are thus the origin of all Western civilisation, whilst also being the only nation to retain their original religious faith.[6] But mere antiquity alone would not have guaranteed the French and their king first place among the nations of Europe. Of much more importance were the allegedly sacred origins of French kingship, as set down in the conversion and baptism of Clovis, the first Christian king of the Franks. According to Gregory of Tours, Clovis had been under pressure for some time from his wife, a Christian, to become a convert, but had resisted doing so. Then one day, during a war with the Germans (*Almans*), his army in danger of extermination, Clovis promised God that, if he won the battle, he would become a Christian forthwith. Hardly had he spoken these words, when 'the Germans turned and fled'. Impressed with this result, Clovis made arrangements to be baptised forthwith.[7] At

3. At this time, the story of the Trojan War was known only from Latin sources, particularly Vergil's *Aeneid*, which naturally gave a very anti-Greek and pro-Trojan account of the war. The Middle Ages thus regarded Troy as the embodiment of romantic chivalry (see, for example Chaucer's *Troilus and Criseyde*), and there could be no higher honour for a race than to be descended from the Trojans.

4. Suzanne Citron, *Le Mythe National: L'histoire de France en question*, Paris, Les Éditions ouvrières/Études et Documentations internationales, 1991, p. 119.

5. Ibid., p. 142.

6. Ibid., p. 143.

7. Georges Tessier, *Le Baptême de Clovis*, Paris, Gallimard, 1964, p. 54.

the political level, of course, this amounts to a claim for equality of importance between Clovis and Constantine; the former doing for Europe what the latter had done for Rome.

The legend of Clovis's baptism was added to over the centuries. An account by the ninth-century Bishop Hincmar gives the authorised version: as Bishop Remi was about to baptise Clovis in the Cathedral at Rheims, a dove 'whiter than snow' suddenly appeared, holding in its beak an ampoule filled with oil, which gave out the most marvellous odour. The oil was used to perform the consecration.[8] The ampoule, which mysteriously refilled itself after use, remained at the Cathedral for centuries, and was used to consecrate all subsequent kings of France, up to and including Louis XVI, before it was destroyed in the Revolution. It is even alleged that pieces of it were recovered and used in the coronation of Charles X.[9] From the very beginning, it was understood that this legend implied a direct connection between God and successive French kings, and gave them a special status among their peers – that of *rex christianissimus*, or *roy trescrestien*, or 'most Christian King'. The anointing with holy oil is intended to recall the Old Testament practice, and, like those of Israel, the kings of France were believed to enjoy a special relationship with God, who had chosen them. Thus, the French nation were the Chosen people of the New Testament era, as the Israelites had been of the Old: 'a chosen generation, a royal priesthood, an holy nation, a peculiar people', as the First Epistle of Peter had it.

Later writers placed the building of 'Lutece' (Paris) by the Franks, as far back as 830 BC, at the time of the earlier kings of Israel, and gave the French an equal status to the Israelites as regards their antiquity, as well as divine support for their military and other adventures.[10] To some extent, the French had outside support for these claims. The papacy in Carolingian times called them the 'new sacred people of promise', and their armies were compared to the columns of the Israelites departing from Egypt, to David's army when he fought Goliath and to Gideon's three hundred.[11] It was not surprising, therefore, that when Pope Urban II

8. Ibid., pp. 130–1.

9. Ibid., p. 138.

10. Rosemary H. Gill, *Political Theory at the Court of Charles V of France, 1346–80*, Unpublished Ph.D. thesis, University of London 1987/8, p. 56.

11. Ibid., p. 56. The comparison of France to David against Goliath has been a favourite one, from the stained glass of the Sainte Chapelle in Paris to the nuclear doctrine of the *faible au fort*.

preached the Crusade at Clermont in 1099, he addressed an anguished appeal to 'Frenchmen, beloved and chosen of God'. He recalled 'the exploits of ..."their ancestor Charlemagne ...", and entrusted to them the mission of leading Christianity against the Infidel'.[12]

The mention of Charlemagne recalls the other claim of the French throne. When Charlemagne was crowned emperor on Christmas Day 800 by Pope Leo III, his title explicitly carried with it the succession to the emperors of Rome, and 'in theory the full Roman headship of the world, the universal world rule'.[13] The emperor was the *dominus mundi*, the lord of the world, with dominion over all other kings. All French kings subsequently laid claim to descent (literal or metaphorical) from Charlemagne, and thus to these universalist ambitions. From the thirteenth until at least the sixteenth century writers set out plans for a world government under a French emperor with his seat in Jerusalem.[14] Charlemagne and his successors were seen in a specifically military context, as in the *Chanson de Roland*, which suited French martial traditions, and this lies behind Clemenceau's reference to France as 'once the soldier of God' in one of the epigraphs to this book. That echoes of the ninth century should appear in a political speech a millennium and more later is less surprising in France than a similar reference (say Churchill quoting Geoffrey of Monmouth) would be in other countries. It is the ultimate origin, indeed, of the claims for the pre-eminence of France, its language (the language of God, of course) and its culture that are still made today.

The themes of antiquity, divine election and identification with Israel were synthesised most completely in the writings of a group of scholars in the court of Charles V in the later fourteenth century, largely because of the need to buttress Charles's shaky claim to the throne in the face of a strong challenge from the English, and to find arguments for the Papal seat's being at Avignon, and not Rome, during the Schism. Charles V was represented by these scholars as the new Solomon, which meant that he had the gift of divine wisdom directly from God. Indeed, so nourished was he by this Wisdom that it eventually took possession of him, and turned him into the Wisdom of God *itself*, and thus Christ reincarnate. In

12. Marie-Madeline Martin, *Histoire de l'Unité Française: L'Idée de Patrie en France des origines à nous jours*, Paris, Presses Universitaires de la France, new edn 1982, p. 127.

13. Frances A. Yates, *Astrea: The Imperial Theme in the Sixteenth Century*, London, Routledge and Kegan Paul, 1975, p. 2.

14. Ibid., pp. 122–3.

turn, this gave him a status above that of the pope – not an un-pleasing conclusion politically.[15] Charles also went to some lengths to stress the connection with Charlemagne – which began, of course, with a coincidence of name – and frequently used the kind of visual symbolism appropriate to a pre-literate age. The figure of Charlemagne on Charles's sceptre wore not an open, royal crown, but a closed, imperial one, and was flanked by two imperial eagles.[16] The consequent universal authority of the French king gave him the duty and prerogative of caring for the *pax Ecclesiae* in other kingdoms also. Indeed, the realm of France is the mysterious body of Christ (*corpus Christi mysticum*), in which all believers are incorporated whether they are actually resident in France or not, that prefigures the kingdom of God that will be established on earth at the end of time.[17]

The relative tranquillity of the sixteenth century allowed the writers of the Pléiade era to embellish the myth still further, adding Classical references to the existing corpus of assumptions. Ronsard inserted the Franks into Roman mythology, picturing Jupiter hand-ing down laws to 'the Frenchman … son of Hector'.[18] All of this may appear recondite and quite unrelated to modern concerns. But it is important to recall that this was not abstract scholarly specu-lation, but political propaganda fashioned against internal and external enemies in a political and diplomatic climate as subtle and murderous as anything in later French history. And it set up pat-terns that are clearly recapitulated in later times, and that clearly relate, for example, to the rhetoric of Louis XIV's coronation, cited above. These patterns of thought are still influential today.

Against what might have been expected, the Revolution did not sweep all these theories away: rather, its theorists, practitioners and hagiographers took all these themes and remodelled them for a secular world. This is why the special sense of France did not dis-appear with the coming of the Republic: the soldier of God simply became the soldier of Humanity. Although later generations have tended – rightly – to emphasise continuity of thinking after 1789, France was believed by the theorists of the time to be the prototype of a new society, a *nation*, in the sense of a group of individuals who had chosen to live together, and in whom all sovereignty lay,

15. Gill, *Political Theory*, p. 51.

16. Christopher Allmand, *The Hundred Years War: England and France at War c.1300 –c.1450*, Cambridge, Cambridge University Press, 1989, p. 144.

17. Gill, *Political Theory*, p. 72.

18. Martin, *Histoire de l'Unité*, p. 187.

as opposed to earlier societies, which had simply been the possessions of a ruler, to be traded according to whim. The nation thus had a kind of virtual existence, whether recognised or not, independent of the torturing of chronology to create unlikely Gallo-Frankish dynasties. 'The nation', said Sièyes, 'exists before everything, it is the origin of everything.'[19] This thinking was to have dire consequences for the national unity, as will appear in a moment. Danton claimed that France itself had natural boundaries – the ocean, the Rhine, the Alps, the Pyrenees.[20] The result of this was a France that did not need to be defined or created, since it existed already, and always had, an 'uncreated entity'.[21]

The main actors of the Revolution had no doubts about its universal significance. The *Declaration of the Rights of Man* was specifically intended to be universal in its application. The preamble claims that all misfortune and corruption is the result of the 'ignorance, neglect or misunderstanding' of the rights of man,[22] which had been identified in France, but were assumed to apply to everyone at all times. It was assumed that the new constitution that accompanied the declaration would 'bring happiness to France, and, in the imitation thereof, to all peoples'.[23] It was taken for granted that a fundamental change was in motion that would spread to the rest of the world in due course. It therefore seemed appropriate to start a new calendar, beginning from the Year I (1793), as a concrete manifestation of a new beginning for the whole world. The Revolution was seen as 'an apocalyptic moment in history, the most important event in the career of man on earth, totally different from such episodes as the Cromwellian and American Revolutions, outbreaks prompted by local grievances and driven by limited aims'. And on more than one occasion, Robespierre claimed that Revolutionary France was thousands of years ahead of all other nations.[24]

But if the Revolution was so important, and France so advanced, what would the nature of its relations with other states

19. Emmanuel Sieyès, *Qu'est-ce que le Tiers état: édition critique avec une introduction et des notes*, ed. Roberto Zapperi, Geneva, Droz, 1970, p. 180.

20. Citron, *Le Mythe National*, p. 155.

21. Ibid., p. 156.

22. Unless otherwise indicated, all constitutional texts cited are from Debbasch and Pontier, *Les Constitutions de la France*. This quotation is on p. 8.

23. Durand-Maillane, *Histoire apologetique* ... (1791), cited in Tristan Todorov, *Nous et les Autres: La réflexion française sur la diversité humaine*, Paris, Seuil, 1989, p. 215.

24. J. T. Talmon, *The Origins of Totalitarian Democracy*, Penguin edn, London, 1986, p. 134.

be? In theory, the position was simple enough: Title VI of the 1791 Constitution said, reassuringly, that 'The French nation renounces the undertaking of any war with the intention of conquest, and will never employ its forces against the liberty of any people' (p. 37). But of course, most (if not all) other nations were not yet free, and thus had no liberty to lose. Accordingly, decrees of 1792 promised aid to a people rising against its king, and 'to all peoples who wished to recover their liberty'.[25] The wars of France were therefore fought for the common good, and it was to be hoped that other nations would recognise and applaud this. Moreover, given that the theories that lay behind the wars had been rationally deduced, and that any rational being unhampered by prejudice would arrive at the same conclusions, the inhabitants of other nations must understand that their duty was to welcome French armies as liberators and pay for them. Therefore, the 15 December 1792 decree warned that 'a liberated population that failed to adopt the institutions of liberty and popular sovereignty thereby declared itself a friend of tyranny and an enemy of France in the global war'.[26] Naturally, it was felt, French officials would be sent to arrange elections and take charge of affairs until the indigenous population had advanced to the same stage of enlightenment as France itself.

These concepts are not new; but they are expressed in a different vocabulary. What had happened was that it had been decided that, in the words of the 1793 version of the *Declaration*, 'Sovereignty resides in the people' (p. 46). But sovereignty had previously been incarnated in the king, and there were no powers held by anyone that were not specifically delegated from him. The result of 1789 was thus to 'move the nation from the absolute sovereignty of the King to the absolute sovereignty of the people'.[27] Since this sovereignty was the result of divine election, the divinity passed, with the creation of the Republic, from the king to the people, but in a secularised form. The people of France were above all others, as the French king (who at one stage had been called 'Emperor') had been above all others. Napoleon probably recalled this when he styled himself emperor also. His decision thus to proclaim himself, as well as the detail of the ceremony, were both heavily and explicitly rooted in the detail of the past.

25. Cited by Todorov, *Nous et les Autres*, p. 216.
26. Talmon, *Origins*, p. 131.
27. François Furet, *Louis XVI Roi des Français*, in (various authors), *L'Election du Chef de l'Etat en France*, Paris, Beauchesne, 1988, p. 69.

Specifically, Napoleon wished to lay claim to the same relationship of equality with the pope as the old French kings had had, and therefore revived an old imperial tradition, summoning Pius VII to Paris. For political reasons, Pius decided to come, although Napoleon performed the actual coronation himself.

Napoleon's propagandists quickly picked up this point, and chose traditional, if somewhat unimaginative, ways of depicting the emperor's pre-eminence. Early in his reign, the propagandists produced illustrations representing all the nations of the earth paying tribute to him:[28] there are commonplaces of sycophancy, as in everything else, and such illustrations had been produced for many previous French monarchs. The meaning was clear enough, and continuous from the earliest days of the Revolution: the armies of the Revolution had history and progress on their side, in the same way that the armies of the Franks had God on theirs, and to take issue with the Revolution and its unfolding purpose was no more acceptable than to take issue with God and his purpose. These assumptions found their way into the popular history books of the nineteenth century, notably in the case of Michelet (1798–1874), the Macaulay of French history. His massive works presented a synthesis of the meaning of French history 'revealed to itself by the Revolution',[29] which dominated historical thinking for decades afterwards. Michelet saw France as the universal fatherland, a new incarnation of God himself. The history of France, he argued, was in effect the history of the world. She had continued the work of the Romans and of Christianity, and the Revolution had performed what the church had only promised, in the Second Coming of 1789.[30]

It followed from this that France had a special status. France was destined to be the 'pilot of humanity's boat', conducting the modern world 'on the mysterious road to the future'. Its vocation was to 'set the world free' and to 'deliver (*enfanter*) each nation to liberty'.[31] This special status of France was qualified only by history. Michelet was prepared to admit that ancient Greece was in some senses a precursor, and a comparison could be made between the Revolution and the first appearance of Christianity. But 'the religion of man revealed by the Revolution is to modern times

28. Jean Tulard, *Napoleon, the Myth of the Saviour*, trans. Teresa Waugh, London Weidenfeld and Nicolson, 1984, pp. 224–6.
29. Citron, *Le Mythe National*, p. 18.
30. Ibid., p. 19.
31. Todorov, *Nous et les Autres*, p. 238.

what the Christian religion was to antiquity'.[32] And Michelet reflects, again, the idea of a kind of 'geographical predestination' of France, of a 'pre-existing France', a 'virtual' nation before a real one. It was after the Revolution that the common periphrasis for France, 'the Hexagon', began to be widely used.[33] The term is still commonly employed today, and is powerfully resonant of an ordered and harmonious geographical space that could not have arisen by chance, a 'Promised Land' into which the new Israelites would doubtless eventually find their way.

Other writers flung themselves into the praise of France as the nation leading the way into the future. Auguste Comte, for example, set out how he believed his theory of positivism would spread around the world. Once the truth of everything had been established in France, (the 'kernel of humanity') it would be ready for export, initially to the nations of Western Europe, and ultimately to the rest of the globe. National peculiarities would be respected, and states given time to evolve as far as the French had; but the end-product would be a universal state constructed along principles developed in France.[34] If there is a single word that represents what it was believed that France stood for at this time, it is probably 'civilisation', which implied a social, economic and political programme directed towards the future. Under the Second Empire, Napoleon III presented every technical advance as a triumph for this 'civilisation', and every political act of France as proof that it was the 'advanced sentinel and first soldier of civilisation'.[35] Even the French language – still, at that date, the universal language of international affairs – was considered a blessing for all mankind. The French language was supposed to express the French virtues of logic and clarity, inherited from Descartes. Other nations, as a consequence, lacked the facility of abstraction.[36]

Finally, and in addition to the urge to colonise as a means to recover French grandeur after 1815, it was often argued that the historic mission and the innate virtues of France gave her no choice but to be a colonial power. 'Among all nations', intoned Etienne Clémentel in 1906, 'France seems predestined … her mission imposes itself so clearly, so imperiously, that she sees it less as the work of her own genius than as the expression of eternal

32. Ibid., p. 241.
33. Raoul Giradet, *Mythes et Mythologies Politiques*, Paris, Seuil, 1986, p. 157.
34. Todorov, *Nous et les Autres*, pp. 46–49.
35. Theodore Zeldin, *France, 1848–1945*, Vol. II, p. 8.
36. Ibid., p. 30.

laws.'[37] Above all, France had no commercial reasons for embarking on colonialism, unlike other nations, such as the British. Rather, she would lead other, more primitive peoples towards the light; and they, for their part, would be delighted to follow. Such was her genius, that wherever 'a Frenchman has placed his foot, even if only for an instant, he has made French the soil upon which he has trodden'.[38]

The National Myth

What I have so far presented does not amount to an unchallenged orthodoxy. Many Frenchmen remained monarchist and Catholic, suspicious of the claims of the Revolution and unattracted by Michelet's strident anti-clericalism, just as some, for various reasons, opposed colonies. Indeed, they went so far as to argue that post-Revolutionary France had actually forfeited its place as the beacon of the world and guardian of universal principles, because of the modernist and secular policies it had adopted. But it did not occur to them to question the special status of their country as such. It was because of this, and because of the trauma of the defeat of 1870, the loss of Alsace and Lorraine and the foundation of the Third Republic, that those who took power afterwards oversaw the creation and promulgation of what Suzanne Citron has called 'The National Myth'. This was the myth of a France united, its origins lost in antiquity, whose central event was the Revolution. It 'exalted the feeling that France had an extraordinary destiny, and nourished a deep nationalism'.[39]

It was propounded mainly in school texts, some of which remained in print until the middle of the present century, until they were eventually replaced by other texts that had, in their turn, been heavily influenced by them. Generations of French schoolchildren were thus taught a history profoundly Franco-centric and didactic in its orientation, which referred to other nations only as they affected France itself. There is not a great deal of point in quoting at length from these texts: they say nothing new. What is

37. Cited in Raoul Girardet, *Le Nationalisme français: Anthologie 1871–1914*, Paris, Seuil, 1983, p. 120. Banalities of this sort often sound better in French, but, on this occasion, not much. The whole quotation is somewhat longer, but I see no reason to inflict all of it upon the reader.
38. Ibid., p. 89.
39. Citron, *Le Mythe National*, p. 1.

interesting is the way in which they take up the themes sketched out above and rigidly schematise them, leaving out any elements that do not fit or do not help the didactic purpose. But a few extracts will help to give a flavour of how generations of French schoolchildren were encouraged to view the world. By far the most influential of these writers was Ernest Lavisse, whose works were reprinted well into this century. His various books provide a simple, linear picture of a France slowly assembling itself over the centuries, from the point where 'two thousand years ago, France was called Gaul'. Once Clovis became king 'Gaul changed its name. It was called France.'[40] After this, 'The kings' then slowly unified France, and, 'obeying the same king, the French began to understand that they were one people'.[41] The French then distinguished themselves in the Crusades, which appear to have been an entirely French affair. The pope called on the French: 'You are the bravest of nations. You are the ones who will chase the Turks out of Jerusalem'; which they promptly did.[42]

The Revolution, of course, is the apotheosis. It was 'after the Revolution that France is really a nation (*patrie*)', and that event 'put into the souls of the French the love of justice, equality and liberty. Our fathers believed that France would deliver all peoples from the evils they were enduring. They were proud to be a great people, responsible for showing the way to other peoples'.[43]

Above all, the texts are didactic in tone: hectoringly so. Long lists of heroes are given, like Vercingétorix, Clovis, Charlemagne, Joan of Arc, Louis XIV and Napoleon, who unified the nation and expelled invaders. A textbook of the 1950s lists all these, as well as modern figures like Foch and Clemenceau, with an injunction to 'remember the names of the great leaders (*chefs*) of our country from the beginning of its history up to our time'.[44] One effect of these texts, with their schematic presentation of French history, of temporary defeats followed by salvation at the hands of a *chef*, must, of course, have been to create a typology of historical events that students could expect to find reproduced in their own lives. It is difficult to believe that saviours and would-be saviours, from Boulanger to de Gaulle, would have been quite so readily accepted had the ground not been so well prepared for them.

40. Ibid., pp. 30–31.
41. Girardet, *Le Nationalisme Français*, p. 81.
42. Citron, *Le Mythe National*, p. 61.
43. Girardet, *Le Nationalisme Français*, p. 83.
44. Ibid., p. 43.

Moreover, the *chef*-based paradigm of history both discourages a belief in the efficacity of a parliamentary system, and helps to create a constant yearning for a decisive figure (usually with a military background) to assume the reins of power. The demand for such figures exists independently of the supply of them, and if a *chef* of distinction is not actually available, a lesser figure will be subconsciously invested with the same mystical powers.

Contemporary textbooks, although more measured in their approach, retain many of these features, and these ideas, presented with varying degrees of intellectual rigour, were – and to some extent still are – part of the mindset of those who directed the policy of France; traces of them are to be found everywhere, as will become apparent in the discussion of post-1919 history with which this study is chiefly concerned. In the meantime, a couple of examples may be of interest. Perhaps the most famous is that of the first pages of de Gaulle's *War Memoirs*, which take their inspiration directly from the schoolbooks of his youth. The thought of France's having 'an exalted and exceptional destiny', and the idea of the 'genius of the land' will be by now familiar. If de Gaulle thought of France 'in a certain way', it was the way in which he had been encouraged to think of it.[45] Raoul Girardet detects the influence of Michelet in particular in these pages, especially in the evocation of Paris, closely modelled on a description in Michelet's *Le Peuple*.[46]

But it is less important that de Gaulle thought this than that others did also; otherwise his appeal would have been less than it was. And his predecessors, with the same kind of education and assumptions, may have pursued (for various reasons) different policies, but their assumptions about France, its history and mission and its place in the world, would probably have been similar. This applies in the most unlikely areas. In 1944 the (clandestine) French Communist Party issued a policy statement on the kind of France it would like to see after the war, as part of a debate with the Socialists. In the section on foreign policy it identified the 'essential problem' as 'the maintenance of the unity of France and the restoration of its grandeur'.[47] Even given the nationalistic tone

45. Charles de Gaulle, *War Memoirs*, Vol. I: *The Call to Honour*, trans. Jonathan Griffin, London, Collins, 1955, p. 9.

46. Girardet, *Le Nationalisme Français*, p. 24.

47. Henri Michel and Boris Mirkine-Guetzévitch, *Les Idées politiques et sociales de la Résistance: Documents clandestins 1940–1944*, Paris, Presses Universitaires de la France, 1954, p. 230.

that Communist parties were encouraged to adopt by Stalin at the time, it is difficult to think of any other Communist party, of that or any other time, that would have expressed itself in quite the same way. There are practical political consequences of the widespread promulgation of this myth in the ways in which the French have conducted themselves in their dealings with other nations. A nation whose history and destiny are so extensive and so glorious is likely to expect other nations to take it at its own valuation, at least in part. But the story of France's international relations in the period since 1919 has been the failure of the objective facts of international life to follow obediently after the glorious image. As I will show, the contrast between the role to which France aspired (essentially the same role it had clung to for a millennium and more) and the brute facts of economics and military strength produced a tension in Paris whose consequences are noticeable today. In addition, there were other, home-grown reasons why France sometimes failed to live up to its glorious destiny, and the rest of this chapter is concerned with how this occurred and how the French tried to deal with it.

The Nation, United

Nothing is more divisive than unity: the strains of trying to reconcile opposing views and opposing factions are a problem for any nation, and the French have found it (or claim to have done so) more difficult than most. There are three ways in which unity has been a preoccupation. The first of these is geographical, and arises from the sense of the 'virtual France' referred to above. If, in fact, France is an immanent design that is slowly being revealed, then the loss of part of the territory once its natural limits have been reached, like the amputation of a limb, is especially difficult to bear, as well as being contrary to nature. Certainly, it is otherwise difficult to understand the depth of agony that was felt over Alsace and Lorraine when, in 1870, after two hundred years of being French, they were annexed to Germany.

The second is social: the disagreements and sometimes violence between different areas of the country, between different sections of society, and between different social and economic groups. Comparative judgements are difficult, of course, but the French experience – which has included open warfare – is probably at least as bad as any. The third is ideological. Although a foretaste was provided by the wars of religion in the sixteenth and seventeenth centuries, it was really at the Revolution that this fault line was opened, and it remains a problem to this day. Moreover, the consequences of disunity are always regarded, by the French, as uniformly terrible. When Frenchmen are fighting Frenchmen, the country becomes weak, and foreigners invade. And when Frenchmen ally themselves with foreigners rather than each other (as has happened, often, from the Hundred Years War to Charles de Gaulle), the results can be catastrophic for the nation. Since the consequences of this disunity and efforts to overcome it remain of importance even now, I will spend a few pages on the French view of the value and difficulty of national unity, and on the myth and the ideology.

A suitable place to start is the Hundred Years' War, which to the French is rather more significant than it is to the English. The war was fought over much the same terrain as that of the First World War, and its effects on the population, the social fabric and the environment were just as devastating, as well as much longer drawn out. Moreover, Frenchman was fighting Frenchman, except that one group of Frenchmen, the Burgundians, were allied to the English. And, at different stages of the war, the Anglo-Burgundian cause was widely supported, not least by the University of Paris, the intellectual powerhouse of Western Christendom at the time, and the first official body to move against Joan of Arc. Yet both sides believed themselves to be patriots, with the good of the realm at heart. The Burgundians pointed – with some justice – to the decadence of most of the Valois kings, and proposed themselves as the healers of France. They were happy to have the help of the English, of course, but only on their own terms. The king of England would unite the nation, should they win, but he would not, for this purpose, be king of England. Rather, he would be king of France, ruling through the Parlement in Paris. This was not how the English saw it, and for the first, if not the last, time the English were annoyed at the conditions the French tried to put on the acceptance of aid that was sorely needed.

The war is the origin of the strife between the French and the 'English' (rather than British), which is one of the major themes of French historical writing. The relationship is often presented as a struggle between two different conceptions of life: the cerebral, idealistic French being constantly defeated and betrayed by the pragmatic, commercially oriented English. Thus, one recent writer argues that the Revolution itself can be seen as partly the doing of the British, both through covert encouragement and financing, and more widely through the influence of political ideas from the Glorious Revolution and from English Freemasonry. By financial chicanery and by causing the emigration of French naval officers after 1789, the English brought about the disaster of Trafalgar, after which 'France was never able to threaten Great Britain at sea again'. The eventual defeat of Napoleon reduced France to the 'status of the nations subject to the whims of London'. It was not until de Gaulle's veto on British entry to the Common Market in 1963 that France dared to 'stand up' to Britain once more.[48]

The war also raised, for the first time, the question of treason and collaboration. With large parts of the nation under long-term foreign occupation, perfect loyalty to the House of Valois was a lot to ask. Moreover, the English – as the Germans were to do some-what later – encouraged the development of regional identity in areas like Normandy, as a way of frustrating French efforts at uni-fication. Individual Frenchmen who collaborated were executed, but when the English were finally driven out, the French crown took a liberal attitude to the provinces – especially Normandy – that had collaborated, accepting that, for the most part, individu-als had little choice anyway. The reconquest of France as a result of the moral dynamism of Joan of Arc has been a consistent theme of French history and propaganda (where they can be distinguished) through the ages, and the unity that she brought has been reinter-preted afresh by each age for its own purposes. Although the Enlightenment largely adopted a policy of amused disdain about Joan's experiences, and the Revolution suppressed her cult, First Consul Bonaparte felt it politically prudent to reintroduce the cel-ebration of her feast in Year XI (1803), and to commission a new statue that would portray her as a Revolutionary heroine, snatch-ing a flag from an English soldier. He also took the opportunity of her feast on 8 May that year to make an appeal for unity: 'United, the French nation has never been conquered. The Illustriousness of Joan of Arc has proved there is no miracle that cannot be accom-plished by the genius of the French when the National Indepen-dence is threatened.'[49]

This interpretation of Joan of Arc remains the authoritative one to the present day. Her importance was less in giving victory over the English – she died before that happened – than in sowing the

48. Tristan Doelnitz, *La France hantée par sa puissance*, Paris, Belfond, 1993, pp. 50–51.

49. Marina Warner, *Joan of Arc: The Image of Female Heroism*, London, Penguin edn, 1983, p. 253.

seeds of French unity, not least in the sense of the immanent geography to which I referred earlier. According to Lavisse in the nineteenth century, at the end of the Hundred Years' War 'Our nation was not yet complete (*achevée*). The different provinces did not know each other well. They all had their own laws.'[50] Nonetheless, the foundations had been laid. Joan of Arc, as it is universally accepted, had 'saved France'. The same formulations crop up as late as the 1960s: Joan 'saved France. She died before her country was completely free, but she made the French understand that they had to unite to defend their country. They attacked the English everywhere, and forced them everywhere to flee'.[51] At a somewhat higher intellectual level, Marie-Madeline Martin's nostalgic and quasi-royalist *History of French Unity*, published at a time, in the 1940s, when such unity was not everywhere apparent, and garlanded with praise and prizes, maintains that 'the English kings wished to be king of France and the union of two Monarchies in one would practically assure their domination of the West. [England], so well isolated and protected on its island is the rival designated to halt the progress of France on the continent'.[52]

However, the ultimate effect of the Hundred Years' War was positive, since it caused the French to abandon their identification simply with their own region or locality, and caused the rise of a 'French nation, a people conscious of participating in the same heritage'.[53] Joan remains to this day the most powerful symbol of unity for the French, and it is not without interest that she also functioned as a symbol of resistance to the Germans. Her home had been in Lorraine, and when part of that province was lost to the Germans in 1870, the cult of Joan became entwined with the desire to reclaim the lost territories: the Prussians were seen as the exact descendants of the English, and Joan's help was sought to eject them.[54] The experience of the Hundred Years' War and the life of Joan have often been used for partisan political purposes, not least during the Second World War. De Gaulle's canny appropriation of the Cross of Lorraine for the Free French is well known, but Vichy also exploited the myth. Its propaganda films presented the D-Day landings as a new English (or more properly Anglo-Saxon) assault on France, with de Gaulle playing the part of the Burgundians,

50. Citron, *Le Mythe National*, p. 46.
51. Ibid., p. 48.
52. Martin, *Histoire de l'Unité*, p. 165.
53. Ibid., p. 175. Emphasis in the original.
54. Warner, *Joan of Arc*, p. 237.

dividing France and laying it waste. Vichy, on the other hand, represented the unity of France, and Joan was pressed into service in its support. A Vichy propaganda poster of 1943 of a burning town that has received the attentions of the RAF, with the image of Joan superimposed on it, carries the legend 'Murderers always return to the scene of their crime.'[55] It is probably not a coincidence that the first capital ship to be launched in France after de Gaulle's return was named the *Jeanne d'Arc*.[56]

The unity that Joan symbolised was never easy to accomplish. The wars of religion, which lasted for forty years from the end of the sixteenth century, devastating as they were themselves, provided a foretaste of what the Revolution would bring. For the first time in French history (with the possible exception of the Albigensian crusade), the disputants were divided on ideological lines: the dispute was not about the right to the throne or the independence of provinces (although such complications inevitably arose), but about what interpretation of religion was correct: there could, of course, be no compromise. The inevitable happened: as France tore herself apart, the Spanish invaded from the south, the English from the north, each under the guise of protecting their co-religionists. One French writer of the time feared that the country had 'almost lost king and kingdom, all things being changed, for the ruin of the country'.[57] It is no wonder that, after this episode and the civil strife of the Fronde which followed, propagandists of the reign of Louis XIV should have enthusiastically praised the unity and completeness of the realm, now at peace and now, with the annexation of Alsace and Lorraine, having reached its ordained geographical extent.

King and kingdom were definitively lost at the end of the next century. The Revolution marks the definitive rupture in French society that persists until the present day, and which lies behind most, if not all, of the events traced in the remainder of this study. At first sight, it is not clear why this should be so, since many other nations have had revolutions and emerged strengthened by

55. There is a useful compilation of Vichy propaganda films by the director Claude Chabrol, called *L'Oeil de Vichy* (1993). The poster is reproduced in Warner, *Joan of Arc*.

56. Joan's infinite adaptability has led to her re-invention by the French Right in the 1980s. In the eyes of the *Front national* she expelled illegal immigrants and fought heroically against a 'cosmopolitan' and 'multiracial' Europe. See Robert Gildea, *The Past in French History*, London, Yale University Press, 1994, pp. 164–5.

57. Martin, *Histoire de l'Unité*, p. 210.

them, or at least reconciled to them. The origins of this rupture lie in the ideology of the Revolution, which was itself an unusually complete marriage of theory and practice. This ideology in turn resulted from the nature of the French monarchy in the age of absolutism, which has been described thus:

> The king retains all the powers of the State: he is the sovereign legislator, in charge of internal administration and foreign relations, of finance and the army, and all justice comes from him…. In practice, the king is helped by many agents, but they have no power of their own: the king cannot give away (*aliéner*), but only delegate his prerogatives, and he can always, therefore, suspend the delegation and take back the exercise of the power he has delegated.[58]

It might have been possible to change this absolutist system for something along the English model, and thus share and diffuse power between different groups. But this did not happen. The absolute and indivisible nature of power was continued, but it was now to be exercised not by the monarchy, but by the people.

In *The Social Contract*, Rousseau begins his argument with two chapters (Chapters 1 and 2 of Book II) that argue successively that 'Sovereignty is Inalienable', and that 'Sovereignty is Indivisible' – exactly the position under the monarchy. Sovereignty he then defines as the 'exercise of the general will'.[59] It is important to understand that this concept is not a statistical or populist one: it is not the sum total of individual wills – still less is it a compromise between their different aspirations. It follows that many individual wills may each be different from the general will, and that those who happen to identify with the general will may be a minority. This does not matter, since the general will is always and by definition right and perfect. However, since 'the people is never corrupted, but it is often deceived' there is often 'a great deal of difference between the will of all and the general will'. This would not arise if 'the people, being furnished with adequate information, held its deliberations [and] the citizens had no communication one with another'. Such conditions would result in the appearance of the general will and 'the decision would always be good'. However 'when intrigues arise, and partial associations are formed at the expense of the great association, the will of each

58. P. Timbal and A. Castaldo, *Histoire des Institutions et Faits Sociaux*, Paris, Dalloz, 1984, pp. 338–9.

59. Jean-Jacques Rousseau, *The Social Contract* and *Discourses*, ed. G. D. H. Cole, new edn, London, J. M. Dent, 1973, p. 200.

of these associations becomes general in relation to its members, while it remains particular in relation to the State'.[60] And such associations (parties as we would now call them) are inimical to the discovery and articulation of the general will.

Three conclusions flow from this. Firstly, if the general will is a concrete fact and not just a pragmatic compromise, there is no room for opposition or even agnosticism. It is necessary that 'whosoever refuses to obey the general will shall be compelled to do so by the whole body'.[61] This is not even the tyranny of the majority; it is the tyranny of the enlightened, who know what the general will is, even if you, yourself, do not. However, as George Steiner has put it, 'no revolution is unanimous'.[62] Thus, disagreement with those who claimed to represent the popular will was forbidden – since rational argument had no place – as well as, under the Revolution, being terminally dangerous. Secondly, political debate, political parties, contending orthodoxies and elected governments are of dubious validity and can be positively harmful. The most that Rousseau is prepared to grant is that elected deputies, while they cannot be *representatives* of the people, are allowed to be its 'stewards', and passively to implement laws and policies that it is inconvenient for the mass of the people to have to spare the time to do together. This tendency to abominate factions has remained a fixture of French political life to the present day, and has done much to undermine parliamentary democracy in that country. Finally, since the general will cannot be measured, but only deduced, all are free to put themselves forward as the incarnation of the general will, without opponents having any grounds, apart from brute force, for challenging them. And a succession of leaders, from Napoleon to de Gaulle, have done exactly this; none of them have felt the need to use opinion-poll findings to justify their activities.

Rousseau was writing in the abstract; but Sieyès produced his book as the Revolution was getting up steam, and *What Is the Third Estate?* was seized upon as a programme for action. Sieyes asked, in the context of France in 1789, in which parts of society the popular will resided. His answer was unambiguous: it resided in the Third Estate – i.e. all those who were not of the nobility or the

60. Ibid., p. 203.
61. Ibid., p. 195.
62. George Steiner, 'Aspects of Counter-revolution', in G. Best, ed., *The Permanent Revolution: The French Revolution and Its Legacy, 1789–1989*, London, Fontana, 1988, p. 129.

clergy. These latter two Estates oppressed the nation – i.e. the Third Estate – and it was too late now for any kind of conciliation with them. One reason for the superiority of the Third Estate lay in the fact that they were the descendants of the original inhabitants of France – the Gauls and the Romans who remained. The position of the nobility and clergy was owed to the conquest of the nation. Once the nation had been 'purified' by the removal of these elements, it would be able to take comfort from the fact that, once more, it was of solely Gallo-Roman heritage.

When the Jacobin stage of the Revolution was reached, these principles began to be put into practice, with the Messianic and Manichaean fervour that so characterised the main actors, especially Robespierre. The latter argued, in effect, against democracy, because of the likelihood that people might be misguided. His argument amounted to saying that

> as long as the people were hungry, dominated and misled by the rich, their recorded opinions could not be taken as reflecting [the general will].... the task was ... first to create the conditions for a true expression of the popular will. This involved the satisfaction of the people's material needs, popular education, and above all the elimination of evil influences, in other words, opposition. Only after that would the people be called to vote. There could be no doubt about the way they would vote then. In the meantime, the will of the enlightened vanguard was the real will of the people.[63]

Robespierre even argued that a trial of Louis XVI was unnecessary, since the general will had found him guilty, whether or not the population at large were aware of having done so. In his view, therefore, only the sentence remained to be carried out.[64] And although he was ideologically against the death penalty, he emphasised that 'Society affords protection only to peaceful citizens: in the Republic there are no citizens other than Republicans. Royalists and conspirators are, to her, strangers, or rather they are enemies.'[65] Such people – and 'conspirators' in this context meant anyone who opposed him – thus deserved to be guillotined. This attitude made enemies of huge sections of French society, often not for what they did, but for who they were and what they thought. In practice, anyone who failed to give uncritical support to the Jacobins was a traitor, an accomplice of other nations, and

63. Talmon, *Origins*, p. 106.
64. George Rudé, *Robespierre: Portrait of a Revolutionary Democrat*, London, Collins, 1975, p. 34.
65. Cited ibid., p. 166.

deserving of the worst penalties. The result was to polarise the nation, and to alienate more moderate opponents of the monarchy. And indeed, the Revolution was not everywhere popular. For much of the 1790s, France was in a state of civil war, particularly during the peasant risings in the Vendée in 1793 and 1795, supported unsuccessfully by an English fleet. When Napoleon made his appeal for unity in 1803, that unity had only barely been established, and the country more or less pacified. These struggles were not about local independence or the succession to the throne: the Breton peasants rose to express their loyalty to the *idea* of monarchy, and against the concept of republicanism. Although the full rigour of the Jacobin ideologues was attenuated after Robespierre was overthrown in 1793, the divisions at the heart of French society were already so profound as to be unbridgeable. Much of the antipathy of those who had fought against the Republic, and remained abroad as exiles or sullenly at home, was personal in origin. And they had long memories. Auguste Thiers, whom we will meet shortly as the suppressor of the Commune of 1871, was the child of parents who had lost a fortune in the Revolution, and he was in due course a conservative historian of the period. He was able eventually to revenge himself on the descendants of those who had ruined his family, and the symbolism of his army's being based at Versailles would not have been lost on anybody.

The fervour of the Revolutionaries had tended to produce a corresponding violence of attitude in their enemies, and the Restoration, when it came, was handled without very much tact or finesse. There were massacres, expulsions, purges and a thousand petty acts of revenge that would be remembered for decades to come. Yet the Restoration was not complete. What was restored was a monarchy, but a constitutional one, with many of the attributes of Napoleon's régime: thus neither side was really satisfied. The effect of the whole, as one French historian has suggested, was that 'France will for many years be divided into two enemy peoples'.[66] This division was essentially between the past and the future. It was between republican and monarchist, Catholic and atheist, teacher and priest, town and country, and even Paris and the rest of France. Often there was little choice in where you stood, or were thought to stand, all because of some incredibly arcane distinction long ago. 'Losing your fortune to inflation and paper money, or making a fortune by speculating in them, going to a

66. Cited by Tulard, *Napoleon*, p. 446.

church served by a constitutional priest or refusing to do so; holding an office or a commission from this or that régime; any of these could mark a family, a clan, a village, for generations.'[67]

Already, the conspiratorial theories of history that have so disfigured the twentieth century were receiving their first outings. As early as 1797, the Abbé Barruel had argued that the Revolution was the result of a plot first undertaken by the Templars in the sixteenth century, subsequently with the help of the Freemasons, to overthrow all the monarchies of Europe. With the rise of Napoleon, another ingredient was added. Why was it that, in every nation under Napoleon's power, the Jews had been emancipated? Obviously, it was because the Jews had helped to bring the Revolution about; an insight confirmed when Napoleon summoned an assembly of prominent French Jews in Paris in 1806. By calling it the Grand Sanhedrin, after the supreme Jewish court of antiquity, he demonstrated to the satisfaction of many that there always had been a Jewish world government, which numbered the Revolution among its more recent atrocities. It was a simple progression for French exiles in London to associate Napoleon with the Antichrist, at the head of a Jewish legion bent on world domination. Later versions of the myth were more elaborate still: by his death in 1820, Barruel was fantasising about a Europe with a Masonic lodge in every village, pursuing a Judeo-Masonic conspiracy aimed at world domination.

It may seem incredible that any sane individual could believe this rubbish. But, of course it was necessary that '[t]hose who identified themselves with the *ancien régime* had to account somehow for the collapse of a social order that they regarded as ordained by God. The Judeo-Masonic conspiracy supplied the explanation they craved'.[68] And the view of the Revolution (and therefore democracy, education and the modern world) as a Judeo-Masonic conspiracy of the Antichrist led a robust existence in conservative circles well into this century. It was part of the mental furniture of a large number of army officers until at least the Vichy régime (Pétain believed himself to be opposed by this conspiracy), and perhaps as late as the colonels of the OAS who tried to assassinate de Gaulle. It was a component part of Vichy ideology. George Steiner has gone so far as to argue that 'Explicitly in

67. Eugen Weber, 'The Nineteenth-Century Fallout' in Best, ed., *Permanent Revolution*, pp. 161–2.

68. Norman Cohn, *Warrant for Genocide: The Myth of the Jewish World-Conspiracy and the Protocols of the Elders of Zion*, Penguin edn, London, 1979, p. 34.

its rhetoric, in its educational revisionism, in its agrarian-Catholic repudiation of Paris, in its authentically nationalist Jew-hatred ... the world of Vichy and Pétain was that dream fought for by the counter-revolutionaries of 1793 and 1795.' And he notes that many of the most murderous clashes between Vichy and the Resistance took place in the very same communities where their ideological ancestors had butchered each other after 1789.[69] Finally, it is worth adding that the Revolution seems to be the origin of the fantasies of hidden armies, hundreds of thousands strong, waiting for a signal to plunge the nation into anarchy.[70] From the 1790s to the 1940s the same ideas recur constantly.

'For sixty years' wrote a historian just before the disaster of 1870–71 'our history is nothing more than a history of civil war.'[71] He had not seen the worst of it. But France had already been convulsed twice, in 1830 and 1848, with a change of régime on each occasion. Lyons had been a particular source of trouble, and in 1834 an insurrection broke out there that took the army six days to crush. Significantly for the future, the grievances of the rebels were to do with their conditions of work.[72] The army was occupied fairly constantly in putting down such uprisings, but they reached a new peak in and after the revolutionary year of 1848. It took 50,000 troops most of a year to put down a tax revolt in central France. Strikes were widespread in the capital, prompting fears of a second Terror. After further industrial unrest, barricades were raised, and fifty thousand Parisians took to the streets in June 1848. Fifteen hundred were killed, and twelve thousand arrested before order was restored.[73] Yet nothing like the worst had been seen yet. In 1870, the Prussians invaded and quickly routed the French. Napoleon III was captured and abdicated. Bazaine, one of the régime's foremost generals, had been trapped in Metz and surrendered there. A new government was formed, and more armies were raised in the spirit of 1792; but they too were defeated in turn. Thiers, the effective prime minister, negotiated the humiliating Treaty of Frankfurt, involving the loss of Alsace and most of Lorraine, and the payment of a huge indemnity. The inhabitants of Paris, disgusted by the humiliating surrender, and seething with discontent for domestic reasons, rose

---

69. Steiner, 'Aspects', in Best, ed., *Permanent Revolution*, pp. 134–5.
70. Gildea, *Past in French History*, p. 22.
71. Martin, *Histoire de l'Unité*, p. 343.
72. R. Magraw, *France 1815 –1914: The Bourgeois Century*, London, Fontana Press, 1983, p. 96.
73. Ibid., pp. 122–9.

up in a revolt that was universally presented as a reprise of 1789, and elected a revolutionary Commune. Once again, France hesitated nervously on the verge of revolution. But, while the Communards bickered amiably among themselves, Thiers sent the army in. Displaying, it has to be said, more *élan* than it had shown against the Prussians, the army fought its way into the capital through the poorer suburbs, leaving some 20,000 to 30,000 Parisians, mainly non-combatants, dead in its wake. In turn, the Communards executed the hostages they had taken. The last 150 to surrender were shot against the wall of the new Père Lachaise Cemetery in eastern Paris, near where the last stand was made, and buried in a mass grave where they fell. The site rapidly became a memorial, the *Mur des Fedérés*, and a shrine for those on the political Left. Even now, fresh red flowers always decorate it. The episode is not stressed in many French history books, especially the kind used in schools, and was regarded as still so sensitive that the government would not permit a commemoration of its hundredth anniversary.

Left and Right drew opposite conclusions from this episode. Thiers himself was very clear that what had concluded was primarily an ideological conflict. 'We have got rid of Socialism', he said of the crushing of the Commune.[74] History was to demonstrate that this was a premature view; but it expressed very well the prevailing assumption on the Right that, henceforth, the main enemy was to be found in the heart of the very French nation they were supposed to protect. Many felt that they had only providentially escaped total anarchy and a repetition of 1793. Those responsible must therefore be hunted down mercilessly: *Le Figaro* called for the 'extermination' of what it termed the 'democratic vermin'.[75] What was clear was that in any future war, significant sections of the nation simply could not be relied on, and burgeoning trades unions and other associations were a threat to the safety of the state. And France must not lose another war: if she did, the country might collapse into total anarchy. But many on the Right felt the problem went deeper. They explained the defeat by the obstinate clinging to democratic and Revolutionary principles, and the weakness of a France cut off from its roots in the face of what they saw as a disciplined, monarchist Prussia.[76]

74. Alistair Horne, *The French Army and Politics: 1870–1970*, London, Macmillan, 1982, p. 14.

75. Magraw, *France 1815–1914*, p. 203.

76. Ibid., p. 255.

Something of a religious revival set in. Even before the Commune itself, a vow was taken to build a church to the *Sacré Coeur*, the 'sacred heart'. It was built in Montmartre, a working-class area and one of the centres of Communard resistance, but also the highest point in Paris and thus the closest to heaven. It was a piece of punitive architecture, encapsulating the belief that a chastened nation, in moral and political decline since 1789, would now turn again to God and king. Those responsible for its building saw it as 'a reproduction of the ark of the covenant', which reminded the French of their 'engagements undertaken for all time with the God of Abraham, Isaac and Jacob'.[77] It was in this spirit that the national vow was composed and immortalised in stone inside the church, where it can still be seen. A small classic of flagellatory self-abasement, its notional speakers 'humble ourselves before God ... We recognise that we are guilty and have been justly punished'. Moreover, 'to make honourable amends for our sins' the church will be built.[78] The idea of democracy as a sin punishable by defeat was to reappear, almost unchanged, in 1940.

On the Left, opposite conclusions were naturally drawn. The army was no longer trusted, and was seen as an instrument of the state and the middle classes against the workers, more interested in maintaining order than in protecting the nation. The Commune was the culmination of a steady disenchantment with the army, which was to remain powerful for decades, and whose after-affects are still visible. Given the importance of this theme for much of the rest of this study, I will say a little about this now.

In Anglo-Saxon political cultures, books with 'Army' and 'Politics' in the title would be brief and uninteresting. But the French tradition, especially since 1870, is different and much bloodier. The army has often felt itself the guardian of the real interests and the conscience of the nation, usually against squabbling politicians, and the threat or reality of intervention has always been present: the philosophical origin of these attitudes will by now be clear. This led essentially to two conceptions of the army, both politically charged. Until the Revolution, compulsory military service was

77. Raymond A. Jonas, 'Constructing Moral Order: The *Sacré-Coeur* as an Exercise in National Regeneration', in *Proceedings of the Western Society for French History*, No. 19, 1992, pp. 191–201.

78. The *amende honorable* was the traditional process by which the condemned man publicly and solemnly acknowledged his crime at the doors of churches before his execution. See Michel Foucault, *Discipline and Punish: The Birth of the Prison*, Penguin edn, London, 1991, p. 43.

unknown, and one of the things that the Right most distrusted was the innovation of the infant Republic in coining the concept of the 'nation in arms'. Two months after Napoleon's abdication in 1814, the Charter of Louis XVIII abolished conscription. A professional army was to be set up, and guns kept out of the hands of those who might point them the wrong way. The army of the Second Empire was recruited by a kind of involuntary professionalism: those chosen put in six or seven years with the colours, after which they were regarded as politically reliable. (It was noticed, during the Commune, that the fiercest resistance came from the militias that had been raised to defend Paris against the Germans.)

The Left had a concept that was diametrically opposed to this. The army, in spite of its failure against the Germans, had performed well on various occasions against its own people. The answer to this lay in the concept of the citizen in uniform, and a return to the popular armies of the Revolutionary era. However, these armies should do as little formal training as reasonably possible, to prevent them being indoctrinated with suspect ideas, and should rely rather on patriotic fervour. In addition, the Left regarded the army as a conservative, hostile force that incarnated all the political attitudes they themselves feared and despised; and they believed the sentiments to be reciprocated. This distaste for a conservative professional army, with a folk memory of being on the receiving end of its attentions, is the essence of the anti-militarism of the French Left, which still endures in some quarters. It is not to be confused with pacifism; the Jacobin heritage is too strong for that. Thus, the Right wanted a long-service professional army and the Left a short-service conscript one. In the face of increasing German power, the army the Right wanted would have been too small, the army the Left wanted, ineffective. As things turned out, a compromise of sorts was possible. The monarchy was not after all restored, and the Third Republic, slightly to its own surprise, survived until 1940. There were no more insurrections, whilst the army, as if chastened by what it had done, stayed out of politics, refusing, for example, to support the comic-opera coup of Boulanger in 1889. The Left accepted the army, in spite of the massacres of the Commune; the Right accepted conscription, in spite of its fears about revolution. Really, there was no choice: the common desire to recapture Alsace and Lorraine could obviously only be fulfilled by the army, and so people had better learn to love it. And a professional army was clearly not going to be big enough to do the job.

The quarter-century after 1870 is, fairly, regarded as the 'golden age' of the French army. Partly this was because of its unprecedented popularity, but partly also because it did make a definite effort to renew and transform itself. The *École Supérieure de Guerre* was founded in 1875 as a way of training General Staff officers. A serious interest in military questions was encouraged, and sweeping changes in military equipment were made.[79] Thus, albeit only temporarily, the army became, as its nickname had it, the 'Ark of the Covenant', above political strife.[80] But problems were already developing. The army was growing steadily apart from society. Ironically, the very prestige of the army was attracting a more and more conservative, often monarchist officer corps, increasingly from the aristocracy, and often former pupils of Catholic, rather than secular, schools. And, in the new Republic, most other public careers were barred to young men from such a background, whilst at the same time their economic standing and security declined as rents and income from land generally fell.[81] Coming from such a background they, for their part, felt increasingly alienated from a secular Republic that now seemed well established.

It was into this background that the Dreyfus affair erupted, a collective outbreak of insanity that convulsed France for a decade, in a way that now seems almost impossible to understand. But the real issue was never whether Captain Alfred Dreyfus, the first Jew ever to serve on the General Staff, had passed secrets to the Germans. Rather, it was an opportunity for enemies and supporters of the Republic to plead their cases and destroy their opponents. On the Right, the affair seemed to confirm all their worst fears. Anti-Semitic propaganda had been on the rise, and the Anti-Semitic League was founded in 1890. Its founder Drumont, author of *La France Juive*, launched a campaign in his newspaper *La Libre Parole* against 'Jews in the Army'. He claimed that the intention of the Jews was to take control of the army, which would then be the servant of the Rothschilds. The newspaper had half a million readers: one fifth of them Catholic priests.[82] But the Jews were only an initial target: the hope of many on the Right was to challenge the very existence of the Republic itself. At the start, the moderates and the Left were scarcely interested; but, as the affair developed,

79. Paul-Marie de la Gorce, *The French Army: A Military-Political History*, trans. Kenneth Douglas, London, Weidenfeld and Nicolson, 1963, pp. 9–10.
80. Horne, *Army and Politics*, p. 15.
81. de la Gorce, *French Army*, pp. 221–4.
82. Ibid., pp. 32–33.

they began to see that it was a wonderful opportunity to bring to heel the army, the most recalcitrant of the organs of the state.

Once it started to become clear that Dreyfus was innocent, the army began to fake evidence against him, and the struggle reached new heights (or depths) of bitterness. The easy tendency to identify a personal view with the general will lent a particular stridency to the debate. 'Drumont and Maurras dismiss Jews and Protestants as artificial Frenchmen, outside the nation; Zola at his trial sets his view of France and his values against those of the military leaders ... The claim of them all is that their vision of France is, or should be, the general one. The conflict is fundamental.'[83] Yet for many in the country, views and values were irrelevant. Their fear was a simple one: the army would not survive the overturning of the case against Dreyfus, and the destruction of the army would leave France undefended. Thus, the guilty verdict must be maintained in the national interest: it was expedient that one man should suffer for the good of many. But not content with this, many of the Republic's enemies argued that there was indeed a plot – not to frame Dreyfus, but to destroy the army itself. For Barrès, the guilty men were 'intellectuals', 'rostrum anarchists' and 'metaphysicians of sociology' [sic], who 'treat our generals as idiots, our social institutions as absurdities and our traditions as unhealthy'.[84] The popular press had no difficulty in identifying the culprits: who benefited from the weakening of the army? Why, the Germans, the Jews and the Freemasons.

After the suicide of Colonel Henry, one of those who had forged documents and was subsequently discovered, La Libre Parole opened a subscription list to support his 'widow and orphan against the Jew Reinach [a Dreyfusard politician]'. The response was enormous, and many contributors added a message of their own, as well as personal details. An assiduous journalist collected and classified the information into a book of nearly seven hundred pages, arranged by category, and it was published in 1899. For the most part, the contributors were those – retired officers, small businessmen, conservative peasantry, priests – who felt excluded from the Republic and apprehensive about social and economic changes. Their voice is the authentic one of a group who were to be the bedrock of the Vichy régime half a century later. Here are a few examples:

83. H. R. Kedward, The Dreyfus Affair: Catalyst for Tensions in French Society, London, Longman, 1965, p. 30.
84. Cited ibid., p. 38.

- two old soldiers of 1870 and five seeking revenge, who hate the yids.
- a small tradesman ruined by the Jews.
- 'God grant that our unfortunate Nation tear itself away from the grip of Jews and Free-Masons.'
- 'Joan of Arc help us to expel the new English.'
- a country priest who prays most ardently for the extermination of the two enemies of France: the Jew and the Free-Mason.[85]

By the end of the affair, with Dreyfus released, if not fully exonerated, some calming of the waters might have been in order. But the opportunity for revenge was too great to miss; not only against the army, but against the whole of the Catholic/monarchist/conservative section of French society that was identified with the anti-Dreyfus cause. Many Catholic schools were closed, church and state were formally separated, and the army was ruthlessly purged. Secret files were kept on all officers, based mostly on gossip and rumour, and those thought to be insufficiently republican and secular were denied promotion and sometimes worse. And, with stunning political ineptitude, the files were kept, for security reasons, in the headquarters of the most powerful Masonic organisation in France, of which many leading republican politicians were members. The ensuing scandal brought down the government in 1906, and the worst of the heat began to go out of the issue. Partly this was because of fears of the growing electoral power of the Socialists, who polled 830,000 votes in that year, which brought them 113 deputies. Many republican, but non-socialist, politicians decided that it was time for fence-mending. Moreover, industrial militancy was increasing, and, for the first time, there was talk that trades unionists in different countries would declare an international strike to prevent a war breaking out between France and Germany. A sign of the times was that the government held back from ordering the army to break down the doors of churches in order that an inventory of property could be made, as was necessary after the legal separation of church and state. Thus, 'the Army could once more assume its normal place within the Nation and the state. Every time public order was threatened by working-class militancy, the government called out

---

85. Pierre Quillard, *Le Monument Henry* (1898). The examples cited are from among those reproduced by Girardet, *Histoire du Nationalisme Français*, pp. 179–181; Kedward, *Dreyfus Affair*, p. 83.

the troops against the strikers. On each occasion it could be seen ever more plainly that the government had to rely on the Army'.[86] Excluded from this reconciliation were, of course, the ordinary people, in whose eyes the standing of the army sank ever lower. Yet when war did come in 1914, the country reacted with a unity that few had suspected. The mass uprisings and strikes did not take place, and the precautionary arrests of politicians and trades union leaders did not have to be carried out. Barely 2 per cent failed to respond to the call-up. A government of national unity was established. And France won: or at least, she was on the winning side. The message was clear, and not new; no matter how threadbare the *Union Sacrée* had been in practice, no matter how low morale was in 1917, unity had been the French secret weapon. When they were united they won wars; when they were disunited, they were invaded and occupied by foreigners. Yet the *Union Sacrée* was only a temporary truce, and dissensions continued to smoulder just below the surface.

The Sovereign

If the natural high destiny of France was forever being obstructed by outbreaks of disunity, leading to invasion and occupation of the country, what could be done to promote the desired unity? The traditional symbol of unity was, of course, the king, whose rule was absolute in the sense that it could not be challenged and that he did not need to account for any of his actions to the people. As Bossuet, the theoretician of divine right under Louis XIV put it: 'Consider the prince in his cabinet. From there issue the orders that set in motion together the magistrates and the captains, the citizens and the soldiers, the provinces and the armies by sea and land. This is the image of God who seated on His throne in the highest heavens sets the whole of nature in motion.'[87] This extract also points out, helpfully, the *universal* character of the king's authority. No decision could be taken unless taken by him or in his name. The concept of the exercise of power that did not derive from the king was not only treasonous, it was impossible. Nonetheless, the power of the king, although absolute, was not arbitrary. In practice, it was

86. De la Gorce, *French Army*, p. 61.
87. Cited by C. B. A. Behrens, *The Ancien Régime*, London, Thames and Hudson, 1967, p. 85.

limited by the fundamental laws of the nation, the influence of the Royal Council, custom, and privileges and indemnities granted long ago, as well as the sheer difficulty of getting the desires of the king actually carried out.[88]

Although the amateur psychoanalysis of whole nations is seldom valuable, and may be downright misleading, it does seem legitimate to point out that France has had inordinate difficulty in trying to move away from this paradigm of an absolute monarchy with practical limitations, and it has been partly re-invented under different guises several times since 1789. There is an observable tendency for power to be concentrated back in the hands of an individual after a period when it is more widely dissipated. Some French theorists of a dialectical persuasion have discovered what they see as a dialectical tendency for French régimes to move from the highly centralised to the highly decentralised, and finally to a compromise state, after which the process begins again. However this may be, there does seem to be a tendency for French régimes to be constructed essentially as a reaction to the faults of the previous régime, and, after a while, to seek an equilibrium not necessarily in a dictatorship, but around a unifying symbol, incarnated in an individual who may or may not wish to play this role.

Rousseau's original idea was to replace the will of the king with the general will: the replacement of one unitary concept with another. The word Rousseau chose to express the concept of the active general will was 'The Sovereign', with all its overtones of royalty. The individual members of the Republic put themselves 'in common under the general will', and thus create 'a collective body ... receiving from this act its unity, its common identity, its life and its will'.[89] In many ways the Sovereign is described much as an absolute monarch might be described. The public are bound to the Sovereign, but the Sovereign cannot be bound to itself. And the Sovereign need give no guarantee to its subjects, because it cannot have an interest contrary to theirs. Once events moved from the theoretical level to the practical, however, the obvious political difficulties arose. If the general will is not a statistical concept, and if, in consequence, representative democracy and the compromises inherent in it cannot identify the general will, how, in practical terms, is the Sovereign to act? A temporary solution,

88. Timbal and Castaldo, *Histoire des Institutions*, pp. 339–40.
89. Rousseau, *Social Contract*, p. 192.

foreseen by Rousseau and enshrined in the Constitution of 1791, was to make the king subordinate to the general will. The nation 'from whom alone all powers emanate' (p. 13) delegates the 'executive power' to the king (the legislative power is delegated to the National Assembly). Thus, the king, from having been the source of all power, is reduced to the status of an agent.

But whereas it is conceivable for an *individual* to delegate powers to others, it is difficult to see how an abstraction can do so. The Constitution of 1791 insists that the nation has delegated certain powers to the king; but of course, this remains an assertion of a relationship at the symbolic level, not a description of a process that objectively happened. Needless to say, this rather unsatisfactory compromise did not last. In perishing, and in removing the last individual symbol of unity, it began a debate that has not yet concluded about the distribution of powers and the relationship between them. Applied with full rigour, the principles of the Revolution would have made a parliament largely redundant. Indeed, its only real function was the mundane one of passing laws that reflected the general will, as an agent of the nation. Yet it was difficult to see how – even in France – an abstraction could visibly and effectively run the country. And from a political point of view, some form of concretisation of the new spirit of popular sovereignty was clearly desirable. At the most practical of levels, someone had to direct the policy of the state, and this was not something that a large and varied legislative body could, in practice, do. For this reason, the 1793 Constitution proposed a *Conseil executif* of twenty-four members, from a list suggested to the National Assembly.

From this point, there began an inexorable slide towards the individual rule of the Emperor Napoleon I a decade later: from the Committee of Public Safety, to the Directory, to the three Consuls, to the sole assumption of power by the first consul. And his acceptance by the French began a pattern whereby, periodically, a Sovereign figure is sought to rescue the nation in times of (usually military) danger. I will have some more to say about the qualifications for sovereignty in a moment; but first it is worth saying a word or two about how and why Napoleon was able to take power. After the overthrow of Robespierre and his colleagues in 1793, the Jacobins declined in influence to the advantage of the Thermidorians, so called after the Revolutionary month in which they had taken power. But France was still divided, the Royalists had only narrowly been prevented from making a comeback, the economy was in decline, French armies were defeated everywhere, the Thermidorians of the Directory were split into factions, and there was the real risk of a coup from at least one quarter. Napoleon had a variety of qualifications for taking a public role at this stage. First, he had not been in France for most of the time since Thermidor: he had been successively with the army of Italy and the army of Egypt, and therefore was uncontaminated by failure at home. Secondly, his absence made him little known. People of varying persuasions could fashion him in their own image. He therefore attracted, as one perceptive contemporary observer noticed 'all the men of no allegiance, all the discontented'.[90] Thirdly, insofar as anything was known of him, he was thought to be a successful general, and success in any field was unusual in 1799. Napoleon claimed to have saved the Republic, and also to incarnate the general will. But he also described his role using concepts and a vocabulary that deliberately echoed the royal heritage. Napoleon was probably the first modern general to understand propaganda and to realise that, on the political level, what counts is not victory or defeat, but public perception. While he was commanding the army of Italy in 1797, Napoleon set up two French-language newspapers that had among their functions the strengthening of his own position, often by deliberately mythologising him. He is described thus by one publication: 'He flies like lightning and strikes like a thunderbolt. He is everywhere and he sees everything.' Napoleon (for he is the effective author) is both describing himself in the guise of a Classical hero, and also laying specific claim to a corpus of iconography about Jupiter, the king of the gods. The comparison to Jupiter was not only a continuation of the Classical references that had delighted the later Louis, it was also an acceptably republican way of laying claim to the divine status that the kings of France had claimed in their time.

From the time when Napoleon was proclaimed first consul, in the Constitution of Year VIII (1799), the attempt at some kind of collective leadership without a central rallying point was abandoned. Thereafter, there was a monarchic or republican head of state at all times. He might be very weak, like the president of the Third Republic, or very strong, like the president of the Fifth; but he was henceforth a fixture. This required the separation – or at least the differentiation – of powers to be discussed, and nowhere more importantly than in those traditionally royalist areas, war and diplomacy. The way in which the powers were divided up

90. Tulard, *Napoleon*, p. 6.

depended, in turn, on how the debate about the way in which the general will should be exercised was progressing. From the moment of the Revolution, some had argued for a balance of power on the British model and a consequent increase in the status of the legislative body: both Robespierre and Sieyès expressed themselves in a contradictory fashion on this point. St-Just put his finger precisely upon the weakness of the general will concept. Who is to define it? How is it to be recognised? Rather, 'The general will, properly so-called, and in the language of liberty, is formed of the majority of particular wills.'[91] It is therefore a statistical, not a mystical, concept, and an elected assembly is the way in which it expresses itself. These concepts recur time and again over the next two centuries, never really reaching a resolution.

It is possible to follow the progress of these ideas in the successive texts of constitutional laws from the fall of Napoleon onwards. In the preamble to Louis XVIII's Charter of June 1814, it was argued that only a 'supreme authority' could provide permanence and efficacy in the institutions of the nation. As a result 'Executive power belongs to the King only', who is 'the supreme head of state, he commands the army and navy, declares war, makes treaties of peace, alliance and commerce, names all holders of public offices and makes rules and ordinances for the execution of laws for the safety of the state' (p. 116). This is in many ways a restatement of the traditional powers and roles of the king (although it also closely resembles the description of the functions of the first consul in 1799, and is, in turn, largely repeated in the Orleanist Charter of 1830). But what is interesting is the way in which these attributes are successively disaggregated and recombined under republican governments. The first attempt at defining a presidential office, in the Constitution of 1848, creates a semi-monarchical figure, whose power is nonetheless carefully qualified. Executive power is 'delegated' to him by the French people, who elect him directly. He 'has available' to him the armed forces, but may not command them in person. He is concerned with the defence of the state, but cannot undertake a war without the agreement of parliament. Ambassadors are accredited to him, and he names and dismisses ministers, military commanders, ambassadors and other functionaries.

This constitution was rapidly overtaken by the coup of President Bonaparte, and the 1852 Constitution describes his role *almost*

---

91. Cited by Talmon, *Origins*, p. 85.

word for word as the king's had been described in 1814: '[He] is the Head of State; he commands the army and navy, declares war, makes treaties of peace, alliance and commerce, names all holders of public offices, makes rules and decrees necessary for the execution of laws.' In addition, he is allowed to declare a state of siege in one or more departments. All ministers are appointed by him directly, and all officials have to swear allegiance to him personally.

The Constitution of the Third Republic represents a clear break with this model. The president negotiates and ratifies treaties, but needs an affirmative vote of parliament in support. He can only declare war with their approval. He is elected by parliament and can be impeached by them. He is not the commander of the armed forces (no one is so designated), and he names all military and civilian employees. It was not surprising that the calamitous collapse of the Republic in 1940 produced atavistic yearnings and the desire for a more monarchical leader. This role was played by Pétain with relish, and he promulgated many laws with the royal *Nous*. In particular, the law of 11 July 1940 concentrated powers of defence and security in his hands. The description of his powers closely resembles those of Napoleon in 1848: he names all ministers, who are responsible only to him, he has the armed forces available to him, he can declare a state of siege, negotiates and ratifies treaties without reference to anyone, but can declare war only with the permission of the 'legislative Assemblies' – not a major limitation in 1940.[92] He subsequently insisted on a personal oath of loyalty from all state servants.

Since the bulk of this study is concerned with events after 1940, I propose to save an analysis of the Constitutions of the Fourth and Fifth Republics for later chapters. But it can already be appreciated that they fit into the trends already described. The 1946 Constitution was a parliamentary one, limiting the power of the executive; the 1958 Constitution, by contrast, set up a Sovereign, a secular God-King figure, as president, recalling in the description of his powers the attributes of monarchs and emperors past. In this sense, the flip comment that the president of France is an elected monarch has more analytical value than its originators might have supposed.

Those Sovereign figures who have from time to time exercised these very considerable powers have always sought to justify

---

92. Dominique Rémy, *Les lois de Vichy: Actes dits 'lois' de l'autorité de fait se prétendant 'gouvernement de l'État français'*, Paris, Romillat, 2nd edn, 1992, p. 41.

them by appeals to popular support. There are obvious attractions in the use of a plebiscite: the terms of the question can be suitably loaded, and the very institution provides a way of bypassing the loathed political parties and of appealing to a higher authority, that of the people themselves. The substitution of a simple yes/no answer, in place of the normal range of choices in a democracy, often works to the advantage of the plebiscite-holder, especially if it is presented as a choice between order and chaos. The Revolution itself had made much use of plebiscites, and Napoleon continued the tradition in asking the French whether they wished him to be consul for life. Arrangements in those days were primitive, the franchise was limited, and the voting procedures were not secret. But what is interesting is that Napoleon should have thought the enterprise worth the effort.[93] It was frequently imitated thereafter, notably by Napoleon III in 1851 and 1852, and was practised more recently, of course, by de Gaulle. The election of a president by universal suffrage and the frequent recourse by Sovereign figures to plebiscites are both reflections of the old idea of a mystical bond between the king and the nation. They are consequences of the widespread traditional French distrust of political parties and factions, and of disenchantment with the weakness and division that have been characteristic features of parliamentary-dominated political systems in France. They also enable Sovereign figures to claim to be above the tawdry compromises of politics, and to incarnate the spirit of national unity, especially at a time of tension.

In his book on political myths, Raoul Girardet distinguishes four models for what he calls the 'Myth of the Saviour' – what I have called the Sovereign. (In practice, of course, these models are often combined.) The first is that of Cincinnatus, the unwilling dictator from the plough, summoned back from a well-merited retirement, or from duty being carried out abroad, to save the nation in its time of peril. The second is that of Alexander, the man of action, whose legitimacy comes from the sword, and who is possessed of heroic and seemingly divine attributes. The third is that of Solon, the giver of laws, who comes to the fore after order has been restored. (And it is interesting that every Sovereign figure, from Napoleon to Gaulle, has produced a constitution, and often much else besides, once their hold on power was secure.)

93. Claude Langlois, 'Napoleon Bonaparte', in *L'Election du Chef de l'Etat en France*, pp. 81–93.

Finally, there is the model of Moses, the seer, granted privileged insight into the future, able to see where the destiny of the people and the nation lies.[94]

As Girardet himself notes, some blurring of reality at the edges is usually necessary to turn real individuals into one or more of these models. It is interesting to see what a variety of (often-unassuming) individuals had to bear the burden of such enormous expectations. Only specialists now remember the names of presidents like Doumerge (1934) or Pinay (1952), yet quite disproportionate hopes were invested in them (and Pinay in particular) for the future of France. This is because, as I noted above, the demand for Sovereigns exists independently of the supply, and so mediocre figures are necessarily invested with supernatural attributes. To the extent that they are ambiguous and even shallow figures, they are the more acceptable. And French politicians have always been historically literate and able, therefore, consciously to manipulate these historical models. Pétain was nothing more than a malevolent nonentity, yet it was precisely his lack of depth and definition that made him almost universally acceptable in 1940: he was a blank screen on to which the French could project their deepest desires, and he consciously set out to fulfil their expectations – themselves, of course, the product of past events.

From the above, it should be clear that de Gaulle's accession to power and the policies that he then pursued were not accidents. They were entirely comprehensible in terms of the grammar of French history that I have, very briefly, been summarising. The extravagant expectations of glory based on divine election, the brutal collision with real military, political and economic weakness, the confusion and disunity of the nation and its political life, the restlessness of the army, the search for a redeeming Sovereign, the coming to power, the confirmation by popular acclaim, the vigorous overhaul of the state, the restoration of national prestige – all could describe not only de Gaulle's tenure, but half a dozen previous episodes also. Among other things, the rest of this study traces the evolution of all these factors in rather more detail. But it might be worth stressing, before we begin, the special nature of the Gaullist construct in the light of what has been discussed so far. As one textbook used by trainee French bureaucrats notes, the acceptance 'of the institutions of the Fifth Republic by all the French political groupings – obvious since the arrival of the Left

94. Girardet, *Mythes et Mythologies Politiques*, pp. 73–80.

in power in 1981 – seems to have buried the quarrel about systems of government that almost continually divided the French from 1789 to 1958.'[95]

The Gaullist Republic is the first that no significant section of the population has regarded as invalid and has wished to see overthrown. Not only did the Left accept the institutional inheritance, the transfer of power passed off much more quietly than could have been foreseen twenty years before. The first properly elected Socialist-Communist government was sworn in without fuss; the army stayed in its barracks, and the crowds in the streets were celebrating, not building barricades. Something of why this was not a typical outcome of French history will already be clear. I now turn in more detail to French security concerns, politico-military relations and relations with other countries, in the period from the end of the First World War to the present day.

95. François de La Saussay, *L'Heritage Institutionel français, 1789–1958*, Paris, Hachette, 1992, p. 3.

2

GRANDEUR AND MISERY

Grandeur and Misery of Victory

Title of a book by Clemenceau

Such a complete misunderstanding aggravated by acerbic, sour, and persistent criticism, I have rarely seen.

French ambassador in Washington, 1922

The United Kingdom would have the greatest difficulty in accepting any plan which involved the creation of a super-State.

Sir John Simon, 1932

It begins with the defeat of 1940, the 'strange defeat' of which Marc Bloch was subsequently to write. But this defeat, in turn, was interpreted at the time as the consequence of, or as a judgement upon, a whole range of events that took place between the two wars, many of which have retained their controversial nature to this day. Because French security policy since 1944 has been very largely an attempt to avoid a repetition of the mistakes of the inter-war years, it is worth briefly sketching in what these events were, and how they appeared to contemporaries. In the process, it will be clear that there are surprising similarities between the difficulties and crises experienced in Paris in those days and more recent events. In this chapter, I focus on the era immediately following the First World War. In the next two chapters I deal with the approach of the Second World War. The complexity of the issues is such that, rather than attempt a (necessarily breathless) complete narrative, I have focused in some detail on a few important episodes, passing in silence over much else.

In the immediate aftermath of the First World War, the main themes that were to dominate French security policy for the next forty years were already in place. These themes were: economic weakness and political conflict, fear of Germany, fear of Communism (or 'Bolshevism', as it was then called) and difficult relations with the United States. First, however, it is important to understand how the French viewed the victory of 1918 and their part in it. When Clemenceau read the text of the Armistice to the two houses of the French parliament, he added the kind of postscript that was the common currency of patriotic French oratory at the time: 'As for the living ... we await them for the great task of social reconstruction. Thanks to them, France, once the soldier of God, today the soldier of Humanity, will always be the soldier of the Ideal.'[1]

This appears to have been the prevalent view: France had sacrificed herself massively and bled herself white, not just for her own sake but for the sake of Western civilisation as a whole. Just as in the days of Charlemagne, she had taken the leading role in facing down the barbarians from the East. Some saw it as 'perhaps the final victory of the French Revolution'.[2] And on the morrow of the victory parade, on Bastille Day 1919, *Le Temps*, the semi-official daily newspaper, owned by industrial interests and not given to lyricism for its own sake, hymned a

> Nation always ready to fight and work for the advancement of universal civilisation and the continuance of human progress, enamoured of justice ... ready for any sacrifice in order that peace should conform to the demands of conscience and the eternal rules of law ... resolved, in spite of her preference for peace, to see total war through to the end if a barbarous invader should come to menace her territory ...[3]

This attitude may seem merely exaggerated, and even bizarre, even for an age when the rhetoric of nationalism came easily to the lips; but its practical political effects were profound. It amounted to saying that France had a special status, and because of this and the degree of its suffering, had more rights than other nations, and these rights should be respected, not only by its vanquished foe, but

---

1. *Journal Officiel, Débats, Chambre des députés*, (henceforth *JO*, etc.), 11 November 1918, p. 2660.

2. Jean-Pierre Azéma and Michel Winock, *La Troisième République: 1870–1940*, Paris, Calmann-Lévy, 1970, p. 179.

3. Cited by Jacques Nobécourt, *Une Histoire Politique de l'Armée, Vol. 1, 1919–1942, de Pétain a Pétain*, Paris, Seuil, 1967, p. 38.

by its allies also. The story of subsequent years is of a bewildered people coming to realise that this view was not shared by others.

Studies of the inter-war years frequently begin by remarking on the contrast between the splendour of the victory parade and the miserable practical situation in which France found itself. There is much relevance in this contrast. For a spectator, the sight must have been heartening. There were twenty nations in the parade: not only the familiar British and the increasingly familiar Americans, but Greeks, Portuguese, Poles, even Japanese, all come to the help of France, yet all seeming no more than auxiliaries to the mighty army of the French, whose contingents were led by the semi-divine figure of Pétain, victor of Verdun, appropriately mounted on a white charger.[4] Yet, even here, the perceptive observer might have thought it interesting that, because the contingents marched in alphabetical order, it was the Americans who led the parade. A nation not even considered a military force in 1914 had, by the end of the war, come to be the determinant of victory.

The French, who had borne the brunt of the fighting, who had emerged at the head of a coalition that had won a victory of unprecedented completeness, and who were now the foremost military power in Europe, might have been expected to display a certain self-confidence and hope in the future. Yet, beyond the pomp and circumstance, political and military leaders looked to the future with foreboding. They were aware, firstly, of the economic and financial weakness of the nation. The war had been fought on French territory, and specifically in the only large industrial area in 1914, the two departments of Nord and Pas de Calais. This area, and thus much of French industrial potential, had been devastated. A British Treasury study put the *direct* cost of the war to the Allies at some £24,000 million, and damage to the French infrastructure alone at some £2,000 million.[5] One expert has calculated that the effect of the war was to lose fifteen months of national income: some 55 billion francs at 1913 prices.[6] The human cost had been stupefying. France had lost a higher proportion of its population than any other combatant: 1.35 million dead, several times that many wounded, many invalided for life. Beyond the human tragedy, the financial cost, in pensions and benefits,

4. Ibid., pp. 14–16.
5. Alan Sharp, *The Versailles Settlement: Peacemaking in Paris, 1919*, London, Macmillan, 1991, p. 76.
6. See Philippe Bernard and Henri Dubief, *The Decline of the Third Republic, 1914–1938*, trans. A. Forster, Cambridge, Cambridge University Press, 1988, p. 80.

and in the lack of a workforce for the reconstruction, imposed enormous strains on the economy. And France had opted to pay for the war by selling foreign assets (thus forfeiting income in later years), and by loans from abroad, which would have to be repaid with interest.

The situation was bad in absolute terms, but in relative terms it was even worse. German territory had been untouched by the war, and its modern industry was completely intact. Its population remained significantly higher (some 70 million, as against about 40 million in France), and among men of military age the disparity was more like 2 to 1. In addition, the German birthrate was respectable, while the French remained stubbornly low. And finally, Germany had financed the war primarily by domestic loans: these debts soon dwindled to nothing as a result of rampant inflation. In terms of population, military and economic potential and financial strength, then, the advantage lay clearly with Germany. An outsider, knowing nothing of recent history, might well have concluded that it was Germany, and not France, that was the victor. The inevitable conclusion was that, for much of the interwar period, France was in a state of chronic economic crisis and weakness. Even when the economy improved, as in the late 1920s, the financial and political problem of war debts – especially to the United States – haunted every government and complicated international relations.

These same leaders were aware, secondly, of the weakness of the political system. For these were the dog days of the Third Republic and of the Constitution of 1875. As is usual in such cases, the arrangements in force were adopted as a reaction to the previous régime – in this case the dictatorship of Napoleon III – rather than for any intrinsic merits they might possess. Thus, a highly decentralised, parliament-based system was created, with a weak executive and an impotent presidency – what modern analysts have called a *régime d'Assemblée*. The disunity of French politics and the multiplicity of political parties combined to make coalition governments inevitable. Governments changed frequently (about every six months on average), but tended to resemble each other closely nonetheless. The situation would have been easier if there had been any kind of party discipline; but there was not. Until 1910, it was even possible to be a member of more than one parliamentary group at the same time – or a member of none. This, combined with the need for constant coalition governments, made any sense of collective cabinet responsibility on the British model impossible.

In the circumstances, the job of the prime minister[7] became much like that of a modern chief whip. He stood or fell by his ability to create and sustain a coalition, and by the skill with which he allocated portfolios to individuals according to their needs, if not necessarily their abilities. This did not leave a great deal of time for the formulation of policy, nor, indeed, did the brief tenure of most French governments encourage long-range thinking. The prime minister had no executive powers, and was little more than a chairman. His personal staff was small, and there was no secretariat to issue minutes of meetings: it was therefore normal for participants to leave with quite different ideas about what had been decided. Generally, a prime minister would also take on an important department himself – foreign affairs, war, finance – purely to give himself a power base, and often without being able to play an effective role in such subjects. International relations were difficult enough, given the weakness of the French position. But they were greatly complicated by the short lives of governments. Ministers and officials setting out for a negotiation could find that the government changed while they were away. And other nations were always tempted to play it long, in the hope that a more acquiescent (or simply weaker) government would soon appear.

Politics became little more than a game. The most admired manœuvre was the resignation skilfully timed to avoid the responsibility for a difficult and unpopular decision. For its full effect, this resignation would be followed by a triumphant return to power over the carcass of the intervening government, destroyed through taking the decision you yourself had avoided. Increasingly, towards the end, the deputies shunned the making of difficult decisions entirely, and voted 'full powers' to the government, thus excusing themselves personally from participation in unpopular measures. Moreover, the sheer quality of the *hommes politiques* of the inter-war years was depressingly low. There was a practical reason for this: the war had devastated the ranks of the graduates of the *Grandes Écoles*, the institutions of higher learning, which have a higher status than universities and provided then (as they do now) the brightest and best of the

7. Known at the time as 'President of the Council' (of Ministers), and thus apt to be confused, in books of French origin, with the president of the Republic, a political nonentity elected by parliament to fulfil mainly ceremonial functions. The post of prime minister was not created until the 1958 Constitution, but I have, on this occasion, preferred clarity to pedantry.

political class. But between 1914 and 1918, many of them never made it out of the trenches, to the eternal impoverishment of French politics. Although such comparisons are difficult, it is doubtful if there was ever a time when the French political class was held in such low esteem by the mass of the people. The traditional French dislike of parties and interest groups, described in the previous chapter, was never stronger, and had a poisonous effect on the credibility of the entire political system. It was this popular disdain for politicians that made Pétain's accession to power in 1940 so straightforward. Similarly, the way for de Gaulle was opened in 1958 by many who thought that the political system of the Fourth Republic too closely resembled that of the Third. The single most dominant party of the period was the (conservative) Radical Party. Its full title was the *Parti Républicain Radical et Radical-Socialiste*, although it was in reality neither radical, socialist nor a party. It had an ideology of sorts, representing as it did the secular and republican political forces of the late nineteenth century. It was supported by middle-class professional men (women did not have the vote until 1944): lawyers, teachers, doctors, dentists, civil servants, the self-employed – it was especially the party of the 'little man'. This distinguished it from the obscurantist parties of the Catholic right, who had yet to accept the nineteenth century, let alone the twentieth, and from the socialists; but any coherent political philosophy had vanished by 1919, when its programme (with the introduction of income tax) had effectively been implemented.

By the 1920s, the party had become little more than a machine, whose main purpose 'was to be in government'.[8] Here, at least, it could claim some success. Although it was more disciplined than most, it was still less a party than a collection of factions, whose leaders hated each other more than they did the other parties, with whom they were anyway forced into coalitions. With such a political system, France would have found it difficult to deal with even the modest challenges of a time of peace and plenty. Faced with the strains of the inter-war years, the system progressively fell apart, until it finally committed ritual suicide in July 1940.

---

8. Oliver Bernier, *Fireworks at Dusk: Paris in the Thirties*, London, Little, Brown and Company, 1993, p. 26.

The Germans Will Pay

Even before the killing had stopped in 1918, the three victors (four if Italy is included) had begun to think about the shape of a settlement with Germany. For the French, there were two issues of overwhelming importance: future security, of which more later, and the question of paying for the war. All precedent on reparations pointed in one direction. War before 1914 was rather like a civil court case: the loser was expected to pay the winner's costs; as had, indeed, happened after the Franco-Prussian war of 1870– 71, when the Germans had exacted a large indemnity from the French, and stayed until it was paid off.

The issue of reparations was a key one for several reasons. First, the finances of the French state were in a very bad way. Income tax had only been introduced, under pressure, in 1917, and was only sporadically enforced. Even together with indirect taxation, revenues only covered about one-eighth of the total budget. Everyone therefore knew that tax reform was inevitable, but no one wanted to be politically responsible for it. This situation would have been bad enough if government commitments had been static or declining; but reconstruction, loan repayments, widows' and invalids' pensions and a necessary minimum of social betterment were about to place unprecedented strains on the public finances.

Politically, the problem was insoluble, since it was impossible to assemble a majority for any particular way of raising the money. For financial, political and historical reasons, therefore, it was inevitable that the government's response would be that of Klotz, the finance minister, that 'l'Allemagne payera': the Germans will pay. In December 1918, Klotz told parliament that, instead of preparing a budget, he was drawing up a list of restitutions and reparations to be extracted from the Germans. These would fund the necessary expenditure on social reforms and reconstruction. Only if the reparations proved to be insufficient would the question of taxes be revisited.[9]

This was predominantly a political response to a political problem. It avoided the sensitive question of tax increases before an election, and punted the whole issue forward into the indeterminate future. It was not based on any genuine analysis of what Germany

9. *JO*, 3 December 1918, p. 3236, cited by Arno J. Mayer, *Politics and Diplomacy of Peacekeeping: Containment and Counterrevolution at Versailles, 1918–1919*, London, Weidenfeld and Nicolson, 1968, p. 650.

could afford, or even what the size of the eventual bill would be. It was less a policy than a means of avoiding having to formulate one: a typical manœuvre, in fact, of the time. It was also a policy that was born of an ignorance of economics which was then almost universal, and from which finance ministers were by no means exempt. Economics had a low status in France, and was scarcely studied – even in its Classical guise (Keynes was not translated until after the Second World War). The economy was run by practical men who knew that you could not spend more than you earned, and that, provided the budget was balanced, all would be well. Beyond that, they really had no theories at all, and it is not surprising either that the French economy during the war was very incompetently run, or that, at Versailles, the French demands were economically illiterate.

Yet the fact remained that Germany could not pay. The sums involved, however calculated, were so unbelievably enormous that they were bound to be beyond her means. And, ironically, Germany would only be *able* to pay if France was prepared to wait until the German economy grew. But would a strong Germany have any incentive to pay anyway? Moreover, such a policy would have needed the agreement of France's allies. Although there was support, especially in Britain, for the idea of squeezing the Germans, foreign politicians had other policy imperatives as well, and these frequently led them to take a softer line on reparations.

Conflict on the Left Bank

Even before the conclusion of the war, the French had glumly decided that victory alone would not be adequate. In addition, some means had to be found of permanently altering the strategic situation in France's favour. The reattachment of Alsace and Lorraine, whilst politically essential, would not improve the situation very much. The answer, obviously, was to detach from Germany the provinces on the left bank of the Rhine, which had been forcibly joined to Prussia in 1815. It would have been desirable to annex them to France itself; but diplomatic fashions had changed in the last century. Clearly, however, an independent state or states on the left bank would give France an effective obstacle between itself and a rebuilt German army. It is clear that this conclusion had been reached by early 1917, since the French ambassador in Moscow raised in February of that year with the Tsar his government's desire to 'attain the political separation from Germany of her trans-Rhenish districts and their organisation on a separate basis *in order that in future the River Rhine might form a permanent strategical frontier against a German invasion'.*[10] This was essentially the proposition that the French government took to Versailles. To be effective, of course, there would have to be a mechanism by which the independent states would be allied to France and allow French troops on their soil in times of tension. Marshal Foch proposed to his political masters, therefore, that several states should be set up 'relatively independent and bound to the western countries by economic accords and by treaties of military alliance which would automatically place them at the side of France, if there should be any war against Germany'.[11]

This became France's official proposition to its allies. A memorandum of 25 February presented the argument in the following terms:

> Germany could by-pass France's natural defences in a few days by invading Belgium and Luxemburg; if the first battle was lost by the French Army, continental Europe would fall into the hands of the German Army, and it would be difficult for the American and British forces to establish bridgeheads in Europe. Consequently, the Rhine was the only possible frontier, not only for France, but for the whole group of western countries.[12]

Few texts can have predicted more clearly and succinctly the events of 1940–44. The motives of France in making this proposal were presented as being largely altruistic. This was because, as the title of Part V of the memorandum put it, there was an 'identity of the collective interest and the interest of France'. Moreover, although this security perimeter was 'a vital necessity' for France, still

> In this question, France asks nothing for herself: not an inch of territory, nor any right of sovereignty. She has no wish to annex the left bank of the Rhine…. What she proposes is the creation, in the general

10. Text of Russian government record of the conversation on 12 February 1917, printed in H. W. V. Temperley, ed., *A History of the Peace Conference of Paris*, 5 vols, London, Hodder and Stoughton and Oxford, Oxford University Press, 1920, Vol. 1, p. 429. Emphasis in original.
11. Cited by Paul-Marie de la Gorce, *The French Army: A Military-Political History*, trans. Kenneth Douglas, London, Weidenfeld and Nicolson, 1963, p. 147.
12. Ibid., p. 148.

interest, of a protection common to all the peaceful democracies, to the League of Nations, to liberty and to peace.[13]

Even so, it was not clear that the French army, by itself, would be able to defend the country successfully, even with the Rhine as a barrier. It was already clear that British and American troops would be based in Europe for several years; but a number of Frenchmen began to wonder whether something more permanent might not follow. *Le Temps* excitedly looked forward to an 'Atlantic Alliance watching over the Rhine'.[14] Such a prospect would have delighted the French government. The wartime coalition had been formalised, by 1917, to the point where there was a Supreme War Council, with representatives of France, Britain and Italy, with observers from the United States, and with a military sub-structure as well. It would have suited France to continue these arrangements, and no doubt there would have been no objection from Paris to Foch's continuing into peacetime his wartime role of supreme commander. When Wilson cited the League of Nations as the future foundation of French security, the French pointed to the need for it to be supplemented with an army and planning staff of its own.[15] In the event, of course, the League was to have no real military dimension at all.

The guiding principles of all this gloomy French analysis were fear and weakness. France was less conscious of having won a great victory than of narrowly avoiding a catastrophic defeat. Already, we can see evidence of the mood of helpless pessimism and neurotic weakness that typified French thinking about their relations with Germany in the 1920s and 1930s: eventually they will be strong; when they are strong they will invade and occupy us. This, more than any other single factor, helps to explain the desperate search, not so much for peace but for un-war, of the French governments of the next two decades. Once a nation is convinced that it is weak and bound to lose a war, and once a generation of decision-makers has grown up with this perception, only extraordinary circumstances can rescue it.

13. Ministère des Affaires Etrangères, *Documents Diplomatiques: Documents Relatifs aux Négociations Concernant les Garanties de Sécurité Contre une Agression de l'Allemagne, 10 Janvier 1919–7 Décembre 1923*, (henceforth *DDF-Sécurité*), Paris, Imprimerie Nationale, 1924, No. 2.

14. Nobécourt, *Histoire Politique*, p. 21.

15. Melvyn P. Leffler, *The Elusive Quest: America's Pursuit of European Stability and French Security, 1919–1933*, Chapel Hill, University of North Carolina Press, 1979, pp. 3–6.

Even today, French historians present the events of the inter-war years as nothing more than a pause while Germany recovered its strength. They assume an unbroken continuity between the Germany of Weimar and the Germany of Hitler, a nation bent on revenge from the moment of Versailles onwards. All disarmament conferences were doomed to failure, all peace moves pointless, once the French were 'abandoned', or 'betrayed', according to taste, by the Anglo-Saxons. This perception was to have substantial political consequences in the future, not least after the Second World War, when much the same problem arose. One interesting figure – from whom I will quote from time to time – is Georges Bonnet: man of Munich, arch appeaser, collaborationist during the war and apologist for Vichy thereafter. Bonnet was about as distant from de Gaulle in political beliefs as it was possible to be, yet he easily surpasses de Gaulle in bilious paranoia about the Anglo-Saxons, and demonstrates, in so doing, how widespread these perceptions, today often narrowly associated with one individual, actually were.

Versailles

These, then, were the objectives with which the French approached the negotiations, as far as they affected the security of its eastern border: massive reparations for France, the detachment of the left bank of the Rhine, and some form of tangible security guarantee from the British and Americans. That they were disappointed in all these objectives is the product of a number of very different factors. First, the Versailles conference was confronted with a vast range of problems of enormous complexity, ranging far beyond the Franco-German quarrel. Although many of the participants looked back in desperation to the Congress of Vienna for any lessons they might learn, their task was infinitely more complex than simply making the world safe for absolutism.

There were new nations to be shepherded into existence, old quarrels to be patched up, and unrest and revolution in all parts of the world. The main actors – using the diplomatic machinery of a bygone age – were in that situation of policy overload with which we are more familiar today: it was unclear which problem was the most urgent, and any settlement of one issue raised a host of problems in other areas. France's obsession with its own security, therefore, was only one element in a situation of unprecedented complexity.

Second, the conference saw, for the first time, the involvement of the United States. This had obvious practical implications for the ease with which French objectives could be attained. Of the five powers who effectively dictated the peace conditions with Germany (for there was no negotiation as such), Italy and Japan were not major players. Decisions were, in practice, taken by Wilson, Lloyd George and Clemenceau, and for the first but by no means the last time, the French found themselves in a minority against the Anglo-Saxons. Moreover, since the French desperately needed a British and American commitment to their future security, and since the French were heavily in debt to the Americans, and moderately so to the British, their hand was not a strong one. And their temper cannot have been improved by the decision, for the first time in a major conference, that French was not to be the sole official language. In a decision replete with symbolism for the future, English was henceforth to have equal status.

The Americans, and Wilson in particular, were in any event antipathetic to much of the thinking behind the French demands. Wilson did not believe that the future lay in a continuation of balance-of-power concepts and games played with provinces. Rather, he tried to persuade the French that their future security would be better assured through the international mechanism of the League of Nations.[16] And even the French had to concede that it was difficult to reconcile the forcible detachment of the Rhineland with principles such as self-determination, which the victorious powers claimed to have gone to war to defend. If the Poles were allowed to decide their own future, why not the Rhinelanders? And if the latter wished to reunite themselves with Germany at a later date, were they to be prevented from doing so?

Then there were many who argued that, in any case, a rapacious reparations policy was doomed to fail. J. M. Keynes – a Treasury official at Versailles – is the best known expositor of this view, but in reality it was not very difficult to conclude, as Lloyd George did in a memorandum to his colleagues, that 'we cannot both cripple [Germany] and expect her to pay'.[17] These remarks were seen in France as 'shameful slanders actuated by evil designs and sordid interests'.[18] Finally, there were many who doubted whether the French position, either financially or militarily, was really as

16. Ibid., pp. 3–5.
17. Cited by Sharp, *Versailles Settlement*, p. 32.
18. Bernard and Dubief, *Decline*, p. 81.

bad as the French themselves made out. Traditional British wariness of the French had not been entirely expunged by the war, and fears of hegemonistic designs on Western Europe remained – not least in the Foreign Office.

A representative view is that of Sir G. Grahame, writing from Paris in September 1919. He notes public unease about the future, but ascribes it largely to the results of a press campaign designed to extract concessions from the British and Americans by playing up French vulnerability, and to the irresponsible antics of the opposition. But he believes that the 'great strengths' of the French position in Europe 'are gradually becoming more apparent to the generality of French men'. It is clear that 'France is the only great military Power on the Continent', whereas Germany has 'been deprived of the means, for a long period of time, of becoming a strong military power'. Germany had lost territory, mineral resources, population, colonies, her fleet and her merchant shipping. These 'catastrophic events', together with the return of Alsace-Lorraine, 'ought, it would seem, to remove any French fears of a successful war of revenge...'. If there was a danger, in fact, it was not of a weak France but a strong one. They might be tempted to 'abuse their predominant position in Europe, which the chauvinistic Frenchman has always considered to be a natural one for his country', by seeking to dominate Italy or Spain, for example.[19] There was a certain scepticism in Washington also, and this made dealings between the US and France – not for the last time – somewhat fraught. In return, the French suspected that the English were reverting to their traditional balance-of-power policies, and that 'the recovery of Germany, up to a point at least, was desirable from the standpoint of British interests, whether commercial or political'.[20] By themselves, these factors would have made France's security objectives hard to attain. But there was a much greater factor at work also: fear of Bolshevism.

The Bolshevik Threat

Difficult as it may be, nowadays, to think ourselves back into the minds of statesmen, diplomats, and generals as the Russian

19. *Documents on British Foreign Policy, 1919–1939*, (henceforth *DBFP*), First Series, Vol. V, London, Her Majesty's Stationery Office, pp. 565–7.
20. René Albrecht-Carrié, *France, Europe and the Two World Wars*, New York, Harper, 1961, pp. 70–71.

Revolution unfolded during 1917, it is important to try to grasp something of how they saw it. First, such a revolution was not unexpected, albeit not necessarily in Russia. Europe had, after all, been convulsed by revolution in 1830 and 1848, the red flag had been hoisted over Paris in 1871, and smaller-scale risings had been put down throughout the Continent regularly thereafter. Secondly, Russia was an important partner in the war against the Central Powers. Even before the new Bolshevik government sued for peace, it was apparent that turmoil in Russia could only harm the Allied war effort, and the Treaty of Brest-Litovsk was greeted as a duplicitous betrayal, the more so since Britain, France, and Russia had agreed in 1914 not to make peace separately.

Thirdly, it was clear that the lines of battle that were being demarcated were ideological and not geographical. If the 'disease' of Bolshevism – as it was usually referred to – were not immediately eradicated, it would spread quickly to other nations, bringing chaos and civil war in its wake. The inflammatory rhetoric of the Bolsheviks encouraged this view. Finally, it was not necessarily assumed that the Revolution was home-grown. To the obvious *cui bono* argument that Germany had both sent Lenin to the Finland Station and benefited enormously from the results of that journey, was added a whole series of misperceptions about who the Bolsheviks were and what they wanted. The view of the London *Times* that the Bolsheviks were 'adventurers of German-Jewish blood in German pay' was representative,[21] and it appears, from testimony given to the Senate in November 1917 by the foreign minister, that this was, in fact, the official French government analysis also. According to Barthou, the Bolsheviks were 'in German pay and ... most of them do not use their real names. They are mostly Jews of German origin, with German names which they have turned into Russian. My counterpart as foreign minister calls himself Trotsky, but his real name is Braunstein'[sic]. And Clemenceau himself went on to claim that 'he [Trotsky] was prosecuted here as a spy, but was protected by certain members of Parliament'.[22] Thus, Germans and Russians, Prussian autocracy and Bolshevism were combined into a single enemy: which made excellent sense from the psychological perspective, even if from no other.

21. John Silverlight, *The Victors' Dilemma: Allied Intervention in the Russian Civil War*, London, Barrie and Jenkins, 1970, p. 21.

22. David Robin Watson, *Georges Clemenceau: A Political Biography*, London, Eyre Methuen, 1974, p. 270.

Nowhere were the events of 1917 followed more closely than in France. The ideological connections between the ideas of the two Revolutions will be apparent, even from the brief outline of the previous chapter, and were fully appreciated at the time. A well-known historian even wrote a series of newspaper articles in which he 'tried to identify individuals and parties in Russia with their equivalents in the French Revolution ...'.[23] There was a particular resonance in these events for the army and other elements of the traditional Right. The Bolshevik ideology appeared, on the surface as least, to be similar to that which Thiers claimed to have vanquished in 1871. But there were many other features, which, as they were understood in Paris, seemed to imply the very birth of Antichrist in Russia. It was as though Bolshevism represented, in one handy package, the distillation of everything they had feared and fought against for decades.

Bolshevism was militantly secular, even atheistic in nature. It was aggressively modern in many of its social attitudes, such as the emancipation of women. It was the product of a close-knit intellectual conspiracy, with its code names, hidden structures and secret doctrine. And, most of all, it was masterminded by the Jews, or so everyone assumed at the time. And given assumptions about German involvement in the plot, could anyone now reasonably doubt that the same Judaeo-German-Masonic conspiracy, which had narrowly failed to destroy the French army at the time of Dreyfus, had now triumphed in Russia?

For the army and its political soul mates, therefore, the situation was straightforward: whatever the threat from Germany might prove to be in the future, there was a far more dangerous threat from Bolshevism now. And it was not only, or even mainly, a territorial threat – it was an ideological one. Having seen how a few revolutionaries could destroy the existing structures of a society and bring its war efforts to a halt, they were terrified that the same kind of thing might happen to France. The mutinies of 1917 – suspiciously contemporaneous with similar events in Russia – were only a mild foretaste of what was to come. Thus political ideas that resembled, even if only slightly, what they understood those of the Bolsheviks to be would have to be sternly repressed, and their

23. Douglas Johnson, 'The Twentieth Century: Recollection and Rejection', in Geoffrey Best, ed., *The Permanent Revolution: The French Revolution and Its Legacy, 1789–1989*, London, Fontana Press, 1988, p. 187.

expositors summarily silenced, in case the German-Jewish-Bolshevik conspiracy should sweep over France next.

These fears were not entirely fantastical. There were quite widespread risings and insurrections throughout France, as well as large-scale industrial strife. And at the Tours conference of the Socialist Party, held in December 1920, the majority of the delegates voted to support the (Leninist) Third International – the Comintern – and left the Party, taking with them the newspaper *Humanité* – to this day, the newspaper of the *Parti Communiste Français* (PCF). The Antichrist now had a base in France itself.[24]

And there was no shortage of violent rhetoric from the Comintern itself, even if it was almost never translated into action. Its policy, defined the same year, was to be based 'primarily on bringing together the proletariat and working classes of all nations and countries for the common revolutionary struggle for the overthrow of the landowners and the bourgeoisie. For only such united action will ensure victory over capitalism'.[25] These fears were not confined to the army. They were also widely distributed in the church, and in professional circles, and were actively disseminated in the media. They formed the mental furniture of a significant number of Frenchmen in 1940, and their influence has by no means disappeared.

This consciousness of a new threat was held in other capitals also, and it was the principal complicating factor in any attempt to hammer out a policy on Germany on which the French, British and Americans could all agree. The essential argument was that of Lloyd George's Fontainebleau memorandum, which argued that too harsh a policy towards Germany might lead that nation 'to throw in her lot with Bolshevism and place her resources, her brains, her vast organising powers at the disposal of the revolutionary fanatics, whose dream it is to conquer the world for Bolshevism'. Were this to happen, all of Eastern Europe would

be swept into the orbit of the Bolshevik revolution, and within a year we may witness the spectacle of nearly three hundred million, organised into a vast red army under German instructors and German generals, equipped with German cannon and German machine guns, and prepared for a renewal of the attack on Western Europe.

24. Azéma and Winock, *Troisième République*, p. 196.

25. Cited by Anthony Adamthwaite, *The Lost Peace: International Relations in Europe, 1918–1939*, London, Edward Arnold, 1980, p. 39.

This result could be best prevented by the offer of 'a peace, which, while just, will be preferable for all sensible men to Bolshevism'.[26]

Confirmation of these fears was to be found everywhere. Sir A. Hardinge wrote from Madrid in October 1919 to report a German-Bolshevik plot to destroy the industry of the country. Although the objectives of the 'Russian Jewish element' were only 'useless mischief and destruction', the Germans were supporting strikes and disruption in the hope of benefiting commercially in Spain, as in other markets to be attacked in the same way.[27] Views in Washington were similar. Even before the Armistice was signed, Robert Lansing, Wilson's secretary of state, had argued for a policy of prudence, noting that 'in Eastern Germany Bolshevism is raising its abominable head, and a Germany crushed might become a prey to that hideous movement. If it did, Europe might become a seething mass of anarchy....'[28] Fear of Bolshevism became a cynical negotiating tool, used by states to frighten each other into making concessions. The Germans themselves, with nothing much else in their hands, used it to try to extract concessions from the West. In early 1919, the German Supreme Command, according to a telegram to the Foreign Ministry, thought it 'extremely important that President Wilson and all of America be filled with horror at the spread of Bolshevism in Germany'. To which the Foreign Ministry replied that they had already thought of this idea. Ambassadors in other countries were asked to reinforce the message.[29]

During the next twelve months, it increasingly became clear that the answer, if there was one, was to 'inoculate' Germany against the 'virus' of Bolshevism, by providing economic aid, and particularly food, whilst providing some support to anti-Bolshevik forces in Russia. Such a policy was hardly going to allow the pillage of Germany in order to rebuild France.

For all nations, the tension between fear of Bolshevism and fear of Germany was very real: for the French, it was worst of all. It was complicated both by the fact that France was, geographically and emotionally, in the front line, and by the fact that the politicians and the generals were effectively on different sides. Clemenceau had, on the whole, a realistic attitude. He was not attracted by Bolshevism, but he was worried much more about Germany.

26. Cited by Sharp, *Versailles Settlement*, pp. 31–32.
27. *DBFP*, First Series, Vol. 5, pp. 763–5.
28. Cited by Mayer, *Peacekeeping*, p. 61.
29. Silverlight, *Victors' Dilemma*, p. 126.

Even his willingness to involve France in the wars of intervention originated in the fear that Germany might expand eastward into a disintegrating Russia. The original motive of the Western powers for intervening in the Russian Civil War was their strong desire to keep that country in the war against Germany, so ensuring that many German troops would continue to be kept away from the Western front. Given that the White leaders promised to continue the fight, it was clearly in the West's interest to support them. It was for this reason that Western troops were sent to Russia: a battalion of the Middlesex regiment – rather to its own surprise, no doubt – found itself fighting in Siberia on Armistice Day. Troops from a dozen countries were fighting on the same side – if that concept has any meaning – at a time when keeping Russia in the war had ceased to be of any importance. French, Italians and Japanese were involved, as were 70,000 Czechs, for reasons too complex to set out here.

The question evidently arose of what to do now. Political inertia kept the troops where they were for the time being – a feeling that their presence might still be useful, a hope that perhaps the Soviet régime was anyway on its last legs. And there was also an unhappiness about abandoning former allies. But no national leader seriously contemplated large-scale operations aimed at overthrowing the Soviet régime: the money was not there, and enthusiasm among the voters for such an undertaking varied from the limited to the non-existent.

Foch and the General Staff, on the other hand, had something much more ambitious in mind. Foch bombarded the Supreme War Council with successive proposals for large-scale intervention. There would need to be a quick, preliminary peace agreement with Germany, after which Americans or subsequently Finns, Poles, Czechs, Romanians and Greeks would be sent against the Bolsheviks. This would result, Foch assured the national leaders, in 'the end of Bolshevism' during that year.[30] It goes without saying that Foch massively exceeded his powers with these proposals, as he was to do elsewhere. The Anglo-Saxons were scandalised at his behaviour. But Clemenceau could do little to rein him in: the fact that the French army had stayed out of politics since 1871 was only partly by their own choosing; successive administrations had tried to avoid provoking them. In politics, after all, the most effective threat is the one that is never articulated. Eventually, political

30. Ibid., p. 154.

reality and Wilson's personal scruples ensured that Foch's grand design was scaled down to a defensive programme of assistance and training, in an attempt to establish a *cordon sanitaire* beyond which Bolshevism would not be allowed to spread. By the summer of 1920, as the Whites' military position crumbled, the last Western troops were withdrawn.

The episode had a lasting effect on politico-military relations in France, and on the formulation of one of the political truths that I defined earlier. The military blamed the politicians for lacking the courage to intervene massively, to wipe out the 'disease' at its source, before it eventually destroyed France too. It led, among other things, to the indecent enthusiasm of the General Staff for fighting the Soviet Union, rather than Germany, in 1939–40, the subsequent vocal (and occasionally practical) support of Vichy for the German struggle against the 'Bolshevik Threat', and the corresponding lack of enthusiasm for de Gaulle, whose priorities lay elsewhere.

The Atlantic Alliance Fails

For all these reasons, the Versailles settlement failed to meet French aspirations, especially as it affected the Eastern frontier. The Rhineland was to remain part of Germany, albeit it was to be occupied by an international force for fifteen years, and longer if French security appeared to be threatened at that point. This was a curious outcome, since it provided France with security at a time when Germany was weak and arguably otiose, and withdrew that security at a time when Germany might be expected to be strong again. Foch felt no need to reconcile himself to this outcome, even if his political masters had, and looked on approvingly while General Mangin, chief of the French occupation forces, strenuously promoted the Rhineland separatist movement during the negotiations themselves, and took the opportunity to renew these efforts when French troops moved into the Ruhr in 1923.

Instead of this dismemberment of Germany, Lloyd George and Wilson offered, in its place, separate security treaties, each of which contained a clause promising 'to come immediately to [France's] assistance in the event of any unprovoked movement of aggression against her being made by Germany'.[31] The British

31. The texts are in Temperley, *History of the Peace Conference*, pp. 337–40.

guarantee was, however, only to come into effect once the treaty with the US was ratified. Clemenceau was delighted, believing the treaties to be a better outcome than dismemberment of Germany would have been. Not much thought appears to have gone into the treaty from the US side, and there were certainly divided counsels within the US delegation on the point.[32] Colonel House, Wilson's special emissary, was highly doubtful if the Senate would accept the treaty, but judged that 'it satisfies Clemenceau and we can get on with the real business of the Conference'.[33] In fact, the treaty was a classic diplomatic rush job, a fix developed to avoid inter-Allied problems. The US and British did not believe in a renewed threat from Germany (or at least one that the League could not deal with), and thus regarded the treaty as unlikely to be invoked, but useful for keeping the French quiet. There is no need, however, to assume, with Georges Bonnet, that Lloyd George deliberately misled Clemenceau into accepting a treaty that, he knew, 'American opinion would not have allowed its Government to underwrite'.[34] In the event, of course, the US Senate declined to ratify the treaty, which meant, in turn, that the British guarantee failed also, leaving the French (as they saw it) with the worst of all worlds, and with a rapidly increasing sense of the perfidiousness of all Anglo-Saxons.

The issue of reparations was beyond the ability of the Big Four to solve among themselves, let alone in negotiation with the Germans, and a compromise of truly classic proportions was eventually settled on and imposed on the Germans. Article 231 of the Treaty, the much-criticised 'War Guilt' clause, read: 'The Allied and Associated Governments affirm and Germany accepts the responsibility of Germany and her allies for causing all the damage to which the Allied and Associated Governments and their nationals have been subjected as a consequence of the war imposed upon them by the aggression of Germany and her allies.' The following article, although recognising that 'the resources of Germany are not adequate ... to make complete reparation ...', required Germany to undertake 'that she will make compensation for all damage done to the civilian population of the Allied and Associated Powers and to their property during the period of the

---

32. Arthur Walworth, *Wilson and His Peacemakers: American Diplomacy at the Paris Peace Conference, 1919*, London, W. W. Norton, 1986, p. 322.

33. Watson, *Clemenceau*, p. 351.

34. Georges Bonnet, *Quai d'Orsay*, (trans. not given), Isle of Man, Times Press and Anthony Gibbs and Philips, 1965, p. 28.

belligerency...'. But the treaty did not specify how much was to be paid. It set up (Article 233) a Reparations Commission, which was to carry out this imposing task and report in time for the bill to be presented to the German government on 1 May 1921.[35]

The reparations provisions were never to work properly. For a long time, the Reparations Commission could not even agree how to proceed, let alone what the sums owing were: German obstruction did not help. It produced a report of sorts in May 1921, theoretically calling for the payment of 132 Bn gold marks (about $33 Bn) to the Allies. Everyone recognised that such a figure was unrealistic, and by the spring of 1922, payments had already broken down, closely followed by the German economy. The most promising way forward appeared to be to tie the sum to Germany's ability to pay, but Poincaré, Clemenceau's hard-line successor-but-one, would not hear of such an idea. He was obsessed with his domestic financial situation, and needed reparation payments to balance the budget and stabilise the franc. A solution of sorts was provided by the Dawes plan of 1923, which, whilst not changing the overall sum agreed in 1921, confined the amounts to be paid over the next few years to sums between 1 and 2 billion marks, with no time-limit for completing payments. Poincaré was obliged to sign up to the plan, essentially because the weakness of the French economy, and the consequent need to borrow from the US, undercut the French bargaining position. His 'surrender' was strongly criticised in Paris.[36] In the end, the sums that were received from the Germans were nothing like what had been hungrily anticipated.

Even today, French historians present the compromises made by France at Versailles, and the later unravelling of the treaty, in a pained fashion. A historian of French diplomacy of the period argues that 'France, who at the time of peace negotiations had sacrificed the real guarantee, which the separation of the left bank of the Rhine would have constituted, then found herself deprived of anything which could have ensured her security'.[37] Seeking to rebut the charges of 'some who have even maintained that French demands ... greatly contributed to the desire for revenge in Germany and to the final victory of Hitler', he notes that 'it is impossible for a Frenchman, even today, not to consider that the principle

35. The text of the treaty is quoted from Temperley, *History of the Peace Conference*, Vol. III, pp. 214–5.

36. Bernard and Dubief, *Decline*, p. 115.

37. J. Néré, *The Foreign Policy of France from 1914 to 1945*, London, Routledge and Kegan Paul, 1975, p. 26

of reparations was perfectly just'. And a French study of 1946 concluded that the 1921 reparations figure was a fair estimate of the damage Germany had done, and not excessive at all.[38] French historians have also criticised (with some justice) the inability of Wilson and his collaborators to deliver the Senate. One recent study accuses Wilson of ignoring American public opinion, and presenting the treaty to Congress 'very clumsily'.[39] The warnings of a number of French political and military figures at the time are often regarded as prophetic. Thus, Foch's warnings about the need to retain the left bank of the Rhine are praised by one writer, who argues that 'today, we know very well that Foch described perfectly accurately the defeat of June 1940'.[40]

A Complete Misunderstanding

The pattern set during and after the Versailles negotiations was continued in the 1920s. In general, a France obsessed with its own security concerns felt isolated, ignored and unjustly treated. It believed that Britain's policy was 'one of thwarting France and of weakening her in every way ... while at the same time encouraging German reconstruction'.[41] French writers still maintain that, until 1938, the Anglo-Saxons had an agenda that involved 'the disarmament of France, which still had the largest armed forces, rather than preventing Germany from re-arming'. Such a policy was acceptable in London, since the Germans had no fleet able to threaten England.[42] The Anglo-Saxon countries, impatient with what they thought a morbid preoccupation with her eastern borders, made a number of proposals that France, through economic weakness, was then brought to accept through gritted teeth. The French were particularly worried by the new (Republican) Harding administration, which took power in 1921; and Briand (then prime minister) sent a high-level representative to plead for continued US involvement in Europe. But public support for France was waning, and the US had already made clear that building up a prosperous and democratic Germany, within the League, was a better policy than uncritical support of France.

38. Ibid., pp. 33–35.
39. Bernard and Dubief, *Decline*, p. 102.
40. Nobécourt, *Histoire Politique*, p. 25.
41. Bonnet, *Quai d'Orsay*, p. 47.
42. Tristan Doelnitz, *La France hantée par sa puissance*, Paris, Belfond, 1993, pp. 84–85.

In pursuing this policy, they had an ace in their hands: France was heavily in debt, and the US was much less inclined to smile upon the remission of war debts from France than reparations from Germany – naturally, since the latter were of no financial interest to them. Moreover, the US government – particularly under Harding – tried to exert pressure on the French to make compromises in all kinds of fields, including trade and economic policy. The Republicans were willing to interest themselves in Europe, but felt that the time for automatic support of France was over. In April 1921, therefore, Harding announced his opposition to the League, and declared that he supported moves in Congress for a peace treaty with Germany: this led to the Treaty of Berlin a few months later. One way of demonstrating this engagement was to call for a disarmament conference, which would have the extra benefit, if successful, of reducing spending on armaments, and thus freeing resources for something more useful.

At the resulting Washington naval conference, Briand played a mediocre hand badly. Wrongly advised, he had hoped to mediate between the British and Americans: in fact he found that, again, they made a united front against him. The American, British and Japanese delegations worked out an agreement limiting capital ships virtually without consulting the French, who were allocated parity only with Italy, and not, as they had hoped, with Japan. The French were extremely concerned that their navy – which had not received much emphasis during the war – should be returned to its former importance. The delegation's negotiating instructions, sent from Paris, stressed that 'the naval situation of France is, at the present time, very inferior to her political and geographical situation', and that France, as the second most important colonial power, needed a larger navy than she then had.[43] When the French argued in this fashion, Hughes, the secretary of state, made one of history's less subtle threats: 'At this point, when we are anxious to aid France in full recovery of her economic life, it would be most disappointing to learn that she was contemplating putting hundreds of millions into battleships.' And he emphasised the economic benefits that would accrue from naval disarmament.[44] Briand gave way and accepted an agreement that 'was interpreted as a humiliation by the French public', and led directly

43. Ministère des Affaires Etrangères, *Documents Diplomatiques: Conférence de Washington, Juillet 1921–Février 1922*, Paris, Imprimerie Nationale, 1923, No. 113. Henceforth *DDF-Washington*.
44. Leffler, *Elusive Quest*, p. 35.

to his own downfall.[45] More importantly, perhaps, public opinion reacted against reported French intransigence, and the press portrayed the French as 'the militaristic villains of the drama'. The ambassador wrote sorrowfully that he had 'rarely seen' such 'a complete misunderstanding aggravated by acerbic, sour, and persistent criticism'.[46] It was not the last occasion that such comments would be made.

In March 1919, the wartime financial arrangements by which the British and Americans supported the French franc came to an end, and that currency at once fell dramatically. For the Anglo-Saxons, the end of the war meant a welcome return to classical liberal economics, and their action had no ulterior motive. The French, of course, did not see it that way, and regarded the act as economic sabotage. It served to usher in a contentious period when the political and military factors outlined above were hopelessly entangled with financial considerations. The French regarded reparations as a life-and-death matter for the economy (and for those in government), and became steadily more worried as the months passed without a definitive settlement. Indeed, Briand told Lloyd George in April 1921 that the French government 'had to settle a budget and they could not make it balance. Unless Germany produced some positive and definite proposal they were faced with ruin and bankruptcy'.[47]

Given this vulnerability, the French felt that it was unreasonable for their allies simultaneously to take a soft line on reparations and to press for loan repayments. During this period, one of the objectives of French diplomacy was to link reparations and debts: a linkage that the Anglo-Saxons would not accept. Thus, many Frenchmen felt that if their 'allies, through blind selfishness, assisted the Germans in their manœuvres to avoid paying their just retribution, those allies in their turn should not expect to be repaid debts which, after all, were contracted for the better defence of the common cause'.[48]

The reparations question was settled, at least in theory, with the Young Plan of 1929, although only after much arm-twisting by the eponymous author. A highly complex settlement, it called for the payment of fifty-nine 'annuities', the last twenty-two of which

45. Bernard and Dubief, *Decline*, p. 111.
46. Ibid., pp. 35–36.
47. *DBFP*, First Series, Vol. 15, No. 70.
48. Bernard and Dubief, *Decline*, p. 82.

were to coincide with debt payments by the Allies.[49] The Americans had thus accepted something of the principle of linkage, whilst the Allies (and particularly the French) accepted that they would receive less than they had hoped. In part, the more balanced outcome reflected the fact that the French economy had recovered substantially in the late 1920s, and her political strength had increased commensurately. But the plan was conceived on the very eve of the Great Depression, which was soon to undermine it.

By the middle of 1931, a growing conviction in Washington that Germany faced complete collapse within days caused President Hoover to propose – effectively without consultation – a one-year moratorium on all forms of debt repayment. Although the initiative met French demands in openly acknowledging linkage, the government of Pierre Laval reacted violently to it. It seemed to the French that they were being penalised financially, since the reparations they were owed greatly exceeded the debts they had to repay. There was also much indignation that the proposal had been sprung on France without consultation – what Laval was to describe to the US ambassador as 'shock tactics'.[50] Briand, then foreign minister, angrily alleged that the moratorium had been proposed out of concern for American private investments in Germany, which might be casualties of any collapse. The very high level of American private lending to France, and the close connections between the Republican administration and Wall Street, did nothing to make this view less plausible.

For his part, Hoover became extremely impatient with the French, claiming that they had more to lose than anyone from the financial collapse of Central Europe and the Bolshevik take-over of Germany that he presumed would follow.[51] Yet the French remained unpersuaded. The main problem was political: reparations were firmly linked to the 'War Guilt' clause – Article 231 – of the Versailles Treaty, and every pause in payment represented a qualification of the judgement that Germany alone was responsible for the war. Public feeling in France ran high against the 'German-Anglo-Saxon plot', and Laval angrily asked the American ambassador what guarantee France had that 'these payments will be resumed at the end of one year'. In the event, American pressure, including the threat to negotiate moratoria with each country

49. See Leffler, *Elusive Quest*, pp. 210–1.
50. Geoffrey Warner, *Pierre Laval and the Eclipse of France*, London, Eyre and Spottiswoode, 1968, p. 32.
51. Leffler, *Elusive Quest*, p. 241.

separately, forced the French to give in, although Laval survived a confidence vote in the Chamber of Deputies by only one vote, after unlooked-for support from the Socialists.[52] On this occasion, the French were right to be sceptical: the Lausanne conference of 1932 decided to absolve Germany from future payments, not without French opposition. The United States refused to renounce its claims to war debts, although Herriot's government was brought down in December of that year by a chamber that refused to pay any more. No further debt repayments were, in fact, ever made, although the debts were never technically extinguished.

A Federal European Union

In parallel (and hopelessly intertwined) with the contorted financial discussions of the 1920s, there were a separate series of policy initiatives from Paris designed essentially to secure France's position through security treaties with individual nations, and vaguer but much more ambitious schemes for multilateral security organisations.

The logical partner for France would, of course, have been the Soviet Union, as Russia had once been. But for reasons that will by now be evident, such a course would have been out of the question politically. Moreover, the independence of the new Polish state meant that the Soviet Union did not have a border with Germany, and thus could only attack the latter by going through Poland. The Poles were unenthusiastic about this. In the East, therefore, the French set about negotiating treaties with Poland (1921), Czechoslovakia (1924), Romania (1926) and Yugoslavia (1927). The wisdom of these treaties has been debated since: certainly, they provided allies of a kind, but, when the feared German rearmament actually took place, they turned out to be liabilities rather than assets.

Britain, on the other hand, had greater military potential, but would require time to move sizeable forces to France. Yet a formal treaty of alliance might make Germany hesitate before attacking. There were several attempts to devise such a system, but they foundered on two obstacles: first, the common one that the most one side was prepared to offer was less than the least the other was willing to accept; and second, the British unhappiness with

52. Warner, *Pierre Laval*, p. 33.

the broadness (and also the imprecision) of the French plans. There were a series of bilateral meetings between Briand and Lloyd George in 1921–22 that led nowhere for these reasons. Briand's concept, outlined in December 1921, was of 'a very broad Alliance in which the two powers would guarantee each other's interests in all parts of the world, act closely together in all things and go to each others' assistance whenever these things were threatened'. Such an alliance might have three or four powers in it (including Germany), but 'the nucleus should be a complete Alliance between Britain and France around which others should gather'. It was hardly surprising that Lloyd George's response was that 'opinion in Great Britain was hardly prepared for so broad an undertaking as that'. Lloyd George was happy to give a political guarantee against Germany, but was unhappy with the possibility of a commitment to support French activity in Eastern Europe, for example.[53]

The French were put out by this counter-offer, which the French ambassador later described to the British government as 'humiliating in its form and useless and even dangerous in its substance'. The proposals had been 'welcomed coolly', because they were imprecise and did not go beyond Versailles, and also because they were humiliating in that they put France, which was receiving the guarantees, on a lower political level than Britain, which was offering them. Mutual guarantees were all that was politically acceptable.[54] Briand subsequently expanded his own proposal to include the construction of some kind of organisation built around the Versailles signatories, charged with sniffing out trouble – in Eastern Europe, for example – before it appeared. The British response was predictably cautious.[55]

A typical example of the ingenuity with which the two nations managed to manufacture quarrels out of thin air at this time is the question of French submarines. It began with an article by one Commandant Castex, of the *Marine*, which praised the efficacy of the German campaign of unrestricted submarine warfare in the recent war. Sarraut, head of the delegation at the Washington conference, reported sorrowfully to the Quai that the British had drawn conclusions from this article about French naval policy towards them, and were naturally upset.[56] The Quai

53. *DBFP*, First Series, Vol. 15, No. 110.
54. *DDF – Securité*, No. 18.
55. Ibid., Vol. 19, No. 10.
56. *DDF-Washington*, No. 103.

wrote back that Castex had 'no official standing to set out the Navy's ideas', and that, anyway, what he wrote did not support the interpretation that the British had placed on it.[57] The subject arose, naturally enough, in the Lloyd George-Briand bilaterals that were going on at the same time. The former mentioned the submarine question in the context of a possible security treaty 'not as a condition, but as a warning'. Briand, according to the British record, was not at all perturbed: France, he said, 'would be only too happy not to have to make the effort of building a large fleet of submarines'.[58] But bureaucratic folklore in the Quai clearly remembered the exchange differently, and Bonnet (who was not present) was to write some years later that Lloyd George made a security treaty conditional *inter alia* on the condition that France avoided 'any naval rivalry between the two countries. France must renounce her submarine programme'.[59] It was not surprising that the initiative failed, with acrimony and publishing of White Papers on both sides. A further round of discussions between Herriot and Ramsay MacDonald in 1924 made no more progress. The latter, whilst very sympathetic, stressed that opposition to a treaty would be very widespread, not only among the 'experts of the navy, army, air force and Foreign Office', but also among the governments of Sweden, Denmark and Holland. The best that could be agreed upon was what Herriot called 'a moral pact of continuous collaboration', which amounted to very little in practice.[60]

One reason why the discussions made limited progress was the British fear of offending the United States. One Foreign Office paper of 1928 recognised frankly that relations had been strained for a number of reasons, yet attributed some of the differences to the machinations of the Europeans – especially the French – who were 'constantly trying to drive a wedge between this country and the United States'. This had produced a situation where 'except as a figure of speech, war is *not* unthinkable between the two countries' (emphasis in original). As a result, and given the many dangers of a policy that 'permitted things to drift from bad to worse', a 'positive policy' towards the US was regarded as necessary. However, it added that 'Friendly relations with the United States need in no way interfere with that close cooperation with France

57. Ibid.
58. *DBFP*, First Series, Vol. 19, No. 17.
59. Bonnet, *Quai d'Orsay*, p. 49.
60. Cited in Adamthwaite, *Lost Peace*, pp. 67–68.

which is such an important asset in European affairs.'[61] This nuanced approach was lost on the French, who, of course, assumed the existence of a solidly Anglo-Saxon bloc, and saw everywhere evidence of its machinations.

These years saw various international treaties, such as Locarno (1925) and the Kellog-Briand pact (1928); but they were essentially political agreements only that did not provide any tangible security guarantees, yet which tended, little by little, to force the French on to the back foot, and to hasten the process of withdrawal from the Rhineland. Likewise, Franco-German attempts at a *rapprochement*, such as those between Briand and Stresemann in 1926, were probably doomed to failure, since neither side could afford the minimum political sacrifices required for real progress to be made. And in 1930, the last French troops left the Rhineland, rather ahead of the original schedule. The French made several suggestions for multilateral European structures in the inter-war period, in which one can dimly see the outline of such future organisations as the European Union and the CSCE. One such was the proposal for a Federal European Union made by Briand in 1930, although under development in Paris for some years. The proposal was trialed by Briand at the League of Nations the year before, where he argued for 'some kind of federal bond' between Europeans, which would enable them 'to get in touch at any time, to confer about their interests, to agree on joint resolutions, and to establish among themselves a bond of solidarity which will enable them, if need be, to meet any grave emergency that may arise'.[62]

Briand eventually tabled his proposals in May 1930, having previously discussed them with the British prime minister, who had expressed alarm lest there should be anything in the scheme 'which would give it even the semblance of being directed against the United States of America'. Briand assured him that this was not so.[63] Briand's proposal, although elaborately presented, was essentially a political document that gave little indication of how the French scheme for 'a permanent régime of conventional solidarity for the rational organisation of Europe' was to work in practice, or how European interests would be 'harmonised' to enable them to be more collectively effective within the League.[64] The general

61. *DBFP*, Series 1A, Vol. 5, No. 490 (Annexe).
62. Cited in *DBFP*, Second Series, Vol. 2, No. 284.
63. Ibid., No. 185.
64. Ibid., No. 186.

reaction to Briand's proposals was polite but dismissive. For many nations, they seemed to be just another way of setting the Versailles settlement in concrete for ever and ever, disregarding the fact that few nations apart from the French thought this was possible, or even desirable.

The British reaction, publicly polite, was in private dismissive and rather patronising. The memorandum was described in an internal Foreign Office paper as 'a surprising and disappointing work ... permeated by a vague and puzzling idealism expressed in such phrases as "collective responsibility in face of the danger which threatens the peace of Europe", "need for a permanent *régime* of solidarity" and much else which may mean a great deal or may mean nothing at all'. The plan was thought unlikely to interest other European states, since any reinforcement of the postwar settlement would 'offer them no advantages and would ... reinforce France's political hegemony in Europe'. Perhaps, the paper speculated, the real intention was to bring about 'such regrouping of European finance and industry as to assure France and the rest of Europe against the ever-growing strength of Non-European and especially American competition'.[65]

By the time of the long-awaited 1932 Geneva disarmament conference, the leaders of Europe were only going through the motions. The conference again featured acrimony between France and others, although it is an exaggeration to argue, as Bonnet does, that 'France found Germany, England and the United States united against her', or that 'England had no other aim than German re-armament and revenge'.[66] French proposals for an international army and the internationalisation of civil aviation attracted little support: Sir John Simon made it clear to the French that 'The United Kingdom Government would have the greatest difficulty in accepting any plan which involved the creation of a super-State.'[67] But, as the negotiations concentrated progressively more on land weaponry, the French began to feel more uncomfortable. Not only were American attempts to distinguish between 'offensive' and 'defensive' weaponry very contentious (a problem that has recurred), but the French were being asked, as the European military superpower, to give up their existing weapons in return for a commitment from Germany not to build any – a

65. Ibid., No. 189.
66. Bonnet, *Quai d'Orsay*, pp. 98–99.
67. *DBFP*, Second Series, Vol. 3, No. 45.

proposition with which they were understandably unhappy.[68] It was symptomatic that the French proposals were presented not by Briand, who had died shortly before, but by the hard-liner Tardieu, who probably had little faith in them. Laval was already prime minister in France, and the next few months would bring Hitler to power in Germany and Roosevelt into office in Washington. Slowly, the teams who would play the Second World War were starting to assemble.

It is clear that the French perception of their own weakness and vulnerability caused them to demand from others special treatment and guarantees that these others were not able to give. The British and Americans, whilst sympathetic at times, saw French security only as part of a much larger problem of putting Europe back together again. The methods for achieving this were primarily economic and financial, and required a prosperous Germany to play a full role on the international stage. The French might, to some degree, have expected such hesitation from the British, with whom there was already an extensive legacy of distrust and mutual incomprehension. But disappointment with the United States was felt much more keenly, because Wilson's visit and the Fourteen Points had raised extravagant expectations. Lord Tyrell, ambassador in Paris in 1931, wrote perceptively that 'The whole outlook of French policy since 1919 has been deeply influenced, if not determined, by the failure of the United States Government to implement the undertaking given by the United States President to come in to the guarantee treaty.'[69] For the French, the problem was essentially non-economic: they wanted political guarantees of their continued primacy in Europe and security arrangements that would stop a renascent Germany from challenging it. There was never a realistic possibility of these wants being met, but the process of disappointment was to create and enhance tensions and to breed misunderstandings that have by no means disappeared even now.

---

68. Laval's visit to Washington the previous year had gone through some of these issues, without any meeting of minds. The exchanges with Hoover brought out the worst of the latter's Francophobia, e.g. 'France always goes through this cycle. After she is done and begins to recuperate ... she gets rich, militaristic and cocky; and nobody can get on with her until she has to be thrashed again' (Warner, *Pierre Laval*, p. 47).

69. *DBFP*, Second Series, Vol. 2, No. 276.

3

ERRORS NOT TO BE REPEATED, I

M. Prime Minister, I can affirm to you that the Army is in a per-fect condition and can stand up to any other Army.

Marshal Pétain, 1936

Stuff the war ... what I want are ... cars that make money.

Louis Renault, 1940

With Hitler against Bolshevism

Newspaper slogan, 1934

From the moment of the defeat in 1940, successive govern-ments, critics and interest groups identified the period after 1933 as that in which the essential errors had been made. So many potential errors were available for study and classification that there was a choice to suit every political perspective; but no one argued against the view that catastrophic mistakes had been made in those years. Moreover, this was not a merely academic analysis. It was accepted that the period between the rise of Hitler and the fall of France was a kind of repository for disastrous errors from which one could learn important lessons for the future. French security policy since the Second World War cannot be properly understood without realising this.

Although Vichy had its own idiosyncratic and rather comic-operatic attempt to apportion blame – at the Riom trials in Febru-ary 1942 – it was not until the Liberation that a more structured investigation was possible. The nearest to an official text is the report of the National Assembly on what are called, with heroic understatement, *The Events Which Took Place in France from 1933 to 1945*. Its purpose is made unambiguously clear from the very beginning: 'The terrible misfortunes which have overwhelmed the country are not the doing of chance, but the result of errors and mistakes.... It is not too late to attempt to draw some lessons from the catastrophe of June 1940.'[1]

And the apologia of Paul Reynaud for his own conduct during the period, called, without visible irony, *France Saved Europe*, features a list of 'Errors not to be repeated in the future'.[2] Reynaud, maverick Radical politician, supporter of de Gaulle and briefly prime minister in 1940, presents the most formidable and impassioned denouncement of any, and I will take his charge-sheet as a kind of informal agenda for this chapter and the next. It reads, in part:

> Was it not a crime to be unprepared for this war whose spectre grew in size for years, on the horizon?
> France was without allies, unfortified and without an army.
> Why?
> An effective alliance with Russia – the nightmare of the General Staff in Berlin – had been rejected by us when it was offered.
> Why?
> We had not fortified the most exposed part of our frontier.
> Why?
> We entered the war without either of the two new arms of war, the armoured division and the ground-attack aircraft.[3]
> Why?
> We set up a defensive army, incapable of attacking the aggressor of our small allies.
> Why?
> And why, finally, in the field of economics, were we incapable, until the eve of the war, in spite of the lessons of the experience of so many countries, of putting an end to the crisis which weakened France, divided her and shackled her armament?
> What is the cause of this long intellectual and moral enfeeblement?

1. Assemblée Nationale, Document No. 2344 (1947), *Rapport ... sur les événements survenus en France de 1933 à 1945*, Paris, Imprimeries de l'Assemblée Nationale, 1951, Vol. 1, p. 5.

2. Paul Reynaud, *La France a Sauvé l'Europe*, 2 vols., Paris, Flammarion, 1947, Vol. 1, p. 35.

3. The words Reynaud uses are *corps cuirassé* and *aviation d'assaut* respectively. In the discussion of military controversies in the 1930s in the next chapter, I have preferred the translation 'armoured force', because the size of the force proposed (some 100,000 men) would make it, technically, of army rather than corps size. The point Reynaud is making here is that, whilst both sides had tanks, the Germans were the only ones to have tank (Panzer) *divisions*. Likewise 'assault aviation' would be meaningless in English: what Reynaud is complaining about is the lack on the French side of anything like the German Ju-87B (*Stuka*), optimised for ground attack.

And then, the inevitable question of any politician:

Who is responsible?[4]

The guilty men, institutions and social factors are a familiar list: 'our élites', who failed 'at the military, diplomatic and economic level', 'national morale' – not as high as in 1914, 'relaxation of the conqueror after victory', a 'deficiency of the public spirit', and many others, scattered through the book. Noting that no attempt was ever made to learn the lessons of 1870, or of 1914–18, Reynaud argues that such an attempt must now be made, to avoid the possible total destruction of France on a future occasion, and volunteers himself for the role of prophet.[5]

Implicit in this kind of approach are two large assumptions, each of which has been influential, but neither of which is above debate. The first is that great events necessarily have great causes. The fall of France in 1940 was so sudden, so complete, so overwhelming, so inexplicable, that it seems natural to seek a very profound cause for it. This may be treachery by generals and others, abandonment by allies, moral enfeeblement of the nation by the Popular Front or any of half-a-dozen other causes. But clearly, it must be possible to identify a significant factor, or factors, that led directly to the fall, and without which France might have won. And if these factors can be identified and corrected, France, it is argued, will be safer in the future. The second is that there is a connection between the disorganisation and division in France – which was real enough – and the defeat that came later. If only, goes the argument, our defence policy had been better made, our political system less adversarial, our politicians worked for the common good instead of fighting each other, our troops would have been better equipped and motivated and we would have won. Thus, at the conclusion of his study of French foreign policy during this period, Jean-Baptiste Duroselle quotes the following from Montesquieu's *Grandeur and Decadence of the Romans*:

There are general causes, which may be moral or physical, and which operate in any monarchy, raise it up, maintain it or cast it down. Everything that happens is subject to these causes; and if the luck of a battle, which is to say a particular cause, has ruined a

4. Ibid., p. 16.
5. Ibid., pp. 16–17.

state, there was a general cause which brought it about that this state should perish through a single battle.[6]

Each of these assertions is dubious. Firstly, there is a tendency to argue backwards from the result in search of a cause. Because the German victory was so overwhelming, it is argued, the French must have been greatly inferior in strategy, tactics, organisation and leadership. This, I think, is an over-simplified view. As often in war, what is interesting about the Battle of France is how uncertain the result was until the very end. If the Germans had a little less luck, if they had used one of their alternative plans of attack instead, if the French had managed one decent counter-attack, if the weather had been bad for a while, if French communications had been a little better: if any one of these things had happened, then the Germans would probably have been stopped before Paris, as the military leaders on both sides expected, and there would have been a replay of 1914. Given such an outcome – which was perfectly possible – historians would now be praising the very generals and politicians they now blame, and lauding the policies that they now criticise.

Secondly, it is very doubtful that any direct connection can be made between the political and social situation in the country and the performance of its soldiers. We now know that the reasons why men fight well or badly (particularly on the atomised modern battlefield) have less to do with patriotism and ideology than with the dynamics of small groups and such unglamorous features of military administration as leave, promotion and the care that the wounded can expect.[7] There are many cases of armies fighting well in spite of poor equipment or political division at home, and emerging victorious. Such an outcome in the Battle of France was by no means excluded. The failure of the French army in 1940 was essentially a failure of the commanders and the command structure. It was a failure to carry out realistic training and to retain morale. (The one British expeditionary force division that fought well and maintained its cohesion as far as Dunkirk was commanded by Major-General B. L. Montgomery, a noted trainer of troops.) Yet if luck had not failed also, the other failures might not have been fatal.

6. Cited in Jean-Baptiste Duroselle, *Politique Etrangère de la France: La Décadence 1932–1939*, Paris, Imprimerie Nationale, 1979, p. 493.

7. See, for example, S. L. A. Marshall, *Men Against Fire*, New York, 1947; Martin Van Creveld, *Combat Power*, London, 1983; Richard Holmes, *Firing Line*, London, Cape, 1985.

I do not intend to go deeply into these questions, fascinating as they are. I want rather to insist on the way in which these – rather dubious – premises have influenced French strategy since 1945. If you believe that the French lost largely because they lost – which is perhaps the most common view today – then it is useless trying to draw lessons for the future. If you believe that, among other things, a lack of modern weapons, betrayal by allies, a lack of political consensus, a lack of central decision-making and insufficient control over the armaments industry contributed to the defeat, then your subsequent policy might well feature investment in modern weapons, independence of decision-making, pursuit of a consensus on defence, centralisation of defence decision-making and the nationalisation of the defence industry. Thus, it is quite common to be told by French officials and officers 'we have the bomb today, because we did not have it in 1940': telescoping half-a-dozen of these factors into one.

In later chapters, I will deal with the responses of various French governments, from 1940 to the present day, to the defeat, and their reaction to the factors that they believed were responsible. But these reactions make little sense out of context, and so this chapter is concerned with the political, economic and industrial events of the period, and the next with the military controversies, and with the events of the *drôle de guerre*, the 'Phoney War'.

A Strong Franc in a Weak France

It is helpful to begin with the economic situation, since this dictated much else. The world recession that began in 1929 did not at once affect France, and never hurt that nation as deeply as it did some others; but its effects were far-reaching enough. The French franc was overvalued by comparison with the currencies of its major competitors after Great Britain left the gold standard in 1931, and after the United States devalued the dollar in 1933. The result was to make French imports cheap and exports expensive. In such circumstances, speculators judged – correctly – that the franc would have to be devalued at some stage, and, as usual, the prophecy was eventually self-fulfilling. Yet devaluation is never a popular expedient for a government – it is difficult to emerge from it without having lost political capital – and so French governments put it off as long as possible: the *franc fort* is not an invention of the 1980s. Exchange controls would have made the defence of the franc easier, but would have provoked a strong reaction from Britain and the United States, and so were not adopted.

Overvaluation and expensive exports, combined with an economic slump in most of France's trading partners led, not unexpectedly, to a slowdown in the economy and to rapidly increasing unemployment. It also led to a massive and increasing budget deficit, as lower economic activity in turn meant fewer tax receipts. French economic policy is often described as *dirigiste*, and assumed always to have been so. But the truth is more complicated. At the micro-economic level, that of wages, rents, food prices and working conditions, the French government (like some others) had a large regulatory apparatus of long standing. It also sponsored limited projects of public works. But at the macro-economic level, there was no concept of the government actually managing the economy: indeed, it was thought that to do this would be quite wrong. The economy was believed to be inherently self-regulating, and it was felt that unemployment would fall, and finally disappear, when wages had been appropriately reduced. Any other action by the government could only make things worse.

In such a situation, conventional wisdom said that the budget deficit could only be tackled by reducing government spending (tax rises were politically impossible). This would bring the economy back into balance. Laval (himself ignorant of economics) expressed the general consensus very well in a radio broadcast in 1935: 'You don't have to be an expert or a financier to realise that if you want to spend more than you have, you soon end up bankrupt. What is true for individuals is also true for the national community.'[8] The measures that Laval took to combat the budgetary crisis were not voted by parliament, but were introduced by what were called 'decree-laws'. They provided for an across-the-board cut in government spending of about 10 per cent, including reductions in the salaries of all public employees. The inevitable result, of course, was that a great deal of demand was taken out of the economy, as the government and its employees had less to spend. Economic activity declined, unemployment rose and the budget deficit went up, rather than down, to general bewilderment.

The structure of public spending in those days was very different from the present day. In particular, there was little social expenditure to cut: there was no unemployment benefit, for example,

8. Cited in Geoffrey Warner, *Pierre Laval and the Eclipse of France*, London, Eyre and Spottiswoode, 1968, p. 90.

since it was seen, as one Radical luminary put it, as 'a way to reward laziness'.[9] The axe therefore had to be directed elsewhere. In the 1930s, about half of government spending was devoted to debt-servicing (much of the debt contracted for the reasons described in the previous chapter), and around a quarter to defence. Although cuts could be made in the final quarter of spending, on education and similar programmes, defence would obviously have to bear a substantial share. Moreover, defence could not be insulated politically in a financial climate where, for example, old age pensions could not be introduced as promised, in 1937, because there was no money for them.[10]

From the time in 1936 when defence spending started to rise again under the Popular Front, the financially orthodox never ceased trying to rein it in. As finance minister in the autumn of 1937, after the fall of the Popular Front, Georges Bonnet managed to get part of the rearmament programme stopped, although it was later reinstated.[11] As late as July 1939, the head of the Finance Ministry was still arguing that the latest rearmament programme was beyond the resources of the country to afford, and would have to be slowed down.[12]

Salaries of government employees were regarded as a fair target, which meant, of course, that the military – poorly paid to begin with – suffered like everyone else. The political effects of this were important, because reductions in military salaries and defence spending by right-wing governments completed the process of the alienation of the military from all political parties whatever. Inherent political probability would suggest a close association between the military and right-wing political parties at this time, and to a degree this was true after 1918. But traditional French suspicions of *partis*, the unattractive behaviour of many 1930s politicians, and a succession of juicy political scandals combined with these measures to complete the alienation of the French military even from overt anti-democrats like Laval.

Another feature of the economic theory of the period was that industry was best left to industrialists. This not only meant

9. Joseph Caillaux, cited by Oliver Bernier, *Fireworks at Dusk: Paris in the Thirties*, London, Little, Brown, 1993, p. 86.

10. Anthony Adamthwaite, *France and the Coming of the Second World War 1936–1939*, London, Frank Cass, 1977, p. 165.

11. Ibid., p. 27.

12. Jean-Louis Crémieux-Brilhac, *Les Français de l'an 40*, 2 vols., Paris, Gallimard, 1990, Vol. 2., *Ouvriers et soldats*, p. 24.

opposition to attempts to better the conditions of the workforce, it also meant that governments felt awkward trying to direct or cajole private manufacturers into doing anything, even if it was to produce armaments for the defence of the country. Contemporary theory held that, if demand for goods existed, the market would automatically adjust to supply them. But this did not happen, for the most part, with armaments, and no one could understand why. The Popular Front government embarked in 1936 on an enormous programme of weapons procurement: 14 billion francs over three years; yet a good part of this money was unspent or wasted. In the circumstances, it is hardly surprising that the Left scented conspiracy: the truth is more mundane, although not necessarily more edifying.

To begin with, the financially orthodox continued to worry about the state of the civilian economy even up to the outbreak of war. Production and export of civilian equipment were seen to be crucial in permitting rearmament to take place at all, and industrialists were given every encouragement to concentrate on the civil side of their work: even on the outbreak of war, manufacture of war material accounted for only 18 per cent of Renault's output.[13] In any event, peacetime armaments production was not seen as particularly lucrative: orders were insecure, production runs short, and there was no guarantee that the costs of tooling up and buying raw materials would be covered. On the other hand, production for the domestic market was much more lucrative and much more dependable. The companies that would manufacture tanks were also those (like Renault and Citroen) that were volume car producers at a time when the market for cars in France was growing rapidly. They saw no reason to reduce their profits by diverting investments into military equipment that would produce a lower return. This was an attitude that persisted even after the start of the war, most notably, perhaps, in the infamous remark of Louis Renault, who had lost market share to his bitter rival André Citroen by concentrating on the military market in 1914–18, and was not going to repeat that mistake again: 'Stuff the war ... what I want ... are cars that make money.'[14]

Even those industrialists who were prepared to engage in war production often demanded that the state absolve them of any financial risk if they did so, and were markedly reluctant to

13. Martin S. Alexander, *The Republic in Danger: General Maurice Gamelin and the Politics of French Defence, 1933–40*, Cambridge, Cambridge University Press, 1992, p. 121.
14. Cited in Crémieux-Brilhac, *L'an 40*, p. 126.

improve or expand their own facilities. As late as April 1940, there is a record of the exasperation of Dautry, former industrialist and head of SNCF brought in to ginger up industrial production, with 'bosses in the provinces'. 'Two at St-Etienne have refused to install special toilets and canteens for the women. Another has said that he would prefer to close his factory rather than to lay out in advance *without a guarantee* the money necessary to buy machine-tools.'[15] Between the reluctance of the *patronat* (the employers) to invest, the reluctance of the financially orthodox to see investments made and the embarrassment of the government in appearing to second-guess the market, the wonder is not that the French armaments industry was 'shackled', as Reynaud charged, but that it produced as much as it did.

Yet even when the will was there, the means were often lacking. French industry of the time was often small-scale and backward, using outdated machinery and production processes, and with a workforce that was poorly trained and often lacked important skills. The generally adverse economic climate after 1918 had made many companies cut back on training to save money, and apprenticeships almost disappeared. Yet the state was reluctant to interfere with such practical business decisions, and had, moreover, very few establishments of its own where apprentices were trained.[16] Likewise, the number of graduates from technical *Grandes Écoles*, who would go on to higher management, was only about 10 per cent higher in the early 1930s than it had been in 1900, in spite of the explosive growth of industry since then.[17] Consequently, modern weapons often could not be produced to the standard required: the R35 tank, for example, was held up in 1936 because the sub-contractors responsible for making the optical sighting and range-finder systems could not find enough skilled labour. The quality of the armour plating supplied was often also below standard.[18] Such a system was, of course, quite impossible to expand quickly in wartime: training, skills and investment that had been neglected for decades could not suddenly be made good overnight.

Even when the labour was available, it was not always prepared to work conscientiously. Industrial relations in the defence sector at the time were appalling by any standards. Many of the industrial workers were first-generation city dwellers, unused to

15. Ibid., p. 135. Emphasis in original.
16. Alexander, *Republic in Danger*, p. 128.
17. Crémieux-Brilhac, *L'an 40*, pp. 27–29.
18. Alexander, *Republic in Danger*, p. 120.

the long hours and crushing monotony of factory life. The *patrons,* in return, treated their workforces as lazy children who needed coercing into doing anything. As a result, strikes were frequent and the motivation of the workforce was low. When hours of work and working conditions were significantly worsened in the last few years before the war, this had (apart from the effect on production, which is debated) the result of depressing morale and increasing bitterness further. The consequence was that strikes were very common and industrial militancy grew: the Communist Party (PCF) found a ready audience for its propaganda.

Finally, the armed forces themselves cannot escape some responsibility. Armies all over the world have the tendency to fiddle with specifications and demand extra features, and the French in the 1930s were not an exception.[19] And even when the equipment was satisfactorily produced, it did not necessarily find its way into the hands of the troops. The 47 mm anti-tank gun, for example, was in prototype in 1935, but was produced in quantity only in 1940. For some reason unavailable for the French army, they were captured and used to good effect by the Germans.[20]

That the French economy failed to function properly in the 1930s, in a general sense and in the industrial sector in particular, is difficult to deny. As usual, economic failure, unemployment and financial uncertainty provoked political unrest also, and I now want to turn to that point.

Conspiracies

Polarisation of French political life was not, of course, new. Important segments of the population were still not reconciled to the Republic, and to the very idea of democracy. These views were disproportionately common in the church, the armed forces and parts of the business community: they therefore had more impact than might otherwise have been the case. They were joined in the 1930s by an important group at the other end of the political spectrum, which likewise had no faith in the parliamentary system and looked to its violent overthrow. The PCF, which had never been a serious force electorally since its foundation in 1920, and was almost wiped out in the 1932 elections, won 15 per cent of the vote and 72 seats in 1936, two-thirds as many as the Radicals. This

19. Ibid., p. 120.
20. Crémieux-Brilhac, *L'an 40,* p. 56.

increased polarisation led to a proliferation of extra-parliamentary activity, which extended as far as violent running battles in the streets and even political assassination attempts. In the process, it brought about a fatal weakening of respect for parliamentary government (helped, it must be said, by the antics of the parliamentarians themselves), such that, in 1940, the Third Republic and its institutions vanished with the suddenness and lack of fuss of a soap bubble.

In the end, it was the Right that won, both in the street and, more importantly, in the chaos that followed the defeat of 1940. This is, perhaps, a suitable point to review what they stood for. First of all, it is important to realise that the French Right of the 1930s, of Vichy, and, indeed of modern times, is quite distinct from the general run of European fascist movements in the 1930s and since. There were fascists in France at that time; but they were a small minority who were kept out of the mainstream. The majority tendency was a specifically home-grown, traditional Right, whose views were outlined earlier. It was authoritarian (and occasionally royalist), it was Catholic (but not always *pratiquant*), it was violently anti-Semitic and anti-democratic and it looked to sweep away one hundred and fifty years of republican experiments to restore the grandeur and influence of France that the Revolution (sponsored by Jews and Freemasons) had destroyed. It saw the family as the repository of all virtue, and the modern world as the source of all vice. In a later chapter, I shall recount what happened when it came to power in 1940.

By far the most influential figure among this tendency was Charles Maurras, leading light of the organisation and the newspaper both known as the *Action Française*. The organisation traced its origins back to the height of the Dreyfus affair in 1898, when Maurras was one of those who argued that Dreyfus, as a Jew, was *inherently* guilty, irrespective of the actual facts of the case, and that the safety of the nation required that he should remain in prison. In the *Action Française* (which began as a review, and became a daily newspaper in 1908) Maurras proceeded to lay out, with an intellectual rigour that diverted the attention of some from the crudity of his conceptions, a vision of a 'vast counter-revolutionary movement' leading to a restored France.[21] It would be essentially the *ancien régime* restored: a Catholic, absolute monarchy organised on hierarchical lines to re-establish the glory of

---

21. Michel Winock, *L'Action Française*, in idem (ed.), *Histoire de l'Extrême Droite en France*, Paris, Seuil, 1993, p. 134.

the past. Maurras was realistic – even cynical – about both of the main elements of his doctrine. It was imperative to restore both the monarchy and the Catholic faith, not because they were necessarily true or valid, but because they were useful and part of French history.

For an organisation whose programme never had the remotest chance of being fulfilled, the *Action Française* was enormously influential. The fact that its newspaper was, by the (unexacting) standards of its type, well written, gave it a prestige all of its own. It was sold outside churches after Mass, and was to be found in every officers' mess: sometimes the only newspaper to be allowed there. It was sold by the *Camelots du Roi* – the 'King's Hawkers', usually students who combined newspaper-selling with street violence. Its total sales never exceeded one hundred thousand copies (although that was more than *Figaro* or *Le Temps*), but its readership was out of all proportion to its circulation. In the absence of libel laws, it set about its opponents with a venom that we would today find nauseating, especially when they were, or might be, Jews. It is possibly the only newspaper ever to have called overtly and repeatedly for the murder of its political opponents. On one occasion, the wish was almost fulfilled: a group of *Camelots* dragged the sixty-five-year-old Léon Blum from his car one day in 1936, and beat him almost to death before being chased off by some construction workers.

It was not alone in these sentiments. At a more popular level, publications like *Gringoire* – selling nearly 600,000 copies by the time the war began – *La Croix, Le Petit Journal, Je Suis Partout, L'Ami du Peuple* and others, reaching millions of readers between them, preached the same messages of hatred and division. There was little in the way of a responsible, serious press in those days, and the only counterweight to the heavy newspapers of the Right – *Le Figaro, Le Temps* – which often took extreme positions themselves, were *L'Humanité* and *Le Populaire*, which were the organs of the PCF and the *Section Française de l'Internationale Ouvrière* (SFIO) respectively, and thus of little interest to non-members.[22]

The targets of the newspapers and the political forces with which they were associated were the usual ones: the Jews, of course, the Judaeo-Masonic Republic and the Judaeo-Masonic-Bolshevik conspiracy against France. A special venom was reserved for schoolteachers, who were accused of rotting the nation with

22. Crémieux-Brilhac, *L'an 40*, Vol. 1, *La Guerre Oui ou Non*, p. 334, has an interesting table of sales of Parisian newspapers in 1939 and 1940.

pacifism and internationalism. Army officers – serving and retired – were especially worried about the effect of this on the troops. *L'Ami du Peuple* in January 1936 reported that both Weygand and Pétain were worried about 'the situation our army is in, thanks to the more and more accentuated decay of our national education in the schools. An absence of physical education, an almost non-existent moral education, and patriotic education forgotten – unless it is given back to front – that is the situation'. The newspaper looked ahead gloomily to a large left-wing vote in the forthcoming elections as a result. Pétain's views were similar: when in government in 1934, he had originally wanted the education portfolio 'to deal with the communist school-masters'. Several years later, his opportunity arrived.[23]

In the context of this study, the extent to which these views were shared by the military of the time is clearly important. Only impressionistic evidence is available, but some assessment can be made. From the fact that almost the entire officer corps of the French armed forces joined and served Vichy, whose ideology was exactly as set out above, one could assume that these ideas were very widespread in the first place. This is perhaps an over-simplification, given such factors as loyalty, inertia, family ties and sheer difficulty in rallying to the Gaullists – points I will return to later. What can be said is that these ideas were very widely distributed in France at the time, and that they were particularly common in the Catholic middle-class circles from which the army and navy, at least, drew most of their officer entry. In considering the 1930s, it has to be remembered that most of the officers would have lived through the Dreyfus affair, and would have been forced to choose sides in a highly polarised fashion. Almost everyone from their social group chose the same side: that of Maurras. De Gaulle's father, a traditionalist Catholic and an early subscriber to the *Action Française*, yet became convinced of the innocence of Dreyfus: not an easy or popular thing to do in the circles in which he moved. His mother never fully reconciled herself to the discovery that all of her sons were republicans.[24]

As other middle-class careers tended to be dominated by republicans, the tendency of the more traditionally minded to cluster

23. Richard Griffiths, *Marshal Pétain*, London, Constable, 1970, p. 162.
24. Jean Lacouture, *De Gaulle*, 3 vols, Paris, Seuil, 1984–86, Vol. 1, *Le Rebelle 1890–1944*, pp. 15–16. Because the English translation of Lacouture's magisterial biography has been abridged into two volumes, rather than three, I have, on this occasion only, preferred to cite the French original, rather than the English translation.

together for safety in the armed forces would have been accentuated. And they felt that they had good reason to be afraid. The
anti-militarist republican tradition was very strong, and before the
First World War there were proposals – by Jaurès, for example – to
abolish the army as it stood, and replace it with a kind of peoples'
militia. That Jaurès's proposals were serious and intended positively did not make them less alarming. And the shortening of the
period of conscription, urged by the Left to stop recruits being
infected with anti-republican ideas, seemed to be an attack on the
very efficiency of the army, and thus on the nation itself. The
excitable and frequently silly attitude of the PCF only served to
fuel these fears. The party published a newspaper called Le Con-
scrit, aimed at inciting indiscipline in draftees, and led various
campaigns against the imperial wars of the 1920s. All these dangers were much exaggerated at the time, but it is not surprising
that, in the fevered atmosphere of the 1930s, a number of officers
felt that 'a conspiracy, all the more ominous because its precise
limits could not be traced, was undermining all permanent military institutions in France'. To such people, Vichy came as a
blessed deliverance.[25]

Yet few officers took any positive action. Although there were
secret societies devoted to rooting out Communists and subver-
sives in the army, and although ex-servicemen and retired officers
were very prominent in the various extra-parliamentary Ligues
that disfigured the streets of Paris, even the bitterest of the Third
Republic's critics does not seem to have contemplated mounting a
coup, although the possibility was a constant fear on the Left. The
views of many officers were certainly extreme: Weygand, for example, dismissed Gamelin (his successor as chief of the General Staff
and one of the few genuine republicans in senior positions) as 'a
man eternally seeking a compromise and always ready to bow to
the decisions of politicians, even when they went against the interests of the army', an astonishing view of civil-military relations.[26]
Yet, for all Weygand's extremism, he was loyal to the despised
Republic, and was probably typical of his colleagues in this. It is
likely that 'Maurrassian' views were widely distributed in the officer corps, but in a passive rather than an active fashion. Officers
despised their political masters and the régime they served, and
looked forward to its replacement with an authoritarian state in

25. Robert O. Paxton, Parades and Politics at Vichy: The French Officer Corps Under
Marshal Pétain, Princeton, Princeton University Press, 1966, pp. 20–21.
26. Alexander, Republic in Danger, p. 30.

which they would have a large influence. They grumbled, but got on with the job, even when they were faced with what they saw as an appalling provocation: the election of the Popular Front government in 1936.

The Popular Front

The Popular Front was the name given to a coalition government of Radicals and Socialists, with support in parliament from the Communists, that held power from May 1936 until June 1937. It is without doubt the most controversial government of modern French history, and the echoes of its passage and its demise at the hands of the Senate, the upper house of the French parliament, have not yet died away. It came about almost accidentally. Ever since the 1932 elections, there had been a theoretical centre-left majority in the Chamber of Deputies; but the Radicals, under Herriot, instead opted to throw their lot in with the Right, and brought about several right-wing administrations during those years, including those of Laval, mentioned above. Several things combined to rearrange the pieces on the board.

The rise of fascism abroad and extremism at home prompted both the SFIO and the PCF (the latter ventriloquised by Moscow) to look seriously at working together. Relations between the two parties had not been good since the Tours Congress, and the PCF had treated the SFIO, in true Marxist fashion, as their worst enemies: 'social-democratic vomit' was one of their kinder characterisations of Blum's party.[27] These two parties, their differences at least suppressed, made common cause with the Radicals, for fear of a coup from the Right. A massive demonstration by the *Ligues* and others in February 1934, culminating in an attempt to storm the Chamber of Deputies, was regarded as an attempted coup, perhaps to install a military dictatorship under Pétain. Another attempt was expected soon. Whether it is true that 'France in 1936 hid in its depths the potential for a civil war'[28] is uncertain; but at the time the alarm was very real.

The Radicals, under the more left-of-centre Daladier, opted to reposition themselves, and the three parties drew up a common programme after much negotiation. In fact, the results of the election of

---

27. Julian Jackson, *The Popular Front in France: Defending Democracy, 1934–38*, Cambridge, Cambridge University Press, 1988, p. 29.
28. Jean Lacouture, *Léon Blum*, new edn, Paris, Seuil, 1979, p. 259.

1936 were not greatly different from those of 1932, in terms of votes cast. But the French electoral system, with its two rounds of voting, puts a high premium on agreements by parties to withdraw after the first round, leaving the field clear for a better-placed party of similar hue. In 1936, electoral discipline held, and the centre-left were returned with a working majority. Rather against expectations, the SFIO, and not the Radicals, won the greatest number of votes, and so Léon Blum, still recovering from the attack made on him, became prime minister. Blum was in some ways an incongruous character to be leader of a government whose coming to power many regarded as tantamount to the end of civilisation. He was intellectually brilliant and had attended the *École Normale Supérieure*, the training ground for the French political class, before leaving to read law. He had gone on to become a member of the *Conseil d'État*, the administrative lawyers who were the élite of the élite of the French bureaucracy. He was also a dramatic critic and journalist before entering politics full-time after the First World War. He was a considerable orator, was generally modest in his behaviour, and had friends from many parts of the political spectrum. He was also, as far as anyone could tell, that rarity of the time, a completely honest politician. For many Frenchmen, he was the devil incarnate.

Because Blum was Jewish, it followed that he was a leading light of the Judaeo-Masonic-Bolshevik world conspiracy. To be a Socialist and an intellectual to boot was as much proof of this as anyone could reasonably want. As a result, from the beginning of his parliamentary career, Blum was subject to perhaps the most sustained and hysterical campaign of vilification that any modern politician has ever had to suffer. In the 1923 debate over the occupation of the Rhineland, for example, when he opposed the operation, he was accused of acting 'in the name of Germany', or 'in the name of the Jewish international'.[29] The type of invective that the election of the Popular Front government provoked is readily imagined, and would be tedious to illustrate at length. The election was described by the *Action Française* as a 'Jewish revolution', and its leader (ridiculously) as a naturalised German, born one Karfunkelstein in Bessarabia.[30] And one of Blum's fellow deputies

29. Ibid., pp. 178–9.
30. Jackson, *Popular Front*, pp. 250–1. Maurras had, of course, a bottomless contempt for democracy. But his characterisation of the 1936 elections in this way was also the result of a conceit by which many so-called Frenchmen who did not share his views were not really French at all. They were members of the '*de facto* France'

regretted that 'this old Gallo-Roman nation' would be governed by a Jew.[31]

But there was more to opposition to the Popular Front than anti-Semitic hysteria, unpleasant though that was. In the frenetic atmosphere of the summer of 1936, a coup, or even an invasion, from some quarter or other was regarded as likely, if not inevitable. The large-scale, peaceful factory occupations that began immediately after the election were regarded as the harbingers of revolution, or worse. Wild stories circulated of a Communist coup planned for 12 June 1936, of secret arms dumps all over the country and militants ready to rise up in bloody revolt.[32] With that flair for the dramatic so characteristic of their type, the second (intelligence) section of the General Staff circulated in January 1937 'a document of Spanish origin which purported to give Soviet instructions on the methods of carrying out a military putsch'.[33] Those who could afford to do so began to consider leaving the country before the tumbrils arrived.

Nothing happened. There was no revolution and the army did not step in. Blum carefully ensured that none of the important defence portfolios went to the SFIO ministers, and went to great lengths to avoid provoking the military. Gamelin, good republican that he was, succeeded in keeping his colleagues in line.[34] The strikes and occupations rapidly ended as the government – in a display of activism unprecedented in modern French history – convened meetings of unions and employers to agree on improvements in wages and working conditions. The two most important of these, bitterly controversial before and since, were the reduction of the working week to forty hours and the institution of paid holidays for ordinary people. Many later writers, like Reynaud, claimed that the institution of 'the forty hours' had prejudiced French defence production and, indeed, contributed to the loss of the war.[35] But in fact, whilst the 'forty hours' represented a significant reduction of the working week *in theory*, in practice, the state of the economy at the time meant that on average employees worked only a few more hours than that anyway, and many

(the *pays légal*) but not the 'real France' (the *pays réel*). Their views and actions could therefore be safely ignored, no matter how many they were.

31. Lacouture, *Léon Blum*, p. 299.
32. Crémieux-Brilhac, *L'an 40*, Vol. 1, pp. 183–5.
33. Adamthwaite, *Coming of Second World War*, p. 168.
34. Alexander, *Republic in Danger*, p. 84.
35. Reynaud, *La France a Sauvé l'Europe*, Vol. 1, pp. 384–92.

worked less.[36] The only way in which industrial production could be increased was if the government was prepared to find more money, and if industry was prepared to respond. The first happened; the second, initially, at least, did not. And an insufficiency of war material was not the main problem in 1940.

The idea of paid holidays was electrifying. They were unknown before 1936 and were viewed with great suspicion by many employers. In some cases, the argument was purely economic: paid holidays would increase industry's costs at a time when French goods needed to be competitive, and so lead to unemployment. But a more profound argument was that these holidays, combined with shorter hours and cheap travel, would teach 'the French working man to be idle'. Lagrange, the much-vilified minister for sport and leisure, was dubbed by the Right the 'Minister for Idleness'.[37] This was the origin of Vichy's critique of the Popular Front: that by promoting idleness it had sapped the moral vitality of the nation.

In many ways the most important legacy of the Popular Front was little noticed and largely technical. It was nothing less than the attempted modernisation of the government machine. Although it was only partly successful, it does point ahead to the more far-reaching reforms enacted after the Second World War. Blum, who had been an enthusiast for government reform for decades, began by not taking a departmental portfolio for himself, and by strengthening his personal staff at the Hotel Matignon so that he could keep an eye on all areas of his government. The government introduced (unsuccessfully) a bill to set up a National School of Administration, to widen the recruitment of the higher civil service, and to improve their professional skills. The Bank of France was no longer to be responsible only to its private shareholders. Parts of the defence industry were nationalised, and money was invested in new plant and equipment, with corresponding gains in productivity. Some of the results were dramatic: the first real production line for aircraft (for the Morane 406 fighter) reduced the time taken to build it from 30,000 to 8,500 hours.[38] The decision-making apparatus in the defence area was overhauled. As a result of all

36. Philippe Bernard and Henri Dubief, *The Decline of the Third Republic, 1914–1938*, trans. A. Forster, Cambridge, Cambridge University Press, 1988, p. 314.

37. Ibid., p. 312.

38. Francois Chesnais and Claude Serfait, *L'armement en France: genèse, ampleur et coût d'une industrie*, Paris, Nathan, 1992, p. 42.

this, France was somewhat stunned to realise that government, after all, could be positive and effective.

Finally, the Popular Front practised what was called the policy of the *main tendue*, the outstretched hand, to other groups (even the church), by which was signalled a preference for unity and the promotion of consensus. The word most used to characterise the approach was *Rassemblement*, usually translated 'gathering' or 'rally', with implications of common purpose. This was not the first time it had been used in a political context; but it is interesting to recall that de Gaulle used the same word when he founded his *Rassemblement du Peuple Français* (RPF) in 1948, seeking to convey the same sense of the unity of the French people. The memory of Joan of Arc was also pressed into service.

Yet Blum lacked the most important quality in a politician: luck. As if the fragmented state of the country, the delicacy of the coalition and the faltering economy were not enough, the Popular Front government took power just as the Spanish Civil War was becoming a major preoccupation. It was this war, more than anything else, that eventually destroyed Blum's government. The war divided France with extreme bitterness, along familiar lines. The early months of the *Frente Popular* government – even the name was the same – had been full of wild rumours of Communist atrocities and anarchist risings on the Right, and fears on the Left that some French general would soon emulate Franco. All of the Popular Front's sympathies, of course, were with its Spanish analogue: moreover, the government in Madrid was legitimate and democratically elected. Yet, in close co-ordination with the British, Blum's government practised a policy of non-intervention that was so strict that it did much to bring about the eventual victory of Franco.

There were a number of reasons for this behaviour. First, much of the Right identified automatically with Franco. Thus General de Castelnau, hero of Verdun, wrote a commentary on the war for the mass-circulation *Echo de Paris*, much read in military circles, which argued that 'the battle is being waged between the Soviet Revolution directed from Moscow and those who have raised the standard of revolt against Soviet slavery ... it is war between Muscovite barbarism and Western civilisation' and posters of the time made the lesson of such diatribes clear: Spain today, France tomorrow.[39] The consequences of any practical support for the Spanish government would therefore be, at best, bitterly divisive.

39. Cited by Paul-Marie de la Gorce, *The French Army: A Military-Political History*, London, Weidenfeld and Nicolson, 1963, p. 241.

Second, the views of London had to be taken into account. Relations between the two countries had gone through a bad patch in 1935–36, but Britain was still France's only substantive ally. If, as seemed perfectly likely, French support for the republicans were to lead to military conflict with Germany, then British support was a prerequisite, and an open clash with Britain was to be avoided at all costs. There was a considerable body of opinion that thought, as a modern writer describes it, that 'the French Government wished to give practical aid to the Spanish Government in its struggle against the rebels, and came to promote the policy of non-intervention only under pressure from Britain'.[40]

Certainly, the British had decided views on the subject. An influential analysis written in the Foreign Office in August 1936 by the superintending under-secretary of the Central Department is revelatory both of British views on the war, and of London's attitude towards events in France. Sargent argued that there was a risk of Europe's 'dividing … into two blocs, each based on a rival ideology'. To prevent France falling into the Communist bloc as a result of the war

> We ought to be able to strengthen the French Government in its efforts – or indeed bring pressure to bear to force it – to free itself from Communist domination, both domestic and Muscovite. Even though this might involve at a certain stage something very like interference in the internal affairs of France, surely it would be worthwhile running this risk?

He thus concluded that it was important to stop France 'by hook or by crook from "going Bolshevik" under the influence of the Spanish civil war...'.[41]

It is not certain how critical this British pressure really was, but, in any event, in less than three weeks Blum's government became converted from initial sympathy to a strict policy of non-intervention. Although Blum found the decision personally devastating, he was not in a position to risk a general European war without British support, or domestic strife in France even with it. Still, it was convenient to be able to blame the British for the decision: such an interpretation would be readily accepted by a people who considered themselves by now inured to constant betrayals by the Anglo-Saxons. It was easy to assume, as Blum's biographer does,

40. Jill Edwards, *The British Government and the Spanish Civil War, 1936–1939*, London, Macmillan, 1979, p. 15.
41. *DBFP*, Second Series, Vol. 17, No. 84.

that the British were motivated by the sympathy of British conservatives 'for the Falangists, defenders of the "Christian order" and the owners of the Rio Tinto mines, in which British capital had a large stake'.[42] The episode did little for Franco-British relations in the long term.

Hitler and Blum

It might seem strange to some that the Spanish Civil War was so furiously divisive. Surely, no Frenchman could welcome the establishment, on France's borders, of a powerful state likely to be an ally of Germany? Yet there was a clear change in the respective positions of Left and Right by 1936, compared, say, to those of a decade before. It would be an oversimplification, however, to see the two swapping sides: the Left losing its positive view of Weimar, the Right its traditional fears. A more complex process was at work. Although many on the Right came to wish for better relations with Germany *after* the rise of Hitler, this was not necessarily because they had sympathy for German aims or methods as such. There were many, like Laval, who had contempt for democracy and admired the more muscular decision-making style across the Rhine, but were not fascists, still less supporters of German foreign policy.

The origins of this attraction lay in the belief, which the British embassy attributed (probably rightly) to Laval as early as 1931, that Bolshevism constituted 'a menace to our civilisation', and that it was important 'to turn Germany away from Russia', even if Germany itself remained a threat.[43] Some embraced this current of thinking more thoroughly than others. In 1934, *La Voix du Peuple*, owned by the perfume millionaire Coty, campaigned under the slogan 'With Hitler against Bolshevism',[44] but this was more an orientation than a call for concrete action outside France, and represented a minority point of view.

But the twin shocks of the Popular Front and the Spanish Civil War sharpened the dilemma acutely. Domestic strife, even a French civil war, now came to seem a real possibility. As Germany became more powerful, so the risk of provoking her seemed less acceptable, and the consequences of a war more terrifying. During and after the Spanish Civil War, one of the most popular cries of the

42. Lacouture, *Léon Blum*, p. 344.
43. *DBFP*, Second Series, Vol. 2, No. 276.
44. Cited by de la Gorce, *French Army*, p. 234.

Right was against the 'warmongers' of the Left, who were trying to drag the country into a disastrous war against Germany that would benefit only domestic and foreign Bolshevism. The particular horror of such a situation for the Right was the likely collapse of all social order and the coming of anarchy. Politicians feared for the whole of French (and indeed European) civilisation, but they also feared for their personal safety. Bonnet told a friend that 'if war comes, there will be a revolution, and the people will throw me in the river'.[45] The new factor since the last war was the advent of the bomber.[46] In splendid defiance of the facts, German bombers were expected to arrive over Paris and devastate it from end to end, producing destruction of a degree we should now associate with nuclear weapons, and provoking what one French politician feared would be 'another Commune'.[47]

It was this feeling that produced an attitude of mind encapsulated in the saying 'better Hitler than Blum'. If anyone *actually* delivered this judgement, it was probably intended to shock or provoke, not to be a sober statement expressing a desire to be invaded and occupied by Germany. It would be unnecessarily glib to believe that sections of the middle classes were less frightened of Hitler, who would only take away their country, than of Blum, who would take their money. Rather, they felt that the consequences of a further period of left-wing government might be so appalling – probably including civil war and war against Germany and Italy also – that almost anything else was preferable. The Left also underwent a modulation of view. Much of it had remained attracted to Briand's ideas of collective security, believing that traditional balance-of-power diplomacy was dangerous and outmoded. And during the Weimar period there was reason to hope that relations between France and Germany might have taken a permanently better turn. These views lost support through the 1930s, and the French Left, with its Jacobin traditions, found a hardening of its views on defence easier than its analogues abroad did.

What united the two was a pathological dread of the possibilities of a future war, combined with the belief that such a war was very likely, but not certain. We tend, these days, to adopt a patronising

45. Cited by Adamthwaite, *Coming of Second World War*, p. 108.
46. See Uri Bialer, *The Shadow of the Bomber: The Fear of Air Attack and British Politics, 1932–1939*, London, Royal Historical Society, 1980, which concentrates, however, on the British panic. I am not aware of a similar work on the French panic, although that was real enough.
47. Joseph Caillaux, quoted by Adamthwaite, *Coming of Second World War*, p. 108.

attitude to the pacifism of those times, and to see it as a moral weakness widely distributed across Western populations. But those of us who have not ourselves lived through a war should perhaps be careful not to condemn too quickly the fears of those who have. For most of the individuals involved, the pacifism I am describing was not ethical in origin, based on a theory of the superiority of non-violence. Rather, it was based on the horrors of the last war, the infinitely greater expected horrors of the next and the judgement that, on the whole, war had relatively little to recommend it, whereas peace was a somewhat better idea. In such a situation, very great, and even humiliating, sacrifices might be in order to preserve peace, since war could only be much worse. It is important to bear in mind that modern catch phrases about 'standing up to aggression' and 'demonstrating firmness', although used of this period, are not of it. Although there was a hope that Hitler might be bluffing, there was, in the great crises – the Rhineland, Munich – an apparently simple choice between war, with all its unforeseeable horrors, and a political settlement of some kind. And on the one occasion when firmness was tried, in September 1939, it led to war rather than a climb-down.

France Without Allies

Reynaud's claim that France was 'without allies' in 1940 is an exaggeration, but contains an important truth. There were, of course, the formal pacts mentioned above; but the only potential allies who would have made a real difference, Britain and America, expressed good intentions and a total lack of interest respectively. The French fixation with security *before* disarmament, rather than *through* disarmament, made her particularly unpopular with both. Whether it is quite true to talk of France's being 'isolated' at this time, to speak of her being the subject of 'jealousy' and 'hatred' is perhaps doubtful.[48] But exasperation with France and a feeling that she was dragging her feet and being unreasonable were very common abroad, especially in London. Inside and outside government, it was widely thought that 'the short-sighted meanness of selfish foreigners, especially the French, had driven Germany to despair and so to Hitler'.[49]

48. Duroselle, *Politique Etrangère*, p. 182.
49. R. A. C. Parker, *Chamberlain and Appeasement: British Policy and the Coming of the Second World War*, London, Macmillan, 1993.

The British were not ignorant of what a cabinet paper of January 1936 called 'The German Danger', but they hoped to meet it by what would now be called a 'twin track' approach: rearmament, but also an attempt to find a political solution.[50] The British analysis, spelt out in a Foreign Office paper by Sargent and others prepared at about the same time, was that a policy of 'coming to terms with Germany' was superior to the other options available, which were just to drift or to adopt a policy of 'encirclement', both of which were thought to be 'policies of negation and despair'. This path, it was argued, was consistent with British policy since 1919 of trying to 'eliminate those parts of the Peace settlement which, as practical people, we knew to be untenable and indefensible ... the ex-Allied Powers should come to terms with Germany in order to remove grievances by friendly arrangement and by the process of give and take, before Germany once again takes the law into her own hands'. This policy, it was argued, had produced many successes so far, and would produce more in the future. It was also strengthened by apparent signs of a greater French desire for reconciliation with Germany.[51]

The British concept of what needed to be done was quite simple: an international settlement that would bury the Versailles Treaty, give Germany the 'equality' of treatment she desired, together with some colonies, and thus divert her on to the path of peace, introduce wide-ranging measures of disarmament and provide a treaty framework related to the League of Nations within which the French could feel secure. Such an outcome would be a better way to deal with Germany than confrontation, since it would encourage the moderates in Hitler's government, and any moderate tendencies the dictator himself had.[52] Such a scheme was entirely consistent with the self-image of the British government, the Diplomatic Service and the Foreign Office,[53] and with Britain's perception of herself as a great power with matchless experience and a mission to solve the problems of the world in a just and equitable manner. The British pursued it almost until the eve of war, not doubting before the very end that they would succeed.

50. *DBFP*, Second Series, Vol. 15, No. 460.
51. Ibid., Appendix 1(a). The paper was controversial within the Foreign Office, but its arguments endured, largely unscathed, in a cabinet paper of February 1936 (Appendix IV (b)).
52. See, for example, the Foreign Office proposals for the 'terms of a working arrangement with Germany' of February 1936, printed in *DBFP*, Second Series, Vol. 15, No. 522.
53. Then, two distinct institutions.

The French, of course, saw things differently. They were unhappy, as a modern commentator puts it, 'to see England obstinately taking the role of mediator between their country and Nazi Germany. They tried to convince the English to one day support Democracy against Dictatorship'.[54] Yet the French were obliged, by and large, to follow the British lead in the great crises of the 1930s. They did not believe that they could stand up to Germany alone, and were terrified of nothing more than a German-British *rapprochement*, which would leave France isolated and defenceless. French studies of the period paint a picture of a weak, frightened France, passively following the lead of the Anglo-Saxons and being ignored and betrayed in return.

A good example is the British-German naval agreement of 1935. The British had been trying to set up naval disarmament talks for some time, and were trying to attract the Germans in. Ribbentrop arrived in London with a simple proposal from Hitler: Germany should be entitled to 35 per cent of British naval strength on a 'fixed and unalterable' basis. The cabinet accepted the proposal, wondering aloud as they did so whether it would be wise to inform the French. The majority thought not: the latter had caused enough trouble already.[55] The British were pleased that the Germans had accepted one disarmament measure: they looked forward to other nations becoming involved in a larger framework. The French reaction was explosive, as much over the lack of consultation as the content of the agreement. Bonnet constructed a complicated conspiracy theory that blamed the British 'imperialist lobby' for this agreement, 'flouting various peace treaties' to buy German support against Italy.[56]

Hitler's remilitarisation of the Rhineland in 1936 well illustrated the relationship between the two countries. The possibility of such a manœuvre had been apparent for some time, and the French had tried hard to extract promises of assistance from the British, but without success. The French preferred not to negotiate, since that might be taken as a precedent for the future. But they did not want to take any action that might lead to their being labelled the aggressors – the Rhineland was German territory, after all – and they were also concerned to co-ordinate everything they did with the British. As a result, the French government

54. Duroselle, *Politique Etrangère*, p. 143.
55. Parker, *Chamberlain and Appeasement*, pp. 30–31.
56. Georges Bonnet, *Quai d'Orsay*, Isle of Man, Times Press and Anthony Gibbs and Phillips, 1965, p. 122.

decided on a policy by which they would act, if need be, only in concert with their Locarno allies. The possibility of mobilisation was kept alive, but nothing was done. As a result, France was able to avoid 'having to fight alone or take full blame if her friends and allies refused to accept their responsibilities'.[57] The British attitude was quite different. Attached to the idea of a general *détente* in Western Europe, London was reluctant to take the French side so blatantly, thus isolating Germany and fuelling the extremist elements there. A Foreign Office paper drafted by Sargent recommended avoiding a situation where fighting or surrender of the Rhineland would be the only options, but rather negotiating its surrender 'whilst such surrender has still got a bargaining value'.[58] In any event, it was not thought France would actually fight: Vansittart, the permanent secretary at the Foreign Office, thought that France was 'too rotten to honour her bond'. Rather, it was feared that France would plead British hesitation as an excuse to avoid fighting, and try to use the crisis as a lever to extract new security guarantees.[59]

In the event, the Germans moved into the Rhineland in March 1936. Unhelpfully, from the French perspective, this was only weeks before an election. And since the centre-right government in power were probably going to lose to the Popular Front anyway, there was little enthusiasm for an invasion of Germany in support of a treaty hardly anyone now took seriously. There were other factors also. The French military mournfully calculated that German forces were much stronger than their own. They did this on the basis of some extraordinary arithmetic, but the politicians believed them.[60] Moreover, the generals also argued that the army was not ready for an offensive operation, and full mobilisation would be required. This has been adduced as evidence of lack of military backbone and pro-German sympathies, but is probably true. A shorter conscription term and a falling birthrate meant that the army was both too small and composed very largely of reserves. There were not enough ready forces to mount an operation of the size thought to be required, and the logistic and other complications of improvising a large-scale aggressive action across the frontier in an unfriendly environment were probably prohibitive.

57. James Thomas Emerson, *The Rhineland Crisis, 7 March 1936: A Study in Multilateral Diplomacy*, London, Maurice Temple Smith, 1977, p. 54.

58. *DBFP*, Second Series, Vol. 15, No. 521.

59. Emerson, *The Rhineland Crisis*, p. 62.

60. Duroselle, *Politique Etrangère*, pp. 166–8.

Things might have been different if the British had been pre-pared to co-operate, but they were not. They still believed that co-operation was a better option than ostracism. And if Mussolini's brutal invasion of Abyssinia had provoked only wrist-slapping economic sanctions, how could war be justified as a way of pre-venting Germany garrisoning her own territory? The embassy reported that French public and political opinion was more mod-erate over the issue than the government, and that criticism of Britain was largely confined to some newspaper correspondents. Sargent agreed, noting that 'Herriot and the extreme Left ... are of course in the pockets of the Bolsheviks and are playing the Russ-ian game, no doubt with the help of Russian money'.[61] Finally, some of the cabinet, including Baldwin, were nervous lest even-tual German defeat in a war over the Rhineland should cause that nation to relapse into Bolshevism.[62] Without British support, with an election on the horizon, terrified of war and feeling themselves to be heavily outnumbered, the French government decided to do nothing, and was showered with praise from all parts of the polit-ical spectrum for not doing it. Yet there was no disguising the humiliation involved, or the public dependence on Britain. And when Belgium declared its neutrality later the same year, a major prop of French defence preparations since the 1920s was removed at a stroke.

When the Munich crisis arrived, a paradigm of impotence, dependence, fear, and surrender already existed. France had little option after 1936 but to seek an even closer relationship with Britain. The British ambassador, Sir E. Phipps, knew France well, and fancied himself a reliable reporter of French affairs. But he was also a meddler in domestic politics – he intervened to per-suade Daladier to appoint the arch-appeaser Bonnet as foreign minister in 1938 – and was blind to all interpretations of events except his own.[63] And he surprised his colleagues in London by arguing at the time of Munich that nothing should be done to 'encourage the small, but noisy and corrupt, war group here. All that is best in France is against war, at almost any price'.[64]

In the event, the French allowed the British to make almost all the running, the latter being convinced that a comprehensive

61. *DBFP*, Second Series, Vol. 16, No. 129. In so far as these categories have any meaning, Herriot was a right-wing Radical.

62. Emerson, *The Rhineland Crisis*, pp. 146–7.

63. Parker, *Chamberlain and Appeasement*, p. 141.

64. Ibid., p. 172.

peace settlement was still within reach. Public enthusiasm in France for war was in any case limited, and there was always someone in every group to supply the necessary sophistry:

> 'But surely', said Jacques, 'the issue is quite clear: we are confronted by a man – I mean Benes – who is formally pledged to establish Czechoslovakia as a federation on the Swiss model.... Whereupon the said person ignores his commitments, and places ... Germans under Czech administration, law and police. The Germans don't like it and they claim their strict rights. Moreover, I know these Czech officials, I have been in Czechoslovakia, I know what petty tyrants they can be. Well then – the proposal is that France, the land, so they say, of liberty, should shed her blood, in order that Czech officials should continue to torment the German population...'.[65]

The arguments employed by the government, through 'guidance' to the media and open propaganda, were not on a much higher intellectual plane. The American ambassador was told by La Chambre, the air minister, that the Siegfied line 'was already a most formidable fortification', and an attack would mean 'the most terrible French casualties'.[66] Bullitt was subsequently told that the Germans could bomb Paris 'at will', with bombs against which there was no protection except 'at least fifteen feet [*sic*] of reinforced concrete'.[67] The enormous crowds who came to greet Daladier at Le Bourget cheered him not because they applauded the betrayal of a small nation, or because they believed Germany's cause just, but because Munich appeared to have banished the terrible spectre of war – ruin from the air and the end of civilisation. The mood changed when it became clear that war, after all, had only been delayed.

As well as the relations with the British just described, there were also attempts during this period to develop closer ties with both the Soviet Union and the United States. The reasons why Reynaud's 'effective alliance' with the Soviet Union was never given effect are a complicated mixture of domestic and foreign policy considerations. They also included a brute fact of political geography. The independence of Poland in 1919 meant that there was no common border between Germany and the Soviet Union. Military

---

65. Jean-Paul Sartre, *The Reprieve*, trans. Eric Sutton, Penguin edn, London, 1963, pp. 92–93.

66. Orville H. Bullitt, ed., *For the President, Personal and Secret: Correspondence Between Franklin D. Roosevelt and William C. Bullitt*, London, André Deutsch, 1973, p. 257.

67. Ibid., p. 298.

pressure could be brought to bear against Germany only if the Poles consented to allow Soviet troops through their country. This meant that effective military assistance to France would either be contingent on the Poles' agreeing to the passage of Soviet troops – judged to be unlikely – or, if no mention was made of this agreement, would imply a Soviet right to interfere in Eastern Europe, neither of which was acceptable.

This problem did not prevent the signature of the 1935 Franco-Soviet Treaty by Laval (negotiated by his predecessor, Barthou). It was seen as a useful political tool that might worry the Germans a little, and could achieve the helpful domestic political result of neutering the pacifism of the PCF. To many on the right, it seemed a sensible reversion to old-fashioned power politics after the vapid internationalism of Briand. And Weygand and Gamelin both agreed that above all it was necessary to avoid 'collusion between Germany and Russia, with a new partition of Poland as its principal aim'. They were happy with the treaty so long as precautions were taken to avoid it having any repercussions on the 'moral unity' of the army.[68]

But as the 1936 elections approached, and a victory of the Left seemed likely, panic set in among the military and their supporters. Weygand, now retired, spoke out against it, and 'official military opinion' judged it 'a trap designed by the devilish Bolsheviks to provoke war between France and Germany', from which, the Soviet ambassador was alleged to have boasted, 'a Soviet Europe will emerge'.[69] The military always managed to obstruct any real substance being added to the original treaty. Partly this was because of political worries, but they also believed that the Red army had little military utility, Gamelin apparently considering even the Romanian army of more value.[70] This is odd, given that much better (and generally accurate) reports of its capability had been available earlier in the decade.[71] Although some low-level exchanges took place after 1938, it was not until the following year, with war approaching, that the French (and, indeed, the British) began to take the idea of a military relationship with the

68. De la Gorce, *French Army*, p. 257.

69. Philip Charles Farwell Bankwitz, *Maxim Weygand and Civil-Military Relations in Modern France*, Cambridge, Mass., Harvard University Press, 1967, pp. 244–5.

70. Adamthwaite, *Coming of Second World War*, p. 235.

71. It is curious that, whilst concern about the 'Bolshevik Threat' was very widespread before the Second World War, and whilst the Red army probably occupied at least the same quantitative relationship to its immediate neighbours that it had in the 1970s and 1980s, there was little concern about a *military* threat from that quarter.

Soviet Union seriously. Even then, French historians contend that the British were not serious, and that their instructions were much less enthusiastic and more limiting than those of the French.[72] The Molotov-Ribbentrop pact, of course, interrupted any possibility of an agreement that there might have been.

Although contact between France and the United States at this time produced nothing at all, it is in some ways the most interesting of these episodes, not least for the light that it throws on postwar events. As has been the case since, enthusiasm for American popular culture and for the American political system were always much stronger on the Left than the Right, which tended to consider the United States a land of soulless modernity and aggressive individualism, not to mention dubious forms of public entertainment. Blum was a great admirer of Roosevelt, whose New Deal he saw as analogous to his own policies. He had a particularly warm relationship with Ambassador Bullitt, who was then, helpfully, an intimate of Roosevelt. Indeed, Blum's biographer argues that, by June 1936, Blum had chosen 'an Atlantic Alliance *avant la lettre*'.[73] For his part, Bullitt was responsible for some of the more measured and accurate diplomatic reporting from France during this time. Yet although Roosevelt partly reciprocated Blum's feelings, the rest of the Washington bureaucracy was not impressed. The State Department regarded Blum as a 'radical revolutionary'.[74]

There was one problem, however, that was to remain insoluble even after the fall of Blum. Recalling the events of 1917, France, like many other nations, looked longingly across the Atlantic at the United States as a source of stability and even military intervention in Europe. Bullitt's letters and telegrams are full of (often ill-tempered) records of his attempts to persuade various French governments that this would not happen. When he had been in Paris for less than a year, Bullitt was writing to Roosevelt that there was 'a violent nervous desire to get us into the next war'. He claimed that 'French Cabinet Ministers and representatives of all the countries of Europe in Paris talk as if they had with them the same phonograph record – playing the theme, "War is inevitable and Europe is doomed to destruction unless President Roosevelt intervenes."'[75]

72. Duroselle, *Politique Etrangère*, pp. 428–31.

73. Lacouture, *Léon Blum*, p. 313.

74. Irwin M. Wall, *The United States and the Making of Postwar France, 1945–1954*, Cambridge, Cambridge University Press, 1991, p. 14.

75. Bullitt, *For the President*, pp. 184–5.

Bullitt was firmly on the side of appeasement. In May 1938, he thought that France would, in fact, fight at Munich, but that the war would be a long one, and would involve 'England and all Europe. There could only be one possible result; the destruction of western Europe and Bolshevism from one end of the Continent to the other.' He then argued that Roosevelt should sponsor an international conference in the Hague, working through the Washington ambassadors of the powers concerned. He might stress to the Germans that

> France will fight and England will fight, that war in Europe today can end only in the establishment of Bolshevism from one end of the Continent to the other, that your proposed conference will leave the Bolsheviks behind the swamps which divide the Soviet Union from Europe and are Europe's real eastern boundary. I think that even Hitler would accept under such circumstances.[76]

The State Department was also firmly appeasement oriented, especially Assistant Secretary Berle, who proposed British and French concessions at the time of Munich.[77] Washington had already considered a peace conference, and on 26 September, in response to more urgent pleadings from Bullitt, Roosevelt put the suggestion to Hitler, who was unimpressed.

France declared war on Germany at 6 P.M. Paris time on 3 September 1939, following the lead of the British once again. The experiences of the 1930s had left the French with a neurotic sense of being unable to protect themselves, and a feeling of humiliating dependence upon other nations whose view of France appeared contemptuous, and who were likely to betray France whenever it suited their wider interests to do so. Other nations seemed not to understand how much they owed France for her endurance between 1914 and 1918, but rather to prefer to devote their time and effort to building up Germany as a major power again, whilst opposing French attempts to enhance her own security.

76. Ibid., pp. 262–3.
77. Wall, *US and Postwar France*, p. 16.

4

ERRORS NOT TO BE REPEATED, II

Without a professional Army there can be no French defence.

Charles de Gaulle, 1934

The offensive is the supreme form of action.... Only the offensive allows definitive results to be obtained.

French army instructions, 1936

Hitler is waiting for the communist insurrection before he attacks.

Military governor of Paris, 1940

Let's get it over with.

Common saying, 1939–40

The defeat of France in 1940 was primarily a military defeat, and so commentators have looked for military causes for it. Some were obviously immediate (mainly the performance of the French army in 1940), but there are usually held to be deeper causes also, going all the way back to the French army's alleged infatuation with the lessons of the First World War. This line of argument begins from the judgement that victories are won by good armies with good doctrine and good leadership over armies that are less well off in these areas. This can be true; but it is not universally so, and believing it tends to obscure the operations of what Frederick the Great (who knew about these things) called 'His Majesty, Luck'.

For political reasons, it was necessary for de Gaulle and other leaders of post-war France to condemn both the Third Republic and the Vichy régime that followed it. The defeat of 1940 was the occasion that made possible the wholesale rejection of the past in all its aspects. It was not unhelpful politically that Pétain, the villain of Vichy, was also seen as responsible for the military doctrine of the side that lost, nor that de Gaulle had been on the other side of the argument. At his trial in 1945, Pétain could scarcely be charged with promoting an erroneous military doctrine; but it is clear that, in the minds of many, this was among his greatest crimes. In the next few pages, I shall try to put the doctrinal debates of the 1930s into their political context, and then to say something about the organisation of French defence in 1940.

A Defensive Army

It is usual for the military to be accused simultaneously both of wishing to re-fight the last war, and of not learning from experience. The French army after the Second World War could certainly be taxed with these errors in some areas, but, in two very important senses, such an accusation would be wrong.

First, the strategic situation of the country had changed. Between 1870 and 1914, there was a widespread, almost mystical urge towards *La Revanche*, revenge for 1870, and the return of Alsace and Lorraine. This mood was reflected in the army also, in the form of the doctrines of the offensive, and of the superiority of the moral over the material. It did not matter that France was in no condition to wage an aggressive war against Germany; the fact was that, unless French troops were further east at the end of a war than they had been when it started, the lost territory was not going to be reclaimed.

After 1918, all this had changed. Although France had not achieved everything she wanted at Versailles, it was difficult to see how a future war could ever result in a more comprehensive victory over Germany, any better territorial settlement, or any further improvement in the security situation. The task therefore became defensive: in any future war, to hang on to as much territory as possible, while being greatly outnumbered by a better-armed enemy. After 1918, there were no realistic territorial objectives to pursue, and a march on Berlin was scarcely credible. Some plans for limited offensive action were made in the immediate aftermath of the war, but they would have been implemented against an enemy that was effectively disarmed. They were soon abandoned because there were insufficient troops to carry them out.[1] If, therefore, France developed what Reynaud dismissed as a 'defensive army', it was because France was defending, and because an offensive doctrine would have been pointless. A different kind of war was envisaged.

Second, no one felt that a repetition of the last war was possible, in any event. In France, as elsewhere, there was a move towards the kind of new technology that would make trench warfare a thing of the past. In Germany, a land power with a requirement to expand its territory, it was to massed tanks; in Britain, a maritime power that hoped to stay out of future Continental wars, it was to strategic bombing. Between them, they took as targets, very deliberately, the headquarters of the enemy, his command structure, his national decision-making apparatus and his civilian population: the hate-figures of the junior officer of the First World War, as so many of the prophets of these new forms of warfare had been.

The French took a different, but complementary, tack. In their case, technology was deployed not to attack an enemy but to ensure the safety of their own *poilus* in the trenches. The Maginot line is perhaps the only example of the large-scale application of military technology to preserving the lives of ordinary soldiers in battle, and this, more than anything else, explains popular support for it. Although André Maginot was not the minister who conceived it, there was much political logic in naming the line after that Sergeant Maginot, who, like a million other common soldiers, had endured conditions of unspeakable privation not far away in 1916. Indeed, anyone who has been into a Maginot fort, even a small one, must be impressed by the feeling of solidity and protection. It kept the garrisons warm, dry and safe: more than most infantrymen in history have ever been able to expect.

Obviously, French thinking was influenced by their experience in the last war (and victory tends to promote conservatism); but the lessons they drew were not necessarily false. Thus, Pétain's remark that *le feu tue*, 'fire kills', has often been mocked, but no one has ever explained what other mechanism caused the immense casualties of the Second World War. In the end, that war, like its predecessor, was won by firepower and attrition: the Allies won because they had much greater resources of tanks, guns, aeroplanes, industrial production and human beings than did the Germans, and

1. Judith M. Hughes, *To the Maginot Line: The Politics of French Military Preparation in the 1920s*, Cambridge, Mass., Harvard University Press, 1971, pp. 192–3.

they used them to pulverise the enemy with previously unimagined quantities of firepower. Similarly, criticism of a defensive posture implies that an offensive one would not only have been possible (which is doubtful), but also superior. But it is unclear that, during the Second World War, there was any *general* superiority of the offence over the defence. Well-prepared defensive positions, as at Kursk in 1943, could be almost invulnerable.

What seemed to have happened is that the eternal oscillation of the pendulum between defence and offence had reached a certain point in 1939–40, where the creative and vigorous employment of armoured units and air power could disrupt and destroy an army in defensive positions. This advantage did not endure for long, but, in terms of the French experience, it endured long enough. Ever since, the tendency has been to elevate the transitory experience of one campaign to the status of universal rule: helpful in terms of post-war French politics, no doubt, but far from the whole truth.

There was nothing invulnerable about the tank. Many of the tanks that the Germans used in 1940 were PzI and PzII models, little more than training vehicles, so thinly armed and armoured that they scarcely deserved the name. The French already possessed weapons capable of defeating those tanks, and probably the more recent Pz III and Pz IV models as well. And the feared Ju-87B, which had caused such havoc in Poland and France, was subsequently annihilated by the Royal air force, and withdrawn almost at once.

The tendency to generalise from the French experience of six weeks in one year of the war has obscured the fact that much of French doctrine was reasonably adequate *when it was written*, and was subsequently to prove at least as applicable as anyone else's. Thus, it is certainly true that the *Provisional Instructions Concerning the Tactical Utilisation of Larger Units* suggested that a continuous front was invulnerable, and that attacks should only be made with overwhelming superiority and after careful consideration. But the document was published in 1921, and fairly reflected the realities of the time. The army can be criticised for taking so long to change its doctrine: only in 1936 did it decide that 'the offensive is the supreme form of action'.[2]

In 1938, Pétain wrote (or, more probably, signed) a preface to a book by General Chauvineau, a fortification expert, whose title

2. Paul-Marie de la Gorce, *The French Army: A Military-Political History*, trans. Kenneth Douglas, London, Weidenfeld and Nicolson, 1963, pp. 271, 277.

has gone down in history as an ill-timed joke in poor taste. The book was called *Is an Invasion Still Possible?* Part of Pétain's preface to what de Gaulle's biographer calls 'this pathetic lampoon' reads:

> There is a deadly barrier against the passage of tanks: it is the obstacle of mines, together with the fire of anti-tank weapons. What would become of an offensive by armoured divisions if it were to run into divisions of the same type, but deployed and with several hours' preparation, on ground of their own choosing, with an anti-tank fire-plan and natural obstacles reinforced by minefields?

It is true, as de Gaulle pointed out, that France had no 'divisions of the same type'; but Pétain's argument is quite valid.[3] In fact, these were much the tactics used to great effect by Rommel against the British in North Africa in 1941, except that he seldom had anything like the number of tanks the British had, and was forced to rely on dug-in anti-tank guns. Indeed, from that point up to and including the 1973 Middle East war, tanks charging a defensive position without adequate preparation and support from other arms have usually suffered badly as a result. As a 1938 article (in an infantry publication, as it happens) put it: 'even modern tanks can never conduct operations for and by themselves'.[4]

Thus, it would be an over-simplification to describe the French doctrine in 1940 as 'defensive', except in the obvious sense that the French expected to be numerically inferior and to receive, rather than give, the first blow. It was far more than 'the siege-warfare mentality of Verdun and the trenches'.[5] It was not an alternative to a fully worked-out doctrine of the offensive, which would in any case have been beyond the capabilities of the army and difficult to justify in an era when there was much interest among Western governments in trying to identify and eliminate so-called 'offensive' weapons.

In reality, there were at least three debates going on simultaneously in France in the mid-1930s, and their echoes have already been noted. The first was whether tanks had an important role on the modern battlefield at all. Opinion was divided, as in most other armies, and there remained much obscurantism, usually in the cavalry. General Brecart, inspector general of that arm, counselled in 1933 against the 'dangerous utopias' of mechanisation. He would

3. Cited by Jean Lacouture, *De Gaulle*, 3 vols., Paris, Seuil, 1984–86, Vol. 1, *Le Rebelle, 1890–1944*, p. 258.

4. De la Gorce, *French Army*, p. 274.

5. D. C. Watt, *How War Came: The Immediate Origins of the Second World War, 1938–1939*, London, Heinemann, 1989, p. 20.

prefer to retain the horse on the grounds that you knew where you were with cavalry, and that France as a nation had no petrol supplies, but lots of good horses.[6] This battle was largely won by the late 1930s; and in quantity and quality French tanks compared well with the Germans in 1940.

The second debate, related but separate, was concerned with the *employment* of tanks. One theory held them to be essentially a form of mobile protected firepower for the infantry, used in small groups to support the advance. This was a popular theory in Britain in the 1930s, as well as in France. Another, much bolder concept was that of a mass of tanks concentrated in all-arms divisions, operating autonomously ahead of the main army. This is what was later to be called *Blitzkrieg* (or, more precisely, the organisational framework in which it was developed). It was difficult to do well, and required not only mobile and sophisticated equipment, but also excellent communications. Even before 1940, the French had started to reorganise on these lines, and the experience of the war demonstrated (a little too late) that they should have done so before. The third controversy, forgotten today except by specialists, was the question of whether France should continue with its existing arrangements for conscription or should go over to a limited form of professionalism. For reasons that may already be obvious, this was by far the most controversial of the three issues, and I return to its political consequences below. Since de Gaulle, then a lieutenant-colonel, was largely responsible for igniting the last debate (and entangling it hopelessly with the others), it is sensible to give an account of the theories in his 1934 book *Towards a Professional Army*.[7] De Gaulle's book is not original, and many ideas, and even detailed examples, are taken from earlier writers, particularly from General Jean-Baptiste Estienne, who had written some visionary articles in the 1920s. He had commanded tanks in 1916–18, when de Gaulle was a prisoner of the Germans. De Gaulle's importance is thus more as a populariser than as an original thinker. What is his argument?

Briefly, it is that the age of mass warfare is over. Modern war is so destructive that no nation would risk it for the traditional (basically territorial) motives. There will remain a requirement for large conscript armies to be available, to guard against the possibility of

6. De la Gorce, *French Army*, p. 272.
7. The usual English translation is *The Army of the Future*, which conveys some of the sense of the book quite well, but quite misses the politically explosive message for anyone who even glanced at the cover of the original.

large-scale conflict; but increasingly the tendency will be for small, short-notice, violent conflicts for limited objectives, in which the attacker would seek to occupy an area before the defender could respond. Such conflicts cannot be fought by conscript armies, but rather need ready forces. They will need to be forces of the highest technological level, armed with the latest sophisticated weapons. The twin requirements of ready forces and high technology dictate that these forces should be made up of professionals, since conscripts would be unable to handle the sophisticated equipment, and would not be available quickly enough. This has been the trend for some time in the army and navy. Because France's northern frontier is difficult to defend, it is very likely that Germany will try a sudden attack with its (professional) army, perhaps to recover Alsace and Lorraine. Fortifications help, but '[w]ithout a professional army there can be no French defence'.[8]

De Gaulle provides a detailed order of battle for the force (again, drawing on earlier ideas). It would consist of six armoured divisions, each with five hundred tanks, and made up of a heavy armoured brigade, an infantry brigade and two artillery regiments, with engineer support.[9] Yet in spite of all the detail, the presentation of the force is lyrical and poetical, rather than technical: his notional armoured brigade moves 'across country as fast as a horse at the gallop … crossing ditches three yards wide, climbing mounds thirty feet high, felling 40-year-old trees, knocking down walls twelve bricks wide, crushing all obstacles, barriers and hedgerows – this is what industry today can provide for every professional division'.[10]

It becomes immediately clear that the tanks that de Gaulle is describing are not real mechanical devices, which break down, throw tracks, run out of fuel and ammunition, and are followed around by a massive logistic tail. Rather, they are mythical constructs, dreamed up by a writer who had, as far as is known, never been inside one, had no technical training, and had never seen one in action, being a prisoner in Germany when they were first introduced. They are virtual tanks, an actualisation of what every officer on the Western front in the First World War desperately wanted. In this armoured mysticism, de Gaulle was echoing other, equally non-technical, pioneers of armoured warfare, like Liddell Hart.

8. General [Charles] de Gaulle, *The Army of the Future*, London, Hutchinson, [1940?], p. 36.
9. Ibid., pp. 88–89.
10. Ibid., p. 88.

We look in vain for any technical detail – speed, size and penetration of main armament, type of propulsion, thickness of armour
plating – on the basis of which the nation is being invited to place
its safety wholly in the hands of these machines; although there is
one odd (and surely erroneous) technical detail: that modern tanks
hold from three to fifteen men.[11] The characteristics that de Gaulle
describes were well beyond the capability of French industry to
produce, and were to remain so for a very long time. Tanks of the
Second World War could certainly not cross open country as fast as
a galloping horse: they usually kept to the roads, where they could
get up a decent speed. Even if their cross-country performance had
been better, their infantry were usually carried in lorries, which
had little off-road mobility, and not in the tracked vehicles that
were de Gaulle's wildly futuristic concept. And there would have
been no chance of recruiting an extra hundred thousand officers
and soldiers for the force, even if the money had been available.

Yet in a sense this does not greatly matter. The force that de
Gaulle describes is essentially a solution looking for a problem, as
becomes clear when he lists, rather unconvincingly, a whole range
of tasks his force might pursue, including pre-emptive attacks
against Germany, intervention in Europe and abroad, and action
in some kind of international force under the League of Nations.
(De Gaulle gave no thought to the practicalities of transporting
such a force any distance.) For de Gaulle, the force is essentially a
symbol, and it was for him then what the atomic bomb was to be
later: a piece of sophisticated technological wizardry that would
ensure the safety of the country. It was consistent with de Gaulle's
generally progressive orientation and his modern political views,
including firm support for the Republic and involvement in the
early thirties with the nascent Christian Democratic movement,
which was trying to modernise the French Right and to arrange a
truce between the church and the modern world.[12] Many who supported his ideas were likewise attracted rather by their modernity
than their coherence.

It was not the technical deficiencies of de Gaulle's ideas that
provoked debate, however, but their political implications. The
book appeared only three months after the February 1934 attempt
to storm the Chamber of Deputies, and at a time when a fearful
public were expecting a military coup at any moment. To choose
that moment to propose the creation of what was immediately

11. Ibid., p. 58.
12. Lacouture, *De Gaulle*, pp. 229–30.

dubbed a 'mercenary' force was to make a political statement of considerable potency, and it is not surprising that de Gaulle was violently attacked. It is more surprising that he found a political champion in the person of Paul Reynaud, who adopted de Gaulle as his military adviser and introduced, in 1935, a law to set up the kind of force he had described.[13] The opposition it excited was political rather than technical: Léon Blum, for example, who could see some attractions in the idea, was worried that it could far too easily be used to carry out a *coup d'état*.[14]

De Gaulle may perhaps be pardoned his political naïvety (and he certainly had no praetorian leanings himself), but the effect of linking the idea of professionalism to that of a modern tank force was very nearly to sink them both together. Analogies are dangerous, but it is rather as though a lieutenant-colonel in the British army had, in 1934, linked a suggestion for a modern tank force with a proposal that the professional army of the day should be abolished and replaced by a people's militia based on compulsory military service, and had then joined in a public crusade with an Opposition MP to get his ideas implemented. As Martin Alexander puts it, if de Gaulle and Reynaud

> had confined themselves to issuing a clarion call for urgent military re-equipment with emphasis on armoured and motor vehicles, they would have gained the endorsement of Gamelin and Colson. Instead, they aroused the irritation of these and many more senior generals.... This antagonism and suspicion combined to impair the army's ability in the long term to match Germany's build-up of tank forces and evolution of accepted and understood mechanised warfare doctrine.[15]

The fact that de Gaulle was not slapped down firmly at the time demonstrates how fragmented and chaotic the Third Republic's politico-military apparatus was. Yet his ideas were doomed to failure (it is surprising that a politician as wily as Reynaud thought there was any mileage in them at all), and nearly brought down proposals for the modernisation of the army with them. The debate, which is often portrayed as between de Gaulle's vision of a mechanised army and the friends of the Maginot line, was really between supporters and opponents of a professional army. This is

13. The text is in Paul Reynaud, *La France a Sauvé l'Europe*, 2 vols., Paris, Flammarion, 1947, Vol. 1, pp. 324–5, together with an elaborate apologia.

14. Lacouture, *De Gaulle*, p. 248.

15. Martin S. Alexander, *The Republic in Danger: General Maurice Gamelin and the Politics of French Defence, 1933–40*, Cambridge, Cambridge University Press, 1992, p. 38.

clear from the authoritative counter-blast to the de Gaulle-Reynaud hypothesis drafted by the army in July 1936, which sets out, quite reasonably, many practical problems with the professional army, but does not comment at all on the proposals for the use of armoured formations.[16]

The end result of all this conflict was, therefore, probably not to advance the cause of mechanisation, but to hold it up by entangling it with a much more controversial proposal. Certainly, giving way publicly would have looked like a defeat for the army and for Daladier, at the hands, respectively, of a widely unpopular junior officer and of Daladier's bitter political enemy. Such things seldom happen in politics. The affair had considerable long-term implications. It strengthened, if that was possible, de Gaulle's belief in himself and his own rightness, and his assumption that different rules applied to him. It created one of the great alibis for 1940 ('with an armoured force we would have won'). It brought de Gaulle and Reynaud close together, which was to have profound consequences in and after 1940. It also deepened the rift between de Gaulle and much of the rest of the French army, which could tolerate an opinionated rebel, but not one who enlisted politicians in his aid.

During this period, there was one project that summed up the debate for many and that has since acquired a semi-mythical status. The Maginot line has become unmentionable, except as an example of an awful mistake, and an awful warning against trusting to static, linear defence. The accusation that it shows a 'Maginot mentality' is usually enough to sink any new idea, and no more devastating criticism of NATO's defensive posture in the 1980s could have been imagined than to describe it as a 'new Maginot line'.[17] This is curious, since the original objectives of the project were quite modest and were not necessarily invalidated in 1940. Fortifications have, of course, been part of French military thinking since the seventeenth century, and the French have always been very good at them. They were important both in the war of 1870 and in the First World War, and it was natural that French minds should turn inquiringly towards fortifications during the 1920s. In

---

16. *Note du Général, Chef du Cabinet du Ministre de la Guerre au Sujet de l'Armée du Métier*, July 1936, reprinted in *Documents Diplomatiques français 1932–1939*, (hereafter *DDF*) *2ème série*, Vol. 3, No. 9.

17. John Connell, *The New Maginot Line*, London, Secker and Warburg, 1986. Other examples include Sidney Lens, *The Maginot Line Syndrome: America's Hopeless Foreign Policy*, Cambridge, Ballinger, 1982.

the form it eventually took, the Maginot line had its origins in the late 1920s, when it became clear that the Rhineland would be evacuated ahead of schedule. There was a great fear, reflected in de Gaulle's book also, of a sudden attack on the recently recovered frontier regions – the *attaque brusquée*. In a series of speeches in 1929, the deputies Jules Fabry and André Maginot painted a grim picture of 300,000 to 400,000 German soldiers invading these provinces, and wresting them back from France. Certain statements by General von Seeckt, the main architect of the Reichswehr, could be read as implying that this was what the Germans would do.[18] As a result, plans already in hand to fortify Alsace and Lorraine were expanded and expedited.

Interestingly, the Maginot line, as constructed, was *not* an example of static, linear defence. Although Pétain and Foch had argued, after 1919, for a continuous network of lightly defended trenches, similar to those that had withstood German assault in 1918, others argued that a manœuvre defence, based on fortified regions, would be more effective as technology developed, and less expensive in money and manpower. There would be static garrisons in the forts, but the majority of the troops – the so-called 'interval troops' – would be deployed outside, to await the attack. After a long struggle, the latter group won.[19] With the fears of the late 1920s, however, the politics of the line began to change, and successive war ministers allowed the French nation as a whole to come to feel that the line was, in fact, a continuous fortification, and that, as a result, that part of France at least was secure behind a belt of concrete and steel.

With the construction of the line, the threat of the *attaque brusquée* was thought to have been lifted. In turn, however, this directed attention to the northern frontier with Belgium, through which the attack had come in 1914. The soggy ground on the frontier was very unsuitable for concrete fortifications, even if it had been politically acceptable to build them on the doorstep of an ally. At the same time, it was also politically impossible to plan for a defensive battle on the same area of northern France that had been devastated in 1914–18, and that still contained the bulk of the nation's heavy industry. The answer, as was recognised from the very beginning, was to advance into Belgium, to keep the soil of France safe and to meet the enemy as far forward as possible.

18. Hughes, *To the Maginot Line*, pp. 193–4. The figures, of course, were wildly exaggerated.
19. Ibid., pp. 198–201.

Until Belgium declared its neutrality in 1936, this would have been a relatively straightforward affair. Some light defensive works, to create a second line of defence on the border, were also considered, but nothing of importance was ever built, and Gamelin decided in 1940 to try to hold on the line Meuse-Namur-Antwerp, deep inside Belgium.[20] Ironically, the main reason for deciding not to build the fortifications was, as Pétain argued, to avoid the 'danger' of the 'subordination of all war planning ... to existing or intended fortification'. [21] Thus what Reynaud (rightly) called 'the most exposed part' of the frontier was not fortified. When the French troops retreated in 1940, they had no fortifications to fall back on, and only the unpromising defensive features of the border areas to play with. Paradoxically, therefore, the French defeat can partly be explained, not by too much attention to fortifications, but too little.

The Maginot line performed as advertised in 1940, in that the Germans were deterred from launching an attack into the most vulnerable part of France, where the countries had a common border. The French were not, therefore, surprised to find the attack developing elsewhere, and the Germans coming through Belgium: unfortunately, they came through the wrong bit. A word finally, therefore, about the Ardennes.

The French did not think an attack through the Ardennes was likely, and the Germans did not at first plan to attack that way. The notorious undertaking, given by Pétain in 1934, that the sector was 'impenetrable' has often been selectively quoted. What Pétain actually said was that the Ardennes were 'impenetrable so long as we make special provisions in them. We therefore consider this a zone for demolitions.... We should erect blockhouses there'.[22] Pétain was not so obtuse as to imagine that any reasonable geographical obstacle was 'impenetrable', whether or not it was defended. He would have known that there were roads through the Ardennes, and all his assertion really amounted to was that, given the rough ground in the area, advances had to be dependent on these roads, and could thus be obstructed relatively easily if certain measures were taken. Unfortunately, they never were, and the Ardennes remained largely unfortified and only lightly garrisoned.

In summary, it can be said that French defensive plans in the 1930s, although far from perfect, were more logical and coherent

20. Ibid., pp 214–9.
21. Cited by Alexander, *Republic in Danger*, p. 184.
22. Ibid., p. 200.

than is sometimes suggested. But this proved to be irrelevant when the settling of accounts began after the defeat in 1940. The main political and military participants landed mighty blows on each other in the battles of the memoirs, but they all had one crippling political disadvantage: they lost. Against the brute fact of the defeat, the political and military actors could only claim that they had been misunderstood, and that, anyway, it was somebody else's fault and not theirs. Although the Maginot line was a success in its own terms, it could not live up to the myth that its political creators had allowed to grow up around it. Building confidence is easier and cheaper than building fortifications; and that was what the politicians of the Third Republic decided to do. They suffered for it in due course.

A great clearing of the decks was therefore possible, and not only of personalities but also of ideas and techniques. The defeat of 1940 is one reason why France, since the end of the war, has pursued a policy of vigorous modernity, not least under de Gaulle. When Leclerc entered Paris in August 1944, he did so, of course, at the head of an armoured division.

Defence by Committee

One of Reynaud's charges was that France in 1940 had 'neither Ministry nor Headquarters for national defence, nor organisation for High Command'.[23] There is much truth in this accusation, and in similar complaints, although France was far from the only nation in such a situation in 1940. As in most countries, there had previously been Ministries of War (i.e. the army) and of the Navy. In 1928, the Ministry of the Air was added. France's military tradition was essentially a Continental one, and this, combined with the sheer size of the army and the lustre of its *chefs*, tended to make it the most important of the services in the political game in Paris. The vice-president (and senior military member) of the Higher War Council (*Conseil Supérieur de la Guerre*) was always chief of the General (Army) Staff at the same time.

By the 1930s, it was beginning to be realised that the mild form of anarchy by which each service did its own planning and fought separately for funds was a bad idea, and governments started to experiment with improved co-ordination. Maginot, during one of

23. Reynaud, *La France a Sauvé l'Europe*, Vol. 1, p. 452.

his stints as war minister in 1931, first suggested the creation of a Ministry of National Defence, and it made a transitory appearance in the short-lived Tardieu adminstration of 1932 before being buried by its successor. Two other innovations did survive, however: the Secretariat General of National Defence (*Secrétariat Général de Défense Nationale*), where de Gaulle was to work, and the Senior Military Committee (*Haut Comité Militaire*), chaired by the war minister. In both cases, however, they had a co-ordinating, rather than an executive role.[24]

It was in 1936 that the Popular Front reverted to the idea of a defence ministry as part of its attempt to modernise the machinery of government. It expanded and transformed the Senior Military Committee into the Standing Committee on National Defence (*Comité Permanent de la Défense Nationale*), and, for the first time, added both the minister of foreign affairs and the secretaries general of that ministry and the Ministry of Defence. Such a move might strike us as obvious, but at the time it was epoch-making, as was a working-level committee established between the two ministries, and meeting in the Quai d'Orsay.[25] It is interesting to examine the minutes of the first meeting of the Standing Committee and to see how limited the innovations actually were. Daladier began by arguing that 'alone among the great powers of Europe, France has not yet carried out the indispensable coordination of its armed forces. In the dictatorships, a single individual has the overall direction of the forces.... In England, a special minister ... has just been entrusted with the coordination of the three military departments'. Yet, in case the military were starting to shuffle their feet by this stage, Daladier added that 'there was no question, in the mind of the Minister of National Defence and War, of posing the least threat to the autonomy of either of the military Ministries, or creating any kind of subordination among them'.[26]

This was, in the end, all that the market would bear, either in France or abroad. The various co-ordination committees did reasonable work, but could not overcome the vested interests of the services. A fully integrated Defence Ministry and High Command, with the ability to override the service lobbies, was decades away, not just in France but elsewhere. Gamelin was allegedly chief of Defence Staff when war came, but he had no executive power

24. Jean-Baptiste Duroselle, *Politique Etrangère de la France: La Décadence 1932–1939*, Paris, Imprimerie Nationale, 1979, pp. 255–6.

25. Ibid., p. 257.

26. *DDF*, 2ème Série, Vol. 2, No. 369.

except over the army, because the other two services were not prepared to surrender any to a soldier. This kind of behaviour was, however, common all over Europe at that stage and afterwards.

A particular problem that the French had was the size of the cultural and intellectual gulf that separated the civilian politicians from the military professionals. There was (and still is, to some extent) a feeling that the military should concern themselves with technical military matters, the diplomats with foreign policy questions alone, and politicians with only general political questions, leaving matters of detail to the experts.[27] This may sound plausible, but policy-making can only work properly if these distinctions are somewhat blurred in practice. There was then no cadre of civilian officials with an understanding both of politics and defence matters, able to hold the debates together and ensure a reasonable outcome. Although the secretary-general attended important meetings, he tended (as befitted his origin as an inspector of finances) not to become involved in discussions of policy.

It is likely that the disorganisation of French defence planning in the 1930s has been overstated, both relatively and absolutely, as part of the blanket condemnation of everything that was done at that time. De Gaulle, for example, describing the impermanence of political life and the 'feebleness of the State', argues that ministers were prevented 'from achieving that organic whole of continuous plans, matured decisions and measures carried to their conclusion, which we call a policy'.[28] But it is doubtful whether any government at that time achieved this feat, even with greater ministerial permanence. Least of all was it achieved in the anarchy and among the competing hierarchies of the German politico-military system. Likewise, in a much-quoted passage, André Beaufre, who as a young officer worked in the Ministry, left us an account of what he regarded as its disorganisation, in that the 'General Staff was theoretically in command, but had no money, no administration, no personnel and no stores; the Secretary General had the money and the administration, without any responsibility for command; the senior officers had the men and the stores, but no

27. One example is the meeting of August 1939, to discuss what to do about the Polish crisis. It features a meandering discussion which arrives nowhere. The text is reprinted in Assemblée Nationale, Document No. 2344 (1947), *Rapport … sur les Evénements Survenus en France de 1933 à 1945*, Paris, Imprimeries de l'Assemblée Nationale, 1951, Vol. 1, p. 276ff.

28. Charles de Gaulle, *War Memoirs*, Vol. 1, *The Call to Honour 1940–1942*, trans. Jonathan Griffin, London, Collins, 1955, p. 12.

authority.' [29] But this is very much the way in which all defence ministries have to work: no democracy, for example, can allow the military to decide how to spend the defence budget, for which politicians are responsible before their parliament. What distinguishes functioning from non-functioning systems of this type is not organisational clarity – of which the French have, perhaps, been too fond – but the skill and common purpose that the participants use to make the system work.

Nonetheless, it was clear, after 1940, that the system, in spite of some modernisation, had not worked, and it was argued subsequently that this had affected the performance of the French armies. Some interpretations were frankly self-serving – de Gaulle, for example, with his belief in a strong state, reproached the structure he had known for being too weak. But, as will be seen in a later chapter, the reorganisation of national defence was a priority task after 1945 for individuals of all political views.

The War of France Will Not Take Place

Although the Third Republic, like a patient rallying before the final collapse, began to try to reform itself in the last years of its existence, whatever hope for reform there might have been was strangled by the events of 1939–40, when the Republic passed through perhaps the most troubled and least impressive period of its history. The eight months between the declaration of war in September 1939 and the German attack in 1940 are called in French the *drôle de guerre*. This formulation (of which 'phoney war' is not a translation) is difficult to put into English: perhaps 'funny kind of war' is the closest one can come. It was a funny kind of war not only because it was different from 1914, but also because it was different from the way in which it was *supposed* to be different from 1914. Folk memory recalled both the sudden and violent descents on French territory in 1870 and in 1914, and the more recent warnings about the likelihood of massive air attacks with poison gas.

Moreover, for the average Frenchman, and for much of the *classe politique* as well, it was difficult to understand what was supposed to be going on. Why had France abandoned (some said

29. General André Beaufre, *1940: The Fall of France*, trans. Douglas Flower, London, Cassell, 1965, p. 44.

betrayed) the last functioning democracy in Central Europe, whilst going to war on behalf of a rather unpleasant military dictatorship? And, if it had gone to war to save Poland, why had it, in spite of the poses it had previously struck, stood back and watched *Blitzkrieg* devour the country in a few weeks? And if Germany, having digested Poland, did not seem to be threatening France, what was the point in being at war anyway?

> For men of the Right, the fate of Poland had never been worth the death of a single French soldier.... For some of the Left, the extremely suspect zeal of the men of Munich suddenly turned warlike authorized every sort of suspicion.... As for the man in the street ... he was liable to see in the destruction of Poland an excellent chance of ending an adventure now...[30]

It is always difficult to understand great events when they do not conform to patterns with which we are familiar. This was not a war to reclaim Alsace and Lorraine, nor a desperate resistance in the face of the invader. *La patrie en danger*? Perhaps, but where was the *danger*? It was this confusion that made the process of getting parliamentary sanction for the war a grimly tragi-comic affair. On the afternoon of 2 September, when Poland had been invaded but the overwhelming German aerial attack seemed unaccountably delayed, Daladier's government finally, and nervously, gave the horns of the bull a gentle squeeze, and called an extraordinary session of parliament. Curiously, when Herriot, the president of the Chamber, opened the session, he did so with a blistering condemnation, not of Germany, but of the Soviet Union, for having just signed a pact with Germany that 'arouses the condemnation of every right-thinking individual'. This provoked massive applause, even from the ranks of the deputies of the PCF.

When Daladier spoke, he proclaimed general mobilisation, and introduced a text of a *projet de loi* which approved an extra 70 milliard francs in government expenditure 'to respond to the obligations of the international situation'. When Daladier sat down, it was noted that he had not mentioned a declaration of war, nor asked the Chamber to agree to one. And his speech had mentioned 'peace' on eleven occasions, but 'war' only three times.[31] It

30. François Fonvielle-Alquier, *The French and the Phoney War, 1939–40*, trans. with an introduction by Edward Ashcroft, London, Tom Stacey, 1971, p. 98.

31. Guy Rossi-Landi, *La Drôle de Guerre: La Vie Politique en France, 2 septembre 1939–10 mai 1940*, Paris, Armand Colin, 1971, pp. 15–17.

was unclear then – and still is – whether there would have been enough votes in the Chamber in favour of war: in the event, the government decided not to risk it, and, throughout the whole of the *drôle de guerre*, never sought a direct vote on the principle. The Constitution of the Third Republic stipulated that the president could declare war 'only with the prior agreement' of the Senate and the Chamber of Deputies.[32] It was not at all clear that this had been done, and opponents of the war could readily claim, throughout the eight months, that the public's representatives never had a chance to speak.

Why this timidity? First, there had been disunity, even within the ranks of the government itself, over the guarantee to Poland. There had been a faction – led by Bonnet – that had been unhappy about giving a guarantee to the Poles in a dispute not about Polish territory, but about Danzig, which was a Free City. And, even as parliament was meeting, Bonnet was still trying to get negotiations started.[33] Second, there was an almost paralysing fear of what war might amount to: nobody wanted to say the word. All parts of the political spectrum and all classes of society were expecting death, destruction, and the end of all civilisation and civilised values. And quite obviously, those with most to lose, who naturally tended to dominate the debate, felt this fear most strongly. Third, there was no unanimity in this fearful country about the very idea of a military confrontation with Germany. Some Frenchmen certainly agreed with the deputy Marcel Déat that it was necessary 'to erect a barrier against Bolshevism for the safety of Western Europe', and that this could be done by giving the German people some incentive to get rid of the Nazis, 'introducers of Bolshevism into the West', and replace them with a pro-Western government, in a new Federal Europe that would subsequently attack Russia.[34]

Beyond this rather extreme grand design, there were many political groups, anti-Communist, pro-German or both, who deplored the idea of the two nations at war with each other. As Thierry Maulnier, one of the ablest younger spokesmen put it, a German defeat 'would signify the collapse of the authoritarian

32. Article 9 of the Constitutional Law of 16 July 1875, see Charles Debbasch and Jean-Marie Pontier, *Les Constitutions de la France*, 2nd edn, Paris, Dalloz, 1989, p. 194.

33. Georges Bonnet, *Quai d'Orsay*, Isle of Man, Times Press and Anthony Gibbs and Phillips, 1965, p. 265.

34. Jean-Louis Crémieux-Brilhac, *Les Français de l'an 40*, 2 vols, Paris, Gallimard, 1990, Vol. 1, *La Guerre Oui ou Non*, p. 240.

systems which constitute the principal barrier to the communist revolution and perhaps the bolshevisation of Europe'.[35]

Such organisations preached defeat and collaboration under the name of 'realism'. Through the popular press, their spokesmen claimed that defeat was inevitable, since the country was ruined by successive left-wing governments. Better to get out of a war 'desired by the English and International Jewry', and let 'Hitler rid Europe of Communism'. Millions of readers came across these thoughts continuously.[36] For some reason, these sentiments did not attract the wrath of the authorities. But the traditional pacifists were more roughly treated. A number of dissident deputies, trades unionists and intellectuals produced a manifesto in the second week of the war, arguing that 'the price of peace will never be as ruinous as the price of war' and calling for 'peace now'. Several of the signatories were immediately arrested.[37]

The most confused of all these actors were the PCF. In the first few days after the signing of the Molotov-Ribbentrop Pact of 23 August, the party gave it a cautious welcome, whilst continuing to support the government. In spite of the closure of the party's newspapers, it voted unanimously for war credits on 2 September.[38] When instructions arrived from Moscow to denounce the war as an 'imperialist' one, the (increasingly clandestine) party split: many deputies and party officials left in disgust. The remainder tried, with more or less success, to believe that the French nation had 'been assigned the mission of executing the orders of the bankers of London'.[39] Although they were informed that they were involved in a capitalist civil war, fighting not for their country but for the 'two hundred families' who controlled it,[40] they were at the same time urged not to go so far as practising 'revolutionary defeatism'. No wonder they seemed confused.

Fourth, many on all parts of the political spectrum wondered if the sclerotic Third Republic was, in any case, worth defending. Extremists wanted it swept away and replaced by something, perhaps along the Italian model. The more moderate would have

35. Rossi-Landi, *Drôle de Guerre*, p. 115.

36. Crémieux-Brilhac, *L'an 40*, p. 125.

37. Rossi-Landi, *Drôle de Guerre*, pp. 116–8.

38. Ibid., pp. 136–7.

39. Cited by Jean-Pierre Azéma, *From Munich to the Liberation, 1938–1944*, Cambridge, Cambridge University Press, 1984, p. 26.

40. Originally, a reference to the two hundred private shareholders of the Bank of France. It later became a term used by all on the Left to refer to the alleged real owners of the country.

preferred a radical overhaul, or at least a modernisation of the institutions. Even among those who were, in principle, republicans, it was difficult to work up the kind of enthusiasm which would lead you to die for it.[41]

Fifth, there was much confusion about the war aims of the nation, reflected in the fact that the official propaganda declined to publish any.[42] Ministers limited themselves to banalities about peace and security, which no one could object to. But the absence of any detailed war aims meant that it was quite impossible, for example, to know whether there were any circumstances under which France might consider a compromise peace.

Finally, and whatever the war aims might eventually prove to be, there was only limited confidence in a military victory to achieve them. Both the wars of 1870 and 1914 had begun in a holiday mood, in the certainty, however misplaced, of rapid victory. This time it was different. In the popular press, in private journals, in the ranks of the military itself, there was a kind of glum pessimism everywhere to be seen.[43] It infected the highest levels of government: Léger, the secretary-general of the Quai, for example, told Bullitt that he doubted the British and French could win.[44]

In the circumstances, a vigorous and well-directed propaganda campaign would have been needed to unite the people, explain what was going on, and convince them of ultimate victory. Instead, the nation got playwright, diplomat and intellectual Jean Giradoux, 'whose willingness was matched only by his unsuitability',[45] and whose best-known work was the (very unbellicose) play, *The Trojan War Will Not Take Place*. Results were mixed.

Although it is difficult to be sure, there was perhaps a certain underlying logic to all of these fears. Those French people conscious of their history (very nearly all of them) would have been aware of a paradigm that had been in existence for hundreds of years, and that I described in Chapter 1. When the French are united they win, when they are disunited they lose. By this logic, all the conditions were in place for a defeat, and the government and other institutions, as if subconsciously aware of this, seemed

41. Crémieux-Brilhac, *L'an 40*, pp. 110–3.

42. Rossi-Landi, *Drôle de Guerre*, pp. 186–7.

43. Crémieux-Brilhac, *L'an 40*, pp. 114–6.

44. Anthony Adamthwaite, *France and the Coming of the Second World War, 1936–1939*, London, Frank Cass, 1977, p. 339.

45. Jean-Baptiste Duroselle, *Politique Etrangère de la France: L'Abîme, 1939–1944*, Paris, Imprimerie Nationale, 1979, p. 85.

in practice to go out of their way to promote further division and disunity, like a prospective suicide who murders his family first.

For example, one of the most important objectives of the *drôle de guerre* was to maintain and increase the tempo of war production, and this obviously required a well-motivated workforce. The gains of the Popular Front were by this stage a memory: industrial workers were often working much more than the 'forty hours' for no extra pay, although there were no controls on prices and profits rose substantially. Yet when the CGT trade union suggested discussions about ways of increasing productivity – as was happening in Britain – the response of the *patronat* was swift and brutal: management was the responsibility of managers, workers simply obeyed. All that was needed was greater discipline.[46]

Daladier and Reynaud were sympathetic, but frightened to support ideas that might lead, as they saw it, to involvement of the workforce in decision-making, and thus to subversion. Ironically, it was Dautry, the only industrialist in the cabinet, who saw what needed to be done. In one of those flourishes where the Third Republic appeared to look forward, briefly, to the post-war reconstruction, he wrote to all directors of defence establishments, instructing them to regain the confidence of the workers through a programme of better facilities and improved personal contact and consultation.[47] But this was too late and too limited to convince many of the workforce that they and the *patronat* were fighting the same war.

Amongst all these confusions, and in spite of the strange mixture of facile optimism and closet despair that the government presented, the mood of the ordinary people and the morale of the troops were, at the beginning at least, rather better than feared. It has often been remarked that there was none of the rejoicing and none of the facile optimism of 1914, either in the reaction to the declaration of war, or in the traditional departure of hundreds of thousands of young men, who left from the same platforms in the Gare de l'Est on the same route that their fathers had travelled in 1914, and their grandfathers in 1870. There was a grim determination to get on with the job: *d'en finir* – to get it over with – was the watchword of 1939.[48]

One group of government employees were not at all idle during the *drôle de guerre*: the officials of the Ministry of the Interior,

46. Crémieux-Brilhac, *L'an 40*, Vol. 2, *Ouvriers et Soldats*, pp. 256–8.
47. Ibid., p. 259.
48. Duroselle, *L'Abîme*, p. 17.

who listened in to telephone calls, opened letters and wrote reports describing the public mood as they saw it. Now and again,
anti-war remarks were noticed, and the offenders usually imprisoned; but the majority of the population seemed to be in at least
reasonable heart. As a result, the mobilisation went with great
smoothness; almost too much so, indeed, since so many industrial
workers were called up that war production almost came to a halt.
Morale in the army was also quite good. Journalists visiting the
front were surprised to find the troops in good spirits, and an official survey of October 1939, based on a survey of soldiers' letters,
concluded that morale was 'magnificent', and that there was 'an
almost unanimous confidence in the leaders, in the Maginot line,
in our equipment, faith in ultimate victory and a determination to
see it through to the end...'.[49]

This confidence was partly based, curiously enough, on the
results of the Polish campaign. The Poles, it was said, had been
incompetent and their leaders inexperienced. They had deployed
their army badly and had elected to defend on their very long
borders, which they could not cover properly. Even then, it was
noted that the German PzI and PzII tanks had been very vulnerable to anti-tank fire.[50] All this was largely true; and it is also true
that much greater attempts were made to study and drive home
the lessons of the Polish campaign than was once believed. The
problem lay in trying to explain not a new weapon or new tactics,
but a whole new operational philosophy, to which there was, at
that time, no counter. The same optimistic conclusions were
reached by the Senate's Army Commission, presumably on the
basis of military briefings.[51] For its part, the popular press eagerly
reported (and frequently invented) all signs of disaffection and
defeatism from Germany, and published encouraging analyses by
retired generals of the Allies' prospects.[52] Such sentiments naturally made the eventual defeat more bitter and the hunt for scape-
goats more assiduous.

The *drôle de guerre* was not, on the French side, an accident.
There was relief, of course, that the Germans had not attacked
straight away, and that Paris had not been devastated by gas
bombs. But there had never been any intention of launching a
quick strike against Germany, even if the capability had been

49. Crémieux-Brilhac, *L'an 40*, Vol. 2, p. 425.
50. Alexander, *Republic in Danger*, pp. 346–7.
51. Crémieux-Brilhac, *L'an 40*, Vol. 1, p. 210.
52. Ibid., pp. 340–3.

there. Rather, and with recollections of 1914–18 still fresh, it had been agreed that the French and British should hope and plan for a long war in which their greater collective economic muscle would eventually wear Germany down.[53] This was the meaning of the infamous poster found everywhere in France in the winter of 1939, depicting a map of the world with the empires of Britain and France highlighted and the caption 'We Will Win Because We Are the Strongest'. It had been hoped originally that Poland would hold out for some months, but, even then, the Allies did not expect to bring much practical help, particularly as the strength of the Siegfried line had been wildly over-rated. Poland in 1940 was seen much as Belgium in 1914; unfortunately mislaid temporarily, but to be restored at the end of the war. In the end, this vision of a long war won by industrial potential proved to be correct, but not until after rather more had been mislaid than was anticipated.

In the interim, however, it was important not to do anything silly. The British and French leaderships agreed to eschew 'any vainglorious gestures in September 1939 which might erode the capacity of their forces to stay the course and reap eventual triumph'. And even if the will had been there, the means were not. It took several weeks to bring the twenty peacetime divisions up to wartime strength, and they could not undertake much activity, even then, until stocks of ammunition had been built up.[54] The effects of this passivity were not good. There are ways of keeping up the interest and motivation of front-line troops waiting for action, although the French were not very good at doing this. Yet these effects can be exaggerated. Alistair Horne reports a British war correspondent 'infuriated' by the response of a French soldier, asked why he was not shooting at a German soldier bathing. 'They're not bad chaps', he said, 'and if we fire, they will fire back.'[55] It is doubtful whether this exchange has much significance. On the whole, human beings do not commit violence randomly, even in war, and this kind of behaviour was common on every front in the Second World War, even in Russia, when operations were not actually in progress.

There was a tendency also for the unhurried pace of peacetime to continue in the *drôle de guerre*. Staff work continued as before, with attention to detail and presentation. Marc Bloch recalled that,

53. Duroselle, *La Décadence*, p. 464.

54. Alexander, *Republic in Danger*, p. 320.

55. Alistair Horne, *To Lose a Battle: France 1940*, Penguin edn, London, 1979, p. 134.

in all the headquarters of which he had been part, 'Stylistic for-
mulae obeyed the rules of a rigorous tradition. In tables, the figures were aligned in columns, as on a parade. Files were carefully
ordered; correspondence duly booked in and booked out.'[56] But
this kind of attention to detail is common in all armies, and,
indeed, in most organisations. Had the French not lost so abruptly
in 1940, it is doubtful whether examples of this sort would have
been brought forward as exhibits. In any case, only the perverse
would argue that France in 1940 would have been saved by
sloppy staff work.

Enforced inactivity and the strain of waiting for the eventual
attack produced the usual crop of rumours and conspiracy theories. Much of the Right was far more concerned about the internal
menace from Commune and revolution than it was about a German invasion, except insofar as they were seen to be connected.
The PCF, by then outlawed, was naturally the principal target. The
Communists, argued one periodical in January 1940, were not
Frenchmen, but 'soldiers of an Army whose headquarters is in
Moscow … They are simply agents of the enemy, and, as a consequence, our enemies'.[57] A more elaborate version of this charge
was that the Communists were 'a foreign army encamped on
French soil', whose peacetime leaders 'had taken refuge in Germany', and whose leaders now were paid 'half from the propaganda funds of Dr Goebbels and half from the budget of the
Comintern'.[58] This deliberate conflation of Germany and the Soviet
Union was not, of course, new: it goes back to the nightmares of
the earliest days of the Russian Revolution. But, in the context of
the *drôle de guerre* and the Molotov-Ribbentrop pact, the literal
identification of the PCF with the German enemy gave public
opinion an internal enemy to focus on.

The inevitable result was another outing for the conspiracy theories last seen in 1936. The chief of the intelligence section of the
Paris military region HQ claimed to have documentary proof of
plans for a *putsch*, complete 'with assembly areas and lines of
march', making use of arms dumps established in the 1930s. The
PCF had available, it was alleged, more than 100,000 men for these
purposes. The military governor of Paris wrote to Daladier that
Communism was 'the number one enemy', and that 'Hitler is

56. Marc Bloch, *L'Etrange Défaite: Témoinage écrit en 1940*, new edn, Paris, Gallimard, 1990, p. 88.
57. Cited by Rossi-Landi, *Drôle de Guerre*, p. 155.
58. Crémieux-Brilhac, *L'an 40*, Vol. 1, p. 185.

waiting for the communist insurrection before he attacks'. There was probably little actual invention in these assertions; rather, a naïve belief in the integrity of paid informants. This conflation of the two threats gave birth to a whole new vocabulary of 'Hitlero-Communism' and a 'German-Soviet threat'. To be, or to have been, a member of the PCF was automatically, therefore, to be a German agent, for which the penalty had to be death. And these charges were not limited to the Right: various SFIO deputies made similar noises.[59]

As a consequence of this view, it was assumed that Communists, whether acknowledged or not, were actively conspiring against the war effort. Hard evidence for this was lacking, but invention supplied what investigation failed to turn up. *Gringoire* set out for its readers the whole dastardly plot. The 'internal offensive' would be combined with the German attack. According to the theories of Lenin, this would be aimed at fraternisation in the trenches. In parallel, the 'Hitlero-Stalinists' would provoke industrial unrest in factories and on the railways. Meanwhile, Thorez, the leader of the PCF and 'an agent of the German General Staff', would return from Germany at the head of a puppet government, which would sign a peace treaty.[60] At least some of these fantasies were taken seriously by the government. Flandin, one of Daladier's ministers, told the British ambassador in the last days of peace that he knew that 'Communist leaders who are the most active in egging on war are already telling their men that if there were ... heavy air bombardment they would rise up, and declare that France had been betrayed by her Government and set up a Communist régime.'[61]

Much (nugatory) effort was devoted to following up such rumours, and also, for example, to the prevention of industrial sabotage. They also found their way into diplomatic reporting. Bullitt, for example, thought that a German attack against France would not be successful, and that Germany would 'go Bolshevik' (by what mechanism is unclear) 'and summon the Soviet armies'.[62] But they did not affect the mass of the population, or the soldiers at the front. As in all wars, however, they had their own myths of

59. Ibid., pp. 181–5.
60. Ibid., p. 351.
61. Adamthwaite, *Coming of the Second World War*, p. 220.
62. Orville H. Bullitt, ed., *For the President, Personal and Secret: Correspondence Between Franklin D. Roosevelt and William C. Bullitt*, London, André Deutsch, 1973, p. 378.

betrayal and subversion in the rear and by their superior officers. The idea that some French officers knew about, and even welcomed, the German invasion was widespread at the time and formed part of the accusation against Pétain at his trial in 1945. To add to the mystery, Pétain (then ambassador in Madrid) was alleged to have said, on 30 March, 'they will need me in the second half of May'.[63] Certainly, there were persistent rumours of a coup or the voluntary surrender of the government to a strongman, dating back at least as far as Munich. And many deduced, from the ease with which the Republic was jettisoned in July 1940, that the process must have been planned in advance. There were many strange events at the front line that seemed to confirm these fears. Generals (real or false) would appear during the fighting and urge surrender, since the troops would soon be back home.[64] Who were they, and what planning had gone into their mysterious appearances?

Sometimes, there appeared to be more substance to these allegations. It does seem to be the case that Huntziger, commanding the Second army at Sedan, ordered the immediate destruction of all concrete blockhouses blocking an advance to Sedan just a week before the assault. When that assault came, it was recalled that he had apparently been rather dilatory in response to orders to construct fortified frontier posts. Huntziger was killed in an aeroplane crash in 1940 and was thus never taxed with these alleged errors; but the fact that he became a luminary of Vichy encouraged belief that he had been secretly in league with the Germans. In a rather different area, there were persistent rumours that trains on the right bank of the Rhine, coming from Switzerland, were actually carrying cargoes of French bauxite, via Switzerland, for the German aluminium industry. If this was not so, then why were French soldiers forbidden to fire on the trains?[65]

The truth of these assertions will never be known, but the truth is not really important. They are an index of the febrile atmosphere of the time, when different social and political groups were ready to consider each other in league with the enemy. This combination of inactivity, fear and boredom, the willingness to strike but the fear of being wounded, and the eagerness to identify an internal enemy came together in the two most bizarre events of the *drôle de guerre*. Before the war formally started, the newspapers

63. Rossi-Landi, *Drôle de Guerre*, p. 110.
64. Fonvielle-Alquier, *Phoney War*, p. 190.
65. Ibid., pp. 194–5.

of the PCF were banned, and, on 26 September, the party itself was dissolved. Arrests, trials and general persecution followed. Meanwhile, and undiscouraged by the indifferent results previously obtained by Napoleon, the French began seriously to contemplate another invasion of Russia.

Daladier signed the decree dissolving the PCF and its associated bodies, which came into force the next day. At this stage, all that they were accused of was not repudiating Soviet policy towards the war, and being, in effect, pacifists. Fifty-one of the 72 PCF deputies decided to constitute a new party, the French Workers and Peasants Group (GPOF). Most of the remainder were in the front line, and thus relatively safe. A few were arrested, several fled. The GPOF despatched a letter to Daladier, calling for peace, Soviet mediation and the consideration of Hitler's compromise proposals.[66] The effect of the letter was unfortunate. Even Blum – who had opposed the decision to ban the PCF – was outraged. The government closed the session of parliament, thus removing parliamentary immunity, and set about hunting down and arresting the deputies. Thorez deserted, and turned up, not in Berlin, but in Moscow. The party went underground, continuing its clandestine struggle against the 'capitalist war', but much enfeebled by arrests and by mass resignations.

The purge was carried down to local government, where local councils controlled by the PCF were suspended, to the armaments factories, and to the local adminstration, where the prefects[67] were ordered to report on the political attitudes of all of their staff. Although the government decided against mass internment of dissidents under military auspices, it did provide for internment, or exile to another area, of anyone 'reputed a danger to national defence', but against whom there was no actual evidence.[68] As well as purging local councillors, the public service, trades unions and industry, action was also taken against individuals, often on the basis of anonymous denunciations, or for having copies of pacifist authors (like Barbusse) in the house.[69] The purges were successively strengthened by outrage first against the Soviet-German partition of Poland (28 September), and then by the subsequent Soviet invasion of Finland. There was an extended episode

66. Rossi-Landi, *Drôle de Guerre*, pp. 142–3.
67. Local representatives of the government, in charge of all state services in a department, except for the military.
68. Crémieux-Brilhac, *L'an 40*, Vol. 1, pp. 189–91.
69. Ibid., pp. 193–5.

of black comedy when suspect workers were sent from front to factory and back, as the government tried to decide where they would be least dangerous.

Meanwhile, the measures taken against the ex-PCF deputies unrolled at a stately pace. The Chamber met on 9 January 1940 to pass a law formalising their eviction from the body politic unless they renounced and denounced the party's principles. It was attended by the few PCF deputies not in prison or in hiding, but their protestations of patriotism were not taken seriously. Chautemps spoke for the government, and, in an interestingly Rousseauesque formulation, argued that 'These deputies no longer represent their electors, or, if these electors have really remained favourable to these monstrous ideas, they must be opposing the national will.'[70] Amid cries of 'treason' and appeals for the death penalty without the tedium of a trial, the Chamber passed the law by a large majority. The secret trial of the deputies took place from 20 March to 3 April 1940, under a military judge. They were found guilty mainly of reconstituting the PCF under another name, although the government had agreed to this move at the time, and the *Journal Officiel* had publicised it.[71]

It is clear, in retrospect, that the whole episode was a grave political error. Blum, for example, believed the campaign against the party was 'a mistake', adding that it would have been far better to allow it to be condemned by public opinion.[72] What was clear was that the government had knowingly alienated the 15 per cent of the population who had voted for the PCF in 1936, as well as an uncertain number of sympathisers. They had destroyed any chance of a repeat of the *Union Sacrée* of 1914 and had permanently disillusioned a group of individuals, mostly industrial workers and front-line soldiers, who were, in principle, better educated and better motivated than average. Moreover, whilst it would have been relatively easy to present the purge as part of a general crackdown on defeatists in general, the repression was, in practice, only directed against one political party and their supposed sympathisers. No action of any importance was taken against even the most flagrant defeatists of the Right, a fact that destroyed

70. Rossi-Landi, *Drôle de Guerre*, p. 147.

71. The day before the trial, in answer to a senator's question about "Hitlero-Communist plots", the minister of the interior gave a list of thousands of arrests, internments and other sanctions, together with newspapers and magazines closed down: Rossi-Landi, *Drôle de Guerre*, p. 156

72. Jean Lacouture, *Léon Blum*, Paris, Seuil, new edn, 1979, p. 436.

any hope of the purge's being accepted by all as being in the national interest.

Daladier's reasons for the purge were varied. Part of it, certainly, was fear about the effects of pacifist propaganda on a fearful and divided nation, which was at best glumly resigned to the war. But that does not explain the virulence of the campaign, nor its length and thoroughness. The purge also served, however, to provide a focus for many of the fears listed above. It provided a home for unfocused concerns about treason and betrayal, it gave the illusion of activity and decisiveness on the part of the government, it provided a vicarious sense of struggle against the (German) enemy, it could be presented as an act in defence of the country and against an enemy who could not retaliate, at that. In a sense, it also united most of the country, albeit against an enemy rather than for something definite. The PCF was a suitable scapegoat, because, although relatively large, it was without allies, and detested by all the other parties. And, although the end product of the affair was division, the degree of unity displayed against the PCF was very unusual in such a divided polity as the Third Republic.

The bizarre story of plans to invade the Soviet Union overlaps with the purge of the PCF and was part of the same set of reactions and expectations. Daladier was a very strong supporter of both. The plans were never put into action, and never, indeed, given a definitive expression; but, in their most extreme form, they featured a gigantic pincer movement. Several divisions were to land in Finland and march south, linking up with a similarly sized force under Weygand, marching up from Syria. The two would join hands at Moscow, effectively destroying the Soviet Union as an entity, as well as putting it out of the war.[73] Another element of the plan was recounted by Léger to Bullitt. The former complained that the British were 'totally idiotic' if they believed that they could ever obtain Soviet support against the Germans, and the French government had thus suggested 'that the British and the French fleets both should enter the Black Sea and bombard Batum and send airplanes to bomb Baku and thus cut off both Germany and the Soviet Union from supplies of oil'. The British, however, had not been enthusiastic.[74]

Many subsequent commentators have wondered at the collective madness that appeared to have overtaken French military and political figures: 'At a moment when it was very much a

73. Duroselle, *L'Abîme*, pp. 113–4.
74. Bullitt, *For the President*, p. 401.

question of whether it would be possible to hang on against Germany until 1941, to have the time to re-arm, people gladly contemplated gratuitously making a new enemy with 190 million inhabitants, having an army then thought to be of about 200 divisions.'[75] There are explanations for this attitude: they have largely to do with domestic politics.

First of all, support for the Finns was virtually universal: even the fragmented PCF found Soviet conduct hard to justify. The Right looked on it as a chance to complete the work abandoned in 1920, the Left as an opportunity to defend the rights of small nations and to uphold international law. The idea was particularly favoured in parliament, and Daladier, like all prime ministers of the Third Republic, had to pay a great deal of attention to its views. Paradoxically, action directed against the Soviet Union was probably more widely acceptable than action against Germany. Many would have agreed with a contemporary commentator that Finland, 'which many have only just found for the first time on the map, has become, as was Belgium in 1914, as once were Greece and Italy, the symbolic land of liberty'.[76] In any event, as has been seen already, the Soviet Union and Germany were effectively seen as the same entity anyway. Although they had only concluded a non-aggression pact, a relatively lowly form of diplomatic life, this was taken by large parts of public opinion as tantamount to the formation of an aggressive military alliance. An intelligence report of January 1940 reports ('from a good source but with reservations') that, in the next attack on Finland, Soviet troops will be fighting under German officers.[77] To attack the Soviet Union, therefore, was to attack Germany, and to defeat the former would greatly handicap the latter. Moreover, the Soviet Union was seen as the weaker partner of the two: the 'soft underbelly' of the German-Soviet coalition. The Quai believed that, with the German-Soviet economic agreement of February 1940, 'the leadership of the German-Russian association [is] passing from the hands of Stalin to those of Hitler'.[78] Thus, as one air force general put it at the time, by 'striking at the Soviet Union, we deprive Hitlerite Germany of the resources she needs, and at the same time we remove the war farther from our frontiers'.[79]

75. Duroselle, *L'Abîme*, pp. 111–2.
76. Cited by Crémieux-Brilhac, *L'an 40*, Vol. 1, p. 222.
77. Ibid., p. 186.
78. Cited ibid., p. 221.
79. Cited ibid., p. 222.

The last element of this statement is another powerful reason why it was easier to contemplate attacking the Soviet Union than Germany. The former was a very long way away, and the two hundred divisions were only a theoretical threat. Not even the most rabid proponent of aerial bombing really believed that *Soviet* planes had the capability of bombing Paris. Operations against the Soviet Union would require only a handful of divisions, and few if any troops from among those recently mobilised. The performance of the Red army against the Finns had been so lamentable that only a few divisions would be needed to defeat 'a colossus with feet of clay'. This was, as Beaufre says, with some understatement, thinking that 'lacked realism',[80] but it was very widely shared. Daladier himself maintained, publicly, that Soviet society and the Red army were both in a precarious state.[81] Above all this was the need, common to governments in times of stress, to *do something*, even if that something was misguided or silly. Unanimity on anything was so unusual for the Third Republic that any government would have been sorely tempted to do what Daladier's did: ironically, the Finnish episode was his downfall. After the Finns surrendered on 12 March, he had to take the blame. As John Lukacs puts it, he 'had been too slow in committing France to the fatal folly of getting into war with the Russian empire somewhere in Finland'.[82] This was not quite all there was to it, of course: the knives had been out for Daladier for some time, as they were for any long-serving prime minister in the 1930s, and this was a good opportunity. Daladier was replaced by Reynaud as prime minister, although (for complicated reasons of domestic politics) he was able to keep his job as minister of defence.

Reynaud's cabinet was not very different. He made an attempt at a more broadly based government, and six SFIO ministers (but not Blum) were appointed, as were five from the Right. At this stage, Reynaud wished to appoint his old protégé de Gaulle as deputy minister of war.[83] The reasons why this did not happen are not quite clear, but have something to do with the bad relations between de Gaulle and Daladier, dating from the controversy

80. Beaufre, *1940*, p. 168.

81. Crémieux-Brilhac, *L'an 40*, Vol. 1, p. 229.

82. John Lukacs, *The Last European War: September 1939 –December 1941*, London, Routledge and Kegan Paul, 1976, p. 70.

83. French and British ministerial nomenclature are quite different, to the frustration of bureaucrats in both nations. Roughly speaking, the British 'secretary of state' (i.e. head of a department), is in France a *Ministre d'Etat*. Conversely, a British minister of state (number two in the hierarchy) is a *Secrétaire d'État*. There is also

about a professional army. The last cabinet of the Third Republic received an extremely lukewarm vote of confidence on 22 March. The broader base of the cabinet in fact proved to be a weakness rather than a strength, since it was unprecedentedly large (35 ministers), and because the extremes tended to paralyse the business of the cabinet. Fantasies of intervention in the Caucasus still occasionally surfaced, as the cabinet, like the rest of the French people, continued to hope that something would happen that would obviate the need for fighting, so that the war of France need not take place after all.

---

the *Sous-secrétaire d'État*, roughly equating to under-secretary of state in Britain. Other ministerial ranks and statuses also exist. To avoid confusion, I will use the term 'minister' for the *Ministre* and 'deputy minister' for the others.

PART II

HOW

5

DEATH IN THE SOUL

You mustn't fight, the war's over.

Anonymous young woman in Sartre's *Death in the Soul* (1949)

*France will find a place in the new Europe worthy of
her past.*

Laval, 1942

By its struggle against terrorism and communism, [France] contributes to the defence of western civilisation.

Pétain to Hitler, 1943

On 10 May 1940, German troops crossed the borders of Belgium and Holland, beginning their offensive in the West. As anticipated, British and French troops moved into Belgium, and took up positions on their intended line of defence. By 13 May, the Germans (or at least some of their Panzer troops) were through the Ardennes and across the Meuse at Sedan to the south, sweeping up to the Channel coast. On 18 May, Reynaud reshuffled his cabinet, to form the last-ever genuine government of the Third Republic. Pétain was brought back from the ambassadorship in Madrid to be deputy prime minister. Gamelin, whom Reynaud had been trying to get rid of for some time, was replaced by the 73-year-old Weygand, recalled from the Middle East, and now not to invade Russia after all. By 28 May, the Dunkirk operation was under way, and by 14 June, the first German troops had entered an undefended Paris. Reynaud resigned on 16 June from the (then-itinerant) government. Pétain took over, and began to seek an armistice. The French signed an armistice agreement on 22 June; by 10 July, the Third Republic had faded away, and Pétain was in sole charge. 'In the history of warfare few campaigns between great and approximately equal powers have been decided so swiftly and conclusively as the German conquest of Western Europe in May and June 1940.'[1]

It is hardly surprising that few in France, at any level, could understand what had taken place, or that sinister and self-serving explanations were offered immediately. I shall go through the responses of the various factions later; but first, I want to focus on several of the events in May and June 1940 in a little more detail, beginning with Dunkirk.

The British tend to celebrate Dunkirk with a fervour that other nations reserve for victories, but it amounted, of course, not only to a British defeat, but to an abandonment of the French, and the reaction among many politicians and military leaders was one of fury. Not everyone would have gone so far as Georges Bonnet, in describing this period: 'Lord Gort withdrew his divisions from Northern France, thus preventing our counter-offensive. Next, at Dunkirk, the British Admiralty evacuated its own troops in such a way that many of our own troops were made prisoner. Those that did escape and were taken to England have complained that they were very badly treated.'[2] But for the French there were uneasy memories of the British panicking in 1918, and wondering about a move to the coast. The incident appeared to confirm the suspicions that Pétain had entertained about the British ever since.[3] Likewise, few of the main actors were ever to believe that the British had tried as hard as they might to defend France: the troops evacuated from Dunkirk should have been reinserted later, more aircraft could and should have been sent, and so forth.

Even Reynaud, who relates this episode with circumspection in his own autobiography, was apparently very unhappy at the time. He approached Bullitt to see whether Washington could put pressure on the British to do more. Could Roosevelt, Reynaud asked, not press London 'to put into the battle more than one fourth of the British [fighter] planes at a time when the French soldier was bearing the entire brunt of the attack without British assistance

1. Brian Bond, *Britain, France and Belgium, 1939–1940*, 2nd edn, London, Brassey's, 1990.

2. Georges Bonnet, *Quai d'Orsay*, Isle of Man, Times Press and Anthony Gibbs and Phillips, 1965, pp. 293–4.

3. For the awkward relations between Pétain and Haig in 1918, see Richard Griffiths, *Marshal Pétain*, London, Constable, 1970, p. 59.

and when all the blood that was flowing to protect the civilised sections of the earth was French blood'.[4]

These incidents had a considerable influence on the subsequent French decision to seek a separate armistice, in spite of the promise of the two nations, made on 28 March, not to do so. The mood was of rancour that Britain had 'sent us only ten or so divisions. She refused to base most of her squadrons in France. She re-embarked the British before the French at Dunkirk, not forgetting the inter-war years, Waterloo, Canada, India and Joan of Arc'. In such a situation, a separate peace and an abrogation of the earlier promise could seem like 'just reprisals'.[5] The decision to seek the armistice, on 16 June, led to the replacement of Reynaud by Pétain, who made, the next day, the first of his many radio broadcasts to the French. Already, the beginning of one interpretation of the defeat is visible. The army, Pétain insisted, had done its best, against 'an enemy superior in numbers and weapons'.[6]

There were other possible options. It would have been possible to withdraw to Brittany, or to Algeria (legally, part of France), and to continue the fight from there. Either would have been a political gesture, rather than a means of seriously continuing the fight; but it seems that some type of initiative would have been possible, had the will existed.

There were several reasons why this did not happen. One important one was the inability of the structures of the Third Republic to cope with such a violent transformation. The whole political ethos of the time was based on the diffusion of power and the avoidance of responsibility for critical decisions. Those brought up in these traditions were scarcely ready to take the kind of bold and far-reaching decisions required to continue the war. Another lies in the pervasive fear that a continuation of the fighting would mean social revolution and civil war, especially after the government had begun the traditional scuttle to Bordeaux.[7] It was recalled that, in 1870, the war had been continued after the professionals had advised against it, and the eventual result had been large-scale

4. Orville H. Bullitt, ed., *For the President, Personal and Secret: Correspondence Between Franklin D. Roosevelt and William C. Bullitt*, London, André Deutsch, 1972, p. 45.

5. Jean-Baptiste Duroselle, *Politique Etrangère de la France: L'Abîme, 1939–1944*, 2nd edn, Paris, Imprimerie Nationale, 1986, p. 205.

6. *Pétain, Discours aux Français: 17 Juin 1940–20 Aout 1944*, ed. Jean-Claude Barbas, Paris, Albin Michel, 1989, p. 57. Hereafter *Discours*.

7. See, for example, Robert O. Paxton, *Vichy France: Old Guard and New Order, 1940–1944*, London, Barrie and Jenkins, 1972, pp. 13–14.

civil unrest and the Commune. The fear of a repetition had haunted the minds of the military and political classes ever since, and, as we have seen, the official mind had thought on many occasions that the revolution was in fact imminent. Consistent falsification of this fear did not make it go away, because it was not based on logic and evidence, but on very deep feelings of guilt and dread that the descendants of the dead of the Commune would come to take their revenge at last.

Although proof was not strictly required, therefore, a certain amount of 'evidence' for a Communist uprising was available. Much of it was gossip, and Bullitt, usually a good reporter of gossip, was sufficiently influenced by it to ask Roosevelt, on 8 June, to send him 'twelve Thompson submachine guns with ammunition', because 'there is every reason to expect that if the French government should be forced to leave Paris, its place would be taken by a communist mob'.[8] Such fears were a factor in the debate that preceded the decision to ask for an armistice. Weygand claimed to be particularly influenced by these fears, and his own *Exposé succinct*, written on 26 August 1940, records that, as early as 12 June, he had warned the ministers that 'only an end to hostilities can allow a little order and cohesion to be maintained'. Otherwise 'the troops will be cut to pieces, scattered and disordered. And there will be general, as well as military disorder'. He concluded that only an armistice could save the situation.[9] Reynaud gives a vivid account of what happened at the meeting the next day: 'Continually obsessed by the idea of the coming revolution, [Weygand] announced, in a dramatic voice, that Maurice Thorez was installed in the Elysée, and that telephone communications with Paris had been cut. Mandel's entire response was to get up, go into the next room, and return, saying to the President "The Prefect of Police is on the line …".'[10]

After the war, Weygand was to deny that he had tried to mislead ministers in this way. But the fears of the past decades had prepared the ground so thoroughly for nightmares of this type that whether they were ever *expressed* in this form is less important

8. Bullitt, *For the President*, p. 455.

9. *Exposé succinct des faits, depuis l'arrivé du Général W....*, 20 August 1940, printed in Assemblée Nationale, Document No. 2344 (1947), *Rapport ... sur les événements survenus en France de 1933 à 1945*, Paris, Imprimerie de l'Assemblée Nationale, Vol. 3, p. 410.

10. Paul Reynaud, *La France a Sauvé l'Europe*, 2 vols, Paris, Flammarion, 1947, Vol. 2, p. 323.

than that the habit of fear meant that they were in everyone's mind.[11] Weygand's image of the leader of the PCF installed in Paris by the Germans and busy Bolshevising France was the logical product of fears of this sort expressed widely for two decades or more. Equally, part of Pétain's popularity came because he was thought to have saved France from 'the abyss' of revolution.[12]

More important for the decision to seek an armistice, however, was Weygand's refusal to let the army fight on. Partly, he, like others, was concerned that there should be enough troops left to 'keep order'. But, more importantly, Weygand claimed that further resistance was pointless, that neither the Breton nor the North African options were workable, and that resistance should therefore cease. However, his 'honour' would not let him surrender either. Weygand claimed in his memoirs that 'I did not claim the right to impose my will on the Government of the Republic.' However: 'I exercised the right which cannot be refused to a man, still less a commander, to act in accordance with what his feeling of honour and his conscience command. If I was wrong, the Government should have dealt with me accordingly: my will gained the day only through the Government's resignation.'[13] In practice, as Weygand well knew, this amounted to an ultimatum. The government could not afford to lose him, and his refusal either to fight on or to capitulate effectively required an armistice: there were no other options. This was, perhaps, the lowest point in the history of army-state relations in the Third Republic. These had been based on the avoidance of conflict by giving the *chefs* unparalleled status and freedom of action, in return for which they stayed out of politics directly. At the most critical hour of the Republic, however, Weygand broke with these traditions.

He did so, in all probability, for two reasons. First, because like Pétain and others, he believed, in a rather confused fashion, that the civilian politicians were responsible both for launching a misguided war, and, by weakening the moral fibre of the nation, for its subsequent loss. A note Weygand produced after the armistice, and

11. A fear shared, apparently, even by Reynaud and Mandel. The latter urged Bullitt, to obtain from the US 10,000 submachine guns and ammunition for the Paris police, since they now expected 'a Communist uprising and butcheries in the city of Paris and other industrial centres as the German Army draws near'. See Bullitt, *For the President*, p. 434.

12. Paxton, *Vichy France*, p. 14.

13. General Maxime Weygand, *Recalled to Service: The Memoirs of General Maxime Weygand of the Académie Francaise,* trans. E. W. Dickes, London, Heinemann, 1948, p. 213.

which he sent to Pétain, blamed the defeat on everything from 'the class war' which had 'divided the country', to the fall in the birthrate, to declining respect for the family, to flaws in the education system, to the 'wave of materialism which has submerged France': to everything, in effect, except his own failures and those of his colleagues.[14] This led, in turn, to a kind of sour, destructive defeatism. It was characterised by Chautemps, one of Reynaud's ministers, in conversation with the British ambassador as a 'mystical, disinterested mood which leads him to hold that France, having made mistakes, deserves to suffer'.[15] Secondly, and again with many others, he had only contempt for the 'Judaeo-Masonic' Third Republic, and the political class that manned it: he had contributed, after all, to the fund for Colonel Henry. I suggested, in Chapter 1, a division between 'mystical' and 'statistical' views of the national will, and argued that, because French thinking had generally supported the former concept, it was always open to an individual to claim to embody the national will at a time of crisis. This was especially easy for the military, who could claim to be above the sordid world of politics. Weygand's motivation has been described as

> the idea of mystical identification between Army and nation, with the former acting against the régime if necessary to protect the latter.... Weygand became the guardian of the military institution and hence of the French people ... he contemptuously dismissed the régime as the real representative of the country ... he maintained that the 'army was nothing less ... than the Nation', as he wrote at the time in a remarkable passage which in effect declares that the civilian ministers had ceased to represent the 'volonté populaire' because they opposed the armistice.[16]

This idea that an individual (ideally *not* elected) somehow represented the public mood better than squabbling members of political factions had been common since 1789, although it is worth adding the rider that the Third Republic, in its dotage, was especially open to such brusque dismissal. Partly this was because of the acknowledged domination of political interest groups, partly because there was no single unifying national symbol that all could respect – least of all the titular president, elected as he was by the *partis*.

14. Ibid., p. 229.

15. Sir Llewellyn Woodward, *British Foreign Policy in the Second World War*, London, Her Majesty's Stationery Office, Vol. 1, 1970, p. 304.

16. Philip Charles Farwell Bankwitz, *Maxim Weygand and Civil-Military Relations in Modern France*, Cambridge, Mass., Harvard University Press, 1967, p. 319.

The decision to seek an armistice was taken, and it was signed on 22 June. It is interesting that, even at this date, Pétain's government still behaved like a state engaged in a negotiation between equals. This was to be a pattern during Vichy: over-estimation of independence followed by bitter disillusionment, followed by self-deception about the degree of freedom of action actually retained. An example is a 'Brief list of concessions which could not be made without threatening [French] honour', drawn up at the time by the Foreign Ministry. Such unacceptable concessions included the handing-over of the fleet to the Germans (which was avoided) and the 'amputation' of Alsace-Lorraine (which was not).[17] In fact, the negotiators found that little negotiation was possible. They were obliged to accept a division of the country into no fewer than six areas. The two departments of Nord and Pas de Calais were put under the control of the German military governor in Brussels. Alsace and Lorraine were rapidly re-annexed to Germany, and a 'forbidden zone' was set up in the North-East, roughly along the Somme River, to be colonised by German peasants. There was even, agony of agonies, a small Italian Occupied Zone along the Alps. The rest of the country was divided into the Occupied Zone, which included the North, Paris and the Atlantic Coast, and the Free Zone, the only part over which the government had any real control. The Occupied Zone contained some 29 million inhabitants and some 300,000 square kilometres of territory, compared with only 13 million inhabitants and about 250,000 square kilometres in the Free Zone.[18]

While the new French government was digesting this crushing humiliation and getting ready to move to its final seat at Vichy, there occurred another violent episode that has not yet entirely ceased to have implications for Franco-British relations: that of the sinking of the French fleet at Mers-el-Kébir. This episode, little known in the UK, was the outcome of Article VIII of the Armistice agreement, which allowed the French fleet to be retained if it was kept in its normal peacetime ports. Darlan, head of the French navy, sent most of the fleet to ports in the Free Zone, notably Toulon and Mers-el-Kébir. The French had gone to considerable lengths to try to persuade the British that they would scuttle all of their fleet rather than allow it to fall into German hands.

It is not really a question of whether the British believed them or not; rather, they felt that even the smallest possibility that the

17. Duroselle, *Politique Etrangère*, p. 246.
18. Ibid., p. 264.

Germans might take over the fleet was unacceptable, and the only way to ensure this was through the physical destruction of as much of it as possible. Thus, on the morning of 3 July, Somerville's Force H, including the *Hood* and the *Ark Royal*, appeared off Mers-el-Kébir, and offered Admiral Gensoul, the French commander, a range of options, including scuttling, joining the British or sailing to a neutral port. For reasons that are unclear, Gensoul chose to interpret the ultimatum as a choice between scuttling and siding with the British, and refused both. The British fleet then opened fire, sinking many of the ships and killing some 1,300 French sailors. At about the same time, all French ships that had escaped to Britain were boarded, and their crews arrested, not without several fatalities. Some ten thousand French sailors were taken to prison camps near Liverpool.

The French reaction was explosive. Pétain, in a broadcast the following week, claimed that 'England, breaking a long alliance, has unexpectedly attacked us, and destroyed French ships immobilised in our ports, and partly disarmed';[19] and he seems to have been dissuaded only with difficulty from ordering retaliatory attacks, and provoking a state of war. A plan was even considered to seize the Mosul oil fields in Northern Iraq.[20] In the event, retaliation was confined to an abortive air attack on Gibraltar, the home base of Force H.[21] Twenty years later, French officers still referred to the incident as a British 'assassination'.[22] The inevitable result was to rally French support for the government, and to cut to almost nothing the trickle of Frenchmen going to join de Gaulle. Darlan was furious that his word of honour had not been accepted by the British. He had harboured resentment against that nation for some time, since the disarmament negotiations of the early 1930s. He had also been violently upset by an apparent error of protocol that had placed him behind a Chinese admiral at the funeral of King George V.[23] He had feared such an attack for some time, claiming, only a week after the Armistice, that Great Britain had launched a 'violent campaign' to 'put in its hands French colonies and fleets for the defence of its interests alone'.[24]

19. *Discours*, p. 67.
20. Robert O. Paxton, *Parades and Politics in Vichy: The French Officer Corps under Marshal Pétain*, Princeton, Princeton University Press, 1966, pp. 72–73.
21. Duroselle, *Politique Etrangère*, pp. 296–7.
22. Paxton, *Parades*, p. 119.
23. Hervé Coutau-Bégarie and Claude Huan, *Darlan*, Paris, Fayard, 1989, pp. 128–9.
24. Ibid., p. 272.

The last and most bizarre act of the Third Republic's self-immolation now took place. The government and the parliament had now arrived and installed themselves at Vichy, a spa town known previously for pleasure rather than politics, and ill-suited for its new role. It was in the casino, appropriately enough, that the French political class abandoned the nation to an unelected administration, and thereby brought about their own destruction. The Senate and the Chamber of Deputies met together, on 10 July, and agreed, by 406 votes to 80 with 20 abstentions, that 'The National Assembly gives all its powers to the Government of the Republic, under the authority and the signature of Marshal Pétain, to the effect of promulgating, by one or more acts, a new constitution for the French State. This constitution should guarantee the rights of work, the family and the country.'[25]

The main architect of this proposal was Laval, who thought he could run Pétain by remote control: he turned out to be mistaken. Like most violent political changes, all the elements of this initiative had been in waiting for some time. Pétain had been spoken of as an authoritarian saviour of the nation for much of the 1930s, in the political world, in the media and in the armed forces. *C'est Pétain qu'il nous faut* was a common expression: what we need is Pétain.[26] Likewise, the concept of giving 'all powers' to Pétain was not entirely new. It will be recalled that the deputies had been in the habit of giving 'full powers' to previous prime ministers when measures they did not wish to be associated with were thought necessary, and had consented to rule by decree law during Laval's own tenure. In practice, Reynaud himself had run the country largely without parliament. What the deputies were voting for was the logical continuation of their steady retreat from responsibility (as opposed to power) during the inter-war years.

The Strange Defeat

If the deputies on 10 July voted so overwhelmingly for their own demise it was largely because, like most of the rest of the nation, they did not have the slightest idea what had happened to the

25. Dominique Rémy, ed., *Les lois de Vichy: Actes dits 'lois' de l'autorité de fait se prétendant 'gouvernement de l'Etat français'*, Paris, Romillat, 1992, p. 31. Hereafter *Lois*.

26. Griffiths, *Marshal Pétain*, pp. 171–88. One of the first opinion polls ever conducted, in 1935, placed Pétain at the head of a list of personalities who might come to rescue France in a time of danger: see Marc Ferro, *Pétain*, Paris, Fayard, 1987, p. 8.

country in the two months since the German attack. It was not surprising that each element of society blamed all others apart from itself for the debacle, whose extent and suddenness were unprecedented. Large numbers of French troops had never been engaged, and many of those who had did not see an enemy. Casualties were relatively heavy – one hundred thousand dead – but much greater than those of the attacker, against all the customs of warfare. As a result, there was no previous experience to act as a guide. The war of 1870 had been sudden and violent at the beginning, but the army had been defeated in battles that Napoleon would probably have recognised, and other armies had been hastily manufactured in an attempt to stem the tide. The war of 1914–18 had opened in much the same way, but stubborn resistance had paid off in the end. This time, there were no consolation prizes; not even the perverse satisfaction of defeat after a long and bloody struggle, with a high price exacted from the enemy. The Germans seemed to have won almost by sleight of hand.

It is not surprising, then, that a bewildered nation looked around for someone to blame. But, if there was 'a cause' of the defeat, it was not treason by generals, or left-wing schoolteachers, or a corrupt political class, or the Popular Front, or the British, or any of the hundred other reasons quickly offered. Marc Bloch, of all of the contemporary observers, perhaps came closest to the truth, when he suggested that '... our leaders, in the midst of many contradictions, meant, above all, to recreate, in 1940, the war of 1915–1918. The Germans fought the war of 1940'.[27] In other words, the Germans and the French were using different *techniques* of warfare, even although they were using very similar *weapons*. The German techniques of mass armoured attack and the use of aircraft as flying artillery were completely new and psychologically devastating. There was nothing inherently superior in the equipment or the tactics; it was just that their combination was outside the experience of those who were on the receiving end. Tanks were already known to be vulnerable; and the Germans themselves showed, with their light anti-aircraft guns deployed well forward, that air support could be a risky and costly business.

The speed and mobility of the attack were what was most disconcerting, since they resulted in the constant breaching of successive front lines. To be unsure whether the enemy is in front of you or behind you can only be frightening and dislocating for the

27. Marc Bloch, *L'Etrange Défaite: Témoinage écrit en 1940*, new edn, Gallimard, 1990, p. 84.

man in the trench. Anglo-Saxon accounts of the defeat tend to dwell, with relish, on stories of whole units running from the rumour of an enemy; but such a reaction is unsurprising in a group of bewildered men, unsure if they are already cut off and surrounded. Marc Bloch again: 'Last May and June, I very often heard the word "We left because the Germans were there". Translation: there where we did not expect them, where nothing allowed us to suppose that we should expect them.'[28] Yet surprisingly, French morale actually held up for some considerable time, as even the prosecution witnesses at the Riom trials of 1942 had to admit.[29]

In this state of defeat, confusion and uncertainty, the French people turned, for a whole variety of reasons, to Marshal Philippe Pétain, hero of Verdun, blank page on which they could project their fantasies. Pétain managed both to be famous and unknown at the same time. His image was known everywhere, but his opinions were a mystery to all. They were actually few and basic; anyway, he distrusted 'ideas'. Some on the Right were attracted by him as a means to destroy the Republic. More surprisingly, others on the Left thought he might be its saviour, seeing him as a 'Republican' general, unlike Weygand or Franchet d'Esperey.[30] In Chapter 1, I recalled Raoul Girardet's four forms that the Saviour – the figure I have called the Sovereign – frequently takes. Pétain, interestingly enough, corresponds to all of them. He was Cincinnatus, called reluctantly from an (albeit active) retirement, to return to save the threatened nation, and he was Alexander, the warrior-hero. He immediately set about being Solon, the lawgiver, and also Moses, the prophet of better times in the future. Yet he was, and became even more, a repository for other myths also. There was a deliberate campaign to present him at once as

> inheritor of a peasant line, military leader, interpreter of traditional morality and father-protector of the nation, a complete image of France is discovered, the same which the Vichy régime wished to install – or maintain. The myth of the Jewish conspiracy comes to join a whole, organised, explanatory system where are to be found resolved all the enigmas posed by the vicissitudes of contemporary history.[31]

Not all of this was clear at the time, either to Pétain or to the French. But there was a rare confluence of two desires: Pétain's

28. Ibid., p. 78.
29. See for example, Pierre Tissier, *The Riom Trial*, London, Harrap, 1942, p. 19.
30. Ferro, *Pétain*, p. 9.
31. Raoul Girardet, *Mythes et mythologies politiques*, Paris, Seuil, 1986, p. 180.

desire to be a figure of national salvation, and the desire of the French people to find one. It is this that explains Pétain's continued popularity as an individual, in spite of widespread repudiation of his policies and a recognition, at the end, that they had only brought disaster. Like most Sovereign figures in French history, Pétain had only an incomplete sense of what he was doing and why. But he did, very clearly, play up stereotypical elements in his situation that the French could identify, and would accept. In return, the French people attributed to him powers and abilities that he did not possess, but that they needed to believe that somebody did. Pétain had always seen his mission in broadly religious terms, consciously reprising many of the attitudes of the medieval God-King. He had spoken of going to Spain to 'expiate the sins of the *Front Populaire*'.[32] And notoriously, his broadcast of 17 June included a promise to 'make a gift of my person to France, in order to alleviate her misery'.[33]

He deliberately tried, therefore, to continue the traditional identification of the king with France, and with God. The public reaction was commensurate. A bishop was found to remark that 'Pétain is France and France is Pétain'.[34] A cult of Pétain grew up, guided, but not originated or controlled, by Vichy. Songs were written to him, illustrated accounts of his life were popular, and twelve million copies of his portrait were sold in the first year of Vichy, roughly one for each French household. Pétain himself played up the regal overtones of his position. He promulgated decrees with the formula 'We, Marshal of France, Head of the French State'.

Before the end of 1940, Pétain had begun what one of his biographers has called 'the marriage of Pétain and France'. A series of visits around the nation, occupied and unoccupied, brought everywhere enormous crowds, anxious to see what one newspaper called the 'living symbol of a renewed France'. The last journey was to Paris, almost three months after D-Day, when the crowds were as large and as enthusiastic as ever.[35] Yet at the same time, this mystical figure was also involved in practical politics, and in relations with the victorious Nazis. Pétain was an important figure in these developments, but not a very interesting one;

32. Griffiths, *Marshal Pétain*, p. 215.

33. *Discours*, p. 57.

34. Cited by Henri Michel, *The Shadow War: Resistance in Europe 1939–1945*, London, André Deutsch, 1972, p. 159.

35. Ferro, *Pétain*, pp. 228–39.

and I shall therefore widen the focus, in the next section, to the collaborationist movement in France as a whole.

Collaboration; Or, the Revenge of Colonel Henry

All occupied countries collaborated to some extent. In most cases, the government left the country, but the administration otherwise continued. What distinguished France was the organised and thorough-going proposals for partnership that the Vichy government put forward, that the Germans largely rejected, and that many of Vichy's domestic critics thought were too timid. Hitler simply wanted a 'docile and amenable France', whose economy he could gut.[36] In this case, it was not necessary for the Germans to use their normal strategy of turning over stones until something crawled out that was prepared to act as a political figurehead. But they did not expect ambitious proposals for France to be an equal partner, fighting for the survival of Western civilisation, or helping to construct a new United Europe.

The Vichy government's attenuated writ did not run through most of the country, and collaboration was not limited to the areas that it controlled. Groups of extremists who favoured a far more extensive programme of collaboration gathered in German-occupied Paris, where they edited periodicals and sponsored movements critical of the hesitancy of Vichy. Their influence was modest, and they played little part in the formulation of policy, but their periodicals sold hundreds of thousands of copies. I shall therefore consider them briefly, before passing on to Vichy itself. For most of them, the rise of Vichy was, in the words of Charles Maurras, a 'divine surprise', and they made the most of it, preferring the bracing political climate of Paris (with its traditional attractions) to the long, dark, provincial Sunday afternoon of the soul that was Vichy. Unlike Vichy, the Germans were mainly concerned with the preservation of discipline and order, and less with political ideas. There was a visible Nazification of Paris, by the appearance over the façade of the Chamber of Deputies, for example, of the slogan *Deutschland Siegt Auf Allen Fronten* ('Germany is winning on all fronts'). But the city was largely left alone in other ways.

The French literary world largely remained in Paris, and censored itself with much more expertise and enthusiasm than the overworked *Propagandastaffel* could have managed. In September

36. Paxton, *Vichy France*, p. 51.

1940, the French publishers' association voluntarily agreed to publish nothing anti-German, and no book banned in Germany, and to censor new works before publication. This led to the famous 'List Otto', so named after the German ambassador, Otto Abetz.[37] Its purpose was defined as 'the creation of a healthier atmosphere and the concern to establish conditions necessary to a more objective understanding of European problems'. Particularly deplored were books that had 'poisoned French public opinion', especially books by Jewish refugees who had 'promoted war unscrupulously in the hope of furthering their selfish goals'. In practice, the usual left-wing, Jewish and pacifist books were banned, but there were unintentionally comic moments also, as when (until June 1941) books critical of the Soviet Union were banned also.[38] And all of this, it should be recalled, was undertaken by the French publishing industry itself, without pressure or supervision from the Germans.

The universities were not backward, either, in adapting to new ideas. In 1942, the Sorbonne created two new chairs, one of 'Racial Studies' and the other of the 'History of Contemporary Judaism'. In fairness, it should be added that the incumbent of the first – a former conservative deputy of long-unsuspected academic ambitions – received such a limited welcome from the students that the second chair was never actually awarded.[39] Industry was involved also. Between 1940 and 1943, France delivered 31,000 million francs' worth of war material to Germany, the largest part being fighter aircraft.[40] Industrialists who had declined to produce weapons for the defence of France were not backward in doing so for Germany. Overtly fascist groups and a vitriolic collaborationist press flourished. Many of them were overjoyed at the defeat, which promised to sweep away everything that they hated. An example is Laubreaux, who had written in *Je Suis Partout* during the *drôle de guerre* that he wanted a 'short, disastrous war' for France. He was one of a small group whose lip-smacking defeatism was so extreme that even the government could not ignore it, and arrested them on 6 June.[41] With the occupation, they re-emerged in

37. It was typical of the administrative chaos at the time that Germany, unlike every other nation, accredited an ambassador to Paris, where there was no French authority, rather than to Vichy, where there was.

38. Herbert R. Lottman, *The Left Bank: Writers, Artists and Politics from the Popular Front to the Cold War*, London, Heinemann, 1982, pp. 154–5.

39. Pascal Ory, *Les Collaborateurs, 1940–1945*, Paris, Seuil, 1976, p. 154.

40. Azéma, *Munich to Liberation*, p. 132.

41. Ory, *Collaborateurs*, p. 33.

their full splendour, and *Je Suis Partout* was reborn as an openly fascist publication, hysterically anti-Semitic, anti-Bolshevik and anti-British, selling up to 220,000 copies each week.[42]

These groups tended to be small and self-deluding, often ejected from Vichy because of their impatient extremism. They saw themselves as young revolutionaries looking to the future, and were unenthused by the attempt of the Vichy 'gerontocracy' to re-create the past. It was the German invasion of Russia that particularly energised them. After that, collaboration against the Jewish Bolshevists became 'a priority objective, since the Reich was undertaking the mission which justifies its pre-eminence in the new Europe: the definitive crushing of Bolshevism'. And it did so with support from the more extremist clergy that went beyond what the church would normally have tolerated, such as the prophecy of a certain Mgr Baudrillart in 1942: 'Here comes the time of the new crusade. I declare that the tomb of Christ will be freed.'[43]

But these groups were, to repeat, a minority. They had occasional influence, and support from the Germans, but no real power. This power, such as it was, was to be found in Vichy, where it was established so quickly and smoothly that many assumed that it must have been the result of careful preparation, and thus treason and conspiracy. The truth was more prosaic, and the effortless sense of continuity resulted from two particular factors.

The first was the continuity of the government machine itself. Very nearly the whole of the civil, diplomatic and military apparatus that served the Third Republic carried on happily serving Vichy, and felt every sense of pride and legitimacy as it did so. The armed forces, in particular, gave every support to the new régime, and, indeed, many of their senior officers held positions of power in it. At one stage, it looked as if it would not be so, since many senior officers opposed the Armistice, wishing to fight on, notably General Auguste Noguès, the commander in North Africa. Yet in the end, none of the senior commanders broke ranks, and only one, very junior, officer from the North-Eastern front went to join the Gaullists. His name was Captain Philippe de Hautecloque, later to be better known as Leclerc.[44]

Some of the reasons for this remarkable continuity were practical. Immense pressure was put on the military, in particular, to remain at their posts. It was argued that, if this were not done,

42. Ibid., p. 117.
43. Azéma, *Munich to Liberation*, p. 136.
44. Paxton, *Parades*, pp. 24–28.

Pétain's claim to represent all of France, and thus France's negotiating position, would be weakened. It required, in any event, unusual courage to turn your back on your home, family, comrades and career, and strike out for an unknown destiny. Even if courage was available, opportunity was often lacking, since a voyage to England – or even escape from German hands – was often impossible. Then again, it was unfortunate, in the eyes of many, that it was de Gaulle who had decided to incarnate France. He was distrusted, at a minimum, by large sections of French society. He had managed to upset nearly everyone with *Vers l'Armée du Métier*, and those who might have rallied to a well-known general or politician were much less likely to do so to a middle-ranking officer suspected of extreme political ideas. It was also unfortunate that de Gaulle had, of necessity, taken refuge in England; the country that had launched the Hundred Years' War and burnt Joan of Arc; the country of Trafalgar and Waterloo, but also the country of Mers-el-Kébir. The accusation that anyone who wanted to continue the fight was an agent of London – and probably of international Jewry as well – was a commonplace of Vichy propaganda.

There was the whip. A succession of laws made anyone who did take refuge abroad guilty of treason, deprived them of French nationality and seized their possessions.[45] There was also the carrot. Secure and adequately paid jobs were available, in an environment where the disruptive effect of politics was largely absent. For the armed forces, in particular, after several generations of anti-militarist political sentiment, there was a chance to serve a government with a warm regard for the military and its traditions. But most of all, there was the overwhelming sense that Vichy was the legitimate government, and that state servants therefore owed their duty to it. Even after 1945, the men of Vichy affected great puzzlement that anyone could have doubted the legitimacy of the government they had served. The classic text is the statement of Weygand at Pétain's trial in July 1945:

> The government of the French Republic is that which, as a soldier, I have always obeyed; it is the government of my country. I have served my country. I have always obeyed my government. I have never been involved in politics; as a consequence, I never dreamt that there might be another government than the government of the French Republic.... The National Assembly, which is made up of Senators and Deputies elected by the nation, decides by a majority

45. Law of 27 July 1940 (*Lois*, p. 59), Law of 10 September 1940 (*Lois*, pp. 78–79).

on something.... I think that the government which succeeded the other is a legitimate government; I can think nothing else.[46]

This is an argument that de Gaulle never accepted, and that is still dismissed by French governments to this day, on the basis that the Constitution of the Third Republic did not permit the National Assembly to act as it did. This may be true (although the constitutional laws are full of lacunae), but it ignores the fact that Vichy had almost unchallengeable *political* legitimacy, given the vote of 10 July 1940, and that Pétain himself possessed a *psychic* legitimacy that no one else, and certainly not de Gaulle, could have begun to match.

The second reason was that Vichy's ideology did not need to be invented: it was already in place. It is unnecessary to describe it in detail, since we have encountered it before, several times. Although Vichy frequently referred to changes after 1940 as a 'National Revolution', the ideology of Vichy was in fact the *counter*-revolutionary ideology of 1789 and after: anti-republican, anti-democratic, anti-Semitic, anti-intellectual, anti-modern. Its positive goals were defined less clearly, but they essentially involved the attempted return to an era that did not actually exist, but *should* have done so: a pre-1789 idyll of a strong and authoritarian state, and a happy, largely rural population, innocent of the corrupting effects of the modern world and modern ideas.

Vichy's attempts to interpret the defeat of 1940 naturally began from these principles. Pétain's very first public utterances spelt out the essence of the interpretation: the defeat had been caused by moral and political factors, not material ones. The priority was 'to restore France ... Our defeat came from our laxity. The spirit of enjoyment has destroyed what the spirit of sacrifice built'.[47] The disaster of earlier that year was 'only, in reality, the reflection at the military level of the weaknesses and flaws of the former political régime'.[48] And it had been exacerbated by 'systematic sabotage, intended to bring about social disorder or international revolution'.[49] In practice, the accusations were more pointed. Like most politicians, when Pétain said 'we', he meant 'you'. There was never any indication that Pétain or his colleagues felt that the leisured and enjoyable lives they had led before the war had contributed to the defeat. Nor were they offering to share in the sacrifices and the

46. *Procès du Maréchal Pétain*, Paris, Imprimerie des Journaux Officiels, 1945, p. 144.
47. 25 June 1940, *Discours*, p. 65.
48. 10 October 1940, *Discours*, p. 88.
49. 13 August 1940, *Discours*, p. 72.

moral renewal that they decided were necessary. Rather, the criticism was very specific: it was directed against the Popular Front, against paid holidays and forty-hour weeks for the workers, and against a minister of sport and leisure. It was directed against the 'Judaeo-Masonic' Third Republic, and the 'Parties' that competed for office. It was directed against the schools, which had failed to inculcate a sense of morality or discipline.

What, then, was to be done? The first priority was obviously revenge. It is given to few politicians to put their political enemies on trial for treason, but it happened in Vichy at the Riom trial, decided upon soon after the defeat, but not finally under way until early 1942. The main defendants were Daladier, Blum, Reynaud and Gamelin, and the indictment, with which Vichy was not really happy, was limited to 'their responsibilities in the matter of the defeat'.[50] But the press covering the trial were instructed to report that 'the real subject of the trial is the state of affairs which gave rise to the French catastrophe', and were ordered 'to make frequent reference' to the 'obvious fact' that 'France is forced to build a new régime or perish'.[51] In practice, it was Blum, and, to a lesser extent Daladier, who dominated the proceedings. It was an unequal contest of amateurs against professionals. Blum had been a distinguished advocate, and it showed:

> There were three phases to the 1936 legislature: first there was the Blum phase – I am afraid I am obliged to mention myself first, chronology demands it – then there was the Chautemps phase, which lasted nearly a year; then there was the Daladier phase. M. Daladier is here! I am here! And the man who came between us, I repeat, is at this moment entrusted with an official mission of the government or the Head of State.[52]

The trial was an acknowledged failure, and was soon abandoned. Its task was impossible in any event: to convict some of the political and military leaders of the 1930s for the disaster, whilst exculpating others at least as heavily involved in the decisions that had led to it. Perhaps the greatest irony, however, is that the instigators of the trial were themselves to be convicted, three years later, on rather similar charges, again by their political opponents.

Revenge was also pursued at other levels. Under the provisions of the Armistice, the army was to be reduced to 100,000 men. In theory, the massive reduction in the officer corps that this entailed was

50. Tissier, *Riom Trial*, p. 12.
51. Ibid., p. 14.
52. Jean Lacouture, *Léon Blum*, new edn, Paris, Seuil, 1979, pp. 466–7.

supposed to be implemented by weeding out the less capable and those whose units had not performed well in the fighting. In practice, 'dissidents' were purged, and the officers who remained were 'a group measurably nearer the social ideal cherished by senior officers'.[53] And special laws made it impossible for Freemasons and Jews to serve in the army, or to be public servants generally.[54]

The perception that teachers had been responsible for the defeat set off a separate wave of purges. But assertion was one thing, and proof was another: in individual cases, it was next to impossible. A purge was carried out by local prefects, essentially on the basis of hearsay evidence, or no evidence at all. Sometimes the opportunity was taken to get rid of genuinely incompetent teachers, whatever their political views; but more often it was just an excuse for settling old scores. Ever since the 1870s, teachers had been the intellectual vanguard of republicanism and secularism: in many cases, communities were divided by the bitter rivalry between the priest and the schoolmaster. Many of the denunciations came from priests, hoping to close down the local (secular) school as a result. The *Légion Française de Combattants*, set up by Pétain as his 'eyes and ears' in the country, was another fruitful source of the several million denunciations received by prefects in 1940–41.[55]

The purge was carried down to the local level. The naming of streets and squares is a highly political act in France, and many streets named after left-wing or Republican leaders abruptly changed their name between 1940 and 1942, usually to 'Avenue Pétain', or something similar. In the provinces, it became clear that a detailed programme of reprisals for the Popular Front was under way, and that 'one's statements and actions at the time of the events of 1936 and 1938 became the touchstone by which one's probable attitudes towards the Vichy régime might be reckoned'. Anyone speaking favourably of those years, even privately, was likely to lose his job.[56]

But revenge alone was not sufficient. From the very beginning, there was felt to be a need for fundamental change, for the 'National

53. Paxton, *Parades*, p. 45.

54. Law of 31 July 1940, Article 5 (*Lois*, p. 70), Law of 2 June 1941 (*Lois*, pp. 116–23).

55. Roger Austin, 'Political Surveillance and Ideological Control in Vichy France: A Study of Teachers in the Midi, 1940–1944', in Roderick Kedward and Roger Austin, eds, *Vichy France and the Resistance: Culture and Ideology*, London, Croom Helm, 1985, pp. 13–35.

56. John F. Sweets, *Choices in Vichy: The French under Nazi Occupation*, Oxford, Oxford University Press, 1986, p. 38.

Revolution'. I shall devote most of the remainder of this section to a discussion of elements of the Revolution, trying to distinguish those elements that represented an attempted return to the past, and those that pointed to the post-war world. First, a brief word about the political and military context. Obviously, no one in Vichy in 1940 would have believed for a moment that the experiment would last less than two-and-a-half years before the Germans occupied the Free Zone. At both the domestic and the foreign levels, they were anticipating a long innings. Laval expressed this judgement very clearly, at Pétain's trial in 1945: 'Do you really think that in 1940 a sensible man could imagine anything else than a German victory?... The interest of France, at that moment, was evidently to find, with Germany, a way forward which would allow us to escape the consequences of the defeat.'[57]

It was assumed that Britain would collapse quite quickly, and that the United States would not enter the war. This being so, the priority was the spiritual and moral rebirth of France, to enable her to take her place, in due course, as the natural leader of Europe. In the meantime, the precious unity of the nation must be safeguarded, a new national spirit created and a good working relationship with the Germans established. Vichy saw 1940 as a defeat, but not a surrender. France was still a great power, with world-wide possessions and interests, and it was hoped that German behaviour would reflect a recognition of this fact.

The first requirement was the re-establishment of national unity, which Pétain described as 'the first law of patriotism'. It was important, he added, not to have many different ideas of what 'patriotic duty' should be, otherwise 'there will be no more fatherland and no more nation. There will only remain factions in the service of personal ambitions. Civil war, division of the territory, fratricidal disturbances, will follow naturally from this division of opinion'.[58]

It might be thought that unity was not best established by official persecution of very large sections of French society, including Jews, Freemasons, Communists, Socialists, Republicans and most foreigners. But Vichy's concept of unity was essentially the Maurrassian *exclusive* one, in contrast to the *inclusive* policy that Blum had espoused, and that de Gaulle was later to implement. Vichy's argument was that the real spirit of France was to be found before the Revolution, before foreigners (and particularly Jews and

57. *Procès Pétain*, p. 195.
58. *Discours*, p. 129.

Freemasons) had imported the ideas that had led to the nation's downfall. This ideology comes from the 'complete nationalism' of Maurras, who, it will be recalled, favoured the exclusion of those who did not belong to the *réel* (i.e. pre-1789) France. Maurras called such people as Protestants, Jews and Freemasons *métèques*, an untranslatable but ugly word, and held that they constituted an 'anti-France'.[59] Thus, 'in the name of an ideology of national gathering' (*rassemblement*), various 'centrifugal forces' could be disposed of. What remained could then be re-moulded to attain the desired unity.[60]

Existing divisions had to be overcome, particularly those in the economic field. Pétain and Laval were both proud of their peasant origins, and the modern industrial world filled them with horror. Pétain was fond of the saying 'the earth does not lie' (*la terre ne ment pas*), a meaningless, but impressive-sounding, formulation. The society to be created would therefore be an essentially rural one, in which Frenchmen once more lived in harmony with the soil and each other.[61] Nonetheless, a modern nation could not survive entirely by farming, and some large-scale industry was inevitable. But Vichy hoped to 'abolish the class struggle … It seemed that France was divided into two camps: on one side the bosses and on the other the workers and peasants'.[62] Some efforts were made to implement this aspiration, especially through the so-called Charter of Work of October 1941, which instituted 'twenty-nine "professional families" subdivided into five "unique professional syndicates" ("employers, workers, employees, superintendents and engineers, leaders of the administration and commerce")'. The system had a complicated, pyramidical structure, with co-ordinating committees at each level.[63] Interesting similarities have been pointed out between the Charter and the social legislation of the Fourth Republic.[64]

Another force for unity and stability was the family, 'the essential unit of society and the nation'.[65] The modern trend for women to work was deplored, and a law greatly limited its extent.[66] Various

59. Paxton, *Vichy France*, p. 171.
60. Jean-Pierre Azéma, *Vichy*, in Michel Winock, ed., *Histoire de l'Extrême Droite en France*, Paris, Seuil, 1993, pp. 201–2.
61. Paxton, *Vichy France*, pp. 270–1.
62. *Discours*, p. 188.
63. Azéma, *Munich to Liberation*, p. 62.
64. Ferro, *Pétain*, p. 280.
65. *Discours*, p. 72.
66. Law of 11 October 1940, *Lois*, pp. 92–96.

laws were introduced to defend the family from anticipated threats: at least one woman was guillotined for procuring an abortion.[67] On a more positive note, Mothers' Day was celebrated with great pomp, and tax benefits were provided for households with several children.[68] Ambitious attempts were made to re-model the family after a hypothetical past: mother and daughters in the kitchen, father and sons working in the fields.

The church also had a role to play. There was a virtually unanimous church welcome for the new régime, with its emphasis on discipline, patriotism and morality, and its anti-Semitic and anti-Masonic bias. The Vichy doctrine of 'Work, Family, Country' (replacing 'Liberty, Equality and Fraternity') was also welcomed enthusiastically: 'these three words are ours also', said one cardinal.[69] But support for Vichy did not necessarily imply support for German occupation or objectives, and there was always a degree of ambiguity in church-state relations as a result. There were practical changes, however: chaplains were reintroduced into the army, and religion was taught once more in secular schools. The celebration of the Liberation of Paris, with a *Te Deum* sung in Notre Dame, was therefore a slightly awkward occasion, with a number of prominent ecclesiastical absentees.

Finally, education was clearly going to have the major responsibility for reforming the nation. Strong attempts were made to enforce the teaching of the National Revolution in schools (where a portrait of Pétain was compulsory in each classroom). But there were too many notorious republicans in the teaching profession for the whole of the effort to be safely concentrated there, and other initiatives were tried. For Vichy, however, education meant much more than book learning. Pétain thought that it was 'a profound illusion' to believe that 'all that is needed is to instruct minds in order to form hearts and make characters'. Such a limited scheme led to unhealthy individualism. What was needed was more discipline and family influence.[70] Ideally, all young men would have spent some time in the army, repository of all these virtues; but that was impossible. As a result, the *Chantiers de la Jeunesse* were formed, to give military-style training to young people for eight months at the age of twenty. They were run by the

---

67. Azéma, *Vichy*, p. 203

68. Sweets, *Choices in Vichy*, p. 43.

69. Bill Halls, 'Catholicism Under Vichy: A Study in Diversity and Ambiguity', in Kedward and Austin, *Vichy and Resistance*, p. 134.

70. Griffiths, *Marshal Pétain*, p. 256.

militar, and emphasised fresh air, exercise, discipline and communal activities. The army took to this new task with a will, having 'three generations of antimilitarist and antipatriotic lay school instruction to overcome'.[71] Particularly active was General de Lattre de Tassigny, subsequently to be chief of staff under the Fourth Republic. Disappointed not to be able to run the *Chantiers*, he set up his own school, designed to 'produce leaders, a type of dominant personality which levelling democracy had done all too much to repress'.[72] Although the main orientation was physical and moral, some history was taught, in the form of great lives, from Vercingétorix to Pétain. But the Revolution of 1789 was virtually ignored.

All these initiatives arose specifically from Vichy's analysis of the reasons for the defeat, and each was intended to remedy some of the causes. But practical implementation proved difficult, as is usually the case with revolutionary theories, and results were often not what was expected. Paradoxically, the greatest importance of Vichy's use of these ideas was in testing them to destruction, so preparing the ground for their abandonment by the Fourth Republic.

Another limb of the National Revolution was the reform of government structures and political life. The hope was that 'the weakness of the State should cease to paralyse the nation ... the administration will be at the same time concentrated and decentralised ... We shall make an organised France'.[73]

The most obvious effect of the National Revolution was the disappearance of parliament and political parties. Ministers were appointed directly by Pétain for their perceived technical competence. Some ministries were run by former civil servants, and others by the military. There were many officials we would now describe as 'technocrats', from the *Grandes Écoles*, often with an industrial or managerial background. They all believed that 'it was imperative to shake free from the archaism of the economic and political structures of France ... It was Vichy that gave them the chance to put their modernist ideology into practice ...'.[74]

Defence was an area of particular innovation. By 1939, there was an almost universal view that co-ordination of defence needed to be much stronger and better organised. It will be

71. Paxton, *Parades*, p. 185.
72. Ibid., p. 197.
73. *Discours*, p. 69.
74. Azéma, *Munich to Liberation*, p. 56.

recalled that Blum's government had made steps in this direction in 1936–37, and that Daladier and Reynaud had largely continued the system. But each took on so many other responsibilities that they had little time to give to this task. It was clear that liaison had been bad and central direction lacking in 1940. Pétain's government therefore introduced a very notable reform, whose main outlines still endure. A chief of the armed forces was created, and a minister of national defence, each with authority over the individual services, as opposed to a co-ordinating role. Being Vichy, of course, the two posts were held by the same individual: first Weygand, then Darlan.[75] The latter introduced a number of centralising reforms, particularly directed at the army whose arms tended to be little empires of their own. Since they came from a sailor, these reforms were dismissed out of hand by the army; but they did sow the seeds of post-war organisational change.[76] The army itself changed in many ways. There was more concentration on practical soldiering and the 'will to fight' than on book learning, and more attention to a smart appearance and to formal parades. Critically, there was a return, for the first time since 1870, to a professional army. However, drawing lessons from the defeat would have been a problem, since the theories that had so conspicuously failed were closely identified with the marshal, head of the French state.[77]

It would be fitting to record great successes for these initiatives; but little of any lasting importance was achieved. The main reason was that a group of military men and bureaucrats, against the expectations of some, could not run a competent organisation. Jealousy, plots, paranoia and jockeying for position were just as bad, if not worse, than under the late despised Republic. Pétain remained, but the government changed seven times between July 1940 and April 1942. And Pétain listened to many individuals in preference to his formal advisers, not least his personal physician. The Ruritanian atmosphere of Vichy was enhanced by the physical circumstances of government. The town had many hotels, but little else, and bureaucracies were forced to work scattered all over the town in accommodations that were totally unsuitable. (It is no doubt a coincidence that the Ministry of the Colonies was in the Hôtel d'Angleterre.)

75. Paxton, *Parades*, p. 168.
76. Ibid., pp. 262–70.
77. Ibid., pp. 150–62.

France and a New Europe

This rump state, with all its atmosphere of Viennese operetta, was nonetheless recognised by most of the world's nations as an independent country, and conducted a foreign policy of a kind. I want to deal briefly with some aspects of this that are important for French policy in later years. First, there was the restoration of the grandeur of 'eternal France'. No one at Vichy saw the current difficulties as anything except a transitory phenomenon. Darlan, with others, took it for granted that a German occupation was an anomaly in the great scheme of things, and that some time in the future, after the Nazi régime had withered away, France would take its place once again at the head of Europe. This was especially welcome, he told the US ambassador, given 'England's impending disappearance from the continental stage'.[78] In the meantime, France was still, of course, a 'European and colonial power'.[79] She was aware of her duties towards both, and, Pétain assured his fellow countrymen that 'as a civilising power, she has retained, in spite of her defeat, a position of spiritual privilege in the world'.[80] Clearly, therefore, France could not accept a secondary role to any nation, including her temporary conqueror. Whatever important events were afoot, it was felt, France needed to be involved in them, and her grandeur and dignity required her to defend her territory, at home and abroad, against all comers. This kind of attitude was, of course, a typically French one: Vichy's prickly sense of sovereignty and independence made de Gaulle look positively relaxed by comparison. As a result, French negotiators tended to have very unrealistic expectations of what they could achieve with the Germans, and were consequently often disappointed.

Vichy believed that collaboration was an expression of strength, not weakness, and that it would bring concrete benefits to France that no other policy could. It was also regarded as a new and better policy towards Germany. Unnecessary hostility towards Germany was one of the mistakes for which the 'former régime' was so heavily criticised. At the centre of France's concerns, insisted Pétain, was 'the problem of Franco-German relations', which had been 'criminally managed' in the past, but which would 'continue to determine' France's future.[81] Pétain was subsequently to claim that it

78. Cited in ibid., p. 65.
79. *Discours*, p. 132.
80. Ibid., p. 211.
81. Ibid., p. 89.

was 'in honour and to maintain the unity of France – a unity of ten centuries – in the context of a constructive activity of the New European Order that I enter today on the path of collaboration'.[82]

Collaboration was nothing to be ashamed of, but a policy consistent with France's honour and history. It was even argued that Germany recognised France's special status. Laval told the US embassy that he was sure the Germans would not crush France, but that they contemplated rather 'a European federation of states in which France will play an important role compatible with its dignity and traditions'. He repeated as much to Hitler and Ribbentrop, arguing that collaboration might 'lead to France regaining her rightful place in Europe as the first Latin power'.[83] Indeed, Laval claimed that he had specifically warned the Germans against being too harsh with France and trying to crush her, or 'inevitably the French people will find ways and means of working the destruction of Germany'.[84] Laval's interest in good relations with Germany was not, of course, new, and he and several other Vichy leaders pursued an active policy of collaboration. This extended as far as the offer of several hundred French pilots ready to join the war against England.[85] Prominent among the activists was Darlan, who wanted to use his beloved fleet on the German side, and claimed that Hitler had wanted to make him 'Admiralissimo' of Europe.[86]

The policy of collaboration became much easier to defend after the German invasion of the Soviet Union in June 1941. For Vichy, and for collaborationists in general, a struggle to the death between the Nazis and the Bolsheviks required France to choose sides, and decades of hostility to Bolshevism pre-determined what that choice would be. Laval said in a radio broadcast in April 1942 that the invasion had 'revealed the purpose' of the war. If the Soviets won, he asked, would they stop at the French border? Surely not, the choice was either 'to be integrated, with our honour and vital interests respected, in a new, pacified Europe … or resign ourselves to seeing the disappearance of our civilisation'.[87] It was this attitude that produced Laval's most famous – or infamous –

82. Ibid., p. 95.
83. Geoffrey Warner, *Pierre Laval and the Eclipse of France*, London, Eyre and Spottiswoode, 1968, p. 191.
84. Murphy to the Secretary of State, *Foreign Relations of the United States*, 1940, Vol. II, p. 379. (Hereafter *FRUS*.)
85. Paxton, *Vichy France*, p. 67.
86. Couteau-Bégarie and Huan, *Darlan*, p. 408.
87. Warner, *Pierre Laval*, p. 292.

statement a few months later: 'I desire the victory of Germany, for without it, Bolshevism would tomorrow install itself everywhere.'[88] This statement was later held to be controversial and was featured at Laval's trial; but he was simply reflecting the common wisdom of Vichy, as well as the views of most right-thinking Frenchmen of the time. It was taken further by Pétain: as late as 1943, he lamented that the fanatic Churchill, together with the Jews who controlled the United States, were obstructing 'a common German-Anglo-Saxon front against Bolshevism'.[89]

Vichy's coverage of the German invasion was adulatory in the extreme, and reflected the fact that, at last, someone was seizing again the opportunity that had been allowed to go to waste between 1917 and 1920. Exhibitions on the iniquity of Bolshevism were easy to organise. Given the generally low opinion of the fighting capability of the Red army, there seemed a real chance that the Antichrist would, at last, be extirpated from the earth. It was obvious that such an epochal struggle must not exclude the French: but how, with the very weak forces available, and a distinct lack of interest on Berlin's part, could this happen? The answer came not from Vichy, but from the ultras in Paris, who immediately proposed the formation of a *Légion des volontaires français contre le bolchevisme* (LVF), or Anti-Bolshevik Legion. Not deterred by a lukewarm German reaction, the founders talked excitedly of raising a full division of fifteen thousand men to join the German-led crusade. Vichy's attitude was a grudging one, less because they opposed the idea than because, given its origins, they feared they might not be able to control it. Pétain did, however, send a message to the Legion in November 1941:

> I am happy to know that you are aware that you have with you a part of our military honour. There may be no more useful tasks at the present moment than to give our nation confidence in its own power (*vertu*) ... But you will be of service to France in a still more direct manner, in taking part in this crusade, in which Germany has taken the lead, thus rightly attracting the recognition of the world ... You will help to keep the Bolshevik Threat away from us; thus, you will protect your country, while also maintaining the hope of a Europe reconciled.[90]

The Legion failed to live up to expectations: the maximum strength it attained was only about five thousand, with only about half that

88. Ibid., p. 301.
89. Paxton, *Vichy France*, p. 289.
90. *Discours*, pp. 204–5.

number ever seeing active service.[91] Its members wore normal Wehrmacht uniforms with *tricolore* shoulder flashes, and were, in every way, part of the German army.

Nonetheless, Vichy eventually came to see considerable utility in the Legion, and its exploits were regularly covered in newsreels. Eventually, it was absorbed into an official body, the *Légion Tricolore*, for reasons that are interesting and make an instructive contrast with de Gaulle's own motivations. As described by one minister of the time, they were 'to integrate us into the common struggle ... to bridge the gap which separates us from our conquerors ... to ensure, in the final analysis, that the substantial sacrifices we are making without any worthwhile return in the economic field produce beneficial results in the political sphere'.[92] It was very much part of Vichy's thinking continually to emphasise the breadth and depth of the French contribution to the common defence. Thus, at the end of 1943, when Vichy had been placed under the total domination of the Reich, Pétain could still write to Hitler that his policy of collaboration, '[b]y combatting terrorism and communism' contributed 'to the defence of western civilisation'.[93]

After the German occupation of the 'Free Zone' in November 1942, and the subsequent dissolution of the Armistice army, Vichy also created a militia (*Milice*) with the intention of maintaining order against the increasing threat from the Resistance. Its volunteers, generally from those with extreme collaborationist views, fought a vicious and largely political war against the *Maquis*. Its first duty, according to its general regulations, was to 'save France from Bolshevism'.[94] Finally, there were those who joined the Wehrmacht directly. Over the years, thousands had joined unofficially to take part in the great crusade. The most popular sections were the air force and the navy (which a recruiting poster described as 'the Atlantic wall of France and Europe') since these did not entail service in Russia. But still there were not enough openings for the enthusiasts, and so, in July 1943, Laval agreed that Frenchmen should be officially authorised and encouraged to join the *Waffen* [fighting] *SS* 'to fight Bolshevism abroad in formations constituted by the German government'. They were known as the Brigade *Frankreich*.

91. Ory, *Collaborateurs*, p. 243.
92. Benoist-Méchin, cited in Warner, *Pierre Laval*, p. 315.
93. Cited by Ferro, *Pétain*, p. 515.
94. Cited in Sweets, *Choices in Vichy*, p. 108.

Eventually, in February 1945, the remnants of all these different groups were constituted as the 33rd (Charlemagne) SS Division. The last few held out in Berlin, even after Hitler's suicide, having nothing much to come back to.[95]

By making moves towards European integration and towards a Franco-German *rapprochement*, Vichy revealed traditional French distrust of, and hostility towards, the British. This was not necessarily greater than in other epochs, but now there was no need for it to be nuanced for Anglo-Saxon consumption. Partly, it was the traditional story of Anglo-French disagreements from the Hundred Years' War to Waterloo; but it was principally a result of the almost continuous shame, fury and humiliation of French decision-makers at the events already recounted, from Versailles to Mers-el-Kébir. During Vichy, the decades of accumulated pain and humiliation of the political and military classes came pouring out. As I have noted, distrust of Britain seemed perversely to justify the separate peace. Laval's histrionic performance on 10 July, which led to the vote to inter the Third Republic, was full of anti-British invective. Britain, he claimed to great applause, 'got us into this war. Then, having got us involved, she did nothing to enable us to win it ... France was murdered, when we Frenchmen believed we were her allies, you will see how she treated us. I will use the word, it is not excessive, we were scarcely even thought of as mercenaries'.[96]

Vichy increasingly spoke of 'England', in terms commonly associated with de Gaulle, although the latter generally spoke more moderately. Weygand in October 1940 recalled that in 1918 England had 'wanted to avoid an excessive French influence in Europe ... [and] did not wish to weaken Germany'. Vichy propaganda argued that England was waging 'her war' 'without weakness, but without false sensitivity, either, in order to keep her privileged position in the world and her standard of living'. The seizure of French ships was described as 'piracy', and British air raids on French cities as 'acts of savagery'. Speakers referred to the 'betrayal' of France at Dunkirk, placing the incident in what they saw as its extensive historical context.[97]

In case any of his officers should have forgotten about British perfidy in the months since Mers-el-Kébir, Darlan wrote to several of his commanders to ask them to remind their officers of why the

95. Ibid., pp. 264–8.
96. Text of debate in *Les Evénements*, Vol. 4, p. 487.
97. Paxton, *Parades*, pp. 127–9.

break had taken place with Britain. The British, he reminded them, were mainly responsible for their army's defeat, and had since tried to deprive them of their 'remaining riches: gold, the Fleet, the colonial Empire'. This, he argued, was the true motive behind Churchill's sudden proposal for a union of the two nations, which would have led to the destruction of France and the delivery of her empire to the British. After the rejection of her offer, on 16 June, Britain had tried to destroy the fleet that she could not have, and was now trying to conquer the empire.[98]

John Lukacs goes so far as to argue that 'Anglophobia rather than pro-Fascism was the key to the inclinations of the armistice party around Pétain.'[99] One might add that Anglophobia was not limited to this group, but was found, albeit with slightly less ferocity, at many levels of French society.

Another reason for hostility was that Britain was a democracy, and intended to remain so. Democracies, thought most important people in 1940, were weak and would soon succumb to a determined assault by more disciplined nations. Britain was therefore to be despised or pitied according to taste. The Judaeo-Masonic-Bolshevist fantasies, which had occupied the idle moments of the Right for so long, had always powerfully featured the power of the city of London, centre of international Jewish finance, to destroy French governments and bring France to her knees. So it is not surprising that a French general in 1941 should have argued that the British represented 'all those things which almost destroyed us; democratic-masonic politics and Judeo-Saxon finance'.[100]

All these concerns – unity, the National Revolution, building Europe, relations with Germany, anti-Bolshevism, distrust of Anglo-Saxons – came together in Vichy's fear and hatred of de Gaulle and his Anglo-Saxon allies. From the first, de Gaulle was perceived as a great danger to the unity of the nation. Partly, this was because he provided an alternative rallying point to the marshal. And he did so by denying the legitimacy of Vichy, and by claiming to embody this legitimacy himself. It was necessary to make a choice, since each proclaimed the other to be a traitor, in league with a foreign power. De Gaulle's claims were especially subversive, since, if he incarnated France, then the entire Vichy apparatus, of government, army and civil service, was composed

---

98. Couteau-Bégarie and Huan, *Darlan*, pp. 301–2.

99. John Lukacs, *The Last European War, September 1939–December 1941*, London, Routledge and Kegan Paul, 1976 (actually 1977), p. 406.

100. Ibid., p. 408.

of traitors. Vichy's response was to raise the spectre of disunity and civil war, and to recall the historical paradigm, last exemplified after 1870, whereby 'a defeated nation which is divided against itself will die; a defeated nation which can reunite is a nation which will be reborn'.[101] De Gaulle, as an opposite pole of attraction, was preventing this rebirth from taking place.

Partly, also, de Gaulle's activities raised the terrible possibility of Frenchmen firing on Frenchmen, across an ideological divide, for the first time since 1870. These fears were borne out almost immediately, as de Gaulle, with British support, began trying to rally colonies to free France. In a number of cases, from Dakar in September 1940 to North Africa two years later, this involved fratricidal strife between Frenchmen. Combined with the struggle between Vichy and the Resistance, this produced, between 1940 and 1944, a veritable French civil war on ideological lines. De Gaulle also represented a continuing challenge to the National Revolution of 1940, just by existing. For all the post-war attempts to postulate an understanding between de Gaulle and Pétain, it is clear that the two men were totally opposed in all respects. De Gaulle represented modernism, technology and republican democracy, Pétain represented a return to the past, to an authoritarian, rurally based society. There was no point of convergence between the two. Pétain's broadcasts make it quite clear that he saw the Gaullists as a force blocking progress, and Vichy had the gall to characterise *them* as the reactionary party of the past – that is, of the Judaeo-Masonic Republic – inhibiting the necessary transformation of France. 'One must choose', Pétain intoned, between 'the rebel leaders who have chosen emigration and a return to the past', and Pétain himself, who had chosen 'France and its future'.[102]

De Gaulle's activities in the colonies also threatened Vichy's ability to deal with Germany on what it thought were level terms. France's greatest asset was its colonies, and Laval claimed that 'as long as they are there, I can talk to the Germans … That's because they are scared of seeing them go over to the other side. If they disappear, what will they do with France?'[103] A France weakened by the loss of its colonies would not be able to take its anticipated place in the New Europe. De Gaulle was also, of course, seen as fighting on the side of Bolshevism, especially after 1941, and frequently

101. *Discours*, p. 172.
102. *Ibid.*, p. 299.
103. Warner, *Pierre Laval*, p. 222.

(since these two were judged the same) on the side of the international Jewish conspiracy.

Finally, there was the link between de Gaulle and the Anglo-Saxons. Ever since June 1940, Vichy had considered that the war was over, and that France was effectively at peace. Vichy perceived, quite accurately, that de Gaulle could have no practical effect on the war except with help from London, and thus Gaullist operations were effectively attacks by the English on the French, and a renewal of an antagonism stretching back centuries. 'Where', asked propaganda posters, 'will England make French blood flow next?' Thus Vichy interpreted operations to liberate Europe as attacks by the old enemy on France. Pétain announced on D-Day, in 1944, that 'military operations have just been unleashed against our country'.[104] Vichy propaganda films showed French families fleeing from the invaders as they had done in 1940. For a Frenchman, especially a soldier, to associate himself with these attacks was scandalous: no wonder posters for the *Légion française des combattants* urged 'For France against Gaullism', as they urged opposition to 'Parties', to 'The Power of the Jews', to 'Bolshevism' and to other traditional targets.

In trying to bring these disparate elements together, Vichy looked around for a myth and found the most obvious one: that of Joan of Arc. Joan suited Vichy very well for a number of reasons. She was clearly a very early supporter of the National Revolution of 1940: 'Peasant from our Eastern borders, faithful to her soil, faithful to her prince, faithful to her God ... Martyr to national unity, Joan of Arc, patron saint of our villages and towns, is the symbol of France.'[105] But she also took part in an (ultimately successful) attempt to drive out the English, and defeat the treasonous Frenchmen who had allied with them. Let no one forget how France had suffered, and the connections between now and then: 'For a century, France had been enfeebled by internal quarrels.... The country was partly occupied by the English.... Foreign propaganda tried to divide opinion.... France doubted itself and its leader.' Today, one saw 'the same weaknesses, the same divisions, the same self-doubts, the same vain hopes placed in foreigners'.[106] The sub-text was scarcely disguised: the Gaullists were the Burgundians, the English were the English, the consequences of more fighting would be the destruction of the country.

104. *Discours*, p. 337.
105. Ibid., p. 131.
106. Ibid., p. 254.

Something should finally be said about the importance of the Vichy era for post-war French policy, especially in the security field. Vichy, after all, had a very free hand, even if it had to keep one eye on the occupiers. First, Vichy was a test to the destruction of a whole series of ideas that had been around since the Revolution of 1789, but had never been implemented together. During Vichy, the whole counter-Revolutionary agenda was implemented, not by the kind of gangsters who ran much of Europe, but by experienced politicians, diplomats, military men and bureaucrats: some of the best and brightest of the time. This policy was a catastrophic failure, both with the people (among whom it was never popular) and at the level of concrete achievement. As a result, its agenda largely dropped out of serious French politics after 1945, and republican and secular tendencies were reinforced. Likewise, government by nostalgia was discredited as a principle. There could be no more going back to a rural dream world. The new France would have to be modern, technological and well educated, and would produce Concorde, the TGV and nuclear weapons.

Second, and in spite of these same backward tendencies, the modernisation of the country was begun. The government machine was overhauled, technocrats were brought in, an attempt was made to rationalise defence and security decision-making, attempts were made to train administrators for the needs of the future. It was recognised that the industrial trench warfare of the past would have to stop. Thirdly, there were changes at the international level. Vichy clearly saw that the continuing Franco-German dispute was pointless and should be brought to an end. The only way in which this could be done was to develop some kind of new European structure that would go beyond the nationalist rivalries of the past. It was assumed that, in the long term at least, this structure would be led by France. But there was a reinforcement of traditional French prejudices against Anglo-Saxons, and the British in particular.

Fourthly, and complicating the above, the men of Vichy emerged with an enhanced belief in the importance of colonies, which alone had appeared to save French grandeur and freedom of manoeuvre. This belief was mainly responsible for plunging France into disastrous wars in Indo-China and Algeria, the latter bringing down the Fourth Republic in the process. Fifthly, and most importantly, the ideas set out above have significance because they, and those who held them, survived well into the post-war period. I deal with this in more detail below; but here it is enough to say

6

THE FAR SIDE OF DESPAIR

What is not possible is not to choose.

Sartre, 1945

'De Gaulle', see 'France'

Index to 'Foreign Relations
of the United States', Vol. 2, 1944

In spite of the very powerful incentives towards collaboration, and loyalty to Pétain's French state, a significant number of individuals nonetheless declined to collaborate or to be loyal. In this chapter, I will explain who these individuals were, what their origins and motivations were, and what their importance was for post-war France.

There is no agreement among scholars about the nature and extent of collaboration in France during the period between 1940 and 1944, nor are we ever likely to see any. This, in turn, is because it is impossible to agree either on the meaning of 'collaboration', or on the meaning of 'resistance', since each came in a large number of flavours. In particular, collaboration can be differently interpreted depending upon whether we see it as expressing an attitude towards the occupying power, towards the marshal, head of the French state, or towards his National Revolution. At one extreme, collaboration can mean unhesitating support for, and identification with, the German conqueror and his ideology. There were Frenchmen who took this position (those who joined the LVF, for example), but they were few in number and not very important. If this were to be the criterion of collaboration, then Vichy itself would have been part of the Resistance, as some of its apologists have indeed claimed.

Moving leftward from this group, one comes to those who believed very fervently in the National Revolution and were prepared to fight for it, but remained patriotic by their own lights. They joined the police forces or the *Milice* and helped enthusiastically in the persecution and rounding-up of Jews, Communists, and other counter-Revolutionaries. Then there were those who supported the régime, but without fanaticism. They might be members of the *Légion Française*, or they might be assiduous bureaucrats, publicists or youth workers, helping to spread the ideas of the Revolution more widely. Then there were those who tolerated, rather than supported, the Revolution, who continued to do their pre-war jobs, who bought a portrait of Pétain out of a sense of obligation and conformity rather than enthusiasm, and who dutifully listened to Pétain's broadcasts, but listened furtively to de Gaulle as well. Finally, there was the huge mass who, whatever their own loyalties and opinions, rallied instinctively to the marshal, the Victor of Verdun, the God-King who interposed his own body between them and the Germans, and would protect them in the future as he had in the past.

It is impossible to say at which point collaboration truly begins or ends; but it is clear that there was a large area in the middle, occupied by those who just wanted to get on with their lives. Equally, it is not clear where resistance began. Since the rest of this chapter is mostly about the varieties of resistance, I shall only note, at this point, that it is a term that could encompass everything from defacing a poster to shooting a soldier in the back, and therefore of restricted general usefulness. What can be said, is that few Frenchmen occupied the extremes. Most of them wished the Germans would go, and were indifferent or cool to the National Revolution of 1940, but identified strongly with Pétain as an individual. What differentiated them from each other was, essentially, their attitude towards the National Revolution. It was perfectly possible for given individuals to be French patriots, to use whatever flexibility their jobs or statuses gave them to oppose the Germans, to be unsympathetic to the National Revolution, and yet to regard Pétain as a great man who had saved France. There is, therefore, no necessary connection between adulation of Pétain and support for his policies, any more than the legitimacy or popularity of a French king was affected by the acts of his ministers. The paradox that Pétain was always much more popular than his régime or his Revolution is only an apparent one.

This is not surprising, when we recall that Pétain immediately started to implement the whole of the counter-Revolutionary agenda since 1789. He, therefore, divided France on traditional lines, and in a way that would have made it very difficult to be uncommitted, even if the traditions of French politics had made uncommitted positions easier. Thus, internally and externally, France was split for four years between those who took their inspiration from the Revolution of 1789, and those who took it from the Revolution of 1940, with only very limited positions available between the two. Moreover, if we use as a criterion the elections of 1932 and 1936, Vichy represented a minority view in any case, since only the parties of the extreme right (typically some 20 per cent of the electorate) offered a programme anything like Vichy's. These elections had been clear victories for the Left, if we mean by that the republican and democratic tendencies. Whilst there were certainly regional variations in support – the countryside being typically less democratic than the town – it would be hard to argue that there was any substantial part of the country where Vichy's ideas had majority support. Even then, the ideology of Vichy was both complex and incoherent, and seldom accepted or rejected as a whole. At the very least, therefore, Vichy began from a position of minority support for its authoritarian and anti-democratic tendencies. This was not necessarily a problem theoretically, since the *volonté populaire* was not seen as a statistical phenomenon; but it was a considerable problem from the standpoint of practical politics. It is no wonder, therefore, that support for the régime was limited, and that the first signs of resistance began hesitantly to appear.

If widespread resistance appeared only slowly, however, it was partly because most of the early signs of Vichy were comforting. The war was over, and some of France was intact. Pétain himself had unchallengeable legitimacy, and had been around since anyone could remember. Weygand was a famous figure; Laval was not widely liked, but he was well known. Together with other, more minor hangovers from the Third Republic, they projected an aura of stability that the general tendency towards administrative continuity helped to endorse. At first, it seemed as if this was only another government of the Right, as after the riots of 1934. And even when the National Revolution was under way, millions of Frenchmen went to great lengths to rationalise their continued support for Pétain by arguing that the marshal was being deceived and manipulated by Laval. The ideological orientation of Vich, and its sense of continuity largely dictated the kind of individuals who would resist, as well as their ideological background. It is common to look at de Gaulle and his followers as representing the 'Right' of the Resistance, and the domestic Resistance as representing the 'Left'. Like all such generalisations, there is some truth in it; but it ignores the fact that what might be called the 'traditional' Right – of Laval and the counter-Revolution – was scarcely represented in the Resistance at all. Practically all of the resistance was from the 'Left', in the French sense of support for democracy, secularism and republicanism. We have seen how de Gaulle was associated with the nascent Christian Democrat movement in the 1930s. This movement also constituted an important strand in the Resistance, and led, in turn, to a major political party of the Fourth Republic, the *Mouvement Républicain Populaire* (MRP).

Those who resisted tended to be without a great stake in the system. They were very often political, social or intellectual rebels, for whom the isolation, danger or even exile involved in resistance was the more acceptable, since they had less to lose in the first place. Sometimes, they were those whom the Revolution itself had evicted or persecuted. They resisted according to their talents and inclinations: military men found action in organised groups in uniform to their taste, and, given the opportunity, they preferred to join the Free French. Intellectuals, on the other hand, naturally took to running clandestine magazines. They shared an orientation, which was expressed in different ways, but which amounted to a stubborn inability to accept defeat and take no for an answer. Laval was right when he said at Pétain's trial in 1945 that no one, five years before, could have predicted how the war would turn out. In the early days, a whole series of lonely decisions to carry on resisting were taken, with faith, perhaps, but essentially without hope. In Sartre's *The Flies*, performed in 1942, Orestes argues that 'human life begins on the far side of despair',[1] and that is where any *résistant* spent much of the war years. The psychological orientation that this state of mind produced had, I shall argue, a considerable influence on post-war French politics.

1. Jean-Paul Sartre, *The Flies*, trans. Stuart Gilbert, in *Altona and Other Plays*, London, Penguin Books, 1962, p. 311.

Resistance; Or, the Man in the Tower

Resistance was largely a creation of Vichy itself. By that, I mean that the National Revolution alienated very large portions of French society, caused them to become politically conscious, and encouraged them first to organise themselves, and then to make contact with each other. Resistance in the North, a natural consequence of the presence of German troops, was largely self-generating. On the other hand, if the régime in the South had been content to introduce a right-wing government along the lines of previous ones, then resistance would have been sporadic and scattered, and probably not much of a problem. By picking a fight, successively, with major portions of French society, and by deliberately and overtly seeking to overturn the republican, secular and democratic traditions that most Frenchmen respected, Vichy managed to create and organise a powerful opposition force. As H. R. Kedward summarises it, Vichy 'by its internal policy alone, caused dissent and created Resistance, steadily in 1940–1 and rapidly in 1942'.[2] Why was this?

At the most basic of levels, people resisted the intrusively well-scrubbed and aggressively healthy image that Vichy sought to create. Young people, children in the 1930s, were unenthused to hear that the main problem with that decade was that it had been too much fun. In Paris, the 'Zazou' movement sprang up among young people. It was one of the first examples of the fascination of the young and left-wing with American popular culture, and featured a taste for (banned) American literature and films, as well as 'Judaeo-Negro' jazz music. Young men went around in narrow trousers with long hair. To the relief of right-thinking people everywhere, the Zazous were progressively rounded up by the police from the autumn of 1942 onwards.[3] At the level of the individual and the small group, it was soon realised that the population had it in its power to withdraw that mundane co-operation with the occupiers that alone enabled the Germans to hold France down. In the North, it might mean giving a German soldier the wrong directions; in the South, deliberately losing the papers of young men being sent to work in German factories.

2. H. R. Kedward, *Resistance in Vichy France: A Study of Ideas and Motivation in the Southern Zone, 1940–1942*, Oxford, Oxford University Press, 1978, p. 90.

3. Jean-Pierre Azéma, *From Munich to the Liberation, 1938–1944*, trans. Janet Lloyd, Cambridge, 1984, p. 94.

Vichy persecuted the PCF with special enthusiasm; but this was only a question of degree. Beyond hostility to the specific parties of the Third Republic – which was widely shared – Vichy was hostile to the very *principle* of political parties in general, and refused to allow them to function. The régime immediately made enemies, therefore, of all who had been members of parties, who had worked for them, or even thought that they were an important part of a real democracy. Most elected local authorities were suppressed also, thus alienating those who had served on them and those who regarded local democracy as important. A sensible Vichy régime would have exploited the ambivalence of the PCF's attitude to the war in 1940, thus neutering in advance the largest and most disciplined opposition it was ever likely to face. But Vichy was not capable of coherent thought on this issue: the PCF remained the concentrated distillation of everything it had hated and feared for decades. So at a time when the (clandestine) party was hesitating, in the autumn of 1940, the Vichy authorities carried out mass arrests, entirely unprompted by the Germans. Even what was described as 'communist propaganda', such as singing the *Internationale*, was punished by a long spell in one of the political concentration camps then being set up. Ironically, the PCF's choice was therefore made for it, and so was its later orientation. Since all Communists were inherently enemies of the 'real France', then they must be allies of other such enemies, of whom the prime example, of course, was de Gaulle. Thus, *Gringoire*, unsurprisingly now an extreme collaborationist organ, could tax the PCF, amongst its other sins, with fostering illusory hopes of de Gaulle.[4]

Vichy then set out, with some deliberation, to persecute and antagonise the whole pantheon of hate figures of the traditional Right: Jews, Freemasons, Socialists, trades unionists, schoolteachers. In doing so, they simply added more large, and often organised, groups to the list of those whom the National Revolution failed to enthuse. This included the Socialists, as instigators of the Popular Front. Deputies were arrested, and Socialists were purged from local councils and *mairies*. Slowly, the party began to re-form, and a group set up the *Comité d'Action Socialiste*. The party newspaper, *Le Populaire*, was re-launched as a clandestine publication. Likewise, the opportunity to reach out to industrial workers and trades unions was squandered. Vichy's proclaimed hostility to capitalism was real enough, since 'the power of money and the

4. Kedward, *Resistance in Vichy*, p. 55.

growth of large cartels … were seen as alien to the workshop tradition in French industry'.[5] But, in practice, any kind of industrial democracy, even better labour relations, was impossible to reconcile with Vichy's authoritarian, hierarchic temper, and the various arrangements, including the Charter of Work, merely served to strengthen the hand of the employers and encourage conflict.

Thus, large sections of society, who might in other circumstances have rallied to the government, or at least tolerated it, found themselves, willy-nilly, its designated enemies. But that does not mean that all members of all of these groups resisted, nor does it mean that other individuals and members of groups did not. Michel Debré, for example, later to be a prominent Gaullist politician, came from a family of the traditional Right, did his military service in a smart cavalry regiment, opposed the Popular Front, and joined the administrative élite of the French state, whilst still being a prominent *résistant*. Analysis of the membership of resistance networks has revealed a complex pattern, but one in which the educated, the professional, and those members of classes specifically persecuted by Vichy appear most often.[6]

There is a brisk controversy, in which I do not intend to become involved, about whether *résistants* were 'misfits', looking for an excuse for action.[7] Clearly, they were always a minority, and they were not a statistical sub-set of the French population as a whole. Whilst they probably represented very nearly the full spectrum of political views in France, they did not, of course, represent them *equally*. This meant that the political parties that the Resistance spawned left very large sections of the French population to one side, with consequent dangers and difficulties in the Fourth Republic.

Some took to resistance work more easily than others. The PCF had long been used to official displeasure and persecution, its organisation was a disciplined and semi-clandestine one anyway, and its members had little more to lose by resistance. At the other extreme, some military men had particular difficulties with the more muscular type of resistance: war in the shadows could involve shooting soldiers in the back, placing bombs in cinemas and railway stations that could kill innocent civilians, or punishment

5. Ibid., p. 106.
6. Jean-Baptiste Duroselle, *Politique Etrangère de la France: L'Abîme, 1939–1944*, Paris, Imprimerie Nationale, 2nd edn, 1986, p. 419, prints an interesting list of the professions represented in one such network.
7. See e.g. Kedward, *Resistance in Vichy*, pp. 75–81.

shootings of collaborators; these tactics were, naturally, anathema to anyone trained at St-Cyr. Thus, the military tended to be happiest with the more organised *maquis* groups that sprang up in the later stages of the war and fought the Germans more openly. For everyone involved, even in non-lethal resistance, there were severe moral scruples. The French and German security forces were not famous for their good manners, and reprisals were routine. Thus,

> in everything he did the resister was endangering other people; the agent who notified the location of an ammunition dump might cause the adjoining village to be bombed ... a bomb placed in a factory might lead to the workers being deported.... What of the specialist who did bad work without always being sure that the enemy would be the recipient of his deliberately defective products?[8]

It was clear also that all the resistance activity, lethal and nonlethal, was not by itself going to liberate the country or bring liberation itself noticeably close. So why engage in this desperate, dangerous and morally dubious work at all? Why dirty your hands and endanger others? Why not practise the favourite Vichy policy of *attentisme* – 'wait-and-see-ism'? There are two principal reasons why.

The first is simple patriotism, which was the first and the most fundamental motivation for all *résistants*. Many Frenchmen of all persuasions were horrified by the defeat and revolted by the practical application of collaboration, even if they personally supported Pétain. Often, this took the form of a rejection of Vichy's vaunted 'realism', of the assumption of Baudouin, Vichy's first foreign minister, that 'The French people must bow before the German victory, which Germany has deserved.' Those who were unenthused by this policy were dismissed as 'hopeless idealists'.[9] For many, this *attentisme* and realism were not acceptable, since they traduced the very image of France that they had accepted since childhood. Michel Debré recounts in his autobiograpy that, as a student in the 1920s and 1930s, he was brought up on the same texts I described in Chapter 1: '[W]e studied history in the *Lavisse*, and geography in *The Tour of France by Two Children*.'[10] The high status and destiny of France and its universal mission were

8. Henri Michel, *The Shadow War: Resistance in Europe, 1939–1945*, trans. Richard Barry, London, André Deutsch, 1972, p. 254.

9. Andrew Shennan, *Rethinking France: Plans for Renewal, 1940–1946*, Oxford, The Clarendon Press, 1989, p. 22.

10. Michel Debré, *Trois Républiques Pour Une France*, Paris, Albin Michel, 1984, p. 74. The first chapter features an extended panegyric of the geographical variety of

clearly in danger. The first step towards resistance was what some Resistance writers have called the 'absurd refusal' – an interesting choice of adjective, to which I will return. It involved 'a refusal to accept what was offered in 1940 against all the apparent force of reason, common-sense and self-interest'.[11] This refusal, went on one of them, 'enabled us to look at a Russian, English or American soldier without blushing … Never have as many men knowingly run as many risks for so little: a desire to bear witness. Perhaps it is stupid, but it is such stupidities which give our human dignity back to us.'[12]

In brief, resistance was what the French had instead of a victory (or at least a more effective defence) in 1940. Those who went into the shadows did so to try to put up, on a symbolic level, the fight they failed to put up earlier. It was a form of compensation, and a form of expiation that would qualify France to take its place in the front rank of nations once more. 'So long' said one clandestine newspaper 'as France has not regained her rank as a great power, so long as she has not collected her empire around her … the national Resistance will have a role to play.' And it was a commonplace to say, at the time, that the Resistance had expressed 'une volonté de grandeur'.[13] This has also been the judgement of some of those involved. Michel Debré, for example, writes that whilst the French did not play a 'determining' role in the war, nonetheless

> that a country which was invaded, enslaved and pillaged, that a population, grieving for a hundred thousand young dead in an immense battle and deprived of two million of its sons kept in captivity, had found the will to resist, that men and women had voluntarily accepted sacrifices to strike heavy blows, that finally, in spite of the internal divisions of an old people, stunned by their misfortune, the nation rallied around the man who had revived its honour: this is what produces grandeur.[14]

This is a very full and very pure presentation of the 'Myth of the Resistance', as it was told during and after the war. Much of it is

---

France and the wonders of its civilisation, comparable with the more famous example in de Gaulle's *War Memoirs*.

11. Kedward, *Resistance in Vichy*, p. 82.

12. Cited by Henri Michel and Boris Mirkine-Gueztévitch, *Les Idées Politiques et Sociales de la Résistance: Documents Clandestins, 1940–1944*, Paris, Presses Universitaires de France, 1954, p. 49. Hereafter *Les Idées*.

13. Shennan, *Rethinking France*, p. 49.

14. Debré, *Trois Républiques*, p. 270.

true, although, as I shall later describe, certain elisions of the truth were found to be necessary.

Many involved in resistance thought it imperative that this grandeur be re-established, and fortunate that they themselves were on hand to accomplish it. As one Resistance organisation dominated by the PCF put it, France

> by its history, by its prestige, by the confidence which the world retains in its thinking, in its creative and revolutionary genius, France meeting point of the great currents of the world, will be tomorrow, in spite of its temporary humiliation, the only nation capable of making proposals to the world, of attempting before it the synthesis of the economic revolution and of liberty, liberation from the power of money and Trusts harmonised with respect for the human being, the foundation of a new revolutionary human-ism, as far away from the disorder of capitalism and from petit-bourgeois egotism as from totalitarian dictatorship.[15]

Dimly present in these rather overwritten manifestos is the thought that liberation – and the revolution which is assumed to accom-pany it – will be an event of comparable importance to 1789, and that the society that the French will then make will be universally acclaimed and influential ever after.

It follows from the above that it was out of the question for the French passively to await their own liberation by others: that was no way to restore grandeur and self-respect. It was essential that the French should play a role in liberating themselves. There was even a like-minded group within Vichy itself that began to make secret preparations to join in against the Germans after a success-ful Anglo-Saxon landing. At least one senior military commander appears to have thought that 'French national grandeur depended upon military participation' in the liberation.[16] Arms were hidden on a substantial scale; but the whole concept was poorly organised by too few people, and the dumps were discovered after the occu-pation of the South in November 1942.

Beyond this general, rather traditional patriotism and a long-ing to restore national pride, there were also strong moral prin-ciples. They were moral rather than political, at least in the pejorative sense of that second term: i.e. they were associated with ethical and moral values rather than the programmes of political parties. As one Algiers-based journal noted scathingly, it would be

15. *Les Idées*, p. 183.
16. Robert O. Paxton, *Parades and Politics at Vichy: The French Officer Corps Under Marshal Pétain*, Princeton, Princeton University Press, 1966, p. 302.

'puerile' to imagine that anyone had died for the Radical Party, although many Radicals had died for France. On the other hand, 'This is a political war. It opposes two conceptions of life. It opposes liberty to slavery, brotherhood to hatred, equality to inequality, justice to injustice. We are among those who affirm: a single aim, liberty and justice, a single means, victory.'[17]

Such a cause attracted those of strong ethical views, irrespective of how they once voted. Once the real character of the National Revolution was revealed, it was not hard to decide, ethically, which side one was on. Many would have been revolted by the policy of collaboration with an evil dictatorship, by the persecution of the Jews and by the progressive stifling of dissent, who yet did not have clearly thought-out political opinions. Resistance was first and foremost a practical activity.

In France, more than anywhere else, there was a pre-existing corpus of values to which the *résistants* could appeal. They were, of course, the values of 1789; they were also the values upon which Vichy had to unmistakably turn its back. The literature of resistance is full of references to the Revolutionary heritage, and the mere scrawling of the words *Liberté, Egalité, Fraternité* on a wall was resistance of a kind. It helped, of course, to have common political myths to fall back on. For virtually all the groups involved, 1789 was a positive symbol: even the Catholics involved had reconciled themselves to the Revolution. Everywhere, republican tradition was emphasised: more than one clandestine newspaper dated its first issue 14 July. In 1942, *Le Père Duchesne*, the 'father of all revolutionary newspapers', which had been started in 1793 and continued in 1848 and 1871, was re-launched.[18] Such continuity of thought and expression provided a clear framework for action and encouraged responses of a certain kind. Revolutionary exaltation helped to overcome divisions in French society. The appeal to the 'Jacobin spirit' usefully encompassed both the defence of a secular, republican ideology and the physical defence of the country against aggression, and so could be held to be very relevant to the circumstances of 1940–44.

It followed that the revolution that would accompany the liberation would be 'a new French Revolution', which would 'take up the thread of 1789'. There would be 'more liberty, more equality, more fraternity', and the world would look on, amazed as before, at the operation of the French genius. But there was one

17. *Les Idées*, p. 114.
18. Kedward, *Resistance in Vichy*, p. 155.

new ingredient: the next revolution would be inclusive rather than exclusive. Thanks to communal suffering, it would unite all patriots and republicans, and would draw on 'the finest traditions of our history'. As a result, it would be a 'revolution of knights and Jacobins'.[19]

It is this aspect of resistance – ideological, perhaps, rather than strictly political – that leads me to support the view that there was, between 1940 and 1944, a French civil war, fought on ideological lines. This view is controversial: John Sweets, for example, argues that there was no serious Franco-French fighting at the Liberation, because 'there was virtually no one around to fight for Vichy's New Order'.[20] This is perfectly true (although only a total fanatic would have tried to take on an American armoured division), but does not, I think, obscure the equally valid point that there was an explicitly ideological cast to the earlier fighting, as was freely acknowledged by both sides. It would not be the last time that massive intervention by an outside power brought an end to a civil war with little further fighting. For Vichy, there was an internal 'struggle against communism'; this term being, as usual, generously glossed to include anyone sympathetic to the ideals of 1789, or indeed unsympathetic to those of 1940. We have already seen the scope of repressive activity against the PCF from the morning of the defeat. Laval had described the first duty of the reorganised gendarmerie in 1942 as 'the desperate struggle against communism'.[21] When the *Milice* was formally constituted in 1943, its tasks were 'the maintenance of order, guarding territorial key points, the struggle against communism'.[22] Its founder, Darnand, explained in his general regulations that this meant that the *Milice*'s first duty was 'to save France from Bolshevism'.[23] The *Milice* thus spent the greater part of its inglorious existence hunting down 'Communist terrorists', without unnecessary displays of good manners.

The fear of the consequences of 'terrorist activity' was linked in the mind of Vichy with the consequences of the defeat of Germany and the consequent triumph of Bolshevism. In one of his last broadcasts, not long before D-Day, Pétain claimed that Bolshevism

19. *Les Idées*, pp. 149–51.

20. John Sweets, *Choices in Vichy France: The French under Nazi Occupation*, Oxford, Oxford University Press, 1986, p. 84.

21. Ibid., p. 108.

22. Pascal Ory, *Les Collaborateurs, 1940–1945*, Paris, Seuil, 1976, p. 250.

23. Sweets, *Choices*, p. 108.

was 'already present on French soil' and busy committing atrocities. Anyone who joined a resistance group 'compromised the future of the country'. Only by a 'correct' attitude to the Germans could France be saved, as a result of 'the defence of the continent by Germany' against Bolshevism, otherwise triumphant.[24] Millions of Frenchmen shared these views and had probably always done so, even if few were ready to stand in front of a Sherman tank to defend them. The existence or otherwise of a scrappy, undeclared civil war between 1940 and 1944 is an important question, because wars generally have two sides and one loser. If the population of France had uniformly detested the National Revolution and rallied to de Gaulle and the Resistance with fervour, then there would, in effect, have been few if any losers in 1944. But the evidence tends the other way, and the forces that were vanquished at the Liberation did not entirely disappear: they returned to haunt the Fourth Republic.

These were the ideas, experiences and orientations that led people to resist. As the years passed, there were several important developments. The forces of resistance grew in size, became largely united and began to think seriously about France after the war. I now want to discuss each of these elements briefly.

It was Vichy, again, that provided the motive force for the expansion of the Resistance. Previous attempts to get enough volunteers to work in German factories had failed, and the Reich needed more manpower: the *Service du Travail Obligatoire* (STO), which involved two years compulsory work in German factories, was introduced in February 1943.[25] By this stage, Vichy was only a shadow, implementing the decisions of the occupier. But the law was passed by Vichy itself, with the justification, apparently, that sovereignty demanded that one commit evil in one's own territory, rather than allowing a foreign power to do it. The result was an explosion of Resistance membership, as young men decided that life with the *maquis* was more attractive than service in German factories.

Unity was not something that came easily to the Resistance: it was brought about through the work of one remarkable man, at the instigation of another. Jean Moulin was a young, left-wing prefect, who was purged for refusing to rally to Vichy. De Gaulle, needing someone to organise and unite the scattered resistance

24. Philippe Pétain, *Discours aux Français: 17 Juin 1940–20 Aout 1944*, ed. Jean-Claude Barbas, Paris, Albin Michel, 1989, pp. 324–6.
25. Dominique Rémy, *Les Lois de Vichy*, 2nd edn, Paris, Romillat, 1992, pp. 221–5.

organisations, asked Moulin to carry out the task. The latter accepted, realising, in all probability, that he was unlikely to return.
In January 1941, with the significant code name 'Rex', Moulin was
parachuted back into France to organise in the Southern Zone
'united action by all those elements who are resisting the enemy
and his collaborators'.[26] Moulin succeeded better than expected,
uniting the Southern movements and persuading the Northern
ones to co-operate more closely. He founded, and was first chairman of, the *Conseil National de la Résistance* (CNR) in 1943. It included representatives of all eight major resistance movements,
both the trades union federations, and six political parties, including the PCF.[27] All of these institutions, without exception, rallied to
de Gaulle.[28] Almost immediately afterwards, however, Moulin was
betrayed (under circumstances still unclear), arrested and tortured
to death by the Gestapo.

His legacy was an organised and coherent resistance, which
now, with liberation approaching, began to think seriously about
the future. The CNR began a programme of studies into what kind
of a France there should be after liberation had taken place,
notably through an occasional theoretical journal, *Cahiers Politiques*, to which first Marc Bloch and then Michel Debré contributed. At considerable risk, and in great secrecy, an intense debate
took place between resistance organisations, with drafts and comments passed clandestinely around the nation. These debates culminated in the CNR's March 1944 *Programme*, a lengthy document
whose main themes will by now not be a surprise. The first objective of the Resistance was, after liberation, a provisional government under de Gaulle 'to defend the political and economic
independence of the nation, [and to] re-establish France in her
power, in her grandeur and in her universal mission'. This was to
be followed by the punishment and purge of traitors and by various social and economic reforms.[29]

There were various contingent debates on how these aims were
to be best accomplished. The most important of these debates was
about the future political structure, since it was widely seen that
'reform of the state [was] the prerequisite for all other reforms'.[30]
There was, of course, an existing tradition of hostile analysis of the

26. Jean Lacouture, *De Gaulle*, Vol. 1, *Le Rebelle, 1890–1944*, Paris, Seuil, 1984, p. 582.
27. Michel, *Shadow War*, p. 306.
28. See *Les Idées*, pp. 123–8.
29. Extracts are printed in *Les Idées*, pp. 215–8.
30. Shennan, *Rethinking France*, p. 121.

Third Republic, which antedated the defeat of 1940, and its main criticisms formed the point of departure. There was general agreement on the need for a new structure, with a stronger executive that yet enabled individual liberty to be safeguarded. As the *Programme* put it, what was needed was 'a democracy which reconciles effective scrutiny by the elected representatives of the people, with the continuity of government action'.[31] But there was little idea of how this might work in practice, except for one negative element: there was little support for the idea of a directly elected president.

These new structures would not be confined to metropolitan France. All political parties without exception assumed that the empire would continue, and that independence was not an issue. Even the PCF shared the wide consensus that the empire 'required political, economic, and social reform, but above all it demanded to remain attached to France'.[32] Algeria, of course, was part of France and would remain so. In international affairs, there was a general feeling, as in Vichy, that war had reached the end of its usefulness as an instrument of policy, and that some kind of reconciliation with Germany was necessary. What was different was the assumption made about who would win. As *Le Populaire* put it in 1943, 'one does not extinguish hatred by hatred or violence by violence.... The abuse of force creates the desire for revenge'. The only way to resolve the problem of Germany was her 'incorporation into the international community'.[33] This was an aspect of a wider (though not universal) tendency in resistance circles to look for genuinely effective international security organisations after the war, a feeling that Versailles had been a ghastly mistake, and that some kind of 'European Federation' was now required.

Finally, much thought was given to economic and social questions. It has recently been argued that the 'keystone' of the resistance's 'economic and social philosophy was socialism'.[34] As the author notes, the sources of this socialism were diverse, and it would be wrong to assume too much doctrinal influence in an environment where practical experience counted for much more. If anything, 'resistance socialism' probably arose out of adverse judgements on its predecessor, unfettered market capitalism. This

31. *Les Idées*, p. 218.
32. Shennan, *Rethinking France*, p. 164.
33. *Les Idées*, p. 381.
34. Shennan, *Rethinking France*, p. 34.

latter was almost universally held to have failed France in the 1930s, not only in promoting unemployment and human misery, but also in not providing the industrial muscle with which to fight a war. As we have seen, moves to plan the economy more rationally and to overcome class conflict had begun in the very different political atmosphere of Vichy. Many who thought of themselves as socialists were, in effect, little more than supporters of modern economic and social ideas, and in many cases they looked to the United States and the Roosevelt New Deal for inspiration, rather than to anything else that might overtly label itself 'socialism'. And it was clear to everyone that economic rebirth was a basic requirement for the restoration of grandeur. Antiquated and ineffective economic theories could not, therefore, be tolerated any longer. Finally, the whole tradition of the superiority of the general over the particular interest played a role: unfettered market economics had not, it was argued, served the general interest. Such initiatives as nationalisation and the setting up of national plans flowed naturally from these orientations.

I shall be tracing the fortunes of some of these individuals and ideas in later chapters. But I would like, finally in this section, to suggest one way of looking at the inheritance of the Resistance, and its influence on certain aspects of French policy after the war.

I suggested earlier that no one joined a resistance organisation as a career move, but rather as an act of moral choice; with faith perhaps, but without hope. One way of illustrating this frame of mind, and its later consequences, is through a brief digression into existentialism. This is not, I should stress, an attempt to show that existentialism was responsible for the Resistance or even determined its shape. Rather, the relationship is almost the inverse: existentialism is quite a good way of understanding the spirit of the Resistance, in that it was popularised by some who took part in it, and was popular among those who wished to continue its traditions. I am not, of course, dealing with the academic works of Heidegger and Merleau-Ponty, nor with Sartre's *magnum opus*, *Being and Nothingness* (1942), which is a technical book of daunting complexity and really accessible only to experts. Rather, I am concerned with the popular image of existentialism, as it appears in the literary work of Sartre and others, and in popularisations, since these are what people as a whole knew. This is important, because existentialism is, so far as I know, unique in being a philosophy of action, not of contemplation. It had a long tradition, and Sartre had first treated it in his novel *Nausea* (1936). But it was the war that gave the philosophy life. Simone de Beauvoir recalls that, by 1940, Sartre

> had firmly made up his mind to hold aloof from politics no longer. His new morality was called 'genuineness', and he was determined to make a practical application of it to himself. It required every man to shoulder the responsibility of his situation in life; and the only way in which he could do so was to transcend that situation by engaging upon some course of action.[35]

This is what might be called popular existentialism in embryo. Sartre filled in some of the detail in a public lecture that he gave in 1945. Existentialism was so called, he said, because existence preceded essence, i.e. it was up to human beings to create their own essence. We define ourselves only through our actions, and, in acting, we make a general statement about the world and about our view of mankind. We are responsible for what we do and for the choices we make: human nature and the circumstances in which we find ourselves are not excuses. But we cannot avoid choosing, and are free to choose as we will, whether we realise it or not.[36]

This was intoxicating stuff, and clearly reflected elements of the mood of resistance. One of the most common images in resistance writing is that of a prison, whose furthest boundaries the *résistant* sets himself to explore.[37] Sartre's philosophy reflects the realisation that there is always *something* a free individual can do, provided the freedom is recognised. It might be profound; it is much more likely to be trivial, such as scrawling a slogan on a wall, or, as in Sartre's case, acting as an underground journalist.

In *The Flies* (1942), Sartre portrays a profound act of free choice. Orestes returns to Argos to kill Aegisthus, and lifts the curse of guilt and fear that has hung over the town since Agammemnon's own murder. It is a deed any of the people could have done; but only Orestes realised he was free to do it. In the process he greatly discomfits Zeus, promoter of fear and guilt, and a figure with obvious Vichy references.

There is a scene in *Death in the Soul* (1949) that is like a small morality play of resistance. Matthieu Delarue, Sartre's *alter ego*,

---

35. Simone de Beauvoir, *The Prime of Life*, trans. Peter Green, London, André Deutsch, 1962, Penguin edn, 1965, p. 429.

36. Jean-Paul Sartre, *Existentialisme est un Humanisme*, Paris, Nagel, 1946.

37. Cf. Sartre's *The Flies*:

> Zeus: If *you* can brag of freedom, why not praise the freedom of a prisoner languishing in fetters, or a slave nailed to a cross.
> Orestes: Certainly, why not?

who spent the first two volumes of *Roads to Freedom* drifting without commitment, and is now part of a defeated army, decides of his own volition to join a group of Chasseurs in the (apparently pointless) defence of a village tower, long after the fighting is supposed to be over. Although he is aware that the village will probably be destroyed, that he himself will probably die, and that nothing will be accomplished thereby, he is determined to make a stand of some sort, reflecting as he does so that it is his decision alone to make a commitment without hope. What distinguishes Matthieu's sacrifice from that of the Chasseurs is that, as one of them tells him 'If you belong to the Chasseurs, you fight.' They do not choose to fight, as Matthieu does; they merely follow orders. They do not realise that the possibility of freedom of choice even exists.

I mentioned earlier the concept of resistance as an 'absurd refusal' to give way to the realities of 1940. This is Matthieu's attitude, but the vocabulary also recalls the work, and the life, of Albert Camus (1913–60), himself a *résistant* and philosopher of the absurd. In *The Myth of Sisyphus* (1942), the absurd is described as the condition in which we find ourselves, and to which a number of responses, including suicide, might be appropriate. But clearly it was the Occupation itself that prompted some of these reflections, and the image of Sisyphus, forever pushing his rock uphill, is also an image of resistance. Sisyphus is an 'absurd hero', as Camus indicates, but he also symbolises the spirit of resistance: dedication, suffering and courage, without hope. As Camus said in a post-war introduction to the essay, he had tried, writing in 1940, 'amidst the French and European disaster', to show 'that even within the limits of nihilism it is possible to find the means to proceed beyond nihilism'.[38] This is clearer in Camus's greatest work, *The Plague* (1947), an explicit allegory of the Occupation under the guise of a realistic novel depicting an outbreak of plague in Oran in the 1940s. For various reasons, a small group get together to try to fight the plague. They have no idea why it has come, and no real hope that they can defeat it. Some die, and, when the plague eventually goes, the survivors cannot be sure that they have had any influence at all on its passing. But all of them lent a hand because, in various ways, they felt that there was nothing else they could do.

These texts, to repeat, reflect a mood rather than outline a philosophy. Their effect was close to that produced by the Gaullist

38. Albert Camus, *The Myth of Sisyphus*, trans. Justin O'Brien, London, Hamish Hamilton, 1955, Penguin edn 1975, p. 7.

experience, and the two eventually combined. The mood produced by these experiences was one of optimism for the future, but also one that was attracted to the politics of gesture, a belligerent emphasis on independence of judgement, and a sense of self-reliance and self-validation.

De Gaulle; Or, the Constable of France

From the time when temporary Brigadier-General Charles de Gaulle arrived in London, in June 1940, his analysis of the situation, his preoccupations, and his objectives were basically similar to those I have described earlier: he shared some ideas with Vichy and the Resistance, some with the latter alone. I shall therefore concentrate here on those elements that were special to de Gaulle: those which arose from his own experiences and personality, and those which resulted from his operating outside, rather than inside, France.

De Gaulle shared the common view that the eclipse of France was only temporary, and that, after an interval, she should and would be restored to her former grandeur. Unlike Pétain, he did not see this best accomplished by repentance and the expiation of sins. Rather, he agreed with the Resistance that it had to be through playing a practical part in the war. Yet de Gaulle had almost no practical means available to him to do this. De Gaulle's thesis was that France had never surrendered, because the government that had signed the Armistice was illegitimate. He, de Gaulle, represented the continuity of the French state. As I have indicated, this was a doubtful proposition constitutionally, and an almost impossible one politically. Nevertheless, it was the only position he could take, because it, alone, implied that, if Germany were defeated, the French forces that took part would represent a state that had been at war continuously since 1939, and was thus entitled to a seat at the top table. Anything less would reduce France to the status of a country conquered, and subsequently liberated, by outside forces. None of the parties between 1940 and 1944 would have been prepared to go along with that interpretation.

De Gaulle's position in the summer of 1940 was not a strong one, and he was conscious of this. For a middle-ranking army officer and very junior minister to put himself forward as an alternative pole of attraction to a French state presided over by an acknowledged warrior God-King, supported by the massed phalanxes of the armed forces, the church and the bureaucracy, and enjoying overwhelming public support, was a bizarre act indeed. It was quite possible that the country in which he had taken refuge would soon be conquered, and it seemed out of the question that the country he had left would ever be liberated. De Gaulle thus made an 'absurd refusal' of his own – to face the facts as everyone else saw them – and began, with faith, perhaps, but without hope, to take advantage of the freedom he had, to do what he could. Even some of his first colleagues could not shake off a feeling of unreality. René Cassin, charged by de Gaulle with negotiating the first agreement with the British, recalled that he had said, ironically, 'We are the French Army.' De Gaulle corrected him: 'We are France.' Cassin recalls thinking: '[I]f Hitler were looking through the key-hole at this unkempt Professor of Law and this temporary General claiming: We are France, he would surely think that we were ready for the padded cell.'[39]

De Gaulle's task was to impersonate a state and a government, and to do so with few resources, little money and an attitude of wariness on the part of his host government. He also had to guard against the charge from Vichy that he was only a creature of the ancient enemy, and this, in turn, forced him to take publicly independent positions that were perhaps more extreme than he would have wished. By sheer will power, he kept alive the idea of an independent, sovereign and autonomous France, in spite of the facts, and eventually secured a seat at the table when the war was concluded. He did this in the midst of an alien culture that he did not really understand, in a language he spoke poorly, and in the teeth of constant Anglo-Saxon attempts to replace him with someone more malleable. It was an astonishing performance, which perhaps only de Gaulle could have carried through; and it left indelible marks on him, his associates and his victims.

Some of the reasons for this refusal to face facts can be traced to his background and education. As we have seen, there was, on all sides, an inability to accept defeat, a wholly irrational idea that French grandeur would be restored before too long. The differences were about methods, not objectives. They were all products of the same education system, of Lavisse and Michelet, of the eternal civilising mission and the perception of France as a special nation. For all of them, the subjugation of France was a blasphemy against the natural order of things, and cried out to be corrected at

39. Cited by Duroselle, *Politique Etrangère*, p. 395.

the earliest opportunity. In the meantime, the dignity, independence, and sovereignty of France had, naturally, to be upheld. This much was common. What de Gaulle added was an ego of impressive proportions, a rock-like faith in the rightness of his own judgement, and the confidence to follow conclusions to the end. He seems never to have found the time to develop a sense of his own fallibility. This, of course, is what one would expect from the author of *Towards a Professional Army*, who had been in conflict with his nominal superiors for several decades. Oddly, the reaction of those superiors to that controversy was not to defenestrate the rebel, but to promote him – and to the command of an armoured regiment, at that. Thus, after learning the reality, as opposed to the theory, of armoured warfare, he found himself commanding the 507th armoured regiment, 80 tanks and 2,000 men, based at Metz.[40]

Command did not make him more amenable to discipline. Worried that the lessons of Poland were not being adequately implemented, he sent, in January 1940, a duplicated manifesto to some eighty civilian and military personalities, arguing that the government's policy was wrong, and proposing another. It was something of a trial run for the speech of 18 June, after the defeat. As Jean Lacouture notes:

> Here, in effect, was an officer, commanding important forces in the front-line, and who, in the middle of a war, gets mixed up in denouncing the conduct of the war by Headquarters, and openly advocating another, not simply by addressing the military leaders, but dozens of parliamentarians also, especially Socialists. It is too weak to describe this as an act of indiscipline, one must almost speak of rebellion.[41]

He was promoted again, on 7 May, this time to be commander of the 4th Armoured Division, a new formation still working up. Gaullist mythology has tended to make much of the limited success this unit enjoyed in combat: more important for our purposes, however, is the style in which he commanded it. It was de Gaulle's first chance to be a real *chef* and to practice some of his theories of leadership. The results might have been predicted. According to one subordinate, de Gaulle

> exercised a command which was independent, exclusive, authoritarian and egocentric, based on the conviction that, in any situation,

40. Lacouture, *De Gaulle*, pp. 260–1.
41. Ibid., p. 301.

> his judgement was the most, if not the only, legitimate one, which
> led him to doubt intelligence which was precise, but did not con-
> form to his own ideas about the enemy. All decisions came from
> him alone. He would take no advice, and still any less direct sug-
> gestion ...[42]

He would never have tolerated for a second in others the freedom of expression that he demanded for himself. He demanded
this freedom not because it was appropriate for all officers, but
because he was right, and special rules applied to him. It is of
interest, perhaps, that none of de Gaulle's subordinates followed
him to England.

Within a month, however, de Gaulle was out of uniform and in
politics. Pétain had managed to have Daladier sacked as defence
minister, and his demise opened the way for Reynaud to send for
de Gaulle. It was thus that de Gaulle shuttled between France and
England, until, on 17 June, he decided not to go back. Again, Vichy
had constructed its own nemesis. If Pétain had not harboured an
unreasoning hatred of Daladier, because of the Popular Front,
then the latter's continued presence in government would have
prevented Reynaud sending for de Gaulle, who would, most
probably, have been captured and imprisoned again. One can only
speculate how different some aspects of modern history might
then have been.

De Gaulle's own background was perhaps his worst enemy.
Not only was he an outsider, he had also set an astonishing example of disloyalty – some would say treason – by rejecting what his
brother officers saw as the legitimate government, and by calling
for armed resistance against it. His thesis, that he alone represented legitimate France, required him to maintain that hundreds
of thousands of military men, diplomats, civil servants and others
were themselves traitors. This was a necessary position, but one that
scarcely endeared him to his former colleagues: even before Mers-
el-Kébir recruitment from the uniformed was desperately slow, and
afterwards it slowed to almost nothing. Even as the Free French
cause prospered, and the Allies began to win, many French prisoners preferred to go back to Vichy rather than rally to de Gaulle.

De Gaulle's politics were also misunderstood. His profession,
his mania for discipline (if not self-discipline), his demands for
unquestioning loyalty, all served to reinforce the idea that here
was a Maurrassian, a figure of the traditional Right, an extremist

42. Ibid., p. 318.

and an anti-democrat. It will already be clear that this portrait is substantially unfair, even if some of those who rallied to de Gaulle in the early days might have had such sympathies. De Gaulle's insistence that he alone represented France, and his demand for loyalty to that nation, implied, of course, loyalty to him personally as well: he was the state. But, to be fair, de Gaulle was conscious of his lack of status, and, certainly at the beginning, would have given way to a more prestigious figure. But the massed ranks of Vichy remained unbroken, and the Constable of France (as he began to call himself, after du Guesclin, companion of Joan of Arc) took on the role himself.

It was in de Gaulle's nature to demand unconditional obedience, of course; but it is also true that he clearly saw that France would, if unchecked, slide rapidly into civil war and destruction. So grave was the situation that it was essential to avoid separate groups of armed Frenchmen confronting each other, at home or abroad. And if de Gaulle represented the state, then all other parts of the resistance must necessarily be subordinate to him.

De Gaulle's own thinking on the future of France was essentially within the parameters defined by the various resistance elements described above, except for his insistence, for understandable reasons, in a strong executive head of state. That aside, his views would have fitted reasonably comfortably into the ethos of the Catholic resistance organisations. Although there was a brisk exchange of ideas between the Free French and the CNR, there was no detailed 'Gaullist' or 'Free French' ideology as such – the movement was too varied. There was, of course, a general commitment to the agenda of 1789 rather than that of 1940, and a general orientation towards political, social and economic reform. In late 1943, de Gaulle's commissioner for national education, René Capitant, summed up 'Gaullist' thinking:

> the liberation of France will have to be accompanied by the renewal of her institutions. Profound transformations will have to be accomplished in the political order, the economic order, the social order. It is an illusion to believe that liberation can lead purely and simply to a return to the way things were before the war.[43]

These ideas, though important for the future of France, were not regarded by the Allies as controversial, or even especially interesting. It was the political relationship with Churchill and Roosevelt that was the nub of the problem, and which I turn to

43. Cited by Shennan, *Rethinking France*, pp. 67–68.

now. With the benefit of hindsight, it is clear that de Gaulle's importance in modern French history has been profound: that was not anticipated in 1940. London at that time was host to various exile governments; all of them combined were much less trouble than de Gaulle, who was not seen, at the beginning, as a particularly impressive or influential figure. Sir John Colville, then a young and impressionable diplomat, who recorded what he heard around him at 10 Downing Street, noted that de Gaulle's 18 June broadcast had 'preached sedition – an action which I later heard was resented by many Frenchmen'. He 'does not appear to have enough prestige to rally the more determined Frenchmen to himself, and it is a thousand pities that nothing is being done ... to form a really strong Imperial French Government, which could disavow Bordeaux and win the allegiance of military, naval and civil authorities in the French Empire'.[44]

The urge to replace de Gaulle with such a government, headed by someone like Herriot, never really went away, and it was the foundation of numerous attempts to unseat de Gaulle over the next few years. Part of the problem was personal. Bureaucracies and politicians have little leisure to make a detailed analysis of each new foreign leader, and the temptation is to place them into one of a number of pre-existing categories: moderate/hardliner/ radical/conservative/extremist/pro-British/anti-Western/strongman/figurehead and so forth. The difficulty for the British, and later the Americans, lay in understanding what de Gaulle actually was, and thus how to deal with him. Partly, the difficulties were historical and cultural, but partly also they were personality related. What was known of de Gaulle – military background, dictatorial manner, ardent patriotism – made him seem like a crypto-fascist: hardly a suitable French leader.

De Gaulle's abrasive personal style and insistence on being treated as a sovereign power caused great complications for bureaucracies for whom France was only one of a number of problems. De Gaulle, with his background and education, could only share the traditional French fear of 'English' designs on their empire, and the fact that he was not consulted about operations in Mers-el-Kébir, Madagascar or Syria did nothing to assuage it. His reactions to these operations were much more moderate than those of Vichy, but mutual suspicions were still reinforced. De Gaulle's relations with the British were much easier than with the

44. John Colville, *The Fringes of Power: Downing Street Diaries, 1939–1955*, London, Hodder and Stoughton, 1985, pp. 169–70.

Americans, however. He was by upbringing a traditional European; he spoke German better than English; he had never visited the United States. Since he had spent the last few years of the previous war in a prison camp, he had no experience of the US army, and only secondhand reports of their contribution to ending the war. Can one then say that he was anti-American?

Before rushing to defend de Gaulle from this charge, one might reflect on why such a defence is necessary, when defence against charges of anti-Italianism or anti-Brazilianism would not, perhaps, be rebutted as urgently. Anti-Americanism is nowhere defined, but if it means a gut dislike of American politics, society, and culture, then de Gaulle can, with confidence, be pronounced not guilty. Like many men of progressive opinions at the time, he was, if anything, rather favourable: he saw in America desirable features of modernism, individual freedom, a working political system and an activist government. By contrast, Vichy tended to identify America with the worst aspects of progress, democracy, individualism and modern popular music. It is true, on the other hand, that de Gaulle sometimes perceived the Americans to be doing things that were wrong, or misguided, or things that threatened what he saw as French interests, and he spoke or acted accordingly. But presumably this is in any case a right – or even a duty – of any national leader in such a situation.

However this may be, De Gaulle was distrusted by Washington from the beginning. Washington, like many other nations, retained an embassy at Vichy. This was not unreasonable: the war could go either way, and it would be foolish not to maintain contacts with a régime that appeared to have the active support of most of the French people. Moreover, Washington soon fancied that 'it possessed a measure of influence at Vichy, and that the differences between Pétain and Laval were real and profound, ripe for American exploitation'. Laval's dismissal in December 1940 was seen as a total defeat for collaboration.[45] In January 1941, Admiral Leahy, another personal friend of Roosevelt, was appointed ambassador to Vichy. He cultivated good relations with Pétain, and, in spite of eventual disenchantment with the régime as a whole, came to share the latter's view of de Gaulle, whose movement, he wrote to Roosevelt in July, did not have 'the following or the strength that is indicated in the British radio news and the American press'. The 'radical de Gaullists' he had met did

---

45. Julian G. Hurstfield, *America and the French Nation, 1939–1945*, London, University of North Carolina Press, 1987, p. 17.

not have 'the stability, intelligence and popular standing in their communities that should be necessary to success in their announced purpose', and were engaged in unsavoury acts of terrorism.[46] When Leahy was recalled in April 1942, he brought back to Roosevelt only 'continued trust in Pétain, [and] hostility to de Gaulle'.[47]

There was little support for de Gaulle from official Washington either. In December 1941, Under-Secretary of State Welles told the British ambassador that he could see 'no outstanding men with qualities of leadership and initiative' among the Free French. Someone like Herriot might unite the French, but not de Gaulle and his associates.[48] By the following May, Welles had decided that 'The Free French movement as represented by de Gaulle and his associates was rapidly falling to pieces.'[49] And in spite of further British lobbying, he told the ambassador later the same month that, whilst some Frenchmen certainly supported de Gaulle, 'other equally important, if not more important elements of resistance were totally opposed' to him.[50] Similar views were held throughout the State Department. Atherton, chief of the European Division, wrote to Welles of his fear that de Gaulle would 'blindly attempt to force himself and his Committee on the French people, by foreign arms'.[51] The judgement that de Gaulle's popularity was restricted, combined with fears about his political views and a series of highly unsuccessful meetings with Roosevelt, completed the process of disenchantment. But at least Roosevelt and Churchill could comfort themselves that de Gaulle would soon be out of the way, and more moderate individuals would take over. Roosevelt amused himself by wondering what job de Gaulle might then be offered: perhaps governor of Madagascar?[52]

Finally, of course, there was the Communist threat. Hull, the secretary of state, wrote worriedly to Roosevelt that, as a ploy to gain control of the French National Committee (set up in Algiers after the liberation of the country) de Gaulle 'has permitted to come under his umbrella all the most radical elements in France',

46. Cited ibid., p. 77.

47. Ibid., p. 81.

48. *Foreign Relations of the United States*, Washington, US Government Printing Office, 1941, Vol. 2, p. 205. Henceforth *FRUS*.

49. Ibid., p. 512.

50. Ibid., p. 522.

51. Ibid., p. 544.

52. Ibid., 1943, Vol. 2, p. 112.

including the Communists.[53] Fears of a Communist rising after the Liberation haunted Washington for some time, and there was a desperate search for someone who would genuinely unite the nation: Leahy suggested that Pétain should be asked to stay on, to rally the nation.[54] Many believed that de Gaulle was a dupe of the Communists, or even in league with them, and certainly some of his reported remarks on the need for social and economic change seemed dangerously radical. William Bullitt, for example, wrote to Roosevelt that 'Stalin's present policy is to set up a de Gaulle government based on certain elements of the Right and the Communists; to crush the democratic elements between them; and eventually to have the French communists dominate de Gaulle'.[55]

This confusion, shared to a lesser extent in London, made rational analysis of the French situation very difficult. Cultural and historical differences, dissimilar objectives and priorities, genuine ignorance, uncertainty whether de Gaulle was a Communist dupe or an incipient fascist, or both – all these combined to produce a policy that might have been explicitly tailored to feed Gaullist paranoia. They also placed strains on the relationship between London and Washington. The British usually took a relatively moderate line with de Gaulle; the US, under Roosevelt's direction, a much harder one. After varying degrees of resistance, Churchill would usually give way, pleading the overriding need to protect the burgeoning 'special relationship'. As usual in such a situation, the British attracted blame from both sides.

For example, at the time of the North African landings in 1942, it was decided that the French should not be involved. This was probably sensible, in that it avoided the risk of Frenchmen shooting at each other; but it is difficult to understand Roosevelt's accompanying insistence that de Gaulle should not even be told of the landings until after they had happened. The British government generally agreed: the Foreign Office thought that Roosevelt was being 'silly', but did not press the point.[56] The two countries went to great lengths to try to stop de Gaulle taking over in Algiers. Roosevelt and Churchill quite openly backed Admiral Darlan, who happened to be in Algiers at the time, and adroitly

53. Ibid., p. 113.

54. Lacouture, *De Gaulle*, p. 749.

55. Orville H. Bullitt, ed., *For the President, Personal and Secret: Correspondence between Franklin D. Roosevelt and William C. Bullitt*, London, André Deutsch, 1973, p. 581.

56. R. T. Thomas, *Britain and Vichy: The Dilemma of Anglo-French Relations, 1940–42*, London, Macmillan, 1979, p. 141.

switched sides. To keep de Gaulle out, the Americans were prepared to see the Vichy régime continue in North Africa: Vichy
laws remained in force, and the police continued to round up *résistants*. Unsuccessful Vichy politicians began to arrive in Algiers,
hoping for better things. British complaints proved to be ineffectual, and all the resistance forces were horrified.[57] Fortunately, the
situation was resolved by Darlan's assassination on Christmas
Eve. The Anglo-Saxon mantle then descended upon General
Henri Giraud, an escaped war hero of no general appeal whatever,
but with the advantages of being malleable and not being de
Gaulle. Giraud, whose views, as far as he had any, were indistinguishable from Pétain's, existed in an uneasy duumvirate with de
Gaulle, under the French National Committee, until de Gaulle
(whose political skills had improved substantially) managed to
ease him out.

Subsequently, the two leaders also tried, without success, to
frustrate de Gaulle's attempts to set up a provisional government
after the Liberation. Uniquely, France was to be treated not as a
liberated nation, but as a former adversary, to be occupied and run
by an Allied military government. Against British protests, teams
of Americans were intensively trained in democratic techniques so
that they could teach them to the French, as their colleagues were
doing in Germany and Italy. In the event, the Gaullists and the
Resistance were one step ahead. Michel Debré and others had
appointed a shadow administration that took power from the
retreating Germans before the Americans and British arrived. This
was fortunate: an attempt to impose any other leader on the French
(if one could have been found) would probably have started a
civil war. There were a very large number of men with guns in
France, and de Gaulle was the only leader to whom they were all
prepared to rally.

This was not the perception in London and Washington, however. The British were worried about a Communist attempt to seize
power after the Liberation, and thought that a 'strong provisional
authority was necessary' to prevent it.[58] It was believed that de
Gaulle and his colleagues were, in Churchill's phrase 'small ambitious intriguers',[59] and, at first at least, the British did not believe
that they could be trusted with this task. Reluctantly, however, the

57. Ibid., 154–6.
58. Sir Llewellyn Woodward, *British Foreign Policy in the Second World War*, Vol. 3,
London, HMSO, 1971, p. 9.
59. Ibid., p. 3.

British, led by the Foreign Office and with Churchill only half-convinced, decided that de Gaulle's National Committee was the only body with any real support. But the Americans still refused to accept the validity of a body headed by what one official called 'this French Adolf',[60] and resisted British pressure to recognise the Committee (which now styled itself a provisional government) until 23 October, when they did so unilaterally, and without informing London.[61]

The British had great difficulty in understanding the American attitude, and the Foreign Office speculated, with some evidence, that Roosevelt was prepared to maintain the Vichy régime in power in France, as he had in North Africa. Rumours of secret contacts between Roosevelt and Vichy were rife in later 1943, and were regarded in London as credible. Roosevelt's motives are obscure, but he and his advisers did not necessarily share the Vichy fantasy of a negotiated settlement in the West leading to a co-ordinated assault on Communism.[62] More probably, it was a mixture of dislike for de Gaulle and a hope that some kind of negotiated surrender would be quicker and cheaper than war to the end. Moreover, Roosevelt appears to have had some kind of a motive for wanting to shut de Gaulle out: as the British understood it, at least, American objectives for France were to reduce it from the status of a great power and to impose various indignities, such as forcible disarmament, the creation of a Flemish buffer-state on her territory and the loss of much of her empire. Clearly, a more malleable leader than de Gaulle was required. The British view of France's future was very different, of course, but their protests were ignored.[63] In the circumstances, it is not surprising that the British were unable to persuade Roosevelt that France ought to be represented at Yalta.[64] This British failure and American refusal were to sow the seeds of what Alfred Grosser has called the 'most durable, most firmly established, most widely shared [myth] of French political life', that of 'a sort of Russo-American agreement to establish a kind of domination, at once co-operative and competitive, in Europe or in other continents'.[65]

These episodes – of which de Gaulle was quite well aware – had all sorts of unforeseen and negative consequences. One of the

60. Hurstfield, *America and the French*, p. 194.
61. Woodward, *British Foreign Policy*, p. 77.
62. Ibid., pp. 174–7.
63. Ibid., pp. 173–4.
64. Ibid., p. 174.
65. Alfred Grosser, *Affaires extérieures: La politique de la France, 1944–1989*, Paris, Flammarion, 1989, p. 30.

most important was that they encouraged a French belief that the British, whose information and judgement were usually better, would never stand up to the Americans. As a result, de Gaulle refused to negotiate with the British unless the US was present, 'since they would have the last word on the immediate future of France'. The British were unhappy, but they had only themselves to blame.[66] Subsequently, the memory of these episodes helped to build up the image of Britain as the Americans' front man in Europe, and contributed to de Gaulle's veto on British membership in the Common Market.

The wartime period was formative for de Gaulle and many of his colleagues. Inherited suspicion of Anglo-Saxons appeared to be confirmed, and even strengthened, by the events of 1940–44, notably what the French saw as attempts to take away their empire and to meddle with their domestic politics. These suspicions were to be further fed by events that took place during the rest of the war and immediately afterwards. But the war also gave the French some idea of how to deal with the Anglo-Saxons. Cassin, negotiating with the British in 1940, recognised that he had no cards in his hand at all, and decided that, as he put it 'extreme weakness imposes extreme intransigence'. His spectacular intransigence not only shocked the cultivated men of the Foreign Office; it was also very successful.[67] The French had appreciated that the rules by which nations deal with each other are essentially a question of good manners, and cannot actually be enforced. Conventionally, a nation in a weak position, which is under pressure from others or which cannot convince others to share its views, will give way. What the French recognised was that they could choose not to do so, and that the bureaucratic need to make progress could actually work in their favour. Weakness could be converted into a kind of strength, if the occasion were carefully chosen.

Many of those who led France after 1945 were influenced by the spirit of the Resistance, the Gaullists, or both. To a historic pride and sense of mission, a bitter memory of betrayal after 1918, and a pervasive suspicion of Anglo-Saxons were added, variously, experiences of isolation and persecution, a burning sense of moral rightness, a low regard for the critical views of others, a sense that you could and should rely only on yourself, and a belief that resistance activity, external or internal, made you a superior person, fitted to lead a nation reborn to grandeur by the sacrifices and struggles of

66. Woodward, *British Foreign Policy*, p. 57.
67. Lacouture, *De Gaulle*, p. 419.

the war years. Resistance to Vichy strengthened republican and democratic ideals, as well as promoting faith in modern ideas and methods. All of these ideas were to have much influence after the war, especially in the defence and security areas.

Meanwhile, the last act of the civil war was about to take place. The population of Paris had its own views about grandeur, and the resistance forces had risen up on 19 August, against orders, while General Leclerc's division was still outside Paris. The result was the plaques you still see all over the capital commemorating the heroic death of this patriot or that for the freedom of France: perhaps the city's reputation as the centre of ultra-collaboration had to be symbolically expunged. De Gaulle entered the city on 25 August, going, in a moment of stunning symbolism, back to the Ministry of Defence, to the very rooms he had occupied in 1940, the pens still lying on the desk where he had left them. After a stop at police headquarters, he went to the Hôtel de Ville across the way, where Parisian risings were customarily announced. This time, however, he was not to proclaim a republic, but to announce that the Republic had never gone away: he had been taking care of it.

There was a final moment of conflict when Leclerc's American commanding officer tried, unsuccessfully, to stop his division providing the guard of honour for the procession to Notre Dame. But the next day, it was the Second French Armoured Division, under a general who had been a captain in 1940, who lined the route as de Gaulle and others walked down the Champs-Elysées from the Arc de Triomphe, Communist *résistants* somehow temporarily united with Vichy officers who had switched sides. De Gaulle's procession was a symbolic recapitulation and redemption of the nation's past, moving backwards in time from Clemenceau and Napoleon to St Louis, past the stone iconography of French history, back into the mythical past; history, as de Gaulle later put it 'gathered in these stones and in these squares, seemed to be smiling down on us'.[68] No one could tell whether the crowds who lined the route were the same as those who had greeted Pétain only weeks before, and no one really wanted to know. After the *Te Deum* had been sung in Notre Dame, what Jean Lacouture calls the 'consecration' of de Gaulle was complete. 'The Rebel had become the Sovereign.'[69]

68. Charles de Gaulle, *War Memoirs*, Vol. 2, *Unity, 1942–1944*, trans. Richard Howard, London, Weidenfeld and Nicolson, 1959, p. 314.

69. Lacouture, *De Gaulle*, p. 838.

7

WEAKNESS AND FEAR

It is not true that men have to choose between large
political blocs.

Sartre and friends, 1948

Essence of capitalism
The Coca-Cola Company on its product, 1948

When the Sovereign returned to Paris in August 1944, in the baggage train of the Allied armies, it was to a France that was humiliated, bankrupt, physically devastated and in places literally starving. The situation was to get steadily worse. In this environment there were three immediate tasks to be performed: there was a war to be won, traitors to be punished and a country to be rebuilt, all more or less simultaneously. This chapter is concerned, first, with these three processes, and subsequently with the international engagements that France entered into in this environment, leading to the signature of the Washington Treaty in 1949. It follows the usual convention in treating the period between the Liberation and de Gaulle's resignation in January 1946 as an integral part of the Fourth Republic.

As Marc Ferro remarks, there was ambiguity in the victory – or, rather, victories: the conception of victory among the Gaullists, the Communist *résistants* and the Anglo-Saxon armies was not identical. The victory had an ideological component, which that of 1918 had quite lacked, and there was obviously less enthusiasm for it among 'all those who had some ideas in common with the Nazis – even if these sentiments were not clearly expressed, even if these individuals were deeply patriotic and anti-German. The latter, who were above all anti-communists, anti-bolsheviks, even anti-semites, did not miraculously disappear. They hoped to lift up their heads again one day'.[1] They did not have to wait long.

Few, indeed, can have been those who genuinely regretted the expulsion of the Germans; but there were many more who had regarded their anti-Communist and anti-Semitic policies with indulgence, and still retained a loyalty to the ideals of the National Revolution of 1940. It is unlikely that, by themselves, the Free French Forces (FFL) and the Resistance, fighting as the *Forces Françaises de l'Intérieur* (FFI), would have been able to take power in France, even in the absence of the Germans, in the face of the coercive apparatus that Vichy still possessed. The Revolution of 1940 was chased away by British and American bayonets, and the installation of the Provisional Government in August 1944 had much more of the quality of a *coup d'état* about it than many in France were prepared to admit, then or later.

It had been clear for some time that France could not withdraw from the fight once the last German had left her soil. France had declared war on Germany in 1939, and would need to see the struggle through to the end. As Massigli, the Free French commissioner for foreign affairs, told the British government in August 1944, it was 'essential that Germany should not be able to say that she had surrendered only to the three Powers [i.e. Britain, the United States and the Soviet Union]; the terms of surrender should efface once and for all the Franco-German armistice of 1940'.[2] The new government had to spend a lot of time and effort trying to ensure a French Occupation Zone in Germany and a seat on the Control Commission, in the face of hostility from America and the Soviet Union, but with support from the British. Finally, a French Zone was agreed upon, to be created from parts of the British and US zones.

The practical application of this policy, however, required something that the Free French did not have: an army. The tiny Gaullist forces, even buttressed by the unknown potential efforts of the FFI, would not be enough to make a credible force. As a result, it was Vichy's Armistice army that made up the bulk of the French forces from 1943 onwards. The first campaign in which they had fought on the same side as the FFL was the invasion of Italy in 1943, where the majority of the troops were loyal to Giraud, rather than de Gaulle 'with all that [that] implies of direct or indirect attachment to Vichy', and were commanded in most

1. Marc Ferro, *Pétain*, Paris, Fayard, 1987, p. 634.
2. Sir Llewellyn Woodward, *British Foreign Policy in the Second World War*, Vol. 5, London, HMSO, 1976, p. 239.

cases by career (i.e. Vichy) officers, many from the extreme Right.[3] The French corps was commanded by General Juin, who had played an important role in Vichy. A single FFL division took part, but the relationship was not an easy one, involving as it did different loyalties, histories, concepts of honour, traditions and even uniforms.

After the liberation of Paris, the FFI were added to this mixture: here, the clash was even more fundamental. In nearly all cases, the FFI were civilians, who had joined to fight Vichy as much as the Germans. On average, they were as far to the left as the Armistice army was to the right. They had little formal discipline, little respect for authority and little in the way of staff and command skills, but they did have a great deal of practical experience. Many of the FFI were sent off to reduce the German pockets of resistance around the Atlantic ports, a thankless and bloody task; but nearly 150,000 of them were incorporated into the First French army, under de Lattre de Tassigny. He, it will be recalled, had been a rather unconventional supporter of the National Revolution: subsequently, he had been disgraced for wanting to resist the German invasion of the Free Zone in November 1942, and so could appeal to both sides. By common consent, he did as well as anyone could have done in welding together this disparate group of amateur and professional soldiers, desperately short of weapons, into a genuine fighting force.[4]

For equipment, and even for uniforms, the French were reliant on the Anglo-Saxons; especially the Americans. The latter appeared strangely reluctant, in French eyes, to supply the equipment and stores necessary for them to take a major role in the rest of the war. Washington refused to agree to the creation of any new French forces beyond the eight existing divisions. De Gaulle, Juin, Massigli and others struggled furiously to get the decision changed. In November, Juin complained to Bedell-Smith, Eisenhower's chief of staff, that 'the reconstitution of the French Army has a moral aspect. As an imperial power, France cannot end the war with eight divisions in the line'. And he threatened to go ahead anyway. Eventually, in January 1945, the combined chiefs of staff agreed to a French request to form another eight divisions, although Roosevelt remained unconvinced. It was yet another bad

3. Jean Planchais, *Une Histoire Politique de l'Armée: de Gaulle à de Gaulle, 1940–1967*, Paris, Seuil, 1967, p. 57.

4. Paul-Marie de la Gorce, *The French Army: A Military-Political History*, trans. Kenneth Douglas, London, Weidenfeld and Nicolson, 1963, pp. 347–8.

omen for the future. Jean Lacouture, who recounts this episode, sees it as an attempt by the Americans to treat the French as they later did the Vietnamese.[5]

In fact, it is unlikely that there was an ulterior motive to American behaviour. Rather, there was a complete disjunction between the French and American concepts of war. Roosevelt made a sharp distinction between high-level political direction, which he concerned himself with, and everything else, which was left to the military. Eisenhower – whose relations with de Gaulle were good – was encouraged to ignore politics and to make purely military decisions, such as those about the size and shape of his army. This infuriated de Gaulle, for whom politics and the war could not be separated. The French had accepted 'that final authority over French forces lay with the Americans'. Yet, in the representative French view of Jean-Pierre Rioux, 'France accepted freely the discipline of the Allies; politically, however, French sovereignty was henceforth inviolable.'[6] Much of French post-war security policy is contained in the word 'freely', with its overtones of resistance culture: there was all the difference in the world between free recognition that a course was sensible, and forced acquiesence in it, even if the results in each case were indistinguishable from each other.

This passed from being a potential problem to a real one with the German Ardennes offensive of December 1944. The (highly symbolic) city of Strasburg was menaced at one point during the German advance, and Eisenhower, who was showing signs of panic, wanted to abandon it. This might, militarily, have been the right thing to do, but it would have condemned the newly liberated population to reprisals from the Germans. De Gaulle refused to allow Leclerc to withdraw, and, with Churchill's support, won the day. Roosevelt declined to overrule Eisenhower, on the grounds that it was a military question: a response that the French, at the time and since, have claimed to find incomprehensible. As an officer involved said later: 'For General de Gaulle, the political weight of arms was always much more important than their use in combat.'[7] This was a typically French view, of course, and it can stand as a kind of motto for much French policy since that date. It was a view that struck a popular chord also: as early as December

5. Jean Lacouture, *De Gaulle*, Vol. 2, *Le Politique, 1944–1959*, Paris, Seuil, 1985, p. 66.

6. Jean-Pierre Rioux, *The Fourth Republic, 1944–1958*, trans. Godfrey Rogers, Cambridge, Cambridge University Press, 1987, p. 8.

7. Cited by Lacouture, *De Gaulle*, p. 76.

1944, 64 per cent of the population thought France had recovered her place among the great powers.[8]

A Pure, Hard France

From the time of the first stirrings of resistance, it had been clear that one day there would be a settling of accounts. Partly, this was a natural human desire for revenge. Partly also it was a moral view, that many in Vichy had committed crimes on account of which they should answer before a court for what they had done. Partly also, it was a reflection of the idea common to many that the individuals who had failed needed to be swept away if the system were ever to be reformed, and the *France pure et dure* of which they dreamed were ever to be created. In the event, the purge that followed the Liberation was by no means as extensive as it could, and perhaps should, have been. There were many reasons for this failure, most of them practical. The Gaullist doctrine of the illegality of the 16 June armistice, together with the fact that virtually the whole of the government apparatus had collaborated, should logically have implied that the 'Grim Reaper' would visit every ministry, every embassy, every army camp and every police station.[9] Nothing of the kind ever happened, nor was it ever likely to. There were two principal reasons for this.

The first was fear. The idea of France collapsing into anarchy and emerging as a Communist state, remote as it may now seem, was very real at the time. De Gaulle was less inclined to this sort of hysteria than most contemporary political figures; but even he was worried enough to make the maintenance of law and order his overriding priority: it will be recalled that he visited the prefecture of police first, on his arrival in Paris. The police and judiciary had collaborated with gusto, and diligently tracked down, arrested and sentenced thousands of *résistants*. But they were now needed to keep the fabric of the state together, and therefore certain past indiscretions would have to be overlooked. The second was common prudence. The new state was going to have a difficult enough job surviving as it was, and, for all their eagerness to collaborate,

8. Rioux, *Fourth Republic*, p. 10.

9. Peter Novick, *The Resistance Versus Vichy: The Purge of Collaborators in Liberated France*, London, Chatto and Windus, 1968, Appendix A, is a thorough discussion of the legality – or otherwise – of Vichy.

those who had served Vichy were generally competent. Certainly, the insurgent forces lacked large numbers of competent people of their own with which to replace them. The treason of an entire social class produced a problem so enormous that the cure would be worse than the disease. But why was this so?

The army, as we have seen, was very largely the preserve of men of pronounced anti-republican and anti-democratic views, and it was not unusual among the organs of the Republic in being so. All bureaucracies take their tone from those who head them, and the high officials of the French public service in the late 1930s were of a very specific type. The French public service was (and still is) divided into a large number of *Corps*, which you join, and in which you remain for your career. There were by convention a number of *Grands Corps*, which monopolised the top jobs: the Foreign Ministry, the *Conseil d'État*, which specialised in administrative law, and the *Inspection des Finances* and the *Cours des Comptes*, which were concerned with financial propriety. These *Corps* controlled their own recruitment through demanding entrance exams, which only those with an expensive, specialised education had much hope of passing. This virtually dictated that the top jobs were held by individuals from moneyed backgrounds, but also from those in which there was a tradition of public service. Such families were generally of the counter-Revolutionary persuasion, sometimes from the aristocracy, and their progeny were heirs to a hierarchical, authoritarian conception of the state that essentially pre-dated the Revolution of 1789. This was mixed with a cynicism about, and impatience with, the generally lacklustre quality of ministerial material under the Third Republic, and indeed a contempt for the democratic process itself. Of course, all permanent officials should very properly try to avoid identification with a particular political view, and try to serve the public good disinterestedly. But under the Third Republic, a consciousness of serving France, rather than the Republic, was tantamount to taking a position on the extreme Right of the political spectrum, and the *Grands Corps* were well known for the number of monarchists, authoritarians and even quasi-fascists in their ranks. This accounts in part, no doubt, for the readiness of the French public service to rally to the French state in 1940. Moreover, new recruits were selected and trained, as far as possible, according to these principles. Almost all candidates came through the *École Libre des Sciences Politiques*, the famous '*Sciences-Po*', whose teaching staff were selected for their hostility to the Republic. Thus, wrote one republican member of the *Conseil d'État*, 'the Republic confided the training of its highest officials to its acknowledged enemies'.[10]

In spite of these difficulties, a purge of some sort was clearly necessary for practical and political reasons. It had started, in fact, before the Liberation, with methods appropriate to the desperate circumstances of the time. The Resistance targeted officials of the French state; in particular, those involved with the machinery of justice, the militia and various explicitly Pétainist organisations. Vichy prosecutors who showed too much zeal were identified by name in the underground press and over the radio from London, and some were killed by resistance groups, usually after an unofficial trial *in absentia*. By the end of 1943, Vichy claimed that there had been more than seven hundred 'terrorist killings'.[11] As the Liberation began to seem a possibility, various forms of psychological warfare were used to intimidate those who worked for Vichy. Stickers were used to label houses, lists of shops displaying German signs were distributed and personal warnings were given. Collaborators were warned that their conduct was being scrutinised and that, after the Liberation, they would have to answer for it.[12]

The invasion of North Africa in 1942 provided the first opportunity to apply these principles: it was a bungled opportunity, for a variety of reasons. The main problem was that the Americans had opted for an agreement with Darlan and the Vichy régime itself, to speed up the operation and minimise casualties. The result has been described by one French historian as 'the substitution of Vichyism under an American protectorate for Vichyism under German control'.[13] With the death of Darlan, the situation eased somewhat, and de Gaulle was able increasingly to exert his control. In September 1943 a 'Provisional Consultative Assembly' was established, with a strong Gaullist majority, and the purge got under way. It was limited, however, especially in the military area: France needed an army with which to fight, and that army was heavily compromised. Something like 1,500 individuals had action taken against them; but any more sustained purge would have destroyed the army, and, with it, any chance of participation

10. Cited by David Thomson, *Democracy in France Since 1870*, 5th edn, Oxford, Oxford University Press, 1969, p. 58.

11. Herbert R. Lottman, *The People's Anger: Justice and Revenge in Post-Liberation France*, London, Hutchinson, 1986, p. 27.

12. Novick, *Resistance Versus Vichy*, pp. 24–35.

13. Yves-Maxime Danan, cited ibid., p. 43.

in the eventual victory parade. Even the Communists were prepared to rally to this view.[14]

There were a number of arrests and even executions of prominent figures. British and American pressure was sufficient to protect some of Pétain's closest advisers, such as Flandin, but the Free French were determined that Pierre Pucheu, former interior minister, should not escape. Since he had been invited to Algiers under the protection of Giraud, rather than the Anglo-Saxons, the latter did not intervene. Pucheu was sentenced to death, and executed on 20 March 1944, claiming to be the victim of a 'political assassination'. De Gaulle was asked by the judges to exercise clemency, but refused to do so, for 'reasons of state'.[15] The trial was a disquieting precedent: evidence had not been easy to find, and Pucheu had denied the powers of the court to try him, claiming to be a victim of Communism. It was unfortunate that the trial judge had himself taken an oath of loyalty to Vichy.[16]

The invasion of the mainland and the military action by the FFI against the Germans and Vichy were obviously an opportunity for the settling of old scores. All parts of the Resistance were determined that random violence should be avoided, and the FFI were supposed to arrest, rather than kill, known collaborators. But such superhuman restraint was scarcely possible, and reprisals were common against 'members of the *Milice*, officials of the Légion, PPF militants, profiteers, informers, and traitors', sometimes with a formal trial of some sort.[17] The best estimate is that some 4,500 summary executions took place in the months after the Liberation, but that some, at least, of these deaths were in combat between the *Milice* and the FFI.[18]

These episodes were, both at the time and later, considerably inflated into a veritable Red Terror stalking the countryside, bringing massacre and atrocity in its wake. Some of this was due to the propaganda of the Nazis and what remained of Vichy, but much of it was homegrown. It was, of course, the product of decades of accumulated fear of a Communist uprising, raised and disappointed at regular intervals since 1870. For the first time, the fantasies of the past decade – tens of thousands of armed Communist

14. Ibid., p. 54.

15. Lacouture, *De Gaulle*, Vol. 1, p. 756.

16. Novick, *Resistance Versus Vichy*, p. 57.

17. Rioux, *Fourth Republic*, p. 29. The PPF (*Parti Populaire Français*) was an extreme collaborationist group.

18. Novick, *Resistance Versus Vichy*, pp. 71–72 and Annexe C.

militants – had actually come about, albeit as a result of official policy. A bloodbath was gloomily anticipated in some quarters, and, when it failed to occur, the ready-prepared reactions carried on nonetheless. The Red Terror stalked the land in theory, if not in practice, and a coup attempt was expected at any moment. American newspapers talked excitedly of fifty thousand Communist victims in the South-East alone.[19] Ironically, however, on the one occasion where the Communists actually had available the arms and organisation that they had often been credited with, their behaviour was very correct. Partly this was because they were under orders from Moscow, partly because, with millions of heavily armed troops in the country, anything else would have been futile. But the recollections of the fear and the atrocity stories were to have considerable political importance a few years later.

Once the Provisional Government was established in Paris, the purges were put on a more organised footing, and trials began. It was decided to prosecute only for offences that were violations of the criminal code at the time. Quite often, this was Article 75, 'intelligence with the enemy', introduced in 1939. It was argued that, since the decision of 16 June to seek an armistice was illegal, France and Germany had been in a state of war all the time, and Germany remained 'an enemy'. All dealings with Germans, therefore, were crimes under that article. This (slightly strained) line of argument satisfied the jurists, but was obviously open to political objections. Inevitably, the trials turned out to be much more difficult than expected. The most common defence was that the accused had been a resister himself. Many Frenchmen could claim, quite plausibly, that they had remained in their official positions as a way of frustrating the Germans and reducing the damage to France. The courts were accordingly presented with moral dilemmas that they were not intended to have to grapple with: a prefect of police might admit to having drawn up lists of French hostages to hand over to the Germans for execution. But was his crime excused if he had negotiated a reduction in the number of hostages to be shot, and used his position to let known *résistants* escape? And was this defence vitiated by the discovery that most of those whose deaths he had allowed were known or suspected Communists? The courts thrashed around in this moral deep water, and their verdicts seldom satisfied.

It had always been clear that the most important trial would be that of Pétain himself, who was not available immediately. His

19. Rioux, *Fourth Republic*, p. 32.

trial did not start until July 1945, on charges of 'conspiracy against the internal security of the state and of intelligence with the enemy'.[20] The transcript of the trial is a depressing document; the accusers and supporters of the marshal might as well have been inhabiting different planets, and Pétain himself refused to acknowledge the jurisdiction of the court. In the end, none of this mattered: the verdict, at least, was certain, even if the charges were largely unconvincing. So was the sentence: death, and so was the commutation of that sentence by de Gaulle. Pétain's execution would have divided the nation at a time when unity was difficult enough anyway.

The same considerations did not apply to Laval, whose trial followed. It was even scrappier and less satisfactory than Pétain's, and resulted in the same sentence. This time, there was no commutation, since Laval did not have a political constituency that needed to be appeased. This was perhaps a shame, since Laval's own corrosive realism and cynicism prevented him from having much time for the National Revolution, and he certainly lacked the fanaticism of his colleagues: he was a much less dangerous man than Pétain. His end was emblematic: he took poison in an attempt to cheat justice, and was dragged out in front of an improvised firing squad in case he died before he could be shot.

The purge ground its way through the apparatus of the Vichy state. In the case of the army, the results of the purge are difficult to separate from the results of the rapid reduction in the size of the army after the war. According to a government statement in March 1946, 131 general officers had been subject to 'various penalties', including early retirement, and 700 officers of all types were struck off the rolls.[21] Whilst the officers who had been in North Africa and fought next to the FFL were largely left alone, officers who had served in mainland France were obliged formally to ask for reinstatement in the new army. About 10,000 applied, but only about half were accepted.[22] Eventually, only forty general officers were retained, one of whom was demoted.[23] Although these sanctions were relatively severe, it has to be remembered that the army as a whole was solidly Vichyite, and few officers from the FFI or the Gaullists were able to be integrated at a senior level. Most of the FFI soon left in any event: by 1960, less than 1,000 of the army's

20. *Procès du Maréchal Pétain*, Paris, Imprimerie des Journaux Officiels, 1945, p. 6.
21. Planchais, *Histoire Politique*, p. 105.
22. De la Gorce, *French Army*, p. 336.
23. Lottman, *The People's Anger*, p. 207.

30,000 officers could be said to have a resistance background.[24] Other areas of the bureaucracy got off more lightly. At that date, there were some one million central government employees, and about 11,000 suffered sanctions of one sort or another, about half losing their jobs.[25] Sanctions against the Diplomatic Service, a particularly anti-republican *Corps*, had begun even before the move back to France. All personnel decisions and all ambassadorial appointments were declared void. Some eighty individuals were penalised, including a high proportion of ambassadors and ministers.[26]

Areas outside the government were purged also. The most difficult area was the political class, much of which had fawningly embraced Vichy on 10 July 1940. A popular proposal at the time was to exclude all the 569 deputies and senators who had voted for Pétain, but this would have resulted in the disappearance of just about every politician from the Right, which had voted, *en bloc*, for Pétain. In the end, a milder régime was introduced that enabled politicians to be struck off for gross collaboration with Vichy unless they had also been active *résistants*.[27] The sense that the 'old gang' was back caused an outcry, not only among the eighty who had refused to vote for Pétain, but among the public as well. There was also disappointment at the limited sanctions taken against the church, which had taken a solidly pro-Vichy line. In the end, only seven bishops were removed.[28] Some sanctions were also taken against private industry, which had been much more effective supplying weapons to the Germans than to the French. The trial of Louis Renault was awaited with particular interest, but he died just before it opened. In the end, although a few companies (like Renault and the Gnome engine company) were nationalised, most sanctions were restricted to junior employees: the support of their bosses was required if France was to be rebuilt.

In the end, the purge satisfied no one. It was arbitrary and inconsistent: too sweeping for some, too timid for others. It would have been difficult to carry out under ideal circumstances: at a time of war and reconstruction, it was virtually impossible. In any event, a good part of the population was still Pétainist at heart, and, if they were glad to see the Germans go, they were not necessarily pleased

24. Planchais, *Histoire Politique*, p. 104.
25. Novick, *Resistance Versus Vichy*, p. 90.
26. Lottman, *The People's Anger*, pp. 196–7.
27. Novick, *Resistance Versus Vichy*, pp. 94–98.
28. Lottman, *The People's Anger*, pp. 201–2.

to see de Gaulle and the Resistance arrive. Charles Maurras, who had urged more and better collaboration, was imprisoned for this, and, one suspects, for fifty years of emetic journalism as well. 'It is the revenge of Dreyfus', he famously shouted, as he was led away. His attitude is typical of those who were punished during the purges: complete inability to understand that they had done anything wrong, and patronising disdain for the new authorities. It is not recorded that any collaborator who was put on trial ever said that he was sorry, or accepted that his conduct might be open to question. After all, in the view of the Vichyites, neither Jews nor 'Communist terrorists' deserved any sympathy: they were *métèques*, not real people, and certainly not real Frenchmen.

Massive campaigns were launched, demanding clemency for some of the better-known accused; and indeed, very large numbers were pardoned. Far fewer collaborators were imprisoned in France than in any other occupied nation, as a percentage of the population, and the vast majority of death sentences were never carried out (de Gaulle alone commuted 1,300). The majority of those imprisoned had been released by the end of 1948; virtually all by 1951. A succession of amnesty laws, beginning in 1947, sweetened the pill further.[29] This was largely necessary, of course. Even if a more measured view had been taken of the possibility of a Red Terror, the insurgent republicans would still have required at least the tacit co-operation of those who had served Vichy just to keep the state running, let alone to rebuild the nation. But the impracticability of wide-scale purges helps to explain the origin of the Gaullist myth that 'everyone resisted'. If, in fact, 'everybody collaborated', and few were punished, then the inescapable conclusion was that the Fourth Republic was largely run by those who had rallied to Vichy. This would not have been an acceptable conclusion politically, and the Gaullist myth necessarily imputes to the same people a set of beliefs they themselves would have angrily rejected.

Remaking France

Sanctions against individuals, no matter how urgent and well-deserved, were only a small part of the process of transforming France. There was a general desire to throw the whole of the old system away and to replace it with something better and more

---

29. Novick, *Resistance Versus Vichy*, pp. 186–8.

modern. In the eighteen months that followed the liberation of Paris, the Provisional Government introduced a whole range of measures that departed fundamentally from the past, especially in government, administration and the economy, and that subsequent governments pursued. It had been clear for some time that, although France would be a republic, that republic would not be the Third. Logically, and given the way that French constitutions have historically been produced, one would have expected a constitution that differed very sharply from that of the Third, especially in strengthening the executive at the expense of the legislature. In fact, this only happened to a very limited extent, because what the framers were reacting against was not really the Third Republic, but the French state, which had dissolved parliament and ruled in an authoritarian fashion. There was only a limited appetite for replacing one powerful executive with another. In October 1945, a complicated referendum resulted in the definitive rejection of the Third Republic and the setting up of a Constituent Assembly (and a *de facto* government). The parties that corresponded to the various resistance factions swept the board, winning some 80 per cent of the seats: the SFIO, PCF and MRP taking some 150 each. By contrast the Moderates (i.e. the traditional extreme Right) and the Radicals were almost wiped out. The parties of the Resistance then dominated the government, under de Gaulle's continued leadership, and set themselves to devise a new constitution. Inevitably, their draft benefited themselves and elected parliamentarians in general, in that it 'conferred virtually unchecked power on a single chamber'. But the referendum of May 1946 rejected the proposal, to general astonishment. An amended version was eventually adopted by a small majority, but almost as many abstained as voted for it.[30]

The Fourth Republic's constitution has had a bad press, and proposals to amend it came almost at once, but this reputation is not wholly deserved. Although there was a longing for a stronger executive, the possibility of a directly elected president, or even one with substantially stronger powers, was anathema across the political spectrum. There was some strengthening of the president's role – and incumbents themselves were to take full advantage of this – but he was still in a relatively weak position. He was to 'take the title of Head of the Armed Forces', but not the actuality of executive power. He could not initiate legislation, and all of

30. Philip Williams, *Crisis and Compromise: Politics in the Fourth Republic*, London, Longman, 1964, p. 23.

his acts had to be countersigned by a minister. For the first time, the function of prime minister was recognised, but he was still called *Président du Conseil*, and his powers, whilst augmented, were still not large.[31] The inevitable result was to pass political power back into the hands of the hated *partis*: the resulting instability is well known.

Yet the real problem was political, rather than technical. A strong two-party system would have enabled the system to work reasonably well; but French politics continued to be hopelessly split among a number of parties, none of which, in their wildest dreams, could expect much more than about a quarter of the vote. Government was by definition coalition government, among parties that had little love for each other, and by politicians who would bring down the government at once if they thought that it might be in their party's interests to do so. Assembling a majority for the installation of a government was an artificial exercise, and required an *absolute* majority of the Chamber: i.e. abstentions counted against. This was not a great problem initially, but became one with the ejection of the PCF from government in 1947. After that point, 51 per cent of all the votes had to come from the remaining 75 per cent or so of the Chamber before a government could be formed. This inevitably produced shifting coalitions and short-term governments, and ensured that a government almost never reflected the balance of political forces in the country. As a result, the average person's vote made little difference to the complexion of the government, which no doubt explains the lack of enthusiasts ready to die for the Republic in 1958. It was being said as early as 1948 that 'The Fourth Republic is dead: it has been succeeded by the Third',[32] an impression strengthened when a number of prominent Third Republic figures returned to political life.

If the hopes for parliamentary renovation were largely disappointed, moves to modernise the bureaucracy had more success. One of those discreetly associated with the Popular Front's unsuccessful attempt to set up an *École Nationale d'Administration* (ENA) had been the young Michel Debré, then a new entrant to the *Conseil d'État*. Even before the end of the war, Debré had won de Gaulle's backing for a single-stream entry to the highest reaches of the French civil service, through a common examination and

---

31. All constitutional texts cited are from Debbasch and Pontier, *Les Constitutions de la France*, Paris, Dalloz, 1989.
32. Cited by Williams, *Crisis and Compromise*, p. 194.

common training. If this were not done, he claimed, the existing system 'prejudicial to the general interest' would simply continue. The first students were to be 'those who had fought with the Free French or in the Resistance, and those returning from prison camps or from deportation'.[33] Debré believed that France needed 'a more realistic administration', and one which was 'more conscious of its duty to defend, tooth and nail, the interests of France'. It should have a much better grasp of economics than currently, and be 'more conscious of the needs of the nation' than of 'drafting texts at the Minister's request', which had, of course, continued, inexcusably, under Vichy.[34]

The idea was given concrete form by the end of the year: it was regarded as a task of great urgency. In parallel, the *École Libre* was merged with the University of Paris and lost its previous political bias. Thus, ENA, which still today produces those who will dominate the French bureaucracy and politics, was equally a product of the Liberation, and had an explicitly ideological and political cast. Its first graduates, who began to reach positions of influence in the middle and late 1950s, saw themselves both as agents of modernisation and change and as agents of the creation of a new France, restored to her grandeur and influence. Other, less spectacular attempts were made to modernise and overhaul the government machine, which together with the creation of ENA led to what Philip Williams has called a 'silent administrative revolution', the overall effect of which was to make the bureaucracy much more efficient.[35] The strengthening of the prime minister's position was reflected in the establishment of a cabinet secretariat, which, for the first time, took and distributed minutes of cabinet meetings, and co-ordinated ministerial business. The *Conseil d'État* examined government bills before they went to parliament, saving much time and embarrassment. There was also a complete reorganisation of the Quai, which created four new geographical *Directions Générales*, and four others for general functions, including one for policy, which still exists.[36]

Many new diplomats were recruited directly and without examination from those with anti-Vichy credentials. Amid mutterings from traditionalists about 'standards', Bernard Destremau

33. Michel Debré, *Trois Républiques pour une France*, Paris, Albin Michel, 1984, p. 365.
34. Ibid., p. 369.
35. Williams, *Crisis and Compromise*, p. 345.
36. John M. Young, *France, the Cold War and the Western Alliance, 1944–49: French Foreign Policy and Post-War Europe*, London, Leicester University Press, 1990, p. 21.

recalls the excitement of the 'noble mission' of making 'the foreign policy of a victorious France'.[37]

Nowhere was this dynamism and modernism more noticeable than in the area of economic policy. A country as devastated as France manifestly could not wait around for economic recovery to begin naturally, even if that had been the prevailing economic orthodoxy. But in fact the tide was running strongly in favour of interventionist economics, the general judgement being that classical economics had failed in the 1930s. The most obvious sign of this new spirit was the large-scale nationalisations, which began almost at once. There were, however, a whole series of reasons for this process, most of which had their origins in the recent past. There was, first, the need to fight the war, since the state could not wait for a profitable market in munitions to develop so that the private sector would invest to take account of it. Then there was retribution: many of the same companies had worked hard for the German war effort, and it seemed unfair that the shareholders should continue to enjoy the dividends. There was also a strong presumption among resistance activists that nationalisations would be one way out of the bitter class warfare that had convulsed the country for so long. There was, in addition, a desire to modernise the management of the economy, and to sweep away the fuddy-duddy ideas of the past.

Most importantly, however, nationalisation responded to a deep concern in the French psyche about the balance between the individual and the general good. In liberal market theory, the general good was nothing more than the sum total of all the individual goods, and, if each individual economic unit pursued its own individual good, then the general good would benefit. But there was, of course, a strong French tradition that argued the opposite, that the pursuit of individual good actually *harms* the general good and should be controlled. There is also a tradition of looking at the results of economic activity on far more than a narrowly financial basis, and asking whether activities serve the wider, general good, as well as the individual good of the entrepreneur. It was thus thought that 'the principal sources of wealth had to return to the nation'.[38] This, no doubt, is what lies behind de Gaulle's own suggestion, soon after the Liberation, that the nation demand that 'private interests should always be constrained to give way to the general interest, that the great communal sources

37. Bernard Destremau, *Quai d'Orsay: derrière la façade*, Paris, Plon, 1994, p. 62.
38. Rioux, *Fourth Republic*, p. 69.

of wealth should be exploited and developed, not for the benefit of individuals, but for the advantage of all'.[39]

The most far-reaching consequence of the new economic thinking, however, was the National Plan, under a commissariat answerable to the prime minister and headed by Jean Monnet, whose inspiration was the wartime mobilisation of the Anglo-Saxon economies. Another important precursor was Vichy's encouragement of the collection of economic statistics. The plan was not centrally directed, as such: rather, it was evolved through meetings of employers, trades unionists, experts and civil servants, all working, as they saw it, in the same national interest. The main theme of the plan was modernisation. Its analysis of the failures of the French economy was quite different from that of the 1930s: the problem was not high wages or excessive government spending, but rather 'low productivity of labour, outdated technology, over-cautious entrepreneurs, plethoric distribution networks, excessive administrative costs and a too-ready recourse to protectionism'.[40] Evoking memories of the co-operative policies of the Popular Front, the plan identified the priorities for France in increased production and modernisation in six key heavy industrial sectors: consumption would have to wait. By 1952, GNP was 39 per cent above the 1946 level, and growth had averaged 4.5 per cent per year.[41] The success of the plan (it was followed by others) and the triumphal way in which the government announced the meeting of one target after another permanently altered the French debate about economic policy, with consequences that are still visible.

One area where modernisation was less successful was that of defence. For one thing, it was an area of less priority: modern heavy industry had to come first. In any event, the army was not especially popular, since it was, overwhelmingly, the Armistice army, which had performed so appallingly against the Germans in 1940, and only slightly better against its own people thereafter. It was an army that had, in Robert Paxton's phrase, busied itself with 'parades and politics', rather than the serious business of warfare. And it was an army without a mission or an enemy: Germany was prostrate, and the struggle against Communism had

39. The text of de Gaulle's speech is in *L'Année Politique 1944–45: Revue chronologique des principaux faits politiques, économiques et sociaux de la France de la liberation de Paris au 31 décembre 1945* (hereafter *AP*), Paris, Editions du Grand Siècle, 1946, p. 76.

40. Rioux, *Fourth Republic*, p. 173.

41. Ibid., p. 177.

not yet officially recommenced. Threatened by renewed interest in a 'People's Army', poorly paid, purged and neglected, it retreated once more, to sulk in its tent. Unsurprisingly, there was little pressure for modernisation from the army itself. Most of its officers had little interest in training for mechanised warfare in Germany, and wanted to get back to 'real soldiering' in the colonies. De Lattre de Tassigny was the obvious safe choice to lead the army after 1945, and he reorganised its training in line with the theories he had put into practice under Vichy. Instead of using the shrunken army of post-war France as the cadre of a much larger future force, as the Germans had done, de Lattre emphasised the virtues he had always regarded as important: fresh air, physical fitness, cleanliness, hygiene, parades and smartness. This was not necessarily wrong, nor always unpopular; but it left little time for more proper military training, and for conscripts, in their single year of service, there was 'an over-all reduction in training and military instruction, and in the study of armaments and manœuvre'.[42] There was also little interest in learning military lessons from the war, or even studying it in any detail. Rather, there was a concentration on recalling heroic deeds and inspirational personalities. As late as 1956, the *Centre des Hautes Études Militaires* was still using a tactical exercise designed in Algeria in 1943.[43]

In the circumstances, the pressure for modernisation came more from civilians than from the military, who generally preferred a policy of nostalgia. To some extent, this was less true of the air force, which, apart from being inherently more technological, was also by tradition more left-wing (or less right-wing) than the other services. The greatest need, clearly, was for jet aircraft, especially fighters, and the French-designed and French-built jets of the 1950s were largely conceived in the immediate aftermath of the war, especially by the dynamic Communist air minister, Charles Tillon. This was linked with a desire to modernise the structure of defence decision-making, which led to a variety of proposals, from the government and others, in the late 1940s. Their common themes were modernisation of equipment and doctrine, the importance of science and technology, and the need to have a decision-making apparatus that did not leave the last word to the military, as had been the case in the past. For example, the *projet de loi* of the Ramadier government, in June 1947, gave the

42. De la Gorce, *French Army* p. 357.
43. Planchais, *Histoire Politique* pp. 150–1.

overall direction of defence policy to the prime minister, especially the distribution of financial resources. He was given a national defence staff, with civilians as well as officers involved, and a supporting committee structure.[44]

It is a conventional judgement, especially from the Left, that the post-war reconstruction of France largely failed, and the hopes of the Liberation were rapidly disappointed. The limited purges of the system, and the return of the Vichyite Right within a few years are cited in support of this view. But, of course, the hopes of the forces of resistance did not necessarily correspond to the views of all, and certainly not to the aspirations of many in positions of power. There were also practical limitations on what could be accomplished by a bankrupt nation, depending on the largesse of others for simple survival and on the tacit support of enemies of the régime for its continued function. But is it clear, on examination, that the traumatic career, and untimely demise, of the Fourth Republic should not be allowed to obscure the fact that major, and largely successful, attempts were made to restructure and modernise the state, to lay the foundations for economic recovery and to produce a more effective political system. In a benign domestic and international environment, the Republic might well have survived longer than it did; but such an environment never really existed.

The Great Fear

The political circumstances of the Liberation and the 1945 election were highly unusual and artificial, and the outcome was not really representative of the balance of forces and opinions at the time. De Gaulle, by far the most popular figure, had no party machine behind him and was uninterested in being a conventional politician. The PCF was extremely popular, not for its programme, but as a result of its resistance role and the part played by the Red army in the defeat of Hitler. The MRP, whose growth and popularity astonished everyone, was powerful for reasons that were accidental and largely beyond its control. These two parties, together with the SFIO, made up an administration that, especially under de Gaulle's leadership, was bound to fragment as the euphoria of victory faded.

44. *Journal Officiel, Documents Parliamentaires, Assemblée Nationale, 1947, Annexe No. 1871*, pp. 1526–8. Hereafter cited as *JO*, etc. A *projet de loi* is a government bill ;a *proposition de loi*, a bill from any other quarter.

The popularity of the MRP appeared to imply a major change on the Right of the spectrum, towards a Catholic constituency ready to make its peace with modernism and democracy. This was not the case, however. The MRP had its roots in the Catholic social organisations, notably the youth movements, and had taken a very different line from orthodox Catholic opinion towards the fascist régimes of the 1930s. The MRP was founded by Catholics who had been active in the Resistance, and this, coupled with de Gaulle's support for it, gave it a flying start. But only a minority of the MRP's voters actually shared its views. The majority were 'Conservatives for whom MRP was a temporary barrier against Communism and not a permanent home'.[45] In order to try to retain this artificial following, the MRP was forced to move steadily to the right, as its support became more concentrated in conservative areas of the country, and as it had to compete with other parties for the Catholic vote. Moreover, its new deputies themselves increasingly resembled traditional right-wing politicians. Thus, although French politics after 1945 is often seen as more moderate, or even leftish in orientation, in practice, the Right had already reasserted its power by the time of the Great Anti-Communist Panic of 1947, and the signing of various international agreements, including the Washington Treaty, over the next few years.

This situation was further complicated by the activities of de Gaulle. The Sovereign was not suited to being a prime minister in the Fourth Republic, and had no taste for the role. He stayed on for a few months after the October 1945 elections, but resigned suddenly, in January 1946. The ostensible reason was a cut in the defence budget, but the causes went much deeper. De Gaulle was fundamentally opposed to the direction the constitutional discussions were taking, and was finding the task of trying to reconcile the various parties exhausting and unprofitable. The whole political world puzzled over the reasons for his departure. André Siegfried, writing in *L'Année Politique*, was inclined to dismiss him, noting that, like Clemenceau and Churchill, he found peace harder than war. 'Saving a country and governing it, above all reconstructing it, are two different things.'[46] There seems little doubt, however, that de Gaulle was expecting to be summoned back to power quite quickly by a people already fed up with the machinations of the *partis*. It did not happen, and so he began to think of ways of facilitating his return. He would not come back,

45. Williams, *Crisis and Compromise*, p. 104.
46. *AP 1946*, Paris, 1947, pp. iv–v.

of course, without a new constitution, and he launched his ideas in a speech in Bayeux in June 1946. As Jean Lacouture, says, it was a speech that took 'two months to write, twenty-seven minutes to read, twelve years to ruminate on and ten years to put into practice'.[47] The speech was, in many ways, the first recorded sighting of the 1958 Constitution: it argued for a second chamber and a 'Head of State', 'placed above parties', to look after the 'general interest'.[48] It was unnecessary to add that he himself would take such a job if it were offered.

Yet, shortly after, the French people reluctantly accepted the second draft constitution, and the Fourth Republic proper was launched. Inevitably, de Gaulle was offered the largely symbolic presidency; inevitably, he refused, and it went to a respected Socialist, Vincent Auriol. But de Gaulle was not finished: he believed, wrongly as it turned out, that he could play the party game and still be above it. The following year, he launched the *Rassemblement du Peuple Français*. It was not, he insisted, a 'party'. It was rather, according to a declaration of April 1947, a way of gathering together 'all those French men and women who wish to unite for the common good, as they did before for the liberation and the victory of France'.[49] The RPF was an instant and enormous success, but largely at the expense of the MRP. It thus inherited much of the wandering vote of the traditional Right, which looked to de Gaulle as the kind of strong man who would act much as Pétain had done. But there was much less of a welcome in the Centre and on the Left, and the RPF never really managed to convert the rhetoric into reality.

At the beginning, the RPF was advertised as a movement that anyone could join, even if they were already a member of another party. But as deputies started to identify with it, and as it fought elections like any other party, it soon became part of the system that it affected to despise and part of the problem it claimed to solve. Increasingly, it became seen as an extremist party, the right-wing equivalent of the PCF, and went into a decline after the late 1940s. The fall of the Republic to which it looked forward took much longer than expected, and was due, in the end, to factors quite beyond the RPF's influence. As Jean Lacouture implies in calling the second volume of his biography *The Politician*, de Gaulle had made the opposite of the usual political progression.

47. Lacouture, *De Gaulle*, Vol. 2, p. 269.
48. The text is in *AP 1946*, pp. 534–9.
49. Cited by Lacouture, *De Gaulle*, Vol. 2, p. 304.

Most politicians try to finish their careers as statesmen: de Gaulle began as a statesman and finished as a politician, a job for which he proved to have limited talent. It was only an extraordinary series of events that allowed him to learn from his mistakes and to come back for a second try.

One reason for the decline of both the MRP and the RPF was the increasing self-confidence and power of the old Right, as politics drifted slowly in their direction. It is doubtful whether there was any strong rightward shift in public opinion as a whole; rather, right-wing voters steadily deserted parties of convenience, like the MRP, as the parties of the old Right recovered their confidence. There were two, linked, ways in which this was particularly noticeable: the rehabilitation of Vichy, and the renewed purge of Communists. As Henri Rousso has noted, the Occupation and the Liberation were events too charged with tension for them to be commemorated in a way that would please everyone. Quite quickly, the different resistance groups began to fashion different myths. The Communists emphasised the 'anti-fascist' struggle, the Gaullists military aspects and republican legitimacy, the Resistance proper its own struggle. To this was now added a revisionist reading from the Right.[50]

It began as early as 1945, with the circulation of clandestine pro-Vichy newsletters. Most of them had very small circulations, but one, *Paroles Françaises*, was soon selling over 100,000 copies. By 1947, publications of this sort were being sold officially, one with the official sanction of the *Action Française*. They were generally written by those who had been active in the wartime collaborationist press, and devoted themselves to attacking the enemies of Vichy. By the early 1950s, a whole revisionist ideology had been worked out, which simultaneously denigrated the Resistance itself, which had been 'infiltrated by Communists, and was in many ways disreputable and dishonest', in favour of the 'resistance' of the Vichy régime, which had been faithful to French military tradition. They argued that unspecified individuals (better not to mention de Gaulle by name) had plunged France into a civil war, which had started in 1944 and was not yet finished.[51] Even the most dubious elements soon recovered their courage: in 1946, the *Combattant européen*, organ of the Anti-Bolshevik Legion, was back on sale, as was *Drapeau noir*, addressed to surviving members of

50. Henri Rousso, *The Vichy Syndrome: History and Memory in France since 1944*, trans. Arthur Goldhammer, London, Harvard University Press, 1991, pp. 26–28.
51. Ibid., pp. 28–29.

the *Waffen SS* (few in number, one assumes, from the publication's short life).[52]

The attempt to rehabilitate Pétain began while he was still alive. A committee was formed as early as April 1948 to demand his freedom: many of its members were from the *Académie Française*, a notorious anti-republican stronghold.[53] After protests, the group was banned. If anything, the rehabilitation continued more strongly after Pétain's death in 1951. Shortly afterwards, the *Association pour Défendre la Mémoire du Maréchal Pétain* was founded. It was not banned, and has since enjoyed a vigorous life, with a board of directors including prominent military men, politicians and civil servants. Weygand was its first honourary chairman.[54]

The final strand in the counter-attack was the disparagement of the Liberation itself. Robert Aron had already produced the highly influential *History of Vichy*, presenting an indulgent view that was not to be overturned until the work of Robert Paxton, twenty years later. His *History of the Liberation* included wild over-estimates of the death toll at the hands of the FFI (from 30,000 to 40,000) and highly coloured accounts of their 'crimes'. The purge was attacked also, and 'the least rumour, justified or otherwise, about its excesses', was believed.[55] The violence of these reactions may surprise us today, since they came from those who had scarcely suffered, in comparison with many of their countrymen. But those who had been disturbed by the Liberation and inconvenienced by the purge tended to be from the better classes of society, or conceived themselves to be: officers, prefects, diplomats, mayors, judges, bishops, industrialists – what the French call *notables* – had been censured, demoted, or deprived of the right to vote for several years. They were used to the reflexive obeisance of the state, not to being on the wrong end of it. Their reaction was one of rage, followed by the desire to wipe away the slur and revenge themselves on their tormentors. They were, in effect, the losing side in the civil war: what has been called 'offended France'.[56] They were not numerous, but they were very powerful and had many sympathisers in high places.

One priority was an amnesty. Campaigns accelerated through the late 1940s, as the Assembly drifted further to the right. The

52. Paul-Marie de la Gorce, *L'Après-Guerre, 1944–1952: Naissance de la France Moderne*, Paris, Grasset, 1978, p. 367.

53. *AP 1948*, Paris, 1949, p. 59.

54. Rousso, *Vichy Syndrome*, p. 43.

55. De la Gorce, *Après-guerre*, p. 67.

56. Ibid., p. 66.

question of amnesty was important, because, under French law, it is actually defined as 'legal oblivion', and an amnestied person could use the courts to 'impose silence concerning all judgements covered by the amnesty'.[57] It was equivalent to a memory hole: a successful campaign would mean that the crimes had, in fact, never happened. The campaign began in 1948 and culminated in 1951–53, with the passing of amnesty laws that reflected the increased strength of the Right and the increasing weariness of the other parties. The fact that this was the height of the Cold War enabled the initiative to be presented in patriotic, as well as anti-Communist terms: 'in the face of rising perils, union of all Frenchmen is more desirable than ever' said one supportive deputy.[58] Only prisoners who had committed the most heinous crimes were kept in prison after 1953.

The other priority was revenge. This was the occasion of the Great Anti-Communist Panic, which reached its climax in the 'terrible year' of 1947. Although the international situation was becoming worse, and Soviet behaviour increasingly worrying, the paranoia of 1947 was, in fact, a domestic phenomenon, and thus had much in common with the previous panic of 1939–40, especially in the way in which all other political parties joined in with gusto. The panic began from the economic conditions of the time, which were worse than anything that had been experienced during the war: at one point, the bread ration was reduced to 200 grams a day, and prices roughly doubled in the first six months of the year. To the surprise of many, there were bread riots, strikes and demonstrations. Ramadier, the prime minister, chose to interpret these events as the result of a Communist conspiracy, although in fact it seems as if the PCF were as surprised as anyone else. De Gaulle joined in with some ill-judged anti-Communist speeches, raising the prospect of a clash between competing extremist forces.[59]

The PCF had been uncomfortable but essential allies for some time. They had guaranteed industrial peace for reconstruction since 1944, but were now losing support to more extreme elements, who were asking when the promised rewards would come. They became increasingly unhappy with both the Indo-China policy and the policy on prices and wages, and were causing great concern by their policy of trying to infiltrate and capture

---

57. Rousso, *Vichy Syndrome*, p. 50.
58. Ibid., pp. 51–52.
59. Rioux, *Fourth Republic*, pp. 122–4.

various organs of the state. In May 1947, Communist deputies opposed the government in a vote on economic and social policy. By the relaxed standards of party discipline under the Fourth Republic, this was not necessarily a hanging offence; but Ramadier took the opportunity to expel them. The SFIO, after some thought, decided to stay. However, long-term damage had been done to the stability of the Republic, because the MRP and SFIO, by themselves, were unable to muster the votes for a majority. They were obliged to depend upon the votes of the Radicals and Moderates to their right, and so was born the Third Force, the professedly moderate *ad hoc* grouping that was the Fourth Republic's last hope of a broadly based government excluding the extremists of the PCF and the RPF. Establishing such improvised coalitions was desperate and tricky work, and sustaining them even more of a problem. Unsurprisingly, few of them lasted long.

Meanwhile, unrest was increasing, and the government found itself in violent conflict with the (Communist-led) miners in the North. In the end, troops had to be sent in, and the mining regions were placed under virtual military occupation.[60] Ever since 1871, of course, such developments had been assumed to be the start of a bloody insurrection, and consistent falsification of this forecast seemed to have no effect. A new civil war was believed to be about to break out, leading to a Communist coup. All sorts of murky rumours were circulating, mostly, it seems, started by the same military intelligence staffs whose vivid imaginations had caused such problems in the 1930s. Anonymous informants spread excited stories of the re-formation of the international brigades to seize power in France, under the leadership of a former FFI officer and Communist deputy, and with the help of massive Soviet arms stockpiles. Such stories were believed by the press, which denounced the 'Communist peril' daily.[61]

The diaries that Vincent Auriol kept at this time are full of the most lurid details of plots that a popular novelist would have blushed to concoct, and that never came to anything. Auriol, an honourable but not especially bright man, wrote down everything he was told, making little distinction between intelligence reports and newspaper scare stories. (Perhaps, on the other hand, there *was* little difference between them.) The Prague coup of 1948 and the (assumed) murder of Jan Masaryk increased the tension further. In February, he noted excitedly a Belgian newspaper report

60. Ibid., p. 130.
61. De la Gorce, *Après-guerre*, p. 314.

that a coup had been imminent, during which he would have been assassinated, and that fake documents were being produced suggesting a wartime link between de Gaulle and the Germans.[62] The next month, Ramadier, then prime minister, reported to the cabinet the discovery of a 'vast paramilitary organisation' all over the country. It was organised into conventional battalions, manned especially by Italians and Spaniards, and with tanks and guns made in Russia.[63] Needless to say, no trace of such an organisation was ever found. By November the story had altered to Soviet international brigades, officered by former *résistants*, ready to invade Spain and start a revolution. This was the same force – 100,000 strong – that had been on standby to support a Soviet airborne invasion in 1946, inexplicably called off at the last moment. The brigades were next expected to help the Communists take power in France and Spain.[64] And by the end of the year, he was told by the intelligence service that 10,000 men had definitely left to settle the Greek civil war: 'in passing', they would overthrow the governments of Italy and France.[65]

That otherwise sensible people should believe these fantasies tells us something about the atmosphere of the time: it also tells us something about the beliefs and loyalties of the various intelligence agencies. So vast is the range of scare stories at the time, so baroque the invention, and so traditional the fears, that one must suspect a degree of organisation, or even something approaching a conspiracy, on the part of a group who, after all, largely believed this kind of rubbish themselves, and had done so ever since 1917. It certainly had an effect. Not only was the Resistance coalition definitively broken (that was inevitable, anyway), but a purge not unlike that of 1939–40 was started. Communists and those with suspected Communist sympathies were purged from the army, the radio, the civil service and the nationalised industries, and a special section of the Interior Ministry was set up to hunt down and identify others. Many publications suspected of Communist sympathies were closed down. All other political parties joined in with enthusiasm: the SFIO were particularly eager to widen the purge.[66]

Those involved were, of course, re-running fears and hostilities that had become conditioned reflexes over the decades. Yet the real

---

62. Vincent Auriol, *Journal du Septennat, 1947–1954*, Vol. 1, 1947, Paris, Armand Colin, 1970, p. 90.
63. Ibid., p. 132.
64. Ibid., pp. 521–2.
65. Ibid., p. 616.
66. De la Gorce, *Après-guerre*, pp. 327–34.

effects of the Great Panic were largely restricted to a small section of the community. The political and military classes, with assistance from the media and the industrial and financial community, collaborated in scaring each other witless, often using the same ideas and even the same vocabulary employed in the past. But there was little evidence of any *general* anti-Communist or anti-Soviet feeling among the population as a whole, and certainly among the ordinary people: they continued (as they always had done) to be more worried about a revived Germany. Thus, in October 1948, a weekly magazine asked the question 'What would you do if the Red Army occupied France?', and printed a series of responses from public figures over the next few weeks. The majority of responses from outside the ranks of the professionally frightened, however, criticised the question and the assumptions behind it.[67]

Marianne's Choice

While these traumas were taking place, the interest of other nations was attracted, not least that of the United States. As we have seen, that nation had already involved itself in the internal affairs of France during the war. It continued to do so afterwards, and its policy was essentially the same: to encourage stable, pro-American governments without the Communists or de Gaulle. For many years, the United States tried to bring about the formation of an anti-Communist, but otherwise moderate, political party or grouping in France, along the lines of the Christian Democrats in Germany and Italy. They used a variety of means, some overt and some covert, some subtle and some less so. Their efforts became entangled with efforts to achieve many other US objectives, especially those concerned with trade and finance. They failed, and, in failing, left a legacy of bitterness and humiliation that endures.

The United States had been interested in the internal development of France for some time, of course, but the escalating problems of 1946 sharpened this interest considerably. A paper of September that year argued that 'the world drama of Soviet expansion' was being played out in France, and argued for the avoidance of extremes of right (i.e. de Gaulle) and left (the PCF) in favour of an appeal to the 'common people', who were believed to be the

67. Ibid., pp. 359–60.

'natural allies' of the United States. George Kennan, the architect of containment, thought this was too complacent a view. He thought that the Soviet Union 'intended to weaken France in order to render it susceptible to Soviet domination' through its chosen instrument, the PCF. The French people did not, unfortunately, understand this, and a psychological warfare campaign was therefore recommended.[68] This implied covert attempts to 'do everything we can to prevent France falling under Communist domination', and the consequent risk of 'Soviet penetration of Western Europe, Africa, the Mediterranean and the Middle East', as Ambassador Caffrey in Paris put it.[69] (The alternative, a Gaullist dictatorship, was equally unattractive.) Caffrey urged massive economic help. A memorandum of July 1947, by the head of the European Affairs Bureau, worried at the problem of whether something more direct could be done to forestall the Communists' returning to government. Accepting that this was 'substantially a French internal matter', nonetheless Lovett thought it would be so serious a development that aid would have to be cut off. If the Communists were refused a place in government, they might try to destroy the French economy, and civil war could break out. Should the US then intervene? Alternatively, a 'Communist-controlled government' might be attacked by 'non-Communist elements probably under the leadership of General de Gaulle'. Should the US help him? Wisely, the paper offered no firm recommendations.[70]

The judgement that France was a key strategic area, that a Communist attempt to destroy the government was a real possibility, and that the US should seek to do everything it could to prevent it, without being too blatant about it, ran through the policy papers of the next few years. The aim was to help build a strong centre, split the SFIO from the PCF, and keep de Gaulle out. This policy, the resources available to the United States, and the weakness of France, meant that the embassy was 'one of the most important pressure groups in the country'. Thus, as 'American preferences for one or another French policy, or even politician, became known, French protagonists sought to use American desires to their advantage, and even bargained with the Embassy directly in quest of American support and intervention'.[71]

68. Irwin Wall, *The United States and the Making of Postwar France, 1945–1954*, Cambridge, Cambridge University Press, 1991, pp. 58–59.

69. *FRUS, 1947*, Vol. 3, p. 712.

70. Ibid., pp. 720–2.

71. Wall, *US and Postwar France*, p. 36.

The embassy tried to reinforce political stability by putting pressure on opposition politicians not to bring down the government of the day, and on members of the cabinet to stay loyal. There was also a major, and largely covert, attempt to influence French public opinion away from Communism. This included efforts to woo workers away from the Communist-led CGT, and the sponsoring of a non-Communist 'peace movement'.[72] The CIA provided discreet subsidies to various non-Communist organisations and publications, as well as dissident groups of former Communists.[73] If the United States was able to have this degree of influence, it was largely because the French were prepared to concede it: as often is the case in politics, a force expanded to fill a vacuum. Such was the atmosphere of weakness and fear that the French reflexively caved in to even the slightest American pressure, and a visitor from the embassy, no matter how humble, would be fawned over by the highest levels of the Quai.[74]

Given this unprecedented degree of influence, it has been natural to ask whether the expulsion of the PCF was the doing of the United States, as was the case at about the same time in Italy. There seems to be little direct evidence for this, and plenty of reasons why the government should have wanted to eject the PCF anyway.[75] The idea was too instinctively satisfying to die an early death, however, and there may be a scintilla of logic to it, in the sense that there was no need for the United States to say overtly that removal of the PCF would help relations between the two nations: that would have been obvious to any politician. Certainly, media speculation at the time encouraged this idea.[76] But it is doubtful that this was more than a minor element in the decision. More generally, it has often been alleged that the United States tried 'to galvanise the anti-communism and anti-sovietism of the IVth Republic' so as to obtain 'the alignment of France with American policy, which was to establish a Western bloc under its aegis, first economic and political, and then military'. It seems 'more than likely' that intelligence data about possible coups given to the French by the US authorities 'were strongly marked by this concern'. Even if this were not so, 'it is the hypothesis which carries the most political conviction'.[77]

72. Ibid., p. 129.
73. Ibid., pp. 150–1.
74. Destremau, *Quai d'Orsay*, pp. 88–90.
75. Wall, *US and Postwar France*, pp. 67–68.
76. Ibid., p. 70.
77. De la Gorce, *Après-guerre*, p. 331.

As the slightly downbeat conclusion to this formulation indicates, ultimately this is what I have called a 'political truth'. This presentation of it is a fairly subtle one, which avoids the crude (and quite erroneous) suggestion that the United States bullied France into NATO. All one can say on the immediate substance is that apparently the US embassy was receiving very much the same kind of reports, and Caffrey thought that they 'were being fed to naïve military officers by French rightists' looking for political subsidies.[78] This may well be true; but the intelligence branch of the army was notorious for spreading politically motivated stories, and it is quite probable that there was an informal plot of some kind to scare the government into a crackdown on the PCF, to which these colourful stories contributed. But there is no evidence that the United States was the source of these inventions.

As a starving and bankrupt nation, France had little choice but to turn to the United States for financial help. This was provided, at first bilaterally and then through the Marshall Plan; but it became sufficiently confused with other aspects of Franco-American economic relations that it caused further misunderstanding and resentment. It will be recalled that France had equally needed loans from the United States after the First World War, and that the commercial orientation of the American bankers annoyed the French, whose claim to the sympathy of the world in turn disconcerted the Americans. Much the same happened thirty years later. It was agreed that Léon Blum would lead a team to Washington in early 1946 to seek loans for reconstruction: the *Wall Street Journal* commented sniffily that it was 'ironical to see how determinedly the descendants of Karl Marx believe in Santa Claus'.[79] Washington saw some scope for a loan, on basically commercial terms; but, in return, wanted French concessions on trade and tariffs, settlement of lend-lease and other outstanding payments, and freer access to French cinemas for American films.[80] The Blum-Byrnes accords were generally a success, but some of the detail escaped, to lead a vigorous and highly coloured existence of its own.

The 'Coca-colonisation' of France and 'Hollywood imperialism' would between them make an unconvincing scenario for a political satire, but were taken with immense seriousness by politicians and others over several years in the late 1940s. Incongruously, pressure was put on the French to import Coca-Cola, and to pay

78. Wall, *US and Postwar France*, p. 46.
79. Cited by Young, *France, Cold War and Western Alliance*, p. 100.
80. *FRUS*, 1946, Vol. 5, pp. 410–1.

for the import of more Hollywood films, at a time when food and coal were both in short supply. It was charged that the manufacturers of the drink were trying to dominate the European soft-drinks market, and drive indigenous companies out of business. It is known that Coca-Cola wanted to make France its European base, as a 'bridgehead to Europe': *Le Monde* charged that coloured maps on the walls at company headquarters 'outlined a strategic plan for the spread of the beverage'. It was thought to be habit-forming (indeed, to contain cocaine), and legislation was passed through the National Assembly that would have allowed it to be banned. The manufacturers put pressure on the State Department and threatened retaliation against wine and champagne. The quarrel over the cinema was really about attempts by Hollywood to regain a profitable lost market, and French worry about the threat to their industry and their culture from cheap imports. There were highly complex, and often acrimonious, discussions about quotas and screen exposure in the margins of the Blum visit, and at least some on the US side wanted to make the loans themselves conditional on a satisfactory resolution of the issue.

To add to the chaos, there was a strong political sub-sub-text. The owner of the Coca-Cola Company was a politically powerful anti-Communist, and claimed that his product contained 'essence of capitalism' in every bottle. Hollywood meanwhile, reeling under the McCarthy purges, was busy making films (not least newsreels) that followed the developing Cold War line.[81] In the end it was clumsiness rather than a conspiracy; but to the French it appeared that, under the guise of a foreign aid programme, they were being ordered to recycle the dollars in purchasing goods that they did not want, which would rot, variously, their teeth and their brains, and were being forced on them for ideological reasons. All parts of society were up in arms. The deeper reason is not hard to find: the French were only just starting to find out who they were again, when their very identity seemed suddenly to be threatened.

This is the background against which the French government took its fateful decisions about security policy in the late 1940s. What can be said about the objectives, fears and preconceptions that the French would have brought to their decision-making, based on their accumulated experience in general and their inter-war experience in particular? One could assume, even with no knowledge of post-war France, that the main elements of thinking

81. Wall, *US and Postwar France*, pp. 113–26.

in Paris would, in principle, follow something like the following lines. There would be a sense of fear and national weakness, great concern about a revived Germany and a sense of anticipatory inferiority, fears for the unity of the country and the risk of revolution, suspicion and fear of the Anglo-Saxons, together with a desire to seek their protection but not their domination, and fear (at least among certain classes) of Communism and Soviet influence. To this would be added the usual concern for the status of France as a great power, and an expectation that she would be treated accordingly. I am not suggesting that a point-by-point comparison of 1918 and 1945 would show no differences; but there is an unmistakable continuity of thought over that period. The difference lay less in the aspirations than in the surrounding circumstances, which were in every way grimmer than those at Versailles.

The word that haunts all discussion of French policy at this time is 'choice': indeed, a popular French survey of the period is called *Marianne's Choice*.[82] The assumption is that in the late 1940s France 'chose' the United States and 'chose' the West, having previously hoped to remain neutral and equidistant from the two superpowers. I believe that this is misleading, insofar as it implies that there was ever a real chance of France's throwing in its lot with the Soviet Union, or even becoming a non-aligned nation in the Bandung sense. It is true that there was a great reluctance to become a camp follower, and a desire, expressed in various ways, to retain independence of decision-making. For example, Sartre and some colleagues produced a manifesto proclaiming that 'it is not true that men have to choose between large political blocs'.[83] Sartre's own preference was for the creation of some kind of 'socialist Europe'; but the desire to avoid subordination to blocs was a common one. This desire was not the same thing as indifference between political and economic systems: France was indissolubly part of the West, and would inevitably have to seek a close relationship with the Anglo-Saxons. It was not the result of the choice that was a problem, but the requirement to make the choice itself.

Fear of loss of identity, and submergence in a disciplined 'bloc' was very much a feature of the late 1940s. Fashionable theories, such as those of the American 'managerialist' James Burnham, held that the world would eventually coalesce into a few large,

82. Annie Lacroix-Riz, *Le Choix de Marianne: les relations Franco-américains de la Libération aux débuts du plan Marshall (1944–1948)*, Paris, Messidor/Editions Sociales, 1985.

83. Annie Cohen-Solal, *Sartre: A Life*, London, Heinemann, 1987, p. 300.

totalitarian, feuding blocs, each headed by a superpower. George Orwell's *1984*, itself partly a satire on Burnhamism, is a reflection of these fears: Britain has lost even its name, by that date, and is only 'Airstrip One' of Oceania, a totalitarian military and political bloc dominated by the United States. For a nation that had virtually ceased to exist for four years, and was riven by dissent and weakened by poverty, the possibility of losing identity and freedom again, so soon, was unthinkable. For four years, after all, elements of France had been parts of 'blocs', and the country as a whole had been torn into pieces by the experience. It was hardly surprising that there was limited interest in repeating the experiment. The overall orientation of French policy was not in doubt, and there would be close co-operation with, and often subordination to, the United States. But there was a world of difference between forced adherence to a dictated line, and a free decision to support the United States, based on the merits of the case.

We are back to freedom again. To take up the existentialist terminology I used earlier, France now *existed*, in the sense that there was, once again, a legal and political entity with an unchallenged title to that name. But the *essence* of France remained to be determined. Partly this was mechanistic: the need to develop a new constitution and new political structures, and run them in. But more importantly it was moral: the need to work out a relationship with the immediate past, to lay to rest the ghosts of the war, and develop a role for the future. The way in which France would define itself was by free action, the more so since it had so recently been broken into pieces, each one the plaything of a foreign power. The bitterness that the French feel about this period results from the perception that this freedom, and hence this definition of essence, was never really possible, and that the quality of the relationship that developed with the Anglo-Saxons was just a new form of subservience.

There would, in any case, have been difficulties in France's playing a free and independent role, even in a much more benign climate. The British faced a similar dilemma, in that they could no longer claim to be a great power by themselves; but they had a way out. As early as 1942, a Foreign Office memorandum was suggesting that the UK 'must have some powerful ally or allies, or cease to be a World Power'.[84] It was not difficult to deduce who

84. Sir Llewellyn Woodward, *British Foreign Policy in the Second World War*, Vol. 5, HMSO, London, 1976, p. 5.

this ally might be. In a celebrated 'stock-taking' paper of July 1945, Sir Orme Sargent proposed that, whilst Britain should endeavour to follow an independent line on the reconstruction of Europe, and 'We must have a policy of our own', nevertheless, we should 'try to persuade the United States to make it their own', as well.[85] The suggested method of quiet assertion, the transformation of Britain into the 'loyal courtier', fitted British traditions of indirect and pragmatic diplomacy very well. It responded to the perception that the British had (and some have argued they still have) that they are cleverer and more skilled than the Americans, who could supply the brawn while the British supplied the brains.

Even in principle, this was not a possibility for the French. There was only room for one loyal courtier, and the British, with their close linguistic and cultural connections, would automatically fill the role. But in any event, French history and French pride would have ruled out such a humiliating role. This left a concentration on the empire, which was clearly essential but not enough. The only way forward appeared to be an organisation of Europe, under French tutelage, into a group that would have the necessary weight to deal on a basis of equality with Washington, and to stop France being reduced to a servile status. This was the essence of French policy in the late 1940s, and remains so to this day. It presupposes American involvement in Europe, and a large role for that nation in some kind of transatlantic structure; but it excludes a preponderant political role for Washington as a result.

This was the background in Paris when the first whispers of what was to be the Washington Treaty were heard in early 1948. Like other initiatives recounted here, it will be clear by now that the idea of a treaty of a military nature among Western nations, directed against Communism and the Soviet Union, was essentially a reshuffling of already existing elements. Fears of Bolshevism had been widespread among the political and military classes for decades. The idea of a formal alliance against Bolshevism in 1918 had not made much progress, but it had produced the informal alliance of states intervening in the Russian civil war. The failure of that policy had in turn produced the concept of the *cordon sanitaire*, an early version of the 'containment' doctrine. A treaty relationship with the Anglo-Saxon powers had been envisaged in 1919. Much of the diplomacy of the inter-war period had been directed at avoiding the Communist menace: Germany had

85. *DBPO*, Series I, Vol. I, no. 102.

been rebuilt, in the face of French protests, lest she collapse into anarchy and thus Bolshevism. More vigorous approaches had been tried also, such as the projected Franco-British invasion of 1940, and the very tangible contributions made by a number of European nations to the German 'crusade' against the 'Bolshevik threat' in and after 1941. Finally, even before the UN Charter was signed, the idea of a European security organisation, with an association with the United Sates, was already being discussed. France had been involved in all these initiatives, and, against the background set out above, was very attracted to the idea of some kind of Western security organisation when it was first broached.

In particular, a government terrified of domestic conflict and a Communist coup was pleased to hear of proposals for a treaty that seemed to be aimed primarily at the preservation of internal order. The panic throughout the West in 1947–48 was not caused by fear of deliberate Soviet aggression, which was thought unlikely (although fear of war breaking out accidentally was quite real).[86] Montgomery, then about to be commander-in-chief of the Brussels Treaty Organisation, judged in July 1948 that it would be five years before the Soviet Union was militarily ready for war.[87] Washington studied hypothetical scenarios for a European war, but believed that the American nuclear monopoly made them unlikely, at least until the mid-1950s.[88] Even in the stressed political climate of Europe, few actually disagreed: Bidault, the French foreign minister, said in July 1948 that he was 'almost convinced the Soviet Union will not attack us'.[89] In public, and in international negotiations, politicians were more apocalyptic, but this was largely for tactical purposes: as in 1919, they found it useful to threaten each other with the spectre of Communism. This applied particularly to the French, who had every reason to exaggerate their vulnerability to get military and economic aid from the United States. Military aid, in particular, was easier to obtain in an anti-Communist framework than by expressing worries about a rearmed Germany dominating Western Europe.

86. For the atmosphere of the early years of the Cold War, and the (sometimes alarming) plans of the United States to 'roll back Communism', see Thomas H. Etzold and John Lewis Gaddis, eds, *Containment: Documents on American Policy and Strategy, 1945–1950*, New York, Columbia University Press, 1978.
87. Cited by Escott Reid, *Time of Fear and Hope: The Making of the North Atlantic Treaty, 1947–49*, Toronto, McClelland and Stewart, 1977, pp. 13–14.
88. Wall, *US and Postwar France*, p. 131.
89. Cited by Reid, *Time of Fear and Hope*, p. 17.

The real fear was of Soviet domination of Europe by non-military means. Here, the example of Hitler was decisive. As one French official put it: 'Communism is simply repeating what Nazism did [ten] years previously.'[90] The negotiations of the late 1940s were the beginning of the long psychodrama through which the Western political classes tried to atone for their behaviour at the time of Munich. As with the Nazis, it was assumed that Communist tactics would feature threats, rather than the actual use of force, and attempts to intimidate nations into 'going Communist' without a fight. Thus, Bevin's message of January 1948, usually reckoned to have started the process that led to the Washington Treaty, referred not to the danger of war, but to the 'Communist peril', which threatened the 'fabric of the West', and would, if not opposed, lead to 'the piecemeal collapse of one Western bastion after another'. To this, he opposed '[p]olitical and indeed spiritual forces', to 'create confidence and energy on the one side and inspire respect and caution on the other', through the creation of a 'spiritual union of the West' as a 'counter attraction to the baleful tenets of communism'.[91] Similarly, the State Department thought that the risk was of 'internal fifth column aggression supported by the threat of external force, on the Czech model'. It could be combatted, however, if 'non-Communist elements' could be convinced that 'friendly external force comparable to the threatening external force' was available.[92] This was the genesis and main purpose of the Washington Treaty: to steady the populations of Western Europe, to encourage them not to vote Communist, and to demonstrate solidarity in the face of an international campaign of economic and political dislocation, masterminded from Moscow and carried out by local Communist parties, trades unions and covert agents. It is an interesting amalgam of the fears of 1918–20 with the fears of 1936–39.

It was not clear how such an essentially political treaty could be applied at a practical level. One indication is the proposal made by Kennan in March 1948 to prevent a Communist victory in the Italian general elections of that year. He proposed that the Italian government should outlaw the Communist Party, in the knowledge that the latter would begin a civil war, after which the United States would have grounds to intervene. Although there would be

90. Cited by Young, *France, Cold War and Western Alliance*, p. 179.
91. *FRUS*, 1948, Vol. 3, pp. 4–6.
92. Ibid., pp. 40–41.

'much violence', this was to be preferred to 'a bloodless election victory' that would give the Communists control of Italy and 'send waves of panic' throughout the area. The idea was rejected as too risky.[93] The thought of this kind of action was, however, present in the negotiations that led to the treaty, and particularly in the concept of 'indirect aggression'. A State Department proposal of March 1948 defined this as 'an internal *coup d'état* or political change favourable to an aggressor', as well as the use of force *within* a territory by agents of a foreign power.[94] As a result, the treaty was at one stage to have contained a provision on indirect aggression; but this ran into opposition from Britain and France.[95] It only survived in the reference in Article IV to threats to the 'territorial integrity, political independence or security' of any of the parties. The French seem to have opposed a wider provision, not because they did not believe in internal aggression, but because they were suspicious of the use another nation might make of it to intervene in their affairs.

The French were not involved in the earliest stages of the negotiations, which were conducted in great secrecy between Britain, Canada and the United States in March and April 1948, immediately after the signature of the Brussels Treaty. It was decided that the French should be excluded, on US insistence, as a 'security risk'.[96] This was probably the wrong decision from a practical point of view, and was in any case rendered pointless by the fact that one of the British officials involved was Donald Maclean: the Soviet Union, therefore, was probably more *au fait* with the negotiations than the French. The latter had their own perspectives in any event, and this caused some confusion when the negotiations proper started, still amid great secrecy, in July 1948, with the addition of France, Belgium and the Netherlands. French objectives were essentially those of a political class in a state of fear and nervous exhaustion. The French wanted military aid more than they wanted an alliance, because, as in 1918, they were neurotically insecure and frightened of domination by any country with a larger army.

The United States had warmly welcomed the Brussels Treaty, and was encouraging the political and economic union of Europe to strengthen it against what was usually called 'Soviet-directed

93. Ibid., pp. 206–7.
94. Ibid., pp. 63–64.
95. Reid, *Time of Fear and Hope*, p. 159.
96. Ibid., pp. 59–60.

World Communism', and also to make the most effective use of American aid. A necessary component of this was some kind of central administration in Germany, although at that date there was no thought that the nation might be re-armed. For the United States this seemed primarily a practical question; for the French, of course, it was supremely political. General Clay, the American military commander in Germany, was pressing for the creation of a provisional government in 1948, because, he told the French, it was 'the only means to fight against communism'. Robert Murphy complained that an inability to see that the Soviet Union, and not Germany, was the real threat, was causing the French to be awkward about German reconstruction.[97] The French, of course, were frightened of a repetition of events after the previous war, when Germany had been rebuilt as a bulwark against Bolshevism, only to turn on her renovators.

These differences of view led to substantial problems in the negotiations. The French wanted a narrowly focused pact with a firm American commitment, plans to defeat any Soviet attack in Germany (i.e. not in France), massive American aid and more US troops.[98] American priorities were roughly the reverse, and in the end, largely bereft of support, the French gave in on most of the points. The French did gain one or two small victories though, chiefly on the question of the geographical extent of the pact. The French had originally wanted all of their North African territories to be included in the area, but eventually settled for Algeria only. This was important, not only because Algeria was legally part of France, but also because there were already signs of a burgeoning independence movement – or 'indirect aggression', as the French saw it. The failure of the NATO allies to come to France's assistance over Algeria was to be one of the major factors in French disillusionment with the alliance in the 1950s. The French in addition believed that their hand would be strengthened if Italy were also a member, which fortunately for them also happened, for entirely different, and essentially military, reasons, to be the view of some in Washington.

During the late 1940s, weak and frightened French governments played a mostly ineffectual part in the evolution of Western security policy and institutions. A paralysing dependence on the United States made the formulation of any kind of independent

97. Young, *France, Cold War and Western Alliance*, p. 190.
98. Ibid., p. 206.

position on these issues difficult to achieve and almost impossible to sustain. The fear produced by weakness and the weakness produced by fear, together with political and economic disunity, led the French to make a series of concessions, and to tie themselves closely to the United States in a way and to an extent that would otherwise not have been the case. A whole anthology of shameful surrenders and callous betrayals was established and passed down to later generations. Opportunities for the creation of a European Third Force were missed, more because of internal Anglo-French problems than through any opposition from the United States. Most importantly, the fear and confusion of the time prevented the country from reconstructing its identity, as it was trying to reconstruct itself in other ways. There was the disturbing knowledge that the United States (certainly) and the Soviet Union (probably) were active in domestic politics, influencing opinions, financing trades unions, subsidising political parties, and who knew what else. Consistent rumours of coups and insurrections encouraged the frightening belief that the country was no longer controlled by the government, but that its history was now being produced and orchestrated by others.

Yet it was possible to take some consolation from the Washington Treaty, which was ratified with a tidy majority in July. At the domestic level, all parties except the PCF rejoiced that anti-Communism was now embraced as the official Western ideology, and that the PCF's electoral attractions were therefore likely to decline. The Right and the army were overjoyed, of course, since the treaty seemed to them to vindicate the stance they had taken ever since 1917, and to call into question the actions of resistance forces, who had believed (erroneously, as it now seemed) that Germany was the real enemy. It also made the demands for an amnesty harder to resist; clearly, the hunting down of 'Communist terrorists' by the *Milice* had been a wise and prudent thing to do. In more moderate parts of the spectrum, there was satisfaction also: the Anglo-Saxons were now linked by treaty to the defence of France, even if the link was a little tenuous – the culmination of thirty years of effort. Some politicians approved of the treaty because of residual warmth towards the United States, others because of a commitment to multilateral security structures, and a willingness to surrender some sovereignty as a price for joining one. Fear, weakness, domestic politics and idealism combined to produce a highly artificial combination of political forces that was inherently incapable of lasting.

In addition, France did not seem to be too badly placed overall. The rearmament of Germany had not been mentioned, and nobody seemed to think it was in prospect. The treaty had not spawned any kind of supranational bureaucracy, which France would have found it difficult to work with. The signatories had set up a Standing Group, on which France was represented with the United States and the United Kingdom, and which would act as the motor of the Alliance. But neither this body, nor the various regional planning groups, seemed to pose a substantial threat to the sovereignty of the struggling state.

8

THE REBELS AND THE SOVEREIGN

I rebel, therefore we exist.

Camus, *The Rebel*, 1950

We must have a European Army.

Eisenhower, 1951

France does not take orders from anyone.

Pinay, 1952

Algeria is France.

Mitterrand, 1954

The outbreak of the Korean War in 1950 began a chain of events that systematically invalidated the main assumptions made in Paris in the late 1940s about the way in which European security would henceforth be organised. The increasing militarisation of the Atlantic Alliance, the perceived domination of the Anglo-Saxons, and conflict over the colonial wars, all combined to produce a wave of disillusionment with NATO and the American link, of which de Gaulle's actions between 1958 and 1966 were a logical (although not inevitable) outcome. De Gaulle himself came to power over the corpse of the Fourth Republic, itself the most notable of the casualties of this series of colonial wars that split France along what are now familiar lines.

The invasion of South Korea by the North in June 1950 caused a major revision in thinking about the Soviet Union and the security of Europe. For most Western leaders, it was axiomatic that this action was part of the grand design of 'Soviet-directed World Communism', leading to world domination. It could therefore be assumed that a second blow, in the West, would follow shortly. An attack on Europe could come at any time: it could come tomorrow.[1] The Soviet army, although massively demobilised since 1945, was still over two-and-a-half million strong, and considerably outnumbered the forces facing it. Soviet capabilities had not changed, but the Korean War brought about a substantial change in views about Soviet intentions. In the light of this new perception, a massive expansion of military forces and a large increase in military expenditure were thought necessary: social policies and measures to rebuild the European economies and the industrial base would have to come later.

It was against this background that the United States proposed 'the immediate establishment of an integrated force in Europe, within the Framework of the North Atlantic Treaty adequate to ensure the successful defence of Western Europe, including Western Germany, against possible aggression'. It argued that it was 'essential that there be an increase in the forces in Europe at the earliest feasible date'. There should be a supreme commander with the authority to 'insure that the separate national forces' were 'organised into one effective force in time of peace', and the right to command them in war. He should have 'an international staff' in his support. There was also a need for 'greater central direction' of production and procurement.[2]

This initiative was not unexpected, and was generally welcomed by European governments. The appointment of Eisenhower as supreme commander was welcomed also. It was essentially as a result of Korea, therefore, that the operational military structure of NATO, as we now know it, started to be developed; and it was a structure with which the French, almost at once, began to have problems.

By far the most difficult and contentious issue was – as it had been after the previous war – the rearmament of Germany. There were two essential arguments put forward by the United States. One was military: Soviet forces were believed to be 'in an advanced state of readiness for war and could initiate offensive operations without warning'. Over two million Soviet and other troops could strike at any moment. Massive preparations for war

---

1. This was apparently the general view in Washington at the time, held by Truman among others. See e.g. Charles E. Bohlen, *Witness to History, 1929–1969*, London, Weidenfeld and Nicolson, 1973, pp. 290–1.

2. The text is in *Documents on British Policy Overseas*, Series II, Vol. 3, No. 33. Hereafter *DBPO*.

had been detected, including the construction of airfields and stockpiling of fuel and ammunition. In the circumstances, this threat could not be addressed without troops in the numbers that only Germany could provide. And for their parts, the Soviets were already believed to be transforming the *Bereitschaften* (East German para-military police) into a military-style organisation. There was also a (lesser) political argument advanced, that Germany should 'stand up and be counted with the West'. The fear of a Bolshevised Germany, so strong after 1918, had started to haunt Western policy-makers again.[3]

Some attempt was made to cater to the feelings of the French and others. A list of 'safeguards' included the assertions that German units would not be under 'the authority and command' of the German Federal Republic, that they would be 'dependent upon Western nations' for heavy equipment, spares and fuel, and there would be 'no general staff as such in Germany but merely an administrative and logistical agency'. In addition, numbers would be limited and recruitment carefully supervised, and prohibitions on the manufacture of military equipment would continue.[4] The initial presentation of these ideas was inept in the extreme. David Bruce, the new American ambassador in Paris, told his British counterpart that 'the United States military people had got control of the negotiations and had launched the United States plan ... before the State Department had had an opportunity of looking at it from the political angle'. Moreover, 'the Pentagon boys had quite forgotten by now that there had been a war in Germany'.[5] It was another case of the very different decision-taking machinery in Washington giving birth to an initiative for military reasons, and the political leadership feeling reluctant to interfere. It was a way of doing business which the French were unable to understand, and it produced a violent reaction. French ministers questioned whether 'we should be putting ourselves in the position of petitioners' to the Germans, and whether the Germans would accept a subordinate position anyway, as well as predicting

---

3. A useful summary of the US position is a brief prepared for General Marshall, then secretary for defence, for a meeting with his French counterpart in October 1950, and printed in *Foreign Relations of the United States*, 1950, Vol. 3, pp. 1408–12. Hereafter *FRUS*.

4. Ibid., pp. 1410–11.

5. *DBPO*, Series II, Vol. 3, No. 93.

'disastrous reactions' from ordinary people, and probable adverse effects on both the Soviet Union and Germany itself.[6]

German rearmament failed to enthuse any other European nation, and was not a popular cause among their publics. The British government (which had realised, even before the end of the war, that the problem would have to be faced one day) wrestled with the subject all through 1950. One Foreign Office official believed that remilitarisation would start 'a process which would be continuous. That is to say, sooner or later there will be a German Army and a German High Command and General Staff and the appropriate Ministry'. And if 'the Russian peril' were to recede, we could be left 'with a German army and no Americans'. Sir W. Strang concluded that, in agreeing to remilitarisation, we 'confess to ourselves that we believe war to be inevitable'.[7] None of the other nations demonstrated any warmth towards the idea either, but the French were isolated in their total opposition to it. The other treaty members agreed with the Italian foreign minister that French arguments had to be rejected, since Europe was 'in mortal peril'.[8] In such a situation, and faced with the 'inevitable rearmament of Germany demanded by Washington',[9] there was not a great deal that Paris could do. The Quai were concerned that a policy of outright opposition created the risk that 'German rearmament will be accomplished despite us, almost against us'. The principle of German rearmament would have to be accepted, but 'modalities' would be needed, 'permitting the retention of sufficient control on the part of the French government over German rearmament'.[10] This desire was to lead to the ill-fated proposal for a European Defence Community.

The dominant mood in France remained one of unease and fear about the future. One can isolate two strands of thought, often confused then and later, in a way which partly explains the apparent incoherence of French opinion at the time. Firstly, general statements about loyalty to the West, resisting Communism, defending common ideals, assuring adequate levels of armed

6. See for example the record of the North Atlantic Council meeting of September 1950, in *DBPO*, Series II, Vol. 3, No. 32. The French succeeded in preventing any reference to German rearmament being inserted into the communiqué.

7. *DBPO*, Series II, Vol. 3, No. 24.

8. Ibid., No. 32 n.1.

9. Frédéric Bozo, *La France et l'OTAN: De la guerre froide au nouvel ordre européen*, Paris, Masson, 1991, p. 39.

10. Irwin Wall, *The United States and the Making of Postwar France, 1945–1954*, Cambridge, Cambridge University Press, 1991, pp. 198–9.

forces, etc., would *in these terms* have commanded approval from large sections of the population and virtually the whole of the policy-making and opinion-forming élites. At the same time, the predominant mood was of what is now called 'neutralism', and featured considerable wariness about the policies and practices of the United States. The explanation is that, given the overwhelming military, political and financial strength of the United States and the weakness of France in all these areas, general statements about Western unity and common values meant *in practice* subordination to the policies and ideals of the United States. The correlation of forces excluded any other outcome. What was wise and prudent for France, and anyway probably inescapable, was not necessarily attractive or free of danger. The French had traditionally adopted a rather patronising attitude to the Americans, regarding them as naïve and inexperienced in international affairs. The immense American military superiority and monopoly of nuclear weapons now produced the added fear that a US government would behave irresponsibly and destroy the world (and France) in the process. Thus Massigli, the French ambassador, told the British Foreign Office that he was afraid that the Americans 'elated by their success in Korea ... would incline themselves more and more towards the idea of knocking out Russia'. He was especially concerned that a revived Germany might tempt the US in this direction.[11]

To some extent, public pronouncements and press coverage fuelled these fears. In October 1951, *Collier's* magazine caused a great stir in Europe with its special feature on 'The Defeat and Occupation of Russia 1952–60', which included maps and faked photographs of the Third World War, including details of nuclear attacks, and a description of the occupation régime in the former Soviet Union. For once, the attitude of the French media was uniformly hostile towards 'the climate in the United States' and 'the vertigo of war which, it appeared, had taken hold of American opinion, and this addiction to the prospect of an inevitable conflict, which tended to make the conflict itself even more likely'.[12] Similarly, French accounts of the period often mention the bizarre story of James Forrestal, secretary of the navy and then of defence, who, after repeated nightmares of a Communist invasion of

11. *DBPO*, Second Series, Vol. 3, No. 38.
12. Paul-Marie de la Gorce, *L'Après-guerre 1944–1952: Naissance de la France moderne*, Paris, Grasset, 1978, pp. 459–60.

the United States, was eventually hospitalised, and committed suicide in 1949 by flinging himself from the window of his room.[13] This perhaps explains a curious series of opinion polls cited by Paul-Marie de la Gorce in his book on post-war France. Between 1946 and 1953, a constant 70 to 80 per cent of the French thought that 'there is a nation which is trying to dominate the world'. In 1946, 37 per cent felt that the United States was this nation, or that guilt was equally shared with the Soviet Union. By 1953, 45 per cent held this view, against only 22 per cent who felt that the Soviet Union alone was guilty. This view was reflected, in turn, in questions about neutrality. In 1954, 39 per cent opted for neutrality between 'East and West', and 53 per cent for non-involvement in a Soviet-American war, against 37 per cent who wanted to be in the 'Western Camp' and 22 per cent who would fight with the United States.[14] As with similar findings, these need to be deconstructed. For reasons described below, most Frenchmen believed that the 'Western Camp' was simply an extension of the United States, whose belligerent stance might lead it to stumble into a destructive war with the Soviet Union. To be in the 'Western Camp' was to give up independence and to subordinate oneself to the political doctrines of another country, with uncertain but possibly lethal results. 'Neutralism' in this sense is best understood to mean 'independence' and freedom of decision-making. Few Frenchmen seem to have been attracted by the Soviet Union or Soviet policy, and in one of the polls mentioned above only 2 per cent wanted to join the 'Eastern Camp'. But to understand these results one has to bear in mind the difference between a political and economic *orientation*, which was not in doubt, and fears of subordination on the one hand, and of being destroyed in a private US-Soviet quarrel on the other. One could like or admire aspects of the United States whilst still feeling that its activities threatened the safety of the world as much as those of the Soviet Union.

These doubts were not universal, however. If approval for NATO and the influence of the United States were minority enthusiasms, limited largely to the politico-military élites, this minority

---

13. For example Simone de Beauvoir, *Force of Circumstance*, trans. Richard Howard, London, Penguin edn, 1968, pp. 179–80. Some of the wilder stories about Forrestal's behaviour have been partly, at least, discredited. But even avowedly sympathetic accounts paint a disturbing picture of the man responsible for managing America's nuclear weapons: see e.g. Arnold A. Rogow, *James Forrestal: A Study of Personality, Politics and Policy*, New York, Macmillan, 1963.

14. De la Gorce, *L'Après-guerre*, pp. 456–7.

was still somewhat larger than that which had cheered the *Légion des volontaires française* on its way to Moscow. It was helpful, of course, that the Germans were not a credible alternative enemy, still less occupying the country. It was also useful that there was a strong domestic political dimension to NATO membership. But there was one new factor: the feeling that on this occasion, unlike what had happened in the 1930s, the menace had been spotted in good time and preventive measures had been taken. Thus, when Robert Schuman was told by Ambassador Bohlen of the American decision to intervene in Korea, his eyes filled with tears and he exclaimed 'thank God this will not be a repetition of the past'.[15] For such people, the extent, or even the existence, of the Soviet threat was less important than the opportunity it gave them symbolically to rewrite history and to atone for the mistakes they and others had made in the 1930s.

Enthusiasm for NATO was especially strong in military circles. Partly, this was because the dominance of Vichy officers was still very great, and the new structure seemed to them to sanctify officially the stand they had taken, and to put in doubt the judgement of those who had resisted the Germans, including, of course, their present political masters. From now on, it was clear that the old geographical missions of territorial defence and the defence of French interests were outdated. Most of the officers welcomed this, but a number of the more modern and thoughtful ones left the colours voluntarily or were eased out, unhappy that

> traditional patriotism failed to explain the reasons for and objectives of the Atlantic Pact. There was no direct conflict between Soviet Russia and France, and the war against communism pointed both to an external and an internal enemy. It could indeed be regarded as a kind of international civil war whose episodes, as long as they remained 'cold' would consist in the progress of each country not only in armaments and manpower, but also in electoral contests, strikes, ideological struggles and the struggles of the *maquis* in Africa and Asia.[16]

Since the enemy was now, unambiguously, Communism, it followed that the nearest enemy was also the nearest Communist, who was likely to be found in the same town, even the same

---

15. Bohlen, *Witness to History*, pp. 289–90.
16. Paul-Marie de la Gorce, *The French Army: A Military-Political History*, trans. Kenneth Douglas, London, Weidenfeld and Nicolson, 1963, p. 362.

street. Army exercises henceforth assumed that the army would be operating, even at home, in a hostile environment. Added to all this was relief that, after years of uncertainty, the army had at last been given a mission and something to train for. That it was the same mission they had claimed for themselves since 1871 was not unwelcome.

The militarisation of the Alliance and the further intensification of the Cold War increased French dependence on the United States. This was inevitable, since France was not yet able to provide for itself the weapons that it needed. France received some $1,500 million of military aid between 1950 and 1952, which amounted to more than 50 per cent of the military equipment distributed to European nations.[17] It appears, though, that at least a part of this equipment was obsolescent, and came without spare parts. Of 257 tanks in service with the 5th Armoured Division in March 1953, it has been claimed that 40 per cent were unusable, and, in turn, that this figure exemplified 'the state of dependence in which the Atlantic system had placed the European allies of the United States'.[18]

There were strings attached to this aid, however. The United States expected France to conform to its own military priorities: with American air power and British sea power already established, it was logical that France should supply the ground troops in Central Europe. But the French were at least as much interested in preserving their empire, and were unattracted to being the Americans' foot soldiers in Europe. This led to frequent disputes between Paris and Washington over the shape and size of the defence budget and programme. The United States opposed the creation of a domestic armaments industry with American money, or at least claimed the right to determine what the French produced.[19] It proved possible, however, to develop some new equipment for the army and air force: the AMX-13 tanks and the Panhard armoured car were available by 1955, as were the early examples of aeroplanes like the Mystère IV and the multi-role Mirage III.[20]

17. Ibid., p. 188.
18. Jean Planchais, *Une Histoire Politique de l'Armée, 1940–1967: de Gaulle à de Gaulle*, Paris, Seuil, 1967, p. 242.
19. Ibid., p. 201.
20. Jean Doise and Maurice Vaisse, *Diplomatie et Outil Militaire, 1871–1969*, Paris, Imprimerie Nationale, 1987, pp. 416–8.

Atlantic and European; Or, the Need for Love

By the end of 1950, the future structure of Western defence institutions was starting to take shape, but was not yet fixed. There
were a number of choices to be made, and the structure of NATO
as we know it today was in no sense pre-determined: it could
easily have looked very different. This section is concerned with
the extent to which French hopes and aspirations were met, or
not. French objectives for the Alliance never really altered, from
the earliest days. What was needed was a firm American guarantee, American support in colonial wars, a great deal of American
hardware, but no American control. In early May 1950, just before
the launch of the Schumann plan for a European Coal and Steel
Community, Bidault, by then prime minister, presented a plan for
an executive organ of NATO, on which the United States, Britain
and France would have permanent seats: a kind of Security Council, which would 'institutionalise France's claim to be a world
power'.[21] Very similar proposals were to issue from Paris at regular intervals until the 1960s. The proposal was only partly, of
course, to ensure the status of France: it was at least as much concerned with ensuring that France retained a more influential position than a remilitarised Germany.

It is the continuity of these objectives that makes it unhelpful
to think of a dichotomy in French policy between 'Atlanticism'
and 'Europeanism' or 'Gaullism', or to scan the skies of Paris, as
the strategic community still does, for sightings of a genuine
'Atlanticist'. By some definitions, most of the French have always been Atlanticist, and by others, few if any have. Apart from
the PCF (henceforth silently excluded from all these generalisations), all the political tendencies in France eagerly sought American military help, and an American security guarantee, as they
had done since 1919. It was not believed that European defence
did, or ever would, make sense without these two elements. In
this sense, everyone was an 'Atlanticist'. But this attitude was
based entirely on a perception of French national interests. It did
not necessarily imply any warmth towards American civilisation and culture, still less to other American political objectives.
It did not give public loyalty towards American policies and a
ready willingness to bow to American leadership a high priority.
It did not see the need to align its own foreign policy with that

21. Wall, *US and Postwar France*, p. 193.

of the United States as an objective in itself, or to avoid quarrels as a matter of principle, even if it was forced to do all these things from time to time as a result of weakness. Above all, there was no 'Atlanticist' lobby in Paris in the sense that there was in London, and was later to be in Bonn. I mean by that, that there was no group who understood and felt at home in Washington and with American officials, who tended to agree with the latters' evaluations and share their assumptions, who understood how the American system of government functioned and were receptive to American proposals. In this sense, there were very few 'Atlanticists'.

This confusion bedevilled Franco-American relations at the time, and still does. It was a dialogue of the deaf, insofar as the French wanted military support, and the Americans wanted to be loved. Criticism of American policy, or even the American way of life, did not imply, to the French, a desire to forgo American support, or to turn to a more 'European' policy, although the Americans often thought that it did. The situation was further complicated by the very fragmented and variable reactions to the United States in France. Confusingly, right-wing governments could be more difficult to deal with than left-wing ones, and the strongest anti-Communists and supporters of the Alliance could also be the severest critics of facets of American culture and society. Enthusiasm for American popular culture, strongest on the Left and among the young, was seldom matched by a similar enthusiasm for American political objectives: logically, there is no reason why it should have been. Thus, Sartre had been in his youth an avid reader of American detective novels, and chose the name of his periodical, *Les Temps Modernes*, as a tribute to the Chaplin film. It was the radical critics of the *Cahiers du Cinéma* in the 1950s who championed the films of Howard Hawks, and who taught the Americans to recognise and applaud a series of cheap, morally equivocal Hollywood thrillers of the late 1940s as *films noirs*. The Maoist Jean-Luc Godard produced a string of homages to the Hollywood gangster movie and to Humphrey Bogart in particular, most notably in *A Bout du Souffle* (1960), for which he even imported the American actress Jean Seberg, possessor of possibly the worst French accent ever committed to celluloid. In the following decade, Godard saw no contradiction between directing a film like *Alphaville* (1966), a space-age homage to the *film noir* with an American hero, and simultaneously leading demonstrations against the Vietnam War.

There was little attempt, in mainstream politics, at least, to substitute a purely European defence system for the Atlantic one. Conversely, enthusiasm for Europe was common everywhere. A model in which France was the natural leader of an increasingly united Europe, and this Europe formed an entity whose close security relationship with America still left it great freedom of action, would have been accepted by the vast majority of the politico-military élite of the time. The restricted value of the Atlanticist/European distinction suggests that it might be profitable to look for another. I will suggest one in a moment, after a brief excursion into the taxonomy of international organisations.

There are two basic tendencies in such organisations: the classic one of inter-governmental co-operation, and the subsequent model of supranational integration. It is only a slight exaggeration to say that it was the Alliance's progression from the first (represented by the 1949 structure) to the second (represented by NATO) that provoked increasing French disenchantment. The first tendency is the classic method by which nations deal with each other, and involves the most use of the traditional arts of diplomacy. It favours large and powerful nations, and nations that have well-organised and skillful foreign ministries and civil services, as well as those with stable and effective governments. Its usual method of working is by meetings of delegates and working groups, in which traditional bureaucratic and diplomatic skills, as well as political strength, can be decisive. A single powerful nation finds it relatively easy to obstruct an initiative it does not like. There will probably be a secretariat, but its functions will be limited to those of arranging meetings and taking minutes. Its staff will probably be seconded from capitals or brought in on contract, and a corporate spirit and corporate objectives may not be easy to develop. Initiatives will mostly come from nations: either the large and powerful ones, or nations holding a rotating presidency, or both. This model is quite close to the original pattern of the Alliance.

Other organisations have tendencies towards supranational integration. This model is more varied, but the common feature is that nation-states have less room for manœuvre, and that traditional diplomatic skills and sheer size and importance play a lesser role. Smaller nations, those with less effective or well-organised foreign ministries and civil services, and nations with weak or ineffective governments will feel more protected inside it. The secretariat will be larger and more powerful, and its functions may include proposing policy initiatives as well as implementing decisions. Many of its staff will be career officials, and a corporate spirit and corporate objectives are easier to develop. The secretariat, or some other institutional body, may develop as a balancing force to the power of large nations. It may be able to hold national governments to account, criticise them for non-performance, and even exact compliance. The Alliance tended to move slowly in this direction during the 1950s and 1960s.

National preferences for one or the other tendency are not, of course, purely a matter of intellectual or cultural preference, although the extent to which a nation's traditions can accommodate each model will be a factor. The judgement is essentially one of self-interest: which tendency gives the most scope for pursuing the interests of the nation, and therefore in which direction should a given institution be encouraged to develop? There will be a different set of judgements to be made in each case, depending on the structures involved and the nations that are participating. The 1950s and 1960s saw a slow but definite move by French security policy-makers away from a wary involvement with integration and back to traditional policies of co-operation. This involved drawing a distinction (little understood by outsiders) between the acceptable (because inter-governmental) Alliance, and the unacceptable (because supranational) NATO. There are nuances and exceptions to this general scheme, which will be described later. In particular, the French were prepared to be more integrated in institutions such as the European Community (where ways of thinking and acting are largely of French origin), and in the planned European Defence Community, where it was hoped that this would also be true.

There were also certain specificities of French military and bureaucratic culture that lent themselves more easily to co-operation than to integration. As will be recalled, power in France essentially flows downward: those below implement the policies of those above, as defined by the minister and his *cabinet*. This system, combined with the rigidity (then almost complete) of the *Corps* structure, with its vertical hierarchy of loyalties, meant that attempts to establish inter-agency structures at the national, let alone international, level, were bound to be difficult. It was for these reasons that it took until the late 1940s for any equivalent of the British cabinet office to be set up: even then, its functions were more limited. The much looser and more informal British system, where officials move freely from department to department, carrying their loyalties with them, has always been difficult for the

French to understand. Their own system has tended to view departments as sovereign entities, their official dealings carefully regulated, and any exchange of personnel formalised through missions, advisers and liaison officers. The classic French approach to institutional conflict has been to form committees of the various interests involved (often without success), or to rely upon a superior arbitrator (the president, under the Fifth Republic). All of these concerns influenced the way the French hoped the Alliance would develop.

A Kafka-like Monster

There was already an embryonic military organisation in Europe, as a consequence of the Brussels Treaty of 1948. It had been set up as the result of a British proposal, accepted by the French as a way of tying the British to the Continent, and in default of a firm alliance with the US and a military organisation under American command. The British provided the chairman of the Western Union Chiefs of Staff (WUCOS) in the person of General Montgomery; the French supplied de Lattre de Tassigny as ground commander. It was an unfortunate mix of personalities, and resulted in 'a long Franco-British conflict'.[22] De Lattre believed that Montgomery's aim was really to look after the defence of Britain, whereas Montgomery was continually annoyed that the French did not recognise him as a real commander-in-chief.[23] It was not just a clash of personalities, however, but a clash of systems as well. General André Beaufre, for example, who was a staff officer at the Fontainebleau headquarters, complains that Montgomery was 'systematically weaving his web' in an attempt to gain control of the organisation for the British, albeit the majority of the officers were French. As well as the unethical use of his chief of staff, and his habit of promoting young officers to high rank, Montgomery also set up a 'faceless network of committees', which horrified de Lattre, but which was apparently 'how Anglo-American planning had functioned during the war under the basically somewhat supine chairmanship of General Eisenhower'.[24] It was

22. Doise and Vaisse, *Diplomatie et Outil Militaire*, p. 408.
23. John W. Young, *France, the Cold War and the Western Alliance, 1944–49: French Foreign Policy and Post-War Europe*, London, Leicester University Press, 1990, pp. 214–5.
24. General André Beaufre, *NATO and Europe*, trans. Joseph Green and R. H. Barry, London, Faber and Faber, 1966, pp. 27–28. Beaufre is an interesting figure: by

clear that there was a real and fundamental collision of military (as well as political and administrative) cultures, which did not promise well for the future.

This structure was developed further with the militarisation of the Alliance in the early 1950s. The oddest feature of NATO has always been that it is a wartime structure in peacetime, complete with multinational forces and command structures of a type that it took the Allies in the Second World War years to evolve. This is explicable insofar as war in 1950–51 was thought to be imminent: it seemed better to have the structure ready in place. It did mean, however, that the system would necessarily be an integrated one (as wartime structures should be), and that, given the weakness of the French at the time, it would be dominated by the Anglo-Saxons and their philosophies of command and staff work.

The French were therefore confronted, for the first time, with the need to define a policy towards an integrated defence structure. The normal objectives of a nation in this situation are to secure the location of the headquarters, and as many posts as possible at as high a level as possible. The main purpose of the latter (apart from considerations of status) is to ensure that the organisation uses, as far as possible, techniques and procedures you are familiar with, and develops a culture as close as possible to your own. The headquarters were already at Fontainebleau, and so the French could not expect too many senior posts in addition: it was already accepted that the Supreme Allied Commander Europe (SACEUR) would be an American. There is no rule by which posts can be allocated in a way that every nation is happy with, and the French were exceedingly unhappy with the way the jobs were parcelled out. It could be argued, however, that the French were often their own worst enemies, and did not always lobby very competently. In January 1951, neither Pleven nor Moch thought to raise the question of French representation in the NATO structure during calls by Eisenhower: each had assumed the other would do so. About one-third of all of SACEUR's staff were from the United States.[25] The resulting predominance of American forces and effort led to the effective institution of the American staff system in NATO, and the use of English as the working language: both of these factors still apply.

---

no means a classic 'Gaullist' – he criticised de Gaulle in 1966 – his diagnosis of NATO's problems was very similar.

25. *FRUS*, 1951, Vol. 3, p. 106.

The effect on the French of this massive infusion was startling. Beaufre thought that the new Supreme Headquarters Allied Powers Europe (SHAPE) at Rocquencourt, was probably based on 'the tradition of the Pentagon, that Kafka-like monster where no less than forty thousand people work'.[26] Writing in 1966, Beaufre counted thirteen 'important commands', in this 'complex, overstaffed organisation', of which France received only one, compared to seven for the United States and five for the United Kingdom.[27] The strongest French complaint was that the original model of the Standing Group, stuck in Washington, was being circumvented by direct American dealings with other nations, and by the tendency of American NATO commanders to ignore the 'interallied hierarchy' and to 'refer back direct to the Pentagon in their capacity as commanders of American forces'. These developments 'completely vitiated the original NATO plan and placed practically the entire defence organisation under strict American staff control'.[28] Beaufre argued that this American domination was 'an error of judgement which largely explains the recent [1966] reactions of the French government'.[29] American and Anglo-Saxon domination of the nascent NATO military structure was probably inevitable, given the political balance of forces at the time, although it could probably have benefited from a little more tact and sensitivity in its application. But the organisation was bound to develop in a way which left the French worried and puzzled. Its culture and staff procedures were largely American, its language was American military English, and it developed in an increasingly integrated fashion, which was acceptable to the Anglo-Saxons, since they provided most of the senior personnel, but obviously less so to the French, whose disenchantment began immediately.

Politicians and officials are always surprised when the subtleties of their carefully tailored compromises and exquisitely balanced communiqués are not grasped by ordinary people. This was certainly true with the formation of NATO, which was interpreted by the French public as 'an American affair', to the extent that, in a poll of industrialists, many believed that SHAPE was 'a headquarters from across the Atlantic installed in Europe'.[30] In a

26. Michael M. Harrison, *The Reluctant Ally: France and Atlantic Security*, Baltimore, Johns Hopkins University Press, 1981, p. 21.
27. Beaufre, *NATO and Europe*, p. 35.
28. Ibid., p. 39.
29. Ibid., pp. 37–38.
30. Planchais, *Histoire Politique*, p. 237.

way this is not surprising, given that at the same time a very large purely American presence *was* busy installing itself in Europe: France handed over seven air bases in Morocco, and fourteen in metropolitan France, as well as facilities in all the main naval bases. By 1958, there were 50,000 Americans deployed in France.[31] It requires an effort of will, today, to imagine the shock produced by the first-ever stationing of foreign troops in France in time of peace. From the earliest days of NATO, ministers agonised over ways of filling their peoples with the enthusiasm for the Alliance they themselves felt, and, year after year, sponsored initiatives to try to bring this about. But if positive enthusiasm for NATO was less common in France than apathy, it was essentially because much of the public, unlike the élites, perceived it as an instrument of American dominance.

A Brain for the Alliance

It soon became clear that the burgeoning military bureaucracy would need to be complemented by a large and powerful civilian one. A mass of continuous work was needed, especially on the production and delivery of weaponry, and this required something more than the *ad hoc* 1949 structure, occasionally animated by ministers. This structure consisted of the Defence Committee (of ministerial rank), foreseen in the treaty, with a Defence Finance and Economic Committee of Finance Ministers added in September 1949. Whereas the Defence Committee was perambulant, its subsidiary organs, the Military Committee and the Military Production and Supply Board, sat in Washington and London respectively. These committees were supported by officials seconded from capitals. The problems of co-ordination with SHAPE in Fontainebleau can readily be imagined, and it was frequently argued that a 'brain' was needed to co-ordinate the Alliance. A decision was therefore taken by ministers at the May 1950 NAC to create a 'permanent civilian body responsible for carrying out the policies of the NATO governments' between NAC meetings.[32]

A committee of so-called 'Council Deputies' (i.e. deputies to ministers) was set up to recommend how this was to be done. By the end of 1951, the deputies were established in London, together

---

31. Doise and Vaisse, *Diplomatie et Outil Militaire*, p. 413.
32. Robert S. Jordan, *The NATO International Staff/Secretariat, 1952–1957: A Study in International Administration*, London, Oxford University Press, 1967, pp. 21–22.

with a permanent secretariat and the Defence Production Board, while the Financial and Economic Board was in Paris. It was clear, however, that this could only be an interim arrangement, and that, in particular, a secretary-general of status would have to be sought. The Lisbon NAC of February 1952 had to resolve these problems, and considered two ways forward, one from the UK and one from the US. The latter proposed a strongly integrationist model, with an active permanent civilian staff that would participate in meetings of working groups, and a secretary-general who would be permanent chairman of the NAC. Each nation should establish a delegation, headed by an ambassador.[33] This model was much more integrationist than the British approach, and was essentially agreed to in Lisbon: it is visibly the ancestor of the present structure. American support for integration was not a question of ideology, but of managerial efficiency. Given the imminent threat, it was essential that the total resources of Europe should be used as effectively as possible, and an integrated approach was obviously better than laborious bargaining among international working groups. And from the political perspective, US dominance of the organisation was such that integration was not a risk to America's interests.

Co-location of the various organs also made sense, and it was agreed that they would all go to Paris. This was against the strongly expressed opposition of the British government, but in line with the views of the US and of many of the smaller nations. The latter felt that a NATO HQ across the Channel might not be adequately attentive to the defence of the mainland. It was, presumably, as a *quid pro quo* for losing the existing NATO organs that Britain was asked to supply the organisation's first secretary-general. For their part, the US wanted the new headquarters close to the Organisation for European Economic Co-operation, the body distributing Marshall Aid. Although the French thus provided a home for all the important parts of NATO, and might have regarded that as a political victory of sorts, it did them little practical good, and even some harm. Normally, a government with an international institution in its capital reckons to be able to influence it, and develop a close working relationship. In this case, because of the preponderance of US personnel, such a relationship was impossible to establish, and French influence was dwarfed by that of the US. However, the fact that this concentration of institutions

---

33. The text of the memorandum is in *FRUS*, 1952–54, Vol. 5, Part 3, pp. 198–203.

had come to Paris meant that other nations would be very unwilling to see France take any of the senior posts in the organisation, and particularly not that of the secretary-general.

This might not have mattered so much if the secretary-general had come from an administrative culture closer to that of France; but the choice of a Briton, who would have great discretion to fashion the organisation according to his own precepts, virtually guaranteed a clash of cultures. The mantle fell, after the refusal by Sir Oliver Franks, on Lord Ismay, a former soldier steeped in the traditions of Whitehall. Ismay set out, largely successfully, to re-create the system he knew. He imported a private secretary, who was an old acquaintance from the Foreign Office, a British personal secretary, and a British executive secretary, who was another former military man.[34] The British tradition regards the private secretary essentially as his master's business manager, and not a formulator of policy. He is far less than a French *directeur du cabinet*, and less even than a *chef du cabinet*: moreover, he is a permanent official, who stays when the minister goes. Instead of the *cabinet* system, Ismay followed the British practice of using his permanent officials to make policy, especially Coleridge, his executive secretary. This was a system that puzzled and disconcerted most other European nations, used to a clear distinction between the *cabinet*, which made policy, and the permanent officials, who implemented it. The system was difficult for European officials to operate, unused as they were to originating policy options for their superiors.

Without labouring the point, one can say that, by about 1952–53, France found herself in an organisation with strong integrationist tendencies, with a military wing dominated by the United States and using largely US staff practices, and a civilian staff constructed according to precepts that were foreign to her understanding. A substantial French presence at lower levels was not felt to compensate for this. Virtually no interest group in France would have regarded the post-Lisbon arrangements as corresponding to their objectives when negotiations began in 1948. Moreover, France remained in a position of inferiority to the United States for financial reasons, and found herself obliged to go along with many unattractive initiatives from Washington. Of course, American preponderance in NATO meant that all NATO policies would be largely American in origin, and that nuclear policies would be entirely so. But the French were not the British,

34. Jordan, *NATO Staff*, pp. 83–85.

who would try subtly to influence US thinking, nor were they a small nation used to this kind of treatment. France occupied a peculiar, and rather unfortunate niche, her grandiose plans reduced to nothing, the NATO structure seeming to 'consolidate and even emphasise her status as a junior partner'.[35]

Federalism, American Style

In French eyes, nothing dominated this period more than the treatment of her concerns about Germany, and it was in an attempt to escape from what seemed an ineluctable repetition of the events of the 1920s and 1930s that the French, encouraged by the US for other reasons, formulated the proposal for a European Defence Community. The principal motive for the EDC initiative was, of course, to acquiesce to German rearmament without allowing the formation of a German army and without permitting Germany to be a member of NATO in its own right. It would not be wholly unfair to say that the French ideal was of a German army with French officers. Yet there were other motivations as well. Schumann, with his resistance background and his Catholic idealism, sincerely believed that the only way to cure war was to create the conditions where the traditional unit of account of the struggle, the nation-state, was powerless to start hostilities. If there were no national armies there could be no wars. The same mechanism would also provide a safe way of reintegrating Germany into the European system, since the option of a revival of German militarism would have been removed. Finally, the EDC was another attempt to create an organised European structure, under French tutelage, that would foster what the French saw as a suitable relationship with the United States.

Thus, on this occasion, France found herself on the side of integration. But this was a temporary position, assumed for largely tactical reasons, and, as Frédéric Bozo notes, 'because she felt it was in her interest'. The EDC, it was hoped, would be 'a mechanism in the service of the policy and status of France, especially with respect to the Anglo-Saxons'.[36] France could dominate culturally and politically an integrated EDC in a way in which she could not hope to dominate the integrated Alliance. To some extent, one might help to counter-balance the other.

35. Harrison, *Reluctant Ally*, p. 25.
36. Bozo, *La France et l'OTAN*, p. 39.

France was, of course, obliged to surrender some sovereignty, but this was acceptable as long as other nations, and especially Germany, surrendered more. It was when this judgement appeared to be in doubt that feeling in France turned decisively against the EDC.

The EDC conference opened on 15 February 1951, in Paris. France, Belgium, Germany, Italy and Luxembourg were full members; Denmark, Norway, the Netherlands and Portugal were observers, as were the United States, the United Kingdom and Canada. In its final form, the European army was to have consisted of a number of European corps, each about eighty thousand strong, and made up of divisions contributed by three or four nations, together with support elements. There would be a council of ministers to oversee the various corps, together with a (vaguely defined) supranational authority to administer them. There would be common training and doctrine, a common budget and common operational concepts and procurement programmes. It was to be available to SACEUR for NATO tasks.[37] Even this concept represented a substantial defeat for France. The maximum size of national units rose throughout the negotiations, and, as they progressed, it became clear that the objective of preventing the reformation of the German army was becoming increasingly hard to attain. Likewise, there was no agreement on what the supranational authority should be. The French had wanted a single European Defence Commissioner (who would, no doubt, have been French): most of the other nations preferred a more broadly based organisation.

The United States was a firm supporter of the EDC concept, although not an uncritical one. The original Pleven plan of October 1950, which was cobbled together in great haste and without any military advice, was unacceptable. But Washington felt that it should be possible to contrive a scheme that would achieve their main objective of German rearmament in a way that was politically acceptable in Europe. Such an initiative would also further integrate European defence, as NATO was also doing, and make more effective and economic use of American aid and the Europeans' own budgets. It would also guard against a renewed outbreak of nationalism, especially in Germany, should the United States ever leave. Provided it was clearly understood that SACEUR would be able to call on the various Eurocorps as

37. See Schumann's report to the NAC, November 1951, printed in *FRUS*, 1951, Vol. 3, pp. 936–46.

needed, and that each corps could be used in pieces, if necessary, and not only as a whole, Washington was prepared to throw its considerable weight behind the scheme. The United States followed the progress of the negotiation with great care, and frequently intervened behind the scenes. As time went on, and as the French began to lose heart, American intervention became increasingly blatant and threatening. At one stage, the United States even put pressure on the British government, in the form of a letter from Acheson to Eden, to become involved more actively in the negotiation.[38]

This year, 1951, was probably the high-water mark of American influence in Paris. The relationship between the two countries had been one of the most unusual in modern history. The sources of it were, in France, a mixture of fear, weakness and idealism, and, on the part of the United States, a managerial concern for the efficient use of resources and a crusading (if occasionally unsubtle) anti-Communist zeal. A situation in which the United States micro-managed the French defence budget and programme, set requirements for her armed forces, and even influenced the composition of her government was clearly the product of such special factors that it could not last. From 1951–52 onwards, and to Washington's surprise, dealing with the French became much more difficult, as the latter recovered their composure. The enormous power available to the Americans was usually wielded in an attempt to do what Washington saw as the right thing, and without conscious malice, but often rather clumsily. The result was resentment in French society and the French politico-military apparatus that a more subtle policy would have avoided, and that came home to roost with a vengeance after 1958.

The evolution of the structures of Western defence in the early 1950s and the strains of Franco-American bilateral defence relations would, by themselves, have been enough to produce terminal disenchantment in Paris. But a number of other factors combined to make a bad situation appalling: these included the way in which NATO strategy developed, the fall of the French empire, and US pressure over the EDC. Moreover, all these tests coincided with a period of political instability leading to the fall of the Fourth Republic. These tests, this fall, and what followed, are the subject of the rest of this chapter.

38. The text is in ibid., pp. 955–7.

The Yellow Fever

One of the most fundamental facts about the Fourth Republic was that it was constantly at war, first in Indo-China and then in Algeria. The Japanese marched into Indo-China in the last few months of the war, easily ejecting the Vichy garrison. Emperor Bao Dai and Prince Sihanouk proclaimed the respective independences of Vietnam and Cambodia, but the Provisional Government in Paris offered only limited concessions, and many Vietnamese turned to the Independence Front, or Viet Minh, in which Ho Chi Minh's Communists played a substantial role. A general insurrection was launched, and Bao Dai abdicated. A broadly based government of national unity was formed. French attempts to intervene were frustrated by the fact that the Potsdam conference – to which they had not been invited – decided, without consulting them, to divide the country at the 16th parallel, with the British taking the Japanese surrender in the south and the Chinese in the north. De Gaulle despatched Leclerc and Admiral D'Argenlieu to see what could be rescued. Leclerc did extremely well, negotiating an agreement that would have resulted in Vietnam's remaining part of the French Union, with French troops stationed there for five years. If implemented, this settlement would have avoided the whole bloody and frustrating war and would probably have changed the course of modern French history. The settlement was not implemented.

To begin with, there was a split between the two military men. D'Argenlieu was an old Gaullist, like Leclerc, but also a ferocious and rather unreflective anti-Communist, who thought that the struggle against the Viet Minh was 'but one aspect of the struggle against the extension of communism throughout the world'.[39] He also, importantly, stigmatised the agreement as 'a new Munich',[40] so claiming the dubious honour of being the first of a long line of post-war Frenchmen to court military and political disaster by feverishly seeking the most unlikely opportunities to atone for the shame of 1938. Leclerc was more relaxed on both counts, but he was less in tune with the atmosphere of Paris and of the colonists and colonial administrators. The government did not disown

39. De la Gorce, *French Army*, p. 388.
40. Jean-Pierre Rioux, *The Fourth Republic, 1944–1958*, trans. Godfrey Rogers, Cambridge, Cambridge University Press, 1987, p. 93. Interestingly, D'Argenlieu had been a Catholic monk as well as a sailor, and carried, through the Second World War and afterwards, a crusading zeal that sometimes got in the way of his judgement. See Planchais, *Histoire Politique*, pp. 201–2.

D'Argenlieu when he proclaimed the autonomous Republic of Cochin China in June 1946: Ho Chi Minh and his party heard the news while they were on their way to a conference on the future of the region. The conference was a failure.

From that point, both the war and the French defeat were pre-ordained. For political reasons, no government was prepared to send conscripts to fight in Indo-China, so the burden fell on the relatively small professional cadre and on the Foreign Legion. In 1949, the French Expeditionary Corps totalled some 120,000 men, but only about a third were professionals from metropolitan France. Virtually the whole of the Foreign Legion – 15,000 men – was deployed, and the numbers were made up from colonial troops and local levies.[41] They were plunged into a war for which they were not prepared, where there were no front lines and few organised forces, and where their superior equipment and training were largely irrelevant. The war involved taking troops out of Europe in huge numbers, and effectively put paid to hopes of creating the kind of modern, high-tech army of which de Gaulle and others had dreamed. The war was also incredibly expensive at a time when France had many other priorities: it cost France nearly eight billion dollars, or about twice as much as all the Marshall Aid she received.[42]

In the circumstances, only massive American financial aid could keep France in the fight. Not only did this aid entitle the United States, as they saw it, to a large influence on how French policy and military operations were conducted, and even on the choice of French commanders; it also continued and confirmed the economic and military dependence of France on the United States. But, important as this economic assistance was, it was not what the French really wanted: they needed ground troops and air power from other nations, and the United States consistently refused to provide them. It was not that Washington was indifferent to the outcome of the war: far from it. For most of the 1940s and 1950s, American policy on colonies vacillated, as Washington was unable to decide whether colonies or Communism were worse. But there was no doubt about Indo-China, after the Korean War. As a State Department paper of 1952 put it, a French defeat 'would have psychological and political consequences which might result in the relatively swift accommodation of the rest of

41. Doise and Vaisse, *Diplomatie et Outil Militaire*, pp. 437–8.
42. Philip H. Gordon, *A Certain Idea of France: French Security Policy and the Gaullist Legacy*, Princeton, Princeton University Press, 1993, p. 26.

Asia and thereafter of the Middle East to communism'.[43] Such a disaster was to be avoided by all possible means.

Unfortunately, there was no prospect of enough support in Congress for the dispatch of ground troops, and even money and military equipment were sometimes tricky to find. This left the United States with little except moral encouragement and financial leverage to fall back on. Publicly and privately, American ministers and officials spared no effort of rhetoric to acknowledge the splendid job being done by the French; and every speaking note prepared for a French visit to Washington advised the American side to shower the French with compliments. But no practical military help was offered, and the French enquired pointedly why, if the future of the world apparently depended on their performance, the United States was not lending a hand: given, moreover, that France had sent troops to next-door Korea.

Washington was perfectly well aware of the political, military and economic costs of the war to France, and wanted it concluded as quickly as possible. But this must not happen through what a National Security Council paper of 1953 referred to as a 'disastrous French withdrawal', which might lead the US to 'have to consider most carefully whether to take over in this area'.[44] As a result, Washington favoured political and military leaders who could promise victory, and tried to support governments that still wanted to take a firm line, in spite of the increasing war-wearines: of the population. But the Americans could only offer money an(moral coercion, and the lack of any real practical support, espe cially the refusal to use nuclear weapons during the culminatin disaster of Dien Bien Phu, was to strain relations badly, and 1 encourage the more reflective decision-makers in Paris to questic the real utility of the mutual security relationship.

The most disturbing outcome of the war, however, was t effect it had on the French military. In the jungles of Indo-Chii and after decades of talk, the French army finally fought Comn nism – and Communism won. The army that had gone to In< China was, essentially, the Armistice army, the army of Vichy, whom Communism, at home and abroad, had been the ene Everything that its officers experienced there strengthened tl in this belief. As in 1940, they did not believe that the defeat their fault: rather, it was that of the political class, which had

43. *FRUS*, 1952–54, p. 29.
44. Ibid., pp. 714–7.

them there, as one former commander put it, 'without a policy', and subsequently 'stabbed them in the back'. At the same time, given that the war they were fighting was an international ideo-logical one, they expected to be protected from enemies at home, who criticised or even obstructed what they were doing. But, claimed General Navarre, the politicians had 'tolerated the per-manent treason of the Communist Party' and critical coverage in the media.[45] Whatever lingering respect the army may have felt for their political masters died then and there.

Moreover, the army learned at first hand about revolutionary warfare, which, it was clear, would be the pattern of their opera-tions in the future. Far from home, ignored or even opposed by public opinion, starved of political support and recognition, they confronted an enemy who fought a political war in which success or defeat was measured not in ground won or lost but in minds. This experience – in some cases including a spell as a Viet Minh prisoner – completed the transformation of these officers from patriots defending their country to ideological warriors fighting a war without lines against an enemy without uniforms. For many, this vision – coupled with half-digested gobbets of Marx and Mao – amounted to an intoxicating new ideology; they were often said to suffer from *le mal jaune*: yellow fever. Once the techniques used by the Viet Minh were mastered and employed, victory in the next round would be assured. The next round could be anywhere, any time, because, as one officer put it, the real adversary of France 'has acquired the most immediate form, that of an invisible and omnipresent enemy less impressive for the real presence of his arms than for the strength of seduction or subversion exercised by means of propaganda or of undercover passwords'.[46] That many of the officers of Indo-China were to pass through Algeria and into the ranks of the OAS was therefore not surprising.

Declarations of Independence

I have already suggested that the security relationship between France and the United States after the Second World War was so unusual in its origins and its nature that it could not last for any great length of time. The relationship started to unpick itself during

---

45. Raoul Girardet, *La Crise militaire française, 1945–1962: aspects sociologiques et idéologiques*, Paris, Armand Colin, 1964, pp. 162–5.
46. Cited by de la Gorce, *French Army*, p. 401.

the early 1950s, but not in an orderly fashion. The process was one of fits and starts, greatly influenced by the personalities temporarily prominent in the ever-changing government scene. It began in the largely forgotten premiership of one Antoine Pinay in 1952, and there are a number of reasons why relations between the United States and France began to change their nature at this time. Everything eventually provokes a reaction, and the fear and weakness of the late 1940s was no exception. As France began to climb out of the 'Slough of Despond', new voices were heard, one of the most significant being that of Albert Camus. His book *The Rebel* (1951) was a plea for revolt and independence of action, but at the moral and personal level. It was non-Marxist (indeed, it criticised the Soviet Union); but it was far from being a thoughtless product of the Cold War. Camus praised 'the slave who has taken orders all his life', but who 'suddenly decides he cannot obey some new command', because 'this has been going on too long'. He puts 'self-respect above everything else'. Better, he urged, to die on your feet than live on your knees.[47] What Camus was describing was a dawning of consciousness, a realisation that independence of action was possible after all.

By this stage, the immediate hysteria of the Cold War had begun to evaporate. The threatened invasion of Europe had not taken place, in spite of the fact that the required level of Western forces was nowhere near being realised, and the sense of dislocation and incipient civil war that had characterised the late 1940s had started to fade. This greater stability combined with the first fruits of the National Plan to produce a sense of increasing confidence and prosperity. As courage returned, and the country seemed stronger, there was less inclination to conjure up external threats to be afraid of. Then again, the pressures of the Cold War had largely driven out of politics those elements who still clung to the Resistance ideals of integration and supranationality, and who were dubious about the validity of the nation-state. Finally, although war-hysteria had subsided, there were worrying signs from across the Atlantic that the Cold War was to be intensified.

The French, like the British, had been disturbed for some time about the announced policy of 'roll-back', which envisaged (and appears to have involved) covert operations in Eastern Europe and a large-scale programme of psychological warfare. Emigré groups were organised into military units, and risings behind the

---

47. Albert Camus, *The Rebel*, trans. Anthony Bower, London, Hamish Hamilton, 1953; Penguin edn, 1971, pp. 19–21.

Iron Curtain were foreseen, as part of a 'liberation' of the area. Radio Free Europe was set up in October 1951, its president explaining frankly that 'what we wanted to do was to create conditions of turmoil in the countries our broadcasts reached'. This latter development worried the French a great deal, since, as well as courting conflict, it seemed to undermine the essentially defensive rationale of the Atlantic Alliance: as the Western European Department of the Quai put it, in February 1953, although the policy seemed 'more a matter of words than substance' (*plus verbale que réelle*), 'it was not thereby less dangerous'. As well as the risk of war, there was also concern about what would happen if, as in East Germany in 1953, a rising were to take place without Western assistance.[48] The victorious Eisenhower campaign team had charged the outgoing Truman administration with laxity in pursuing the anti-Communist struggle, and the new régime – especially in the formidable shape of Secretary of State Dulles – was committed to a more vigorous policy of 'liberating' Eastern Europe.

These changes of perception in France had not been accompanied by any qualitative change in relations between the two nations. Military and financial aid to France was controversial in the US Congress, where it was felt that the French were showing insufficient gratitude for American largesse. The French economy, it was argued, was insufficiently deregulated and capitalist, the fiscal system archaic and corrupt, and the trades unions excessively dominated by the PCF. The United States regularly tried to use its military assistance programme (now known as off-shore procurement) to pressurise the French into concessions on these issues. Likewise, since they were underpinning the French defence budget, they felt entitled to pronounce on its overall size and its make-up. Finally, American influence was being used to push France ever closer to integrated structures such as NATO and the EDC.

There was, by 1952, a burgeoning sense of independence and a desire to re-balance relations with the United States. What was lacking was an individual to focus these concerns, until in March 1952 there shuffled briefly on to the stage of history the curious, if ultimately unremarkable, figure of M. Antoine Pinay, the 'average Frenchman'. In rather unhelpful political shorthand, Pinay's government was usually characterised as 'right-wing', and it certainly depended for its investiture on the votes of some for whom Vichy

48. Beatrice Heuser, *Western 'Containment' Policies in the Cold War: The Yugoslav Case, 1948–53*, London, Routledge, 1989, pp. 138–42.

was a fond memory. It is true also that Pinay was a bitter anti-Communist, and set in hand a minor key repetition of the great purges of 1939–40 and 1947. But in many other respects he continued the modernist tradition. He talked of cutting government spending, but in practice only a small cut was made, and the corresponding slowdown in growth and rise in unemployment (to 48,000) were both consequently limited. In general, he continued the Keynesian policies of his predecessors, with similar success.[49]

His reward was a quite unprecedented popularity, which seems bizarre to us today: once again, the French had seized on a figure and made him into the Sovereign who would rescue them from their troubles. It was Pinay's very ordinariness that was the secret of his popularity: he was born, *Paris-Match* noted excitedly, in the Massif Central, 'not too far to the North, or the South, or the East, or the West'. He was of humble origins, had been decorated for bravery in the First World War, smoked a pipe, enjoyed fishing and was said to prefer the comfort of his modest apartment to the glamour of his official residence.[50] He was exactly the kind of calming, reassuring, everyday influence the French needed. The massive political legitimacy he enjoyed as a result gave him the strength to take on the United States.

He did not set out to seek confrontation, but confrontations occurred so frequently in those days that he did not have to wait long in any event. Emboldened by his popularity, he felt able to make his own 'absurd refusal', and to take on the largest concentration of political, military and economic power ever assembled in one country. Although the exact circumstances were complex, the essential question was the right, or otherwise, of the French government to decide for itself the level of its defence spending. The United States had consistently tried to tie its military aid to the setting of a budget higher than successive governments believed they could afford, with the result, as the Quai put it in July 1952, that the government was in the 'humiliating position of never being able to meet its commitments by its own means, and always, everywhere, on any occasion, asking for larger amounts of aid'. In October 1952, Acheson sent Pinay a letter regretting that the US would not be able, after all, to make available the expected military aid for 1953. In delivering the letter, however, the ambassador was instructed to say that the United States expected France, nonetheless, at least to keep its defence budget at the expected

49. Rioux, *Fourth Republic*, p. 199.
50. Raoul Girardet, *Mythes et mythologies politiques*, Paris, Seuil, 1986, pp. 64–68.

level, making up the US shortfall from its own resources: indeed, an increase in the budget would be well received in Washington. Such messages had been received before; but this time circumstances were different. A wave of indignation swept through France, and Pinay had the full support of the bureaucracy and the political class in telling the Americans to go away. The French government, said Pinay, could not 'accept that the use of credits voted by Parliament be submitted to the unilateral decision of a foreign government'. France, he added, to the ambassador, 'does not take orders from anyone'. Other political figures from different parts of the spectrum piled in, as the pent-up frustrations burst forth. The government's eventual defence budget proposal was, in fact, within the limits the Americans had suggested; but it was as a result of a free decision on their part, not as a result of foreign pressure.[51] Ironically, it was European rather than Atlantic problems that brought Pinay down. The EDC Treaty was eventually signed under his premiership, but his government, like its successors, dared not submit it for ratification. Even here there was an American connection, since the embassy was by that stage perhaps the only interest group in Paris to support the proposal unreservedly.

In the end, Pinay did not have the personal qualities necessary to pursue a consistently independent policy, nor was the political system of the time conducive to such initiatives. But the process of disenchantment with the American connection and with NATO had irreversibly begun: what was needed was a more imposing figure to channel the resentment in a positive direction. In Pinay, one can already see Mendès-France, and in Mendès-France the outlines of de Gaulle's policies are already clearly visible. And as the early 1950s passed, the range of subjects that left the French terminally disenchanted, and stoked resentment further, continued to grow.

So long as the United States was by far the largest military and economic power in the Alliance, its influence was likely to be preponderant. Since it provided most of the forces, any change in its defence posture would, inevitably, mean a *de facto* change in NATO's policy also, although Washington did not usually pause to consider the international implications of its changes of mind. And since the US had a monopoly of deployable nuclear weapons in the Alliance, NATO's nuclear policy was unavoidably made in Washington. This relationship would have been inevitable even

51. Wall, *US and Postwar France*, pp. 228–32.

without an integrated structure, but, with the American-dominated structure that existed at the time, there was a pardonable feeling on the part of the Europeans that their own forces were out of their control and responding to new doctrines about which they had not been consulted. The classic example of this process is the Eisenhower administration's 'New Look' of 1954. This appears, once again, to have been a military-led exercise (the State Department commented sourly in February 1954 that 'we find ourselves somewhat handicapped by our lack of knowledge of the "New Look" which we understand the JCS has taken at US defense policy').[52] Its essential elements were a greater reliance on nuclear weapons, which were to be used in the same way as conventional munitions, and withdrawal of a substantial number of US troops from overseas. The primary mechanism for deterrence was to be the threat of massive nuclear attack.

For a number of European states – not only the French – this new doctrine was puzzling and alarming. What had become of the massive requirements for conventional forces and consequent huge increases in defence budgets after 1950? What role, indeed, were European forces now to play, if any? Did this new policy mean progressive withdrawals of forces back to the United States? And might it not have been wise of the Americans to have consulted those upon whose territory the nuclear weapons were to be used? In any event, there was no serious resistance to the US proposals, and NATO 'approved this doctrine, decided unilaterally by the Americans' in December 1954.[53]

By that time, the list of Franco-American tensions was a long one: the organisation and policy of NATO, the Indo-China war, German rearmament, French colonies, the European Defence Community, and the French defence budget and programme. On all these issues, the Americans wanted and expected to get their own way; they had been used to doing so for some time. It seemed entirely proper to Washington that its agencies should conduct covert operations within France, sponsor and fund non-Communist groups and publications of all sorts, and seek to educate the French in the virtues of American-style productivity techniques and labour relations. If the French resented this – and they did – they largely had themselves to blame. Ever since 1936, the attitude of France towards the United States had been one of timidity and supplication: successive governments had begged the United

52. *FRUS*, 1952–54, Vol. 5, Part 1, p. 482.
53. Doise and Vaïsse, *Diplomatie et Outil Militaire*, p. 429.

States for political and military support, for American troops and American weapons, and for massive economic aid. In return, and in an advanced state of fear and weakness, they had been prepared to agree to virtually any conditions the Americans chose to attach to their aid.

By the early 1950s, Washington had had a decade and a half to get used to this idea of France: an eternity in bureaucratic terms. No one in Washington had any recollection of a France that did not seem easy to dominate, that was not by turns sulky and weak-kneed. The curious Franco-American relationship was essentially of France's own creating: a less wilting series of governments, less paralysed by fear and weakness, could have taken a much more robust line with the Americans, who, after all, needed the French at least as much as the French needed them. That dealing with the Americans and solving some of France's more pressing crises was essentially a matter of attitude, and a willingness to use the freedom of manœuvre that existed, began to be appreciated from 1954 onwards, when, in Irwin Wall's phrase, France 'declared her independence'. One might say, less aphoristically, that France decided at that point to try to convert its relations with the United States to something more like normal inter-state relations. It needed an unusual leader to accomplish this, but, precisely on time, Pierre Mendès-France duly appeared.

Mendès-France is one of those curious figures who, in spite of leading a nation only briefly, towers over a whole era, and is better remembered than any collection of time-serving hacks. It was obvious from his earliest days that he was going far. Brilliant pupil at the *Sciences-Po*, youngest advocate in France, deputy at the age of twenty-five, minister at the age of thirty-one in the second government of Léon Blum, he was arrested for desertion by Vichy, held in solitary confinement for nearly a year, suffered one of Vichy's nastier show trials, sawed through the bars of his prison cell and escaped via Switzerland to join de Gaulle. He became de Gaulle's economic specialist, and a minister in his Provisional Government: he was then thirty-seven. He had been out of office since 1945, which was a considerable advantage. Mendès-France (like de Gaulle later) had no personal or political stake in the security arrangements France made between 1948 and 1952, nor in the way the bilateral relationship with the US had developed. He was not inhibited or dominated by the memory of the fear and weakness of those years. For several years, a Mendès-France government had been widely expected, and had almost been formed in

1953, when his electrifying speech brought him almost, but not quite, the 314 votes he needed.

Mendès-France is conventionally described as a 'man of the Left', although he was not a Socialist, but an independent Radical, and the SFIO did not join his government. But he was a modernist, an economics specialist (he had taught the subject at ENA), and a man with a blazing determination to carry France forward into the future. None of his major ideas was new, and his politics has been described as 'a hope for renewal, more a state of mind than a politics, and as much a state of feeling as a state of mind'.[54] He represented what the Fourth Republic should have been and might, under other circumstances, have become. He surrounded himself with bright young experts, many of whom had been his students at ENA, and, to cover his parliamentary flank, he relied on the young François Mitterrand, already famous for his political street-fighting skills. In his investiture speech, Mendès-France explained that, from now on, he would choose the government he wanted, and that nominations from parties would not be welcome.[55] No one had treated the *régime d'assemblée* like this before, but they swallowed and accepted it. There was nothing in the vigour and determination of his actions that could not have been accomplished before, had a suitable individual been available.

Mendès-France had set out his political credo in his 1953 speech. It was a manifesto for modernisation, strong on social and economic detail, pleading for a coherent approach to the many problems of France, which, he argued, were themselves interrelated. But there were elements that immediately alarmed Washington. He spoke of the war in Indo-China as unaffordable, and of the burden of defence spending as unsustainable. He spoke of a change in the relationship between France and the United States to replace the current 'dependence', and a need to find common European approaches to problems instead of the current 'Indian file' of European leaders presenting themselves in front of the new American president, each seeking preferential treatment.[56] Washington was duly alarmed, and did what it could

54. Jean Lacouture, *Pierre Mendès-France*, trans. George Holoch, London, Holmes and Meier, 1984, p. 259.

55. Those with a taste for symbolism remarked at the time that the debate to invest the Mendès-France government opened on the fourteenth anniversary of de Gaulle's last flight to London, and concluded on the fourteenth anniversary of his 18 June speech.

56. *Journal Officiel, Débats*, 1953, pp. 2906–12.

to prevent Mendès-France from coming to power. For their part, the governments that held office between Mendès-France's two attempts did not scruple to use the threat of this happening to try to squeeze more help out of the United States in Indo-China.

The fall of Dien Bien Phu in May 1954 made French defeat and a Mendès-France government both inevitable. For the United States, these were both disasters. Dulles claimed that a French collapse was, in prospect, as grave as that of 1940, 'with the distinct possibility of a French government which would collaborate with the Soviets just as the French government of the summer of 1940 collaborated with the Germans'.[57] This was to remain his view of Mendès-France until the end. In his investiture speech, Mendès-France served notice that he would solve the Indo-China problem within a month, and very nearly did so. Negotiations in Geneva had begun already, and Washington was finding it much more difficult than expected to influence the French position. In the end, the United Sates grumblingly went along with the Geneva accords, and even accepted the principle of free elections, which it had always opposed in the belief that the Communists would win. In the end, Washington had no choice, and found itself in the unusual situation of playing second fiddle to an ally, and finding itself manipulated in the process. The gap between France and the United States yawned much wider as a result.

The next problem was the EDC. Mendès-France would have preferred the treaty to be ratified, since he recognised that Germany would have to be brought back into the fold somehow. But, as with Indo-China, his approach was ruthlessly practical. There was no majority for the treaty in the National Assembly, and the position was likely to get worse rather than better. That being so, it was better to have the vote, lose it if that was how it turned out, and look for another way of dealing with Germany. It was with consternation that Washington learned that, before submitting the treaty, he wanted to discuss the future of Germany with the Soviet Union. Comprehensively misunderstanding, Dulles thought that France now favoured German neutralism, and claimed that this would 'undermine the very basis of French-American relations and the future of the NATO alliance'.[58] Mendès-France indignantly tried to set the record straight. This misunderstanding sabotaged the last, frantic French attempt to save the EDC by attaching to it a protocol that would have made it less integrationist and given the

57. Cited by Wall, *US and Postwar France*, p. 262.
58. Cited in ibid., p. 284.

French an effective veto over some of its aspects. The United States put enormous pressure on the other EDC states to reject the French proposals, which they did. With this impasse, there was no hope of saving the treaty, which went down heavily at the end of August. In the last days of the crisis, American lobbying became almost hysterical; but a more self-confident France no longer believed that the Americans would leave Europe in retaliation for a vote against the EDC. In any event, the problem lay not with the executive, but the legislature – a distinction the Americans might have been expected to understand.

With EDC gone, Washington's French policy was now in pieces. The embassy counselled caution: France was ill, and shock treatment might be needed, but only in moderation.[59] But Dulles was intent on revenge, and began a policy of reprisals, including a halt to military aid. He accused Mendès-France of being a Soviet stooge, whose next task would be to 'kill NATO'. At one stage he seems to have considered helping either Bidault or Schumann to overthrow the government.[60] Reports of these latter initiatives inevitably found their way into the press. However, the two nations did co-operate over the resolution of the German problem. It was Mendès-France's idea to revive the 1948 Brussels Treaty, and to invite Germany (and Italy) to adhere, thus achieving many of the benefits of the EDC, but without the integrationist aspects, and with British participation. But when Mendès-France went to Washington in December 1954, the atmosphere was distinctly chilly, and the ritual request for a three-power inner directorate of NATO was abruptly turned down.

In not much more than six months, Pierre Mendès-France, the last, best hope of the Fourth Republic, had disposed of three major problems that, between them, had paralysed French politics for years. In doing so, and although this was not his intention, he had put Franco-American relations on an entirely new footing. Mendès-France did not set out to antagonise Washington: he had simply been out of government when the reflexes of deference were developed in the late 1940s and had never learned them. As Irwin Wall suggests, American hostility was 'a reflection of having to resume the use of ordinary diplomatic channels in dealing with the French government', after a long period when other methods were used. His government looked forward to the Fifth Republic,

---

59. *FRUS*, 1952–54, Vol.6, pp. 1443–5.
60. Wall, *US and Postwar France*, pp. 287–8.

as it looked back to the Popular Front, in its personnel as much as its methods: Mitterrand and Chaban-Delmas were both members. Yet even Mendès-France could not settle the problem that was to destroy the Fourth Republic: Algeria.

The Leopard Men

That the Fourth Republic perished over Algeria was not an accident: in the vicious war against the FLN, and in the political confusion and division that accompanied it, every major theme of this study so far is illustrated. First, Algeria was seen, not as a colonial conflict, but as an internal French matter. Algeria had been legally part of France for almost a hundred years, and was, indeed, divided into three departments, who sent deputies and senators to Paris. Algerian independence was therefore a contradiction in terms, and no French government before 1958 ever seriously entertained the possibility: 'Algeria is France' said François Mitterrand in his capacity as interior minister in 1954, and it was often said that 'the Mediterranean runs through France as the Seine runs through Paris'. Although opposition to the war grew towards the end, and was, inevitably, largely from the Left, the political classes, across the spectrum, largely supported the war, as did most of the media. It was the Socialist government of Guy Mollet (1956–57) that pursued the war most vigorously (and indeed launched the Suez adventure in the process), as well as vigorously censoring newspapers and attempting to silence critics. In short, Algeria adhered to the rule that the French political class united only in favour of policies that led to inevitable disaster.

Algeria therefore had the character of a civil war, and an ideological one at that. The *Front de Libération Nationale* had a rather incoherent ideology that borrowed much of the anti-colonialist and Marxist rhetoric of the time, and was therefore widely seen to be an agent of the international Communist conspiracy, moving to North Africa after its triumph in Indo-China. This was strengthened by the common-sense observation that the FLN could not possibly speak for the bulk of the population: who, after all, would turn their back on the French Union and all the benefits of French civilisation for the dubious rewards of independence? Obviously, a conspiracy was involved. Thus, the French army's involvement in Algeria represented the nearest it ever came to combating the widespread Communist rising it had been anticipating in mainland

France since 1917. The settler community in Algeria shared this assessment; like many such communities, it was politically conservative, and hostile to change and modernisation – Vichy had enjoyed enormous support there. Algeria was the last place to be touched by the post-1945 modernisation: still mainly agrarian, it was a good image of the bucolic, shabby, traditionalist France that the Fourth Republic was trying to replace. The settler community, especially its wealthier elements, were a considerable political force, and could block any moves towards political or economic modernisation.

It is hardly necessary to add that, in this refusal, they had the support of the army. Or rather, they had the support of the still-powerful men of Vichy, the colonels, and the officers of the regular forces, including especially *les paras*, the paratroops. These were the men who had fought, and lost, in Indo-China. They had, indeed, scarcely set foot in France since 1940, and had grown entirely apart, not only from France in general, but even from the new army that was being painfully put together. Their political convictions had changed since 1940 only in their greater intensity. The experience of Indo-China had confirmed their worst suspicions and made them more determined than ever not to lose a second war. Moreover, when they arrived in Algeria, they found a situation very similar to the one they had just left: surely, this could not be a coincidence? It was considered a truism that the Third World War had already begun, and the battlefields were internal, this time, rather than external. Thus, Algeria was part of a wider struggle, but was also the cockpit where that struggle was at present concentrated. France was therefore fighting, on behalf of the whole world, against a pitiless and endlessly resourceful enemy bent on total domination. As General Allard, then commander in Algeria, told SHAPE in 1957, 'the enemy' was not attacking the West directly, but was engaged in a vast flanking movement through 'China, the Far East, the Indies, the Middle East, Egypt and North Africa, with the aim of encircling Europe'. All that was lacking to complete this hideous design was to 'remove France from Algeria'. Then, he added for a largely American audience, Central and South America were next.[61]

Since the entire future of the world was at stake in Algeria, it would not do to be too squeamish about the methods employed. Conventional military operations were uncommon anyway; but

61. Girardet, *La Crise*, p. 177.

they were widely seen as pointless, since the most dangerous enemies were unlikely to be in uniform. The army had taken to heart
the reported judgement of General Giap that they had lost in Indo-
China because they had not become involved in politics, and
decided they must now do so. As one general who fancied himself
an expert on Mao wrote in an official review, the survival of the
world depended upon Western soldiers taking on the kind of ideological role their colleagues behind the Iron Curtain were believed to carry out.[62] This specifically implied a role in domestic
politics, and it followed logically that, if a government were misguided enough to think of pulling out of Algeria, steps would
have to be taken to prevent it.

To this political vision was added a whole series of other ideological beliefs of varying profundity. There was a cult of anti-
modernism and lack of interest in modern warfare. There was a
pervasive sense of betrayal and isolation, a sense of insecurity and
estrangement from normal bourgeois life and values. There was a
military ethic, which, as usual with self-designated military élites,
emphasised the virtues of courage, loyalty and fortitude above
mere military professionalism or even intelligence: the latter were,
if anything, rather frowned upon.

The end result of all this was a swaggering nihilism that seemed
glamorous to some. Paratroopers took to wearing their combat
fatigues in the street even when off duty: these were of a new,
spotted pattern, and gained their wearers the nickname of 'Leopard Men'. Their ideology was much discussed, and a so-called
'paratroopers prayer', alleged to be pinned up everywhere on the
walls of *para* camps, was frequently quoted, with its plea for a life
of insecurity and travail and an early death. Most young men
grow out of these emotions in their early twenties; and it is depressing to learn that the 'prayer', with all its derivative adoles-
cent romanticism, was apparently widely popular through the
army as a whole.[63] But then, in the immobilism of the Fourth
Republic, any kind of philosophy of action was attractive to some.

Yet the Leopard Men were not representative of the army as a
whole. Most of the huge numbers deployed in Algeria were conscripts, occupied on static guard duties. The army's presence
reached a height of 450,000 men in 1957, two-thirds of whom were
French; and there were also substantial contingents from the navy

62. Ibid., p. 184.
63. De la Gorce, *French Army*, pp. 484–5.

and air force. Eighty per cent of these were conscripts, whose engagement had been increased to twenty-eight months. Because Algeria was an infantry war, and because it involved so much of the army, it effectively wrecked any chance of modernising the army and turning it into a major force in Europe. Whole armoured and artillery units abandoned their modern equipment and had to be retrained for an infantry role, finding obsolescent half-tracks waiting for them if they were lucky. Some even had to learn to ride horses.[64]

The effect of all this on France's allies can be imagined. With most of the French troops that should have been in Germany in Algeria, and few German forces as yet available, the Central front seemed dangerously underpopulated. It was unfortunate that the annual review process had begun in 1952, with its questionnaire addressed to nations about the future level of their forces, and their deployment. The spotlight thus fell, in a very public and precise fashion, on France, which was seen for most of the 1950s as the 'bad boy' of the Alliance, even if, as French writers have suggested, the practice of other allies was, in varying degrees, similar.[65] These allies did not give France the material or political support she craved, and, indeed, seemed reluctant to be identified with France when she was hauled before the UN General Assembly, as frequently happened. The French complained bitterly that their support for the United States over Berlin and Korea was not being reciprocated. It was, of course, the Suez adventure that most sharply exposed this contradiction and propelled French distrust for the United States to even greater heights.

There are interesting domestic comparisons between Suez and the unlaunched invasion of the Soviet Union in 1939–40. Both had overwhelming support from all parties except the PCF; both were popular with the public also; both avoided direct combat against a troublesome enemy; both promised to end a war through a quick, indirect attack directed against a weak link (Egyptian support for the FLN in 1956); and both, in retrospect, seem to be actions of governments that had abandoned the habit of rational thought. It is certainly not easy to understand why a Socialist government attacked a non-aligned state in an explicit attempt to defend the commercial interests of private French companies, and in cahoots with its traditional bitter enemy for position and status

64. Doise and Vaisse, *Diplomatie et Outil Militaire*, pp. 454–5.
65. Bozo, *La France et l'OTAN*, p. 47.

in the Middle East. One reason is the traditional excuse of politicians: it seemed a good idea at the time. Anything that united most of the French population was *ipso facto*, good politics for the government that carried it out, and a swift, victorious war would have pleased everybody and expunged the better part of two decades of incessant military humiliation. Even the French army, it was felt, should be able to cope with Nasser. There was another reason also: the search for opportunities to expunge the shame of Munich (in principle, never-ending) ground on. Nasser's book *The Philosophy of the Revolution* was held, particularly by those who had not read it, to be the *Mein Kampf* of the 1950s, and Nasser to be Hitler reborn, bent on gobbling up the Middle East with Soviet backing. The Cold War dimension was also very real, and, whilst not all in Paris would accept the apocalyptic interpretation of the Leopard Men, there was a sense that France, unlike her allies, was actually engaging Communism face to face, and that Suez was amply justified for this reason alone.

A final important element of the Algerian fiasco was the influence of the army. In a way, this is the most important element, since it led directly to the fall of the Fourth Republic. That Republic scarcely even tried to impose any sort of political control over the military, and nowhere less so than in Algeria, where the army applied its techniques of psychological warfare learned in Indo-China. The best-known episode of political surrender is the so-called Battle of Algiers in 1956–57, when mounting turmoil, widespread terrorism and the threat of a Muslim general strike persuaded the civil authorities to hand over full powers to General Massu's Tenth Parachute Division, just returned from Egypt. The Fourth Republic gave a fastidious shudder, turned its back and walked away, not wanting to enquire how an ideological war was to be fought. For the military, as with their colleagues everywhere, it was a matter of technique. The appropriate techniques were the imposition of an effective martial law, the suspension of all civil rights, and the use of unparalleled brutality and widespread torture. Massu and his men demonstrated that, with enough brutality and torture, an urban terrorist campaign could be defeated, and, indeed, the battle was duly won. The Mollet government averted its gaze, contenting itself with seizing publications that criticised what the Leopard Men were doing. Yet, when added to reports of atrocities elsewhere, the Battle of Algiers was one of the factors that produced genuine discontent at last in a population that had previously loyally supported the war.

Sometimes, the military did not wait to be asked. In October 1956, the French pilot of a plane carrying four of the most important rebel leaders to Tunis for a meeting with Arab leaders obeyed the radio orders of a French general to land in Algiers instead, where the FLN party, including Ben Bella, were arrested. This was a short-sighted and ultimately counter-productive operation, typical of those who act before they think. It brought international condemnation, and removed from the game precisely those FLN leaders who might have sought a compromise with France. But what is most important is that – incredible as this may seem to Anglo-Saxons – it was the military and not the politicians who planned the operation, for their own purposes. Accounts vary, but it seems that only one junior minister was even consulted before the operation was carried out. Mollet, 'not informed until the operation was over, decided to underwrite the act of piracy, bowing in effect to the *fait accompli* of the military in Algiers'.[66] By this stage, the more thoughtful knew that the war could not be won, even if it could be continued for some time yet. But the government were too frightened of the power of the army and the settlers to draw the obvious conclusion, and their weakness positively invited these groups to take the initiative. After this, the end came quickly.

In January 1958, French aircraft intending to bomb an FLN camp hit a Tunisian village instead. Shaken by the international outcry, the government was forced to accept a British-American offer of 'good offices' (a thinly camouflaged sign of imminent negotiations with the FLN). Much of the political world condemned this as a 'new Munich', and the government fell.[67] Public opinion turned decisively against the war. Events rapidly spiralled out of control, partly because the very authority of the government itself seemed to have eroded, and it had great difficulty in getting its commands obeyed. An effective coup in Algiers on 13 May instigated the final crisis, as the army prepared Operation *Resurrection*, an air and ground assault on Paris. The system of the Fourth Republic was splintering under the strain. Clearly, the only hope of avoiding civil war lay in attracting a well-known and prestigious figure to take power. But who?

Charles de Gaulle was now sixty-seven, and had been out of power for twelve years. He had recently written his autobiography, it is true; but it was less valedictory than most written at that time of life, and contained, in fact, his political credo and a reminder

66. Rioux, *Fourth Republic*, p. 272.
67. Ibid., p. 298.

that he was still available. And in the streets the murmur had been for months, *c'est de Gaulle qu'il nous faut*: it's de Gaulle we need. De Gaulle's behaviour during May and June was a masterpiece of the political art, and, from the technical perspective, his finest hour: it is likely that he was the only one of the major actors who knew exactly what he was doing. Ostentatiously refusing to take sides, he allowed others to assume what they wanted about his own objectives, and confined himself to general expressions of concern and reminders that he was available. In circumstances that will probably always be obscure, his lieutenants shuttled between different interest groups, wheeling and dealing. At last, on 27 May, de Gaulle declared that he was forming a government. A surprised political class found itself unable to do anything except negotiate the terms of its surrender, pleading with de Gaulle at least to take power constitutionally. Faced with an apparent choice between the general and the colonels, the political class did not hesitate: it ran away. On 29 May, President Coty asked de Gaulle to form a government, threatening to resign if this were rejected. On 1 June de Gaulle appeared before the Assembly, asking for full powers for six months and promising to revise the constitution. He was invested by a large majority, and, on 3 June, full powers were granted.

De Gaulle was the last leader of the Fourth Republic, as he had been its first, and there was a depressing similarity between the situations that he confronted in each case. It is tempting, in the circumstances, to regard the period – or at least the years after 1946 – as the 'locust years', a time of failure and weakness. It is true that much of the life and all of the death of the Republic were unedifying. A political system that desperately needed reform was essentially unchanged, and the nation, weak and frightened, staggered from crisis to disaster, wasting lives, money and credibility on pointless wars. But, now that the Gaullist anathema on the Fourth Republic is itself part of history, we can see that much important work was undertaken during those years to modernise and reform the country. In the security field, the collapse into panic and impotence had been followed by the beginnings of a new assertiveness and a progressive move away from integration. The will to independence was now very clear, demonstrated by one of the last acts of the Fourth Republic, the full development of a nuclear weapon programme. In many ways, this had been Gaullism without de Gaulle, a set of objectives and attitudes that lacked a strong personal focus and a robust political structure to support them.

And what of the returned Sovereign? As foreign ministries struggled to digest events, many in France felt they could already see what was happening. From the *casernes* of Algeria to the cafés of the Boulevard St Germain, it was clear that France was heading for a period of authoritarian, right-wing, personal rule, that the Cold War and the anti-Communist struggle were to be stepped up, and that Algeria would be French for ever.

9

CHARLES THE GREAT AND THE GOD-KING

De Gaulle was the only man we had available. Perhaps the Army made a mistake.

General Massu, 1960

The past is finished. Long live Vichy!

De Gaulle, 1959

Call me God.

Kermitterrand, in French TV's *Bebete Show*, 1994

Anglo-Saxon studies of the Fifth Republic's security policies tend, for understandable reasons, to focus on the slow detachment from the NATO integrated structures between 1958 and 1966, and the quarrels with the United States. Yet, for most of de Gaulle's tenure at least, these were not the first, or even the second, priorities. The overwhelming priority of de Gaulle's early years in power was to find a way out of the Algerian impasse, and a close second was to head off the incipient civil war and political division that Algeria itself had done so much to encourage.

De Gaulle was to claim later a coherence and underlying logic to his Algerian policy that few observed at the time, and that is difficult to make out even in retrospect. Yet behind the many changes of tactics, there are some consistent orientations that governed the way in which he reacted. There are three in particular that are worth dwelling on for a moment, since they demonstrate a certain modernity of thought, and mark de Gaulle out very clearly from his critics. De Gaulle shared the common view of the importance of colonies, and of the special status of Algeria: given his background and experiences, it would be astonishing if he did not. He was part of the consensus after 1945 that saw colonies as a mark of a great power and a means by which a medium-sized nation could retain or regain that status. Yet here, as elsewhere, he had certain negative advantages: he did not share some of the distorting ideology around Algeria from which so many others suffered, and could therefore see the problem in perspective.

First, de Gaulle did not really see colonies as an end in themselves. He was proud of the French Union, and more aware than most of the importance of colonies in the recent war. But colonies were essentially a means to greatness and international respect, as well as to the promotion of pride at home. If colonies no longer fulfilled those functions, then it was questionable whether they were worth keeping. By the late 1950s, it was unclear that France was really receiving any advantages from Algeria, although the disadvantages were obvious enough. Half a million men could ensure a stalemate, but not a victory, at enormous financial and political cost. French unity was a major casualty, as once again the nation divided along Dreyfusard lines, and France's international standing had seldom been lower. The Army was stuck in the ideological slum of counter-revolutionary warfare, planning coups and resolutely refusing to modernise itself. France was attracting criticism rather than support from its allies, both for its policies themselves and for the gaping holes they were leaving on the Central front.

Secondly, de Gaulle felt no personal sense of involvement or commitment in Algeria. He had never served there, never been captivated by the vividness of the sky and the silence of the desert. Nor did he feel any responsibility for the Indo-China disaster. He did not have memories of abandoning France's native allies to the Viet Minh, nor did he feel a burning desire to avenge that humiliation in any way possible. Then again, he bore no responsibility for the conduct of the war until that date. The third difference lay in de Gaulle's conception of what the war was about. The military view was reflected in a map in the office of General Challe, the commander in Algeria, which depicted 'the flanking manœuvre of communism by an arrow from Moscow, which crossed the Middle East and Africa to touch Europe'.[1] De Gaulle, as a modernist and republican, had never accepted the apocalyptic view of the Cold War as a contest between the forces of light and darkness, and was not at all persuaded that the fate of the world depended on the Algerian conflict. He had, it is true, held strong anti-Communist views in the late 1940s; but these were partly for political

1. Jean Doise and Maurice Vaisse, *Diplomatie et Outil Militaire, 1871–1969*, Paris, Imprimerie Nationale, 1987, p. 460.

effect, and partly also because he viewed the PCF as unpatriotic and thus primarily a danger to French unity. Indeed, de Gaulle (who notoriously always referred to the Soviet Union as 'Russia') saw that nation as a secular great power, with normal national interests, rather than the nerve centre of some ideological crusade. De Gaulle thus saw the Algerian crisis for what it was: a problem of nationalism and de-colonialisation. His view of how it might be solved was always realistic, and he realised very early – perhaps as early as 1955 – that Algerian independence was inevitable.[2] The requirement, therefore, was to extricate France with as little damage as possible.

This conviction of de Gaulle's was practical rather than moral: he was not, of course, an anti-colonialist, and would, no doubt, have preferred to keep Algeria French if possible. At least, it might be possible to administer such a shock to the FLN that French prestige could be rescued and her negotiating position strengthened. The first recourse was therefore military, and de Gaulle unleashed the army against the mountain strongholds of the FLN: in parallel, a number of the more extreme officers, such as Massu, were recalled. As usual there was a strong political sub-text to de Gaulle's actions. This course of action meant taking the army away from its selected mission of ideological warfare among the masses, and using it once again in conventional combat against an armed enemy.

Moreover, the assault was spearheaded by the weapon that incarnated de Gaulle's technological muse between the tank and the atom bomb: the helicopter. This was not the first time that helicopters had been used in Algeria; but in the operations of 1959 they were used *en masse*, in conventional combat, and to great effect. At last, although in a way he could not have expected, de Gaulle had the weapon of which he had dreamed in 1934: a machine that could cross any terrain faster than a galloping horse. It was the offensive battle that he had envisioned for a quarter of a century; and some have seen a connection between de Gaulle's enthusiasm for this kind of warfare, and the opposition it provoked in the army, and the Pétain-de Gaulle controversy of the 1930s.[3]

In any event, the operations of 1959 served several purposes. They began the process of weaning the army away from the past and towards the future, they marked the arrival of a leader with his own ideas, they tested to destruction the question of whether

2. Jean Lacouture, *De Gaulle*, Vol. 3, *Le Souverain, 1959–1970*, Paris, Seuil, 1986, p. 50.
3. Ibid., p. 40.

a military solution was, in fact, possible, and they delivered heavy blows to the FLN. But they could not win the war; and so de Gaulle set out on the slow and difficult road to the Evian agreement of March 1962, which recognised Algerian independence with as many safeguards as the French could build in. The willingness to consider a negotiated solution was bitterly criticised, especially by the army and its political camp followers, who believed that they had brought de Gaulle to power in 1958, and thus owned him. This led to the events of 22 April 1961, the only serious attempt after 1870 by the French army to overthrow the Republic.

The attempt began, of course, in Algeria, among the Leopard Men themselves. As with most attempted coups, it was an affair of colonels, although Challe was persuaded to lend his name to the enterprise. It was based on a terrible sense of fear and betrayal: fear that Algeria, and hence the West, was being abandoned; betrayal by the man whom they had brought to power on 13 May 1958. The mood was summed up by an injudicious interview that Massu, victor of the Battle of Algiers, gave to a German journalist in early 1960.

> The Army has the power. It has not shown this power yet, because the occasion has not presented itself, but will intervene with this power if the occasion demands it. We no longer understand the policy of General de Gaulle. The Army had no idea he would carry out such a policy. Our greatest disappointment was to see him become a man of the Left.... De Gaulle was the only man we had available. Perhaps the Army made a mistake.[4]

As well as the air of slightly comic bafflement, there was dangerous self-delusion here, for it was not obvious that Massu spoke for 'the Army', or, indeed, anyone much outside the Tenth Parachute Division. The Leopard Men had massively over-interpreted the events of 13 May 1958, seeing public acquiescence in their coup as support for their own anti-democratic, anti-modernist and neo-Vichyite position, not as the disgust and impatience with the Fourth Republic that it really was. As a result, and 'obsessed by the old Maurrassian distinction between the *pays réel* and the *pays légal*', the ultras built a France in their own image, assuming that the 'true France' was that of the small, if powerful, group attached to *Algérie Française*, and that the views of others did not matter.[5] The significance of the referendum of January 1961, where the idea

4. Cited in Lacouture, *De Gaulle*, p. 88.
5. Jean Planchais, *Une Histoire Politique de l'Armée, 1940–1967: de Gaulle à de Gaulle*, Paris, Seuil, 1967, p. 354.

of self-determination for Algeria was approved by 75 per cent of French voters, appears to have eluded them. Their supporters were a varied bunch, and not always those for whom *Algérie Française* was the main preoccupation. For the white residents of Algeria, the *pieds noirs*,[6] this was a fundamental issue, but part of a wider picture also. Hostility to the modernising trends of the Fourth Republic had been especially strong in Algeria, together with nostalgia for many elements of the past, even Vichy. Right-wing groups had flourished there during the 1950s, and support for the ideology of the Leopard Men extended well beyond the narrow question of whether Algeria should be French or not, to the wider issues of anti-Communism and anti-modernism. In this sense, Algeria had now become a kind of 'anti-France': a gangrenous limb that had to be amputated if the nation as a whole was to survive. On the mainland there were similar sympathies. The modernisation and industrialisation of France in the 1950s had produced its ideological casualties: large groups of the provincial lower middle classes, the *petits hommes*, the 'little men' to whom every French politician had traditionally to appeal. From these sources came support for the movement of Pierre Poujade, whose ideology featured anti-parliamentarianism, anti-Semitism, and most of all anti-modernism, and nostalgia for an imagined pre-1914 world of order and uncomplicated patriotism. It expressed 'the resentment and panic of a backward France in danger of being swept away by modernisation'.[7] Although the movement was able to gain election of a number of deputies – including the ex-paratrooper Jean-Marie Le Pen – a great deal of support was lost to de Gaulle in 1958, and the Poujadists were another group who felt bitterly betrayed by de Gaulle. For the Poujadists Algeria was a perfect issue round which to rally.

Thus the coup of 22 April 1961 was a critical moment in modern French history, since whilst it was formally a product of de Gaulle's Algerian policy, it expressed wider fears about the whole direction of France since 1944. It was a head-on collision between the Revolution of 1789 and the counter-Revolution of 1940, between traditionalism and modernism, between the Republic and its hereditary enemies. Had the coup succeeded, it would have led not only to an *Algérie Française*, but to a *France Algérienne*: that is, a

6. Literally 'black feet', either from the black shoes the first settlers had worn, or alternatively from their unshod, and thus dirty, feet.
7. Jean-Pierre Rioux, *The Fourth Republic, 1944–1958*, trans. Godfrey Rogers, Cambridge, Cambridge University Press, 1987, p. 249.

military dictatorship and the application to mainland France of the same principles of psychological warfare that had so recently graced the streets of Algiers. Yet, in spite of the deep divisions that it symbolised, the coup itself was a comic opera affair, never in the least an equal contest. That the coup failed so completely was due to a strange conjunction of technology and apathy. Technology, since the widespread availability of cheap radios gave de Gaulle the chance to address the troops in Algeria directly and to command their obedience, as well as speaking to the nation as a whole through the new and magical medium of television. Apathy, because the urgent ideological cries of the Leopard Men seemed bizarre and remote to most of the conscripts and to the French population as a whole. Few seem to have understood what Challe had in mind when he alleged that, if the coup were not successful, Mers-el-Kébir would be a Soviet base the next day. In the event, the coup was a complete fiasco. In Algeria, only a handful of regiments joined in, and most of those were from the Foreign Legion. In metropolitan France, grandiose plans for a pincer movement on the capital from Orléans, Rambouillet and Auxerre amounted to no more than a few reserve officers in private cars, who were arrested by the police. Appeals by Challe for American support to 'save the Mediterranean from communist domination' were rebuffed.[8] By 26 April, it was all over.

The defeat of the coup did not mean the end of the crisis. A number of the leaders of the attempted coup fled to join the *Organisation Armée Secrète*, which was then beginning its murderous campaign. We tend these days to think of the OAS in its *Day of the Jackal* mode, as an incompetent organisation of assassins. In fact, it began as an organised terrorist movement in Algiers among the *pieds noirs*, with the objective of forestalling independence through violence, assassination and intimidation. OAS and FLN conducted a grisly round of outrage and counter-outrage in the streets of Algiers: increasingly, the OAS began to attack the mainland as well, which did not stop Le Pen and others from demanding that it be legalised as a political movement. Algeria also provoked enormous crises of conscience among politicians: some old Gaullists, like Debré, resigned. Some went further: Georges Bidault, no less, became chairman of a National Resistance Council, the name chosen to

8. Bernard Droz and Evelyne Lever, *Histoire de la guerre d'Algérie, 1954–1962*, Paris, Seuil, 1982, p. 308. This appears to be the entire foundation for the widespread, if erroneous, view that the United States was behind, or supported, the abortive coup.

recall the organisation he had headed during the war, after the death of Jean Moulin. De Gaulle as Hitler? The Fifth Republic as the Nazi occupation? What on earth could he be thinking of? The likely answer – and it has a general application – is that Bidault, like the rest of his generation, was dominated, even obsessed, by the period from Munich to the Liberation. To the widespread idea that an agreement with the FLN would be a new Munich, Bidault seems to have added the fear that to give away what was legally part of France was somehow to repeat the mistake of Vichy in 1940 in allowing the country to be partitioned.

The overwhelming endorsement of the Evian accords by a referendum in April 1962 meant that the OAS's objectives were reduced to killing people. Since independence for Algeria was now inevitable, the priority became revenge – the execution of the 'traitor' de Gaulle. A self-styled military tribunal sentenced de Gaulle to death for high treason, for the second time in a quarter of a century, and for the same political reasons. In the event, the Leopard Men could not even shoot straight: a dozen or more assassination attempts failed, sometimes in circumstances of farcical ineptitude. Towards the end, foreign mercenaries started to be used, but with no more success. Ironically, the last of the OAS figures to play an active role, Bastien-Thiry, had known de Gaulle since 1937, and been a member of the RPF. He had broken with de Gaulle over what he saw as the handing over of Algeria to 'Arabo-communism', and now saw him as the Antichrist.[9] Bastien-Thiry was captured and shot in March 1963, one of the few conspirators to suffer the severest penalty. As in 1945, de Gaulle recognised that there was still an unaccommodated France that should not be provoked too far.

Nonetheless, the end of the Algerian episode marks a decisive break in modern French history. The failed coup was, effectively, Vichy's last throw, and it revealed how little support the counter-Revolutionary agenda could now count upon. From that point on, the atmosphere of semi-permanent crisis that had existed since 1870 began to dissipate, and the lowering menace of the army seemed somehow less worrying. Indeed, apart from the rather over-interpreted events of 1968, the principal characteristic of the Fifth Republic has been relative peacefulness. The crisis surmounted, the rebuilding of France could proceed. And already, amidst the Algerian carnage, had come a symbol of hope from the deep desert: the first French nuclear weapon had been exploded at Reggane, on 13 February 1960.

9. Lacouture, *De Gaulle*, p. 274.

A Republican Monarchy

When the Fourth Republic was bullied out of existence in 1958, hardly a voice was raised in its defence. Three years later, most of France rallied to the Fifth Republic without hesitation. What had happened in the interim? The simple answer is that de Gaulle was popular in a way in which his interchangeable predecessors had not been, but that is only part of the truth. A political system that does not grow out of the cultural soil of a nation in which it is used will not prosper, and in the French case, after the Revolution of 1789, the challenge was to find a way of somehow reconciling the need to give expression to popular sovereignty with the need to contain the centrifugal tendencies that were likely to result. Individual rule, by Louis Napoleon or Pétain, could be perpetuated, since there was no longer any generally recognised principle of legitimacy or succession. The Third and Fourth Republics, on the other hand, could not contain these centrifugal, individualist, tendencies, and so died of weakness. It has been the achievement of the Fifth Republic more or less to reconcile these opposing requirements, and so to fashion a régime that enjoys a degree of legitimacy unknown for two centuries.

Most of this legitimacy derives from the president. But when de Gaulle took over in 1958, he was not president, only prime minister with special powers. Moreover, he was quite clear that the presidency of the *régime des partis*, necessarily a professional nonentity, had not served France well, and should not be imitated. De Gaulle had promised a new constitution, and it was promulgated in October 1958, and approved by referendum the same month. The Constitution has by now accumulated a small library of exegesis: I will touch here only on a few points that are relevant to themes I have been developing. The preamble of the 1958 Constitution is unambiguous about its republican heritage, declaring the 'solemn attachment' of the French people not only to the Declaration of the Rights of Man of 1789, but also to the preamble of the 1946 Constitution, with its idealistic resistance colouring.[10]

The centre-piece of the Constitution itself is the changed balance between the president and the parliament. The president is a figure above politics in the normal sense, and, crucially, he is not elected by parliament. The president is, in fact, exactly the kind of figure de Gaulle had always wanted, and for which he argued in

---

10. The text used is that in Charles Debbasch and Jean-Marie Pontier, *Les Constitutions de la France*, 2nd edn, Paris, Dalloz, 1989.

his Bayeux speech. French constitutions tend to be textually conservative, and, as Alfred Grosser notes, the powers of the president with respect to defence and foreign affairs are not all new. The Constitution of the Third Republic gave the president the right to 'negotiate and ratify treaties', and he had 'the Armed Forces at his disposal'. It is just that these powers were never used.[11] Some elements are new, however. The president is now the head (*chef*) of the armed forces and chairs committees concerned with defence (Article 15), and he is given sweeping emergency powers in times of danger to the independence of the nation (Article 16). On the other hand, it is the government that 'determines and carries out the policy of the nation' and has available 'the administration and the Armed Forces' for this purpose (Article 20). Most curiously, Article 5 *bis* describes the president as 'guarantor of the independence of the nation and the integrity of the territory', although what magical means he has to accomplish these tasks is not specified. What is going on here?

All this is easier to understand if, taking our cue from the institutional conservatism of texts, we realise that what is being described is the relationship of the Sovereign to his ministers. The Sovereign rules, in the name of the people, but does not burden himself with the actual business of daily government. And whereas the ministers draw their legitimacy from the Sovereign, since they are appointed by him, the Sovereign himself draws his legitimacy from other, more mystic, sources. This is fundamentally the situation under the 1958 Constitution, where the president names and revokes ministers, but has an entirely different source of legitimacy himself. It is the congruency with received ideas that made the post of the president so readily accepted after 1958, and it is possible to see how a mystical embodiment of the nation can defend its integrity, in the sense that the medieval king could, in his literal identification with the country.

But there is one significant difference. The 1958 Constitution makes reference to the *election* of the president, by extra-parliamentary methods: the first time this had been done since the ill-fated experiment that had led to the Second Empire. A strict Rousseauite would have argued that the popular election of the president was unnecessary, and even harmful, since an individual might well express the popular will even if the populace were unaware of willing it. But practical politics ruled out such a purist position; there

11. Alfred Grosser, *Affaires extérieures: La Politique de la France, 1944–1989*, Paris, Flammarion, 1989, p. 151.

would have to be a popular election of some sort. What was unacceptable, however, was election by the hated *partis*. At one stage in the drafting of the 1958 Constitution, it was even proposed that all candidates who belonged to parliamentary parties should be excluded from standing.[12] The original Constitution featured an enormous electoral college of some 80,000 people, in which parliamentarians, although they participated, were a tiny minority. Most of the rest were locally elected mayors and councillors. Almost at once, however, the rules were changed to election by universal suffrage. De Gaulle's reasons for doing this are interesting, and give the lie to suggestions that the 1958 Constitution was designed for his personal use. Rather, as an old man in a hurry, he knew, like any Sovereign, that he had to ensure the succession. He knew, quite simply, that no other political figure was likely ever to have his inherent legitimacy. The only way the system would survive would be through a direct link between the president and the people, a kind of popular sacrament. As he said at the time

> In fact, I have re-established the monarchy in my favour; but, after me, there will be no one as the natural choice. I was elected without the need for a referendum; it cannot be the same after me. It is best to set up a Presidential régime, so that we do not fall back into the struggles of the past. The President must be elected by universal suffrage: that way, whatever kind of person he is, he will have at least a semblance of authority and power during his mandate.[13]

Just as the authority of the king derived not from his personal qualities, but from the mandate of heaven, so the authority of the president would, it was hoped, derive from the mode of his election. Nothing else would provide a symbol of unity and stop the internecine quarrels of the past.

Of course, a simple symbolic restoration of the monarchy would not, by itself, have provided a focus for national unification. France was a republic (and indeed de Gaulle himself was a strong republican), and the experience of Vichy showed that attempts to restore the authoritarian monarchist state lacked general support. Fortunately, the French republican tradition, with its distrust of parliament and parties, has always been able to accommodate the idea of rule by an individual expressing the national will. Fortunately also, there was a body of iconography

12. René Rémond, *La Cinquième République, les partis et l'élection présidentielle*, in *L'Election du chef d'état en France: de Hugues Capet à nos jours*, Paris, Beauchesne, 1988, p. 162.
13. Cited by Lacouture, *De Gaulle*, p. 171.

that de Gaulle was able to take over for the Fifth Republic – one that had variously Revolutionary, Napoleonic and monarchic overtones. One of its most important components was Roman mythology, which turns up in surprising places, as will be seen in a moment. Another was the appeal to distant antiquity. Quite soon after he took power, de Gaulle began to be referred to as *Le Grand Charles* – Charles the Great. In Latin, of course, this is *Carolus Magnus*, hence Charlemagne, who was traditionally believed not to have died in 814 at all, but rather to be sleeping until the moment when he would return to save France in the hour of her greatest need. This was an image immediately recognised in Germany: from de Gaulle's first meetings with Adenauer, he was accused of acting in a 'Carolingian' fashion towards Germany. Certainly, it is interesting that the best-known photograph of de Gaulle and Adenauer had them together in the cathedral at Rheims, where every French king since Clovis had been crowned.[14] Because of his antiquity and mythical status, Charlemagne was not directly associated with the absolutist monarchism of the *ancien régime*, and so was an acceptable incarnation of monarchy for republicans. There was also a Napoleonic echo: Bonaparte himself (who had been a consul, Roman-style) had been crowned emperor in a replica of Charlemagne's regalia.[15] Thus the figure of the president of the Fifth Republic, as sketched by de Gaulle in the early years, was a comfortingly familiar one, with something for everyone to identify with. And the iconographic associations identified the president with the God-King of antiquity, the foremost prince in Europe and the instrument of the divine will.[16]

There was still one component missing, however. The light from the desert on 13 February 1960 was an indication that there might be a way, after all, in which the president could really guarantee the independence and integrity of the country, and in so doing, supply the keystone for the edifice of the Fifth Republic.

14. Lacouture, *De Gaulle*, pp. 291–2.
15. Robert Gildea, *The Past in French History*, London, Yale University Press, 1994, p. 63.
16. Tristan Doelnitz goes so far as to argue that previous French constitutions had been slavishly dependent on British models, and that it was 'necessary to wait for the Fifth Republic for the country to recover an institutional framework closer to that inherited from the first eight centuries of its history'. Can it be an accident, he wonders, that this coincided with the casting off of British 'diplomatic supervision'? Tristan Doelnitz, *La France hantée par sa puissance*, Paris, Belfond, 1993, p. 55.

Fire from Heaven

This section is not – except incidentally – an essay on the development of the French nuclear force and its doctrine. Rather, it attempts to place both of these things in their historical and political context, and to show why they developed as they did, and why they could really develop only under the Fifth Republic, where they fitted naturally in the imagery and iconography of a republic that managed to be both modern and timeless. In saying this, however, it must be conceded that the first steps in the French nuclear programme actually started under the Fourth Republic, and that the reasons why France wanted nuclear weapons were as well understood then as later. In great secrecy, preparations were begun under the government of Mendès-France, and all the arguments that were later adduced for French nuclear weapons had their first outing in 1954.

Mendès-France himself needed little persuasion. Coming fresh to international negotiations, he had been struck by the evident diplomatic advantage that nuclear powers possessed over non-nuclear ones. It was important that France should have this advantage, not least given that Germany (under the modified Brussels Treaty of 1954) was prohibited from enjoying it. The immediate causes of the decision were two American initiatives, the 'New Look' and Eisenhower's 'Atoms for Peace' initiative of December 1953, which would have established a stockpile of American, Soviet and British nuclear weapons for creative purposes. The lesson of the first was that, if a future war was rapidly to become nuclear, then a state without nuclear weapons would have no role except to provide the battlefield. In particular, the security of France would be entirely in the hands of the Anglo-Saxons, and her 'subordination' confirmed. The second was a less direct threat, but was perceived as 'a threat to the freedom of decision of France in the military applications of nuclear power'. Other, less immediate arguments were also deployed. For example, it would make the traditional French desire for equal status with Britain and the United States in NATO easier to pursue, and would additionally hold out the hope that the three nations could between them constitute a directorate that would decide by unanimity on the use of nuclear weapons, thus giving the French an effective veto on the launching of a nuclear war in Europe. And, as early as 1954, it was being argued, in an anticipation of the *faible au fort* strategy, that the menace of a nuclear riposte was sufficient to discourage an

aggressor, 'even one much more powerful'. Although a decision to proceed with nuclear weapons was taken in December 1954, the fall of the Mendès-France government meant that the policy had to be carried forward by others.[17]
In great secrecy, the process of constructing a nuclear force and a strategy to underpin it went ahead. Political interest and support appears to have waxed and waned with changing governments, but it has been suggested that the experience of Suez was decisive. Taken together with lack of support at Dien Bien Phu, it has been suggested that Suez 'made it appear that the United States could not be a reliable ally of their NATO partners in difficulties', and so convinced many politicians of 'the advantages which would accrue to France at the diplomatic level' by 'her accession to the rank of nuclear power'.[18] In any event, construction of a bomber that could carry the bomb (the Mirage IV) had started by the end of that year. The explosion of February 1960 was, then, the culmination of a programme that began long before de Gaulle, and the contribution that he brought to it was not one of concept, but of energy and determination.
At all stages of this programme, the highly political nature of these weapons was recognised by all. Because de Gaulle spoke openly of what was previously kept secret, his remarks have perhaps had more than their due share of attention. His comment that a state that does not possess nuclear weapons 'while others have them, does not control its own destiny', can too easily be interpreted as all of a piece with de Gaulle's fixation with grandeur and *rang*, and to suggest that the function of these weapons is purely symbolic.[19] But such sentiments can be paralleled, almost word for word, as early as the debates of 1954, when it was claimed that soon, no nation would be able to 'claim real political independence' if it did not possess nuclear weapons and the means to deliver them.[20] Such judgements as Wilfred Kohl's, that the French nuclear force was inspired 'more by political considerations than by concern for military security', and that it was only a tool used by de Gaulle 'in pursuit of his larger foreign policy objectives', both risk

17. See Georges-Henri Soutou, 'La Politique nucléaire de Mendès-France', in *Relations Internationales*, No. 59, Autumn 1989, pp. 317–30.
18. Marcel Duval and Yves le Baut, *L'arme nucléaire française: Pourquoi et comment?*, Paris, SPM/Kronos, 1992, p. 27.
19. Cited by Philip H. Gordon, *A Certain Idea of France: French Security Policy and the Gaullist Legacy*, Princeton, Princeton University Press, 1993, p. 42.
20. Soutou, *Politique nucléaire*, p. 326.

misleading the superficial reader into thinking that de Gaulle originated the nuclear forces, and also imply that the force is merely a
token one, for political purposes only.[21] There was more justification
for this view in the time in which Kohl was writing, since the *Force
de frappe* consisted of only a few squadrons of vulnerable aircraft.
But anyone who has actually visited French nuclear forces today
will testify to their professionalism and competence, and to the lav-
ish resources that are poured into them, as well as to the sense of
utter seriousness with which they go about their work.

But more generally, this approach betrays the application of an
Anglo-Saxon, and specifically American, consciousness to a problem with very different origins. For France, safeguarding national
independence is not an arcane political question only. France lost
her national independence between 1940 and 1944 in circumstances that could have led to the extinction of the nation, and was
only slowly recovering it again in the 1950s. Political factors such
as these are at least as important as any purely military ones. In
this connection, a great deal of attention – too much, perhaps – has
been focused on the texts and speeches in which various French
commentators have tried to set out a doctrine for nuclear weapons, in an attempt to isolate and discuss the various factors that
corporately have determined the French attitude. It is necessary to
remember, however, the relationship between theory and practice
in this area: practice comes first. That is to say: policy is what governments do, not what they say. Statements of policy are not law:
they are an acceptable way of describing what governments
already do, or have decided to do. They do not shape action, they
describe it. Thus, the various texts that are often referred to are
attempts by the authors to describe and account for a practice
whose implementation has preceded its description, and to do so
in ways that reflect their background and the type of audience
they are addressing.

The roots of French nuclear doctrine lie, in fact, in history and
domestic politics. They are both a reaction to the defeat of 1940
and a necessary component of the office of president of the Fifth
Republic. I suggested earlier that the defeat of 1940 has had a
determining effect on French security policy since that date, and I
have tried to give examples of how this has been so. It is in the
nuclear field that this perception can be most clearly seen, and
where Reynaud's 'Errors not to be repeated' have been taken most

---

21. Wilfred Kohl, *French Nuclear Diplomacy*, Princeton, Princeton University
Press, 1971, pp. 3 and 6.

clearly to heart. The first and most important component is the perception that France was left alone in 1940, abandoned directly by Britain, indirectly by the United States. This, it was thought, led to dismemberment and occupation, and to a position of weakness and dependency after the Liberation that it took more than a decade to recover from: a repeat performance could scarcely be contemplated. During the late 1940s, a respite from the fear of domination was at hand. For the United States, the preservation of Europe from Soviet influence was such a high priority that it was prepared to station troops there, and to defend its European interests with nuclear weapons. Since no conceivable administration would survive the charge of having 'lost Europe', the threat to use nuclear weapons to prevent this happening was credible.

But with the deployment of a serious Soviet nuclear capacity, these arguments changed, and it was not clear that preservation of a non-Soviet Europe was a greater priority than preservation of American lives and cities. Thus, France faced the possibility of a nuclear Dunkirk. Either the United States might decline to be involved, or, more likely, it would decide not to employ nuclear weapons. Such was the United States' domination of NATO structures that this decision would inevitably mean that NATO as a whole would not use them either.[22] However, if France had a nuclear arsenal, no matter how small, the position might yet be saved. Even a force of 60 Mirage IVs might, at the eleventh hour, avoid a repetition of 1940, perhaps forcing the invader to halt on the very borders of the Hexagon. And the use of French nuclear weapons might in fact force the American hand, and Europe (or at least France) might thus be saved that way. It is clear that this perception is anchored primarily in history, or, to be more precise, the need to avoid repeating it. It is a product of fear and memory, rather than an analysis of the situation of the time. To cite, again, a comment one hears in Paris, 'we have nuclear weapons today, because we did not have them in 1940'. Many other aspects of French policy have a similar orientation, as I shall show in a moment, and one can say that, overall, the purpose of French nuclear weapons has been to prevent the defeat of 1940, in the sense that, by addressing all the weaknesses believed to have contributed to it, the very reality of the defeat itself can be denied.

Some examples can readily be given. It will be recalled that the French nightmare after 1870, and even more after 1918, was the

22. The United Kingdom would not be considered an independent actor for this purpose.

numerical disparity between their own nation and Germany. The French have always been attracted to the idea of nuclear weapons as an 'equaliser', and, as the doctrine of *faible au fort* suggests, they can be seen as the final answer to the problem of forty million Frenchmen facing seventy million Germans. Likewise, the defeat was widely, if erroneously, ascribed to inferior French technology. By putting its trust in nuclear weapons, France was embracing a technology that then represented the height of modernity. These were the early, untroubled days of nuclear power, when everyone wanted a source of energy that was apparently clean, safe, and so cheap it could be provided free.

Similarly, it was widely felt that the defeat had been the result of an inferior and outdated military doctrine, represented by Pétain and his followers. Nuclear weapons offered the possibility of a proactive, aggressive strategy, and would give future French governments a muscular diplomatic option that they did not possess at the time of, say Munich, when a quite erroneous fear of *German* air attack was a factor in the government's behaviour.[23] It is not an accident that, under de Gaulle, the nuclear force was called the 'strike force' – the *force de frappe*.

Moreover, the French pursued a deliberate modernity of doctrine, and were influenced, both in private and in public, by the games theorists of the RAND corporation and elsewhere. This is not surprising, since many of the early games theorists had backgrounds in economics, a subject that was rapidly increasing in prestige at the time in France; and much the same rational models were applied to nuclear theory as the French were already applying to the economy. Thus economic models assume rational behaviour by actors with perfect knowledge of the market, so that, for example, a company will increase staff and produce goods until the cost of producing the last item (the marginal cost) is exactly equal to the expected revenue, at which point it stops. Applied to nuclear strategy, the same model implies perfect knowledge and rational action by decision-makers during a nuclear crisis. The *faible au fort* argument is an extreme case of this, since it relies on what is, in effect, a cost-benefit analysis by an

23. This is what lies behind the famous (or infamous) concept of *tous azimuts*, first developed in an article by General Ailleret in *Revue de défense nationale*, in December 1967. Ailleret is clearly concerned to avoid the mistakes of the 1930s, when rigid adherence to a single plan and threat assumption brought disaster. Over-reliance on NATO, and the assumption that the threat will come only from the East forever, are the modern equivalents.

312 | *Humanity's Soldier*

enemy that the benefits from an attack on France are not worth the possible disbenefits. It may be objected that this is not a good description of how wars actually start, since they are more often launched from positions of weakness than of strength, and by frightened leaders with inadequate information; but an assumption of rationality is a requirement of any theory of nuclear strategy, even if its grip on reality is a tenuous one.

Another important feature of the analysis of 1940 was the power of the army in declining to continue the war. Nuclear weapons took the decision to surrender or continue away from the army – seen to have abused it – and gave it to the president. Henceforth, a conventional military defeat would not be decisive, and no amount of military defeatism would prevent the president's unleashing what French writers call the 'nuclear fire' to save the country. Before 1940, it had been the army that was the guarantee of the nation's independence and survival, and this gave it a status in politics and a degree of leverage over the civil power that few outside its ranks found attractive. Nuclear weapons have fundamentally altered this political reality, by taking the ultimate survival of the nation out of the hands of the men in khaki. Indeed, by confiding it to sailors and airmen, under the direction of a civilian politician, the role of the army in political terms has been reduced out of all recognition. There are well-known photographs of successive presidents, accompanied by a military officer carrying the famous briefcase in which are carried the nuclear release codes. The iconography is not hard to interpret: the military several steps behind the civil power, and subordinate to it.

Then, of course, there was the difficulty the French had in getting hold of weapons from overseas in 1940, especially aircraft, and the problems in getting industry to provide what was needed. A relatively small and very high-tech nuclear force would not suffer from these problems, and the state could invest in the necessary facilities directly, rather than trying to persuade industry to do so, or trying to buy them from abroad. Thus, warheads were designed, developed and tested under government control, submarines were built in state-owned shipyards, and Avions Marcel Dassault would have found it difficult to refuse to build the Mirage IVs.

Finally, there was the question of the very war itself. It will be recalled that in the 1930s, the French were desperate to keep fighting away from the Hexagon itself, which had been so badly damaged between 1914 and 1918. This was the origin of the Maginot line and the advance into Belgium, echoes of which can be seen in the more recent uncertainty about how far forward French forces would fight, and whether French nuclear forces were intended to protect anything outside national territory. The ultimate hope of 1939–40 was that war could be avoided completely, and the territory preserved: clearly, this was an even stronger hope after the infinitely greater devastation of 1940–45. The French insistence that nuclear weapons exist only to deter war, and must never be used, and criticism of NATO doctrines that, in their view, imply the opposite, are both a memory of those periods, and an expression of the fear of total national annihilation in another war. Possession of nuclear weapons, the French hope, can symbolically bring about what was practically impossible in 1940, and expunge the war and the fact of the defeat as though they had never been. We have nuclear weapons today, because we did not have them in 1940....

I suggested earlier that nuclear weapons were especially suitable to the Fifth Republic; and, whilst the Fourth Republic began work on them, it is hard to see how the political limitations of the time would have allowed their use. The endemic confusion over who was responsible for security and defence would have made their use next to impossible: the thought of needing an affirmative vote in the Chamber of Deputies would have given any government pause. By contrast, the centralised Fifth Republic seems as though it was designed expressly to accommodate them. It is now finally possible to see how a single individual can guarantee the independence of the nation and the integrity of the territory, a president who is not so much an elected politician as a 'Nuclear Monarch', who is widely seen as 'Zeus, god of the elements, supreme arbiter and lord of Heaven, alone capable of throwing thunderbolts, guarantor of fidelity to treaties and director of relations with other countries ...'.[24]

Once again, there is a consistent pattern of imagery here. The literal identification of the king of France with Christ did not, of course, survive the Revolution. But there were separate strands of imagery of a more secular nature, particularly Classical: Louis XIV was often painted as one of the Greek or Roman gods. Louis, of course, was believed to be the foremost prince of Europe, and was flatteringly depicted receiving homage from everywhere: much the same was said of Napoleon. Interestingly, there is a medal of 1684 that depicts the bombardment of Genoa, a city-state that had allowed the construction of ships for Spain. It shows Louis as

24. Samy Cohen, *La Monarchie nucléaire: Les coulisses de la politique étrangère sous la Ve République*, Paris, Hachette, 1986, p. 15.

Jupiter, hurling thunderbolts from the sky. A medal struck to commemorate the bombardment of Algiers the year before includes the phrase *Algeria Fulminata*: Algiers struck by lightning.[25] The same iconography was used of Napoleon, as noted in Chapter 1. So it should come as no surprise to learn that the bunker under the Elysée from which the order to release nuclear weapons would be given is code-named 'Jupiter'. Likewise, and after de Gaulle himself had gone, one of the submarines of the SNLE[26] force was baptised *Tonnant* – 'Thunderer', and another *Foudroyant* – 'Lightning wielder': traditional names that perpetuated the concept of the Jovian king of France. And if the president was Jupiter, king of the gods and thus first among the rulers of Europe, then tactical nuclear missiles would naturally be named after his brother, ruler of the underworld (*Pluton*, and later *Hadès*).

The End of the Past

The establishment of the 'Nuclear Monarchy' was not, in itself, going to unite the nation, since the objective facts of recent history were too painful, and the divisions gaped still. As outlined above, Vichy revisionism was in full swing by 1950, partly under the influence of the Cold War. It was de Gaulle's special achievement to canalise this revisionism and to make it harmless, by encouraging the French people simply to forget about the divisions of those years. Henry Rousso has traced the different stages of de Gaulle's own, more benign, myth of the Occupation from 1945 on, with two constant objectives: 'the obliteration of Vichy and the redefinition of the Resistance as an abstraction, an achievement not of the *résistants* but of "the nation as a whole"'. And in 1959, de Gaulle even payed a visit to Vichy itself, preaching to the people about the virtue of forgetting the past: '... history is a continuous thread. We are one people, and whatever ups and downs we may have suffered, whatever events we may have seen, we are the great nation of France, the one and only French people ... the past is finished. Long live Vichy! Long live France! Long live the Republic!'[27]

25. Peter Burke, *The Fabrication of Louis XIV*, London, Yale University Press, 1992, p. 98.

26. *Sous-marin nucléaire lance-engins* (= SSBN).

27. Henry Rousso, *The Vichy Syndrome: History and Memory in France since 1944*, trans. Arthur Goldhammer, London, Harvard University Press, 1991, pp. 71–73.

That the man who had been condemned to death by Vichy should speak thus, was as strange as that the man of 18 June 1940 should begin a deliberate policy of downgrading the importance of various anniversaries of the Second World War. But a Nuclear Monarch has responsibilities as well as authority, and among them was the need to reflect all tendencies in a fragmented society that could not come to grips with the events of the war years, and to promote a healing myth that would make the memory easier to live with.

It is no surprise, therefore, that the history schoolbooks of the 1960s should have 'made Vichy disappear, or minimised its influence'. All the atrocities of the era were attributed to the Germans, and the textbooks claimed that 'most of the French resisted'. Realism began to creep in only during the 1980s, and even then one was likely to read that collaboration was a German idea, and that Pétain was 'badly advised', and 'allowed the Fascists to impose a New Order'.[28] The policy officially encouraged amnesia, given that the act of remembering was itself so fraught with danger. Whilst it would be untrue, for example, to suggest that the cinema ignored the war entirely, it generally dealt with collaboration only indirectly, in such films as Louis Malle's *Lacombe Lucien* (1974). One of the few films to show the extent of French collaboration, Joseph Losey's *M. Klein* (1976) is, not surprisingly, directed by an American.

The creation of myths proceeded at a popular level also. One of the most obvious is the series of cartoon books by Goscinny and Uderzo featuring Astérix the Gaul, which began appearing in 1961. At one level, these books are just wish-fulfilment: the indomitable Gauls, strengthened by their magic potion, defeat the Romans, lend help to the British, and even win all the medals in the Olympic Games (in a year when, as it happens, France did not win a single gold medal). But one can also see the series of books as the creation of a myth of unity and resistance, which idealised the real experience of 1940–44. Certainly, there are episodes where Astérix and his colleagues hand out rough treatment to Gaullish 'collaborators'. Intriguingly, after Uderzo's death in 1980, his colleague openly alluded to a 'great divide', which had cut the village in two.[29]

28. Suzanne Citron, *Le Mythe National: l'histoire de France en question*, Paris, Les Editions ouvrières/Études et Documentations internationales, 1991, pp. 92–93.

29. Rousso, *Vichy Syndrome*, p. 83. One can take exegesis of popular culture too far, but it seems at least possible that there is more detail in the Astérix myth than is often realised. A thoroughgoing interpretation of it might be as follows: the reader can accept as much or as little as he likes. *The Village* is an idealised picture

The Europe of Nations

Strengthened by the liquidation of the Algerian problem, the antic-ipated reception of the 'nuclear fire', and the start of organised amnesia about the past, de Gaulle was ready to begin his changes in foreign policy. Yet the dimension in which he chose to begin was not the Atlantic, but the European. One of the most damaging and misleading myths about Gaullism is that it is (or was) anti-European, a small-minded and xenophobic doctrine for the nar-row promotion of French interests. This is utterly misguided, as are attempts to equate Gaullist attitudes towards Europe with the policies of recent British governments.

The unity of Europe was a consistent objective of de Gaulle's thinking since the 1940s, and in this he was typical of his time. Typ-ical also was the assumption that there was no conflict between European unity and French national interest, since France was, and had been for hundreds of years, the natural leader of Europe. European interests were, by definition, French interests, and, as Europe became stronger and more united, France would benefit accordingly. De Gaulle expressed these views (which he was to claim dated back to 1940) in commonplace terms, in a series of speeches in the late 1940s. At Compiègne, in March 1948, he argued for the formation of the 'free states of Europe' into an 'eco-nomic, diplomatic and strategic grouping', combining 'their pro-duction, their trade, their foreign policies and their defence forces'. The resulting grouping of 250 million people, with common values

---

of France under the Occupation. *The Gauls* represent the republican tradition of the origins of France, as they did for Michelet. The watchword of the village is unity against the enemy. As long as that unity remains they cannot be conquered. *The Romans*, with their huge numbers, represent a generalised threat from the East, and in particular, of course, the Nazis. *The Gauls* are an idealised pic-ture of the nation as a whole. The Chief, *Abracacourix*, is literally a *chef* in the great tradition. He says little, but is admired and respected by all. He sends the Gauls off to battle with conventional adjurations to uphold the honour of the village. *Astérix* himself represents the civil power, intelligent and wily, but also decisive and a nat-ural leader. *Obélix* represents the Army: not so bright, but faithfully subordinate to the civil power. He, alone of all the Gauls, is not allowed to drink the magic potion, since he fell into it as a child. *Panoramix*, the druid, brewer of the magic potion, rep-resents the scientists and engineers who might have saved France in 1940, and sub-sequently worked on the atomic bomb. The *Potion* is, of course, the atom bomb, but more generally it is everything that France did not have in 1940: ingredient X (the recipe is a secret), which would have saved the day. As the druid's name implies, it protects against threats from all quarters.

and possessing large territories overseas, would be the means by which Europe could recover from the effects of the war. Of course, given that the natural boundaries of this Europe would be 'the North Sea, the Rhine and the Mediterranean', it followed that on France devolved 'the duty and the dignity of being the centre and the key'.

Much the same was said by others, before and since, and de Gaulle was expressing a majority view that saw no conflict between European unity and the preservation of French interests. This view was opposed, of course, by a number of those who still shared the Resistance idea that nations themselves were part of the problem, and therefore favoured an integrationist approach to building Europe, rather than the federalist approach to which de Gaulle subscribed. This latter approach required, of course, the retention of the nation-state as the basic unit of account. An integrated Europe, which downgraded the importance of nation-states, would eventually bring about, horror of horrors, a Europe in which France could not find its anticipated role of natural leader. This is the consistent fear behind French opposition to integrated structures in Europe, as it had also been in an Atlantic context. Once it became clear that the EDC would be so integrated that French dominance was in question, opinion turned against it. And a consistent thread runs through French policy from this episode, through quarrels in NATO and the European Community, to French concern that the common foreign and security policy of the European Union should be conducted in an inter-governmental (i.e. federal) fashion, and not in an integrated fashion. This is not, except incidentally, a Gaullist view, but rather a traditional French view that, at that time, had to compete with more integrationist tendencies that have now largely vanished from the political scene.

De Gaulle's manifestation of these objectives was in the so-called Fouchet Plan, launched after an EEC summit in February 1961, and named after the French chairman of the commission that elaborated it. Its preamble indicated that what would be created was a 'Union of States', which would be complementary to the existing integrated apparatus of the EEC and similar organisations, and would be principally concerned with co-operation in foreign policy, defence and culture. A *Commission Politique* of national leaders or foreign ministers would meet regularly, taking decisions by consensus. A parallel commission of officials, meeting in Paris, would be the real government of the Union, and eventually replace the commission in Brussels. Part of the intention was to create a European bloc within NATO that would lead, inevitably, to a re-balancing of that organisation in favour of Europe. The scheme eventually perished because it was too federal for some of the smaller European states, who demanded more integration, and too daring for some in France. It was also obstructed by the desire of some of the small states to see Britain take part, to balance the feared Franco-German hegemony. In spite of praise for the plan as a federal, rather than integrationist, concept, Macmillan refused. But the plan is the origin of the phrase *Europe des patries*, which has been tossed freely around in recent years and often glossed to mean the kind of European free-trade zone that successive British governments have often sought. Nonetheless, as the original con-text makes clear, the *Europe des patries* is a reference to a scheme that is the direct ancestor of the 1991 Maastricht Political Union Treaty, except where it is more ambitious.

It is worth noting that the first hint of what was to be the Fou-chet Plan was given by de Gaulle to Adenauer, the German chan-cellor, in July 1960. From the beginning of his presidency, de Gaulle had realised that a new relationship would have to be carved out with Germany: the fantasies of dismemberment that he had entertained after the war were quietly forgotten. If Germany was to be accepted as a continuing political entity, then Franco-German relations were of paramount importance. But these rela-tions could only, obviously, be entertained if Germany were the subordinate partner: not easy, given the demographic and eco-nomic weight of the larger state. So de Gaulle's policy, whose ori-gins go back to the ideas of the first proponents of the EDC, and whose main lines have been imitated by his successors, was to constrain Germany within structures dominated by French ideas and norms. The two leaders had met very soon after de Gaulle took power – in September 1958 – and formed an immediate attachment. This might not have seemed likely: Adenauer was a pious conservative traditionalist, dominated by anti-Communism and a great admirer of Dulles, whose 'ideological Manichaeanism' he shared. He saw no higher objective than the preservation of the Atlantic Alliance.[30] Yet Adenauer was a Rhinelander, and thus in French eyes a 'good', or at least acceptable, German. He was from that area that the French had always seen as untainted by Prussian militarism, and that was civilised, Catholic and Western: rather like France, really. The man of the Rhineland was an acceptable

30. Lacouture, *De Gaulle*, p. 294.

intermediary between France and a nation that the French were still a little reluctant to accept. Moreover, in spite of Adenauer's gut anti-Communism, he was not an uncritical admirer of NATO, and appears to have shared de Gaulle's view of the need for reform.[31] The actualisation of all this was the Elysée Treaty of 1963, whose inspiration, naturally, came from Paris. It set up a system of Franco-German co-operation in a variety of areas – including defence – that endures to this day. It was, avowedly, the first step in a Europe-wide scheme, and, as such, attracted the wrath of Washington immediately.

The Daughter of Europe

It was suggested earlier that French hostility to integration, although customary, is not absolute. There have been circumstances where the French have been content with a degree of integration, where they have controlled, or largely influenced, the rules by which the integrated organisation works: what I would call the 'operating system' of the structure. In NATO, this domination was never possible, largely because another nation, the United States, was already filling that role. For de Gaulle, as for his predecessors and successors, the NATO integrated military structure, and the other integrated structures of the Alliance, were simply a means to American hegemony, designed to continue the same degree of micro-management of French defence policy that the United States had managed bilaterally up until the early 1950s.

To normal fears about integration, which implied a status for France below her deserts, were added fears that France's defence policy and her armed forces were now not her own, just as had been the case in the immediate post-war period. American numerical predominance in NATO structures and procedures was the origin of this fear: American anger at any proposals for change, or examples of European co-operation, only served to strengthen this perception in Paris. For the British, there were connections of language and culture that allowed them to attenuate the practical impact of American hegemony. For France, there were no such opportunities, beyond the traditional idea of a French-dominated group of European states, which had been rejected a number of times already. Traditional methods for the

31. Ibid., p. 297.

recovery of French sovereignty, it was felt, had been exhausted. It was time for something new.

De Gaulle proceeded cautiously. His first step was a memorandum of September 1958, addressed to Eisenhower and Macmillan, which made four suggestions for a reconfiguring of the Alliance.[32] They were: to enlarge the area of application of the treaty, to question the principle of military integration, to question the American nuclear monopoly, and to seek a Three-Power Directorate, of France, Britain and the United States, to control the Alliance. It will be clear that none of these thoughts is new: each had developed since the late 1940s, and several had been given special force by the crisis of confidence that had followed the Suez fiasco. They represent, in particular, a natural continuation from the French negotiating objectives of 1948–49. They are very much the kind of demands that any new government of the Fourth Republic would have felt ritualistically inclined to make, and, although there are certain differences of nuance in the way in which the propositions are put, it is clear that they have important elements of continuity with the past.[33] Indeed, it is probably best to interpret the memorandum not as the beginning of a process, but as the culmination of one: the end, that is, of attempts by the French to achieve their ends by quiet and private diplomacy. The memorandum's rejection brought about a more public and explosive mode of discourse.

There seems little doubt that de Gaulle would have stayed inside the integrated military structure if he could have secured American and British agreement to its adaptation. For all de Gaulle's reputation for mindless provocation, he was a considerable pragmatist, who would have avoided a break with the Anglo-Saxons if that were possible. Moreover, both Macmillan and Eisenhower were old wartime comrades whom he liked and admired, and his relations with Kennedy were also very good. The idea of a de Gaulle forever gratuitously exasperating his allies from 1958 onwards is simply erroneous. The memorandum was launched privately, without fanfare; and indeed the text was not even published until 1976. In the end, however, it proved impossible to reconcile de Gaulle's vision with something acceptable to other members of the Alliance: such had been the case with successive French demands.

32. That the Germans were not informed of the memorandum's existence is, of course, entirely in keeping with the pattern of Franco-German relations that de Gaulle favoured.

33. See e.g. Maurice Vaisse, 'Aux origines du mémorandum de septembre 1958', in *Relations internationales*, No. 58, Summer 1989, pp. 253–68.

The reasons for this, and especially for the American reaction, were not new; but they were given special point by the arrival of de Gaulle on the scene. Essentially, the problem was a clash of expectations. Like Mendès-France, de Gaulle had been out of power during the years when the habits of subservience had been laid down, and he thus approached his dealings with the Americans without the political baggage and feelings of weakness and inferiority that most of his predecessors had carried. Unlike Mendès-France, however, de Gaulle had also directed the affairs of Free France between 1940 and 1944, had experienced hostility and thoughtless provocation from the Anglo-Saxons, and had fought back using the only weapon that came to hand: intransigence. To traditional French sensitivities and objectives, therefore, he added his own recollection of Anglo-Saxon attitudes and how to deal with them successfully.

Conflict might have been avoided if Washington had been prepared to be flexible and pragmatic in the way in which it treated de Gaulle. This was not to happen, and part of the problem lay in the way in which de Gaulle had irrupted on to the political scene once more, and the strange sequence of events that had brought him there. Sudden and dramatic changes of national leadership are disturbing to other governments, who naturally want to know as much about the new leader as possible: where did he come from? who brought him to power? who are his associates? what policies will the new government follow? Governments seek this kind of information immediately, and do not have the leisure or the inclination to commission deeper studies. The view of a national leader formed in the first few days or weeks will thus be influential for a long period afterwards. Quite often, harassed embassies and bureaucracies will fall back for convenience on the standard models and archetypes described in Chapter 6. The problem was, of course, that de Gaulle did not fit neatly into any of these categories, and his persistent refusal to do so was one of the reasons for the misunderstandings that were so common during his presidency.

By any standards, de Gaulle was a difficult individual to analyse properly, and it is hardly surprising that Washington failed to understand who they were dealing with. They were not helped by their ambassador: Bohlen fell victim to exactly the kind of pigeon-holing described above, as a despatch of March 1963 makes clear:

> ... it is important to remember that de Gaulle is distinctly a product of that half of France (or less than one-half) which has been since 1789, and still is, conservative, hierarchical, religious and military. This was one of the reasons for his bitterness against Pétain. He is

also the product of French military training pre-World War I and II in that he tends to approach a given problem from a highly analytical and rather simple point of view.[34]

As catastrophic misjudgments of modern statesmen go, this is quite a serious example. It was compounded by the fact that there was a folk memory of de Gaulle in Washington from the period 1940–46. De Gaulle would have been recalled as a 'difficult' figure to deal with, prickly and independent, one who was an incipient fascist to some, a tool of the Communists to others, and an enigma to all.

Then there were also the unconscious expectations that Washington would have had of any French leader. In spite of the Mendès-France episode and the strains of Suez, Washington's image of French government had been fixed in the late 1940s, and had not varied much. France, like other European nations, was expected to be grateful for the presence of American troops, and for the expressed willingness of successive administrations to defend their European interests with nuclear weapons. In return, America expected loyalty, or, to put it less kindly, obedience. Europeans should accept American leadership in many areas, not only within NATO but in foreign policy generally, as well as in economic and trade policy. Europeans should accept American criticism of their foreign and domestic policies, and recommendations about how their electorates should vote, without, of course, reciprocating in kind. One does not have to postulate a conspiracy here: these habits were at least as much the result of European timidity as of American assertiveness. But they were habits that de Gaulle had simply never acquired, and his behaviour, even had he been guided by the kindest and most benign of motives, was bound to be misinterpreted in Washington. It was certain to give rise to strains, because his objectives and those of the Americans could not be reconciled. More independence of action for France meant less influence for Washington, both in France, and in the Alliance as a whole. And de Gaulle was the heir to several centuries of patronising ideas about, and behaviour towards, a nation that was still widely thought of as 'the daughter of Europe'.

The decision to leave the integrated military structure of NATO, announced in March 1966, was both a defeat for de Gaulle and an expression of the impossibility of accommodating the conflicting needs of the two nations. De Gaulle's attempts to reform NATO

34. Charles E. Bohlen, *Witness to History*, London, Weidenfeld and Nicolson, 1973, p. 508.

had been rebuffed, and a whole string of developments after 1959 had served to exacerbate divisions that existed already. Most of these were about nuclear weapons, and several were attributed by Paris to American attempts to stop the deployment of independent French nuclear forces and a consequent attenuation of American nuclear hegemony. Certainly, nuclear issues had given trouble from the first months of de Gaulle's tenure. According to a celebrated story, de Gaulle had been briefed in September 1958 by the then SACEUR, General Norstadt, about American dispositions in France. But when de Gaulle asked where American nuclear missiles were based and what their targets were, Norstadt first asked that the room be cleared and then admitted sadly to de Gaulle that he was forbidden to tell him. Other nations' leaders, perhaps other French leaders also, might have taken this with equanimity; but de Gaulle was heir to a tradition that the king of France was 'Emperor in his own domain', and could scarcely accept the implication of subordination that the refusal implied.[35]

For the French, it appeared as if a strong attempt was being made to 'prevent, or at least slow down, the acquisition by other nations of the Alliance of independent nuclear capabilities. In concrete terms, this meant discouraging France from developing a means of national deterrence, and urging Great Britain to reduce her autonomy in this area'.[36] McNamara's swingeing attack on independent nuclear forces at the 1962 NATO Athens summit only served to reinforce this perception. The Multilateral Force (MLF) initiative, first launched in December 1960, would have given European naval crews (including Germans) Polaris missiles to be launched by general agreement. The French interpreted the MLF initiative as 'a concept thrown together any old how, allowing Washington to divide its allies'.[37] Likewise, Kennedy's December 1962 offer at Nassau to sell Polaris missiles to France, as to Britain, was generally seen at the time as a trap that Macmillan fell into, but de Gaulle avoided.

The final element of nuclear dissonance was the adoption by the United States of the system of 'flexible response', which had been in preparation since the early days of the Kennedy administration, and was first revealed by McNamara at the Athens summit. For the French, the unilateral way in which the conclusions

35. Lacouture, *De Gaulle*, p. 466.

36. Bozo, *La France et l'OTAN: De la guerre froide au nouvel ordre européen*, Paris, Masson, 1991, p. 80.

37. Bernard Destremau, *Quai d'Orsay: derrière la façade*, Paris, Plon, 1994, pp. 248–9.

were announced was part of the problem, as was the universal assumption that NATO as a whole would rapidly adopt the strategy as well. French fears about the doctrine were not hard to explain, since it appeared to place in doubt the real commitment of the United States to use nuclear weapons in Europe. The effective American nuclear monopoly within NATO would enable the two superpowers, should they wish, to fight a war for Europe without recourse to nuclear weapons: the Europeans would have no say in the matter, but be confined to providing the 'potential battle-field', while 'sanctuarising the territories of the great powers'.[38] The fears of a nuclear Dunkirk, never far away, were raised once more.

In parallel with the final stages of French disenchantment with NATO, de Gaulle began the process of tentative disengagement. In March 1959, he withdrew French ships in the Mediterranean from NATO command, citing their importance for the Algerian war. He responded to Norstadt's reluctant snub by expelling NATO (i.e. US) stockpiles of nuclear weapons from France later that year. In 1963, de Gaulle withdrew French ships from SACLANT's command, and, after that date, increasingly refused to participate in 'forward defence' exercises on the Central front. When it came in 1966, therefore, the break was scarcely unexpected: it had been in the making ever since the days of Pinay.

Myths and Legacies

It is impossible to say whether any other French leader would have acted as de Gaulle did, and whether, under different circumstances, the break might have been avoided: too many variables are involved. One important fact, of course, is that France without de Gaulle would have been a very different country. If the Sovereign had not returned in 1958, the nation would have staggered from one crisis to the next, its possible futures arranged in a spectrum from a weak, Italian-style government run on corruption and compromise to a military dictatorship. It is quite possible that, even if a strong leader had arisen, he would not have commanded the wide support and legitimacy of de Gaulle, and so not felt able to take on the Americans in the same way. In the purely formal sense, therefore, French practice, as opposed to French objectives, might have been different. On the other hand, the accumulated frustration and tension in Paris, telegraphed as early as the Pinay

38. Bozo, *La France et l'OTAN*, p. 81.

government, would have found an outlet eventually. Because of the assumptions that lay behind the independent nuclear programme, a break of some sort with the United States was also probably inevitable, especially with NATO's adoption of the 'flexible response' doctrine. Finally, if the nation had managed to extract itself from the Algerian morass, it would have had to decide whether to send the half-million returning troops to the Central front to fight 'under American command' or not, and another government might well have decided, as de Gaulle did, to refuse to do so. In all probability then, French policy would have evolved in much the same way, but in a less coherent, more fractious and probably more disruptive fashion.

These reflections lead naturally to an evaluation of the nature of de Gaulle's legacy, and what his successors have done with it. First, however, it is important to be clear about three things: what 'Gaullism' actually consisted of, how far (if at all) it was new, and whether alternative models were available for use, then or later. The three points are clearly all connected. I would suggest that the essence of 'Gaullism' is to be found in two connected doctrines, neither of which is new. The first is that France must never again find herself, as in 1940, abandoned by her allies in the face of a superior enemy. The second is that, in peace and in war, France's co-operation in security and defence matters can be counted on, but should never be taken for granted. The first concern leads naturally to the development of an independent nuclear force, the second generally in the direction of the 1966 break. Everything else is window-dressing.

Of course, like all government policies, these are objectives to be attained to the greatest extent possible, not rigid requirements against which failure can be precisely measured. And like all governments, de Gaulle's seldom felt the need gratuitously to point out to its public areas where the fulfilment of its objectives was difficult or incomplete. It is the failure to understand these points that has bedevilled so much analysis of French policy. The fact that 'during the 1960s, at least, the French deterrent was not very credible', because of its size and vulnerability,[39] may be true, but is not really the point. If the apparatus of deterrence and American protection were to fail, if the nuclear umbrella were to be withdrawn, then anything that might help to keep French soil inviolate was better than nothing. It was possible that the Red army, rolling

39. Gordon, *A Certain Idea of France*, p. 41.

westwards behind the departing Americans, would simply laugh at French threats; but it was also possible that they might not. What was certain was that not even this slim chance would be available if France were to keep all its eggs in the basket of American-led integration. Moreover, de Gaulle, like a large section of French opinion, viewed the Soviet Union without favour, but without a sense of panic either. That is to say, the interpretation of its behaviour identified with Vichy and its followers, that the inherently aggressive ideology of Moscow would lead it inevitably to a gratuitous plunge into attempted world domination, was no longer the leading interpretation in Paris. Rather, war was viewed as unlikely, except through miscalculation, arising perhaps from a superpower disagreement. France herself was not seen as any kind of special target – the reverse, if anything; and in a war of miscalculation, it was possible than even quite a modest nuclear capability would keep her safe.

Similarly, the famous doctrine of 'independence' was relative, rather than absolute. There is a tendency in Anglo-Saxon criticism of de Gaulle to argue that he pursued some kind of ideal and purist notion of national independence that simply refused to acknowledge the influence of other states at all, and that his influence on France, and on the Alliance generally, was correspondingly damaging. It would be surprising if de Gaulle, with his experience in the 1940s, ever thought like this. What independence means in this context is the greatest independence of decision-making possible. We are back, in other words, to the existentialist concept of free action. This was, once more, an objective, rather than a rigid rule, and there have been many occasions in the last thirty years when France has been obliged to sign up to unattractive propositions. But the ideal is of a nation that examines each proposition on merit, and agrees out of a free choice, not because she is forced to do so. The practical result may indeed be identical (which makes this distinction a difficult one for Anglo-Saxons to take seriously); but the process has been completely different. Thus, for many years, France resolutely refused to sign any of the international treaties limiting nuclear weapons or nuclear testing, but made it known, nonetheless, 'by declarations which were unilateral and so non-binding, that she would behave *as though* she was party to these treaties insofar as they concerned the international community'.[40] Once more, it was the process that was more important than the end result.

---

40. Duval and Le Baut, *L'arme nucléaire française*, p. 91. Emphasis in original.

The ability of a state to behave in this fashion was obviously reduced if it was part of an integrated structure, and if some decisions were effectively outside its own control. So long as a structure was receptive to French ideas and working methods (as the EEC largely was), this was a manageable problem. But when the integrated structure was largely owned by another nation, the chances of a free decision were much reduced. As a result, the process by which French forces would fight under US command in a future war had to be altered, although the end result would not change. Thus, immediately after the 1966 estrangement, French officers began to negotiate with the staff of the Commander-in-Chief, Central Front (CINCENT) a series of agreements regulating how the French First Army would actually have been used in the event of an attack on Western Europe. The so-called Ailleret-Lemnitzer accords of 1967 have never been made public, but appear to be very extensive, and to provide, in great detail, for a status for the First Army that is not very different, in practice, from that which fully integrated forces would have. The difference appears to be that there would have been, in addition, some kind of political approval process on the part of the president. It is the difference between Matthieu Delarue joining in the defence of the tower as a free act, and the Chasseurs he joins, who were ordered to fight.

French officials and military men have always insisted that 'of course' France would have honoured her treaty obligations. They have gone so far as to draw a sardonic contrast between nations (like the French), which are integrated in practice but not in theory, and other nations (not specified), of which the reverse, they argue, is true. In any event, the French can, and do, point to a history of loyalty to their allies in incidents ranging from the 1948 Berlin crisis to the Gulf War. They frequently go on to hint, darkly, that it would be nice if the United States had been similarly loyal, in such episodes as Indo-China and Suez. This characterisation of 'Gaullist' policy as one of loyalty tempered by the need to be asked nicely is not, of course, common. More popular is a picture of a disagreeable and bad-tempered partner, the *Reluctant Ally* of Michael Harrison's title.[41] This formulation (which is not borne out by the content of the book) implies that the French were reluctant *to be* an ally of the United States or of their fellow-signatories – a contention that cannot be supported. More plausible is the judgement that the French were reluctant *to behave* as allies of the United States in the

41. Michael M. Harrison, *The Reluctant Ally: France and Atlantic Security*, Baltimore, Johns Hopkins University Press, 1981.

terms that Washington expected, in so far as they had a different view from Washington's of what being allies entailed.

If the essence of 'Gaullism' is as I have described it, and if little of it is new, the next obvious question is whether 'Gaullism' represented any kind of break with the past at all. At the level of objectives, it is difficult to see anything really new. If it is true that, under de Gaulle, French behaviour and French rhetoric were somewhat different, that is because de Gaulle adopted different tactics in pursuit of a very similar strategy. As is usually the case in France, the strategy was expressed in outline terms only, and was as vague as the two postulates that I identified above. As a result, the various decisions of 1958–66 were not policies or strategies themselves, but tactics pursued towards a larger goal. This is something that has always puzzled Anglo-Saxons, who tend to forget how typically the French think in decades.

It is a reluctance to take these kinds of factors into account that leads to an over-simplification of what 'Gaullist' and 'post-Gaullist' security policy is all about. In particular, it leads to a cartoon-like creation, 'Vulgar Gaullism', which is no more than a policy of gratuitously insulting NATO and the United States, of being different from these parties for the sake of it, and pursuing a narrow-minded and warped policy of extreme nationalism. By this interpretation, of course, friendly references to the United States, good-tempered behaviour at NATO summits, or support for integration in Europe can be labelled 'Atlanticist', 'post-Gaullist' or 'European' respectively, when they usually represent either a small modification to rhetoric or a reaction to a completely changed situation. Similarly, there is an excessive tendency to see every detail of French defence policy as part of a specifically 'Gaullist' design. Thus, budgetary problems and equipment cutbacks in recent years have been glibly ascribed to the contradictions of 'Gaullist' policy, even though all advanced nations are having the same problem, and any conceivable French government would also want to retain an (expensive) balanced range of conventional and nuclear forces anyway. Similarly, it is difficult to blame French difficulties in making large numbers of troops available in the Gulf War with 'Gaullism': the French problem was common to all nations with conscript armies, and the French, with a large professional contingent, were actually affected less than some others.

On the other hand, it is also true that some in France have lost sight of the distinction between strategy and tactics in much the same way. It is not impossible that re-entry into a (changed) integrated military structure could at some time seem a sensible move for a French government. But so much political sensitivity now surrounds the issue that, for many people, the tactic that was supposed to safeguard independence has been confused with the independence itself. Similar pointless polemics have taken place about whether or not the Gulf War demonstrated that peacetime integration was essential or not, as though integration were an absolute evil that must never be permitted to have any virtue at all.

It is on this question of tactics that I come to my third point: whether there were, or are, alternative models to pursue. This is particularly important, since de Gaulle's tactics were widely unpopular at the time, in the army, in the Quai, and in parliament and the media. Does this mean that there were large numbers of 'Atlanticists' whose resistance de Gaulle had to overcome? I would suggest that it does not mean this. There were many types of opposition to de Gaulle in 1966, and by no means all the critiques were consistent among themselves. The first, and simplest, was opposition from military men and extreme anti-Communists, for whom any reduction, however slight, in the size and efficiency of the apparatus confronting international Communism was not to be contemplated. In a less extreme fashion, there were also those who, whatever their personal feelings about integration and sovereignty, were attracted by the greater efficiency of an integrated structure, and, usually for military reasons, wished to retain it. Linked with this was a reluctance to give up prestigious jobs and operational commands in the NATO structure. There were the remaining idealists, who still believed that the re-nationalisation of defence was dangerous in itself; and there were those who feared the consequences not of French, but of subsequent German disintegration. There were those for whom change of any sort was anathema; those who were worried about the reactions of other nations and the political damage France might suffer; and those who were frightened of retaliation from Washington and what it might mean.

But there were also more substantial reasons for the differences. The corollary of de Gaulle's accession and the advent of the Fifth Republic was the eclipse of an entire political generation that had ruled under the Fourth. Although the MRP were present in the early years, de Gaulle's accession effectively put an end to the vast majority of the political careers that had begun after 1944. Moreover, an entire political, diplomatic and military generation had either agreed to the dispositions of 1948–52, or had worked with them, and become reconciled to them. As a political position, the argument that you had no choice, and that the arrangements made were the only ones possible, loses much of its force with repetition. Human nature dictated that those who had been involved in the security apparatus created after 1948 would, in time, come to accept it and defend it. Now, de Gaulle was putting the work and the self-image of an entire generation in question. His strictures on NATO were equally, of course, strictures on those who had accepted for France what he regarded as a subservient position. The debate therefore became an intensely personal one very quickly.

Some personalisation would have occurred in any event, since the bitterness against de Gaulle for the destruction of a whole political class was very real. We sometimes look for deeper motives in this debate, forgetting that opposition parties oppose the government because it is their nature, and indeed their duty, to do so. The 1966 decision was far from the only item of Gaullist policy that was violently attacked in those years, and indeed the censure debate of April 1966 was on a far wider range of topics than just the recent decision about NATO. We can see this in the exchange, during that debate, between Pompidou and René Pleven. The former no doubt genuinely believed what was in his brief; the latter had been prime minister and defence minister in the years when the decisions now being attacked had been taken. But the debate is less a principled debate about 'Atlanticist' and 'Gaullist' models than the usual ritual exchange between government and opposition, automatically taking different sides on any issue.

Partly, therefore, and as often in politics, it was a question of generations. New men of the Fifth Republic replaced those who had opposed de Gaulle, and orthodoxies changed. Indeed, after de Gaulle's departure, some of his rusticated opponents in the Quai were brought back, and seem to have adapted themselves well to the new situation. It is also a question of myths. The Gaullist era combines two very powerful myths, that of fall and recovery, and that of the absent king. The first represents the way in which the Gaullist effect on France is generally presented in its popular form: it is the myth of the fall and rise of a great nation, of sin followed by redemption, and of weakness, decadence and disunity giving way to renewed strength. Its power derives from the fact that most people, and most nations, prefer to feel that they are on the upward, not the downward, swing of the pendulum. The second myth is of the king or leader who goes away, and whose country falls into ruin in his absence. As a type of story this is universal:

examples range from Odysseus to the Duke in *Measure for Measure*. The story necessarily ends with the return of the king and his triumphant reception by a repentant people. In isolation, each myth is powerful: in conjunction, they make up a flattering and positive interpretation of recent history that the French are unlikely to want to give up quickly.

The Rose and the Crown

The security policies of the post-Gaullist era have been massively studied, and I propose only to say a few words here about the persistence of themes since 1966. Writing in 1981, Michael Harrison felt that he could detect, by that date 'the gradual emergence of a national consensus on the value of the Gaullist security model', which was based on 'a certain conception of French independence and symbolised by an independent nuclear force and restrained ties to France's Western allies'.[42] It is perhaps better to say that de Gaulle did not so much invent a security model as reconstitute one: that after a dozen uncharacteristic years of fear and weakness, France had begun to move back to traditional models and positions. There was a move away from integration and towards federalism and co-operation, a reassertion of France's leading role in Europe, and a relationship with the United States based less on subordination and more on equality. Beyond this, there was also a conscious reaching back to earlier models of politics, and a reinterpretation of a Sovereign figure in republican terms.

The election of François Mitterrand as president in 1981 should logically have marked a change. This Mitterrand, after all, was de Gaulle's oldest and most effective opponent, who had nearly taken the presidency from him in 1965. He had quarrelled spectacularly with the Sovereign in London, and had led opposition to him in the last days of the Fourth Republic. He had served the régime de Gaulle despised, and, in preparation for his candidacy had penned one of the most scathingly literate pamphlets any national leader has ever had to suffer, elegantly dismissing de Gaulle, his actions in the 1950s and the régime of 'permanent *coup d'état'* that he had created.[43] It is easy to make a list of simple differences. De Gaulle was from the fringes of the nobility and joined the army, Mitterrand from the lower middle class and became a

42. Harrison, *The Reluctant Ally*, p. 2.
43. François Mitterrand, *Le Coup d'état permanent*, Paris, Plon, 1964.

lawyer. In 1940, de Gaulle was a temporary general, Mitterrand an unenthusiastic sergeant. De Gaulle spent the war in London and Algiers, Mitterrand was in the Resistance. De Gaulle spurned the Fourth Republic and tried to destroy it, Mitterrand served it, and tried to save it. Mitterrand scorned de Gaulle's 'bomblet', and opposed the exit from NATO. And so on.

But there are some surprising similarities. Like de Gaulle's, Mitterrand's political origins were equivocal. He was both a Vichy civil servant and a *résistant*. He was not noticeably to the Left for many years, being elected to the National Assembly in 1946 by the votes of those who saw him as less left-wing than the other candidates.[44] He formed and dominated the *Parti Socialiste* more as a vehicle for himself than out of ideological conviction. He therefore had the same indeterminate quality that de Gaulle had, and that every successful Sovereign must have – the ability to attract opposites to him, to act as a focus for widely different aspirations. Both were elderly men when they became president; but there was a domestic, bourgeois quality to Mitterrand that was entirely foreign to de Gaulle: who could imagine applying to de Gaulle Mitterrand's nickname of *tonton* – 'uncle'? It can be said that Mitterrand represented the stage by which the Fifth Republic had settled down, and the Gaullist charisma become routinised. It is also true that Mitterrand, the man of the Fourth Republic, represented the final *rapprochement* of the Fourth and the Fifth; not a synthesis, but a coming-to-terms. Perhaps, as Alan Duhamel suggested, he was Ulysses in the French Odyssey, a character in Corneille, rather than in Racine.[45]

Yet Mitterrand's other nickname was *dieu* – 'God'. If anything, he deepened and strengthened the attributes of the presidency, producing a more rounded and complete Sovereign figure, the essence of a century of French political life and a millennium of political culture. He was not only the God-King, he was also the great builder, the patron of the arts and the man of letters (his official photograph showed him holding a book). Moreover, he inherited the power to call down fire from heaven, and, under Mitterrand, the president's control of security and defence matters was further increased.[46] And he appears to have responded to a

44. Franz-Olivier Giesbert, *François Mitterrand, ou la tentation de l'histoire*, Paris, Seuil, 1977, p. 120. He stood against candidates from the SFIO and the PCF.

45. Alain Duhamel, *De Gaulle – Mitterrand: La marque et la trace*, Paris, Flammarion, 1991, pp. 22–23.

46. See, for example, Samy Cohen, *La défaite des généraux: le pouvoir politique et l'armée sous la Ve République*, Paris, Fayard, 1994.

need in the French psyche: a series of opinion polls during the 1980s demonstrated a clear shift of opinion towards the view that Mitterrand was 'the President of all the French' rather than a party figure. Interestingly, this view was stronger during the 1986–88 period of cohabitation.[47]

A complex process is at work here, rather more than the simple adoption of a pre-existing model. The Fifth Republic that Mitterrand and others opposed was not the real republic being created at the time, but the sum of their own fears, just as de Gaulle was not really another Napoleon III or Pétain. For those who had failed to prevent the demise of the Third Republic, it had been essential to prevent the Fourth going the same way. If de Gaulle had been the kind of person Mitterrand thought he was, then that opposition would have been entirely justified. But it became clear that the 'model' – if that term must be used – had its roots not in the nineteenth century, but in the collective subconscious of France itself. As the years passed, and as the memory of Vichy became less bitter, de Gaulle became more visible in his own terms, and the essentially traditional nature of his policies became clearer. It became obvious that here was no nuclear-armed dictator bent on a narrowly nationalistic defence policy, but someone drawing strength from the patterns of the past. The Left's embracing of the Gaullist heritage is seen most clearly in the work of Régis Debray, at one stage Mitterrand's foreign policy adviser.[48] Stressing that his own political views have not changed, Debray presents a new de Gaulle, not the 'Napoleon III', as he feared at the time, but rather the 'great political myth' of the twentieth century.[49]

This absorption of the Gaullist heritage by the Left has been very noticeable in the areas of defence and security. A number of factors have helped, not least the realisation that much of what was being absorbed was not invented by de Gaulle, but merely recovered and articulated. It is helpful also that the Jacobin tradition on the Left remains strong: after all, the greatest military triumphs of France were achieved by a citizen army. France has never really had a mass pacifist movement. Pacifism and anti-militarism are often confused, but in fact they are quite distinct. Pacifism, in the sense of a principled refusal to fight, has never had a

47. Jean-Louis Quermonne, 'Le profil des candidats et la fonction présidentielle', in *L'élection du chef d'état*, p. 204.

48. Régis Debray, *A demain de Gaulle*, Paris, Gallimard, 1990.

49. Ibid., p. 23.

mass following, even on the Left. There has been, however, a great anti-militarist tradition on that side of the political spectrum, largely as a consequence of the unrestrained use of the army against the Left in the period between 1870 and 1914. That the Left should have conceived a poor image of the army is scarcely surprising in the circumstances, and they reacted by arguing that the traditional military virtues were incompatible with democracy and republicanism. Citizen armies with short periods of conscription were preferred. But this latter attitude did not imply pacifism or lack of patriotism, and its concrete embodiment in the Resistance, at a time when the professional army was cohabiting with the Nazis, demonstrated this quite adequately.

The 'Gaullist model' itself contained a number of features that made it easier for the Left to rally to it. For small nations, faithfulness to an ally or an international grouping can be electorally beneficial. But for a larger power, this is seldom true, and the nationalist focus of Gaullist policy, the formal stress on independence of decision-making, was very difficult to argue with from any part of the spectrum. Since the NATO integrated military structure was generally seen as controlled by the United States, moves towards it were necessarily seen as moves away from independence and towards domination by a foreign power. This was a judgement that could command support almost anywhere. This was true even of nuclear policy, where the Left had most harshly criticised de Gaulle. The process by which the unified *Parti Socialiste* under Mitterrand came to accept nuclear weapons is a complex one. Reasons include the greater credibility of a sea-borne force, financial factors, and a natural political tendency to align with an emerging consensus.[50] The acceptance of nuclear weapons was in any case part and parcel of the acceptance of the Fifth Republic itself, the Nuclear Monarchy that de Gaulle began to build, and which Mitterrand finished off.

It is scarcely surprising, therefore, that the main outlines of Mitterrand's foreign and security policy were what we might think of as 'Gaullist'. It is sometimes suggested that Mitterrand, and indeed Pompidou and Giscard, have pursued a more 'Atlanticist' policy than de Gaulle. On examination, this usually turns out to mean that there were fewer overt collisions with the United States, and that the rhetoric of the relationship was softer. This is hardly a

---

50. Jolyon Howorth, 'Defence and the Mitterrand Government', in Jolyon Howorth and Patricia Chilton, eds., *Defence and Dissent in Contemporary France*, London, Croom Helm, 1984, pp. 94–134.

change in policy. What happened, of course, was that by the late 1960s it was obvious that France's new position in NATO would be permanent, and the arguments (which any government with the same policies would have had) were largely over. A steady state is always easier to manage than a period of transition, and both the international agenda itself, and the personalities of successive French and American leaderships, produced a rather quieter relationship. Mitterrand, in particular, with his extensive political experience under the Fourth Republic, was bound to pursue his objectives with a subtlety and patience that would have been alien to de Gaulle. The heroic age of security policy was over: the lion had departed, and the skills of the fox were more appropriate.

But, beyond the surface differences of tactics, the objectives were very much the same, as Mitterrand's 1986 book on foreign policy clearly demonstrates. The introduction presents with great clarity the mature French view of the transatlantic relationship. 'The worst danger', he argues, 'would be if America were to withdraw from the shores of our continent.' However, this does not

> at all affect my reservations about various aspects of United States policy … the forces of opposition, who seem to be shocked by the fact that one can here approve and there disapprove of our powerful ally, denounce as a contradiction which, in my eyes, constitutes the very coherence of our foreign policy. Really? Can one not, without provoking an outcry, criticise both the level of arms in the Soviet Union, and the interventions of the United States? Must France be limited to taking her choices from those of a master, or a model, and so give up being what the centuries have made her?[51]

In practical terms, once again, this means that France will make a free choice on the issues that confront her. If this choice sometimes leads her to positions similar to those of the United States, this is not 'Atlanticism', nor is the opposite true, either. There are a series of instances that demonstrate this clearly. In the case of Afghanistan, for example, both Giscard and Mitterrand condemned the Soviet invasion absolutely, but only the pursuit of an unreasoningly gratuitous anti-American policy would have led them to any other position. After all, international law and the rights of small nations were ideas that, in their view, were copyright in France anyway. Moreover, the historic antipathy between the Socialists and the PCF would have removed any possible hesitation Mitterrand might

51. François Mitterrand, *Réflexions sur la politique extérieure: Introduction à vingt-cinq discours* (1981–1985), Paris, Fayard, 1986, pp. 9–11.

have felt about criticising Moscow. Similarly, in the Gulf War, France rallied immediately to the side of the United States, because the same principles seemed to be under threat. French forces were freely put under command of the United States, and it is difficult to understand why anyone should have been surprised. In a war in Europe, France would have made a free decision to put its troops under American command, with some political limitations, and this was exactly what happened in the Gulf.

Had the United States attempted to order French participation, of course, the reaction would have been quite different. The converse also applies: French antipathy to American policy in Central America in the 1980s, like that of de Gaulle twenty years before, was based on traditional French foreign policy concerns and a feeling that candid criticism of an ally was acceptable, even when that ally is a superpower – not on a policy of deliberate hostility. The same factors applied to the French refusal to allow US aircraft to use French airspace in the 1985 bombing of Libya.

The most interesting example is that of the NATO decision to deploy American cruise and Pershing intermediate range missiles in Europe in the early 1980s. Mitterrand pressed his allies, including the Germans, to accept these missiles, in the face of overwhelming popular opposition. One might argue that, since France would not be taking any of the missiles anyway, this was an easy case to make; but there were wider factors at work also. The presence of the missiles in Europe made American involvement in any conflict more likely, and therefore corresponded to French policy concerns since 1919. If this caused unhappiness in other nations, that was unfortunate. Moreover, it is interesting that, whilst the various peace movements that sprang up throughout Europe were partly in response to the deteriorating international situation and the increased risk of war, much of the unhappiness was the perception that American missiles were being forced on Europe, without European control of them, and might be launched, in a fit of pique or absent-mindedness, by a president about whose judgement many had reservations. It is hardly necessary to add that these were very much the concerns that had led de Gaulle to demand the withdrawal of American nuclear weapons from France, and contributed to the 1966 decision. Ironically, it might be that France had no sizeable peace movement in the early 1980s because (to the extent that such a movement might have appeared in France anyway) it had been in the government for a quarter of a century already.

No one can write about these issues without a taste for symbolism, or without developing one. Thus, it is appropriate to end with the fiftieth anniversary, in 1990, of de Gaulle's first wartime broadcast from London. All day, a large mock-up of a radio set at the Arc de Triomphe broadcast the famous appeal, and the celebrations were led by none other than de Gaulle's bitterest enemy, now his successor as Nuclear Monarch, François Mitterrand. The 18 June 1940 and the 18 June 1990 are symbolically one: the creation of a model of France, its unity, its security, and its foreign relations can be regarded, as the French say, as *acquis*.

EPILOGUE

The Past and the Future

There is no simple way of approaching the question of how French governments will act in the defence and security area in the future: any firm predictions are likely to be wrong, since they will rapidly be falsified by changes of personnel or by external events. But there are certain political limits beyond which French governments are unlikely to go, unless, as between about 1940 and 1952, they have no choice in the matter. This concluding section looks at what kind of limits these might be.

A word of caution first. So tangled are the defence and security relationships between France and the Anglo-Saxon countries, so full of misunderstandings and sheer ignorance, that it is highly likely that any developments in French policy will be misinterpreted abroad, either in whole or in part. Thus, recent (1993) French moves to take part in NATO military committee discussions on peacekeeping in Yugoslavia were, it appears, interpreted abroad as a move back towards the principle of NATO integration. This is not the case, in fact, since the type of operation and the command arrangements envisaged are entirely different from those that provoked the split in the first place. The common-sense explanation, that France should be in any forum where decisions that affect her interests are being taken, has been ignored by some in favour of the hope that the fantasies of a repentant France begging for reintegration, entertained by some in London and Washington since 1966, may now be coming true. And conversely, there are those in Paris who seem more attached to the purely formalistic aspects of 'Gaullist' policies than to the logic underlying them. This may make it difficult for French policy-makers to adapt to new circumstances as quickly as they would like.

With these caveats, we can proceed to examine what limitations on future policies there may be. It may be worth, therefore, recalling the importance of 'meta-strategy' that I expressed in the Introduction, and trying to define the limits of the meta-strategic envelope in France today. By definition, this meta-strategy is nowhere summarised. It must be sought in pieces, and not in learned journals or in policy statements, but in schoolbooks, popular histories, the media, incidental statements by politicians, inscriptions on monuments, and a dozen other places where the French are talking informally to themselves, often in shorthand with the nuances left out. This is clearly a vast subject, even in relation to one nation alone, and what follow are only some examples and indications.

Thus, whilst the details of the Franco-German relationship and the future construction of Europe both cause problems for the professionals, the desirability of each has entered the collective French unconscious to a point where public pronouncements – say, the arrangements for a routine commemoration of the Liberation of Paris – will contain reflexive references to the centrality of the Franco-German *entente* and the importance of the European construction.[1] Similarly, for a view of the French self-image in the world, we might ignore official government statements for the moment and look elsewhere. Robert Gildea reports, for example, that the Gaullist 1984 election manifesto contained the following, reasonably pure, evocation of the universal mission:

> The impact and influence of France abroad are far greater than its economic or demographic weight in the contemporary world. This is probably due to the radiance of our culture, but it certainly cannot be separated from the fact that we are the land of the Declaration of the Rights of Man. In the domain of policies towards the Third World perhaps more than in any other, 'France oblige'.[2]

The importance of statements of this kind, or of Mitterrand's remark during a 1989 press conference that 'The role of France is to retain its rank',[3] lies precisely in their incidental, marginal quality. They are reasonably unreflecting manifestations of the informal meta-strategy, semi-automatic genuflections in the

1. All the mainstream French politicians who opposed the Maastricht Treaty were concerned to assure voters that, nonetheless, they were fully committed to Europe.

2. Robert Gildea, *The Past in French History*, London, Yale University Press, 1994, p. 153.

3. Ibid., p. 112.

direction of truths that are so obvious to all that they scarcely need to be articulated.

They derive, almost certainly, from a millennium of thinking about the very processes of history itself in a way that is difficult or impossible for Anglo-Saxons to appreciate. It is a teleological idea of history, expressed in such diverse ideas as the medieval view that the 'Second Coming' would be in France, and the modern belief that Europe has a destiny to fill, and that France's role is to conduct it there. The French idea of history as purposive process contrasts strongly with the Anglo-Saxon view of history as, in John Masefield's famous formulation, 'One Damned Thing After Another'. If there is a pattern and a destination to history, then there is a need for Michelet's 'pilot-nation of humanity', to ensure that history steers the correct course and arrives at the right destination. This nation is, of course, France. And it should be noted that the special status of France was always *granted*, first by God, and then by history: it did not need to be earned. It did not have to be demonstrated, it merely *was*. Thus, the heroic exploits of French chivalry were not qualifications for the special status of France and her king – they were proofs and tokens of it. Similarly, history had ordained that the 'Rights of Man' and the idea of the nation-state should be formulated in France, and spread by her armies. What are seen as the civilising actions of France since 1789, and the cultural, political and intellectual gifts presented to the world, are not qualifications for the status of pilot-nation, but rather proofs of it. Grandeur, great power status and the leadership of Europe do not have to be earned; they have been granted, and may always be assumed, irrespective of the sordid facts of economic, political and military power. It is only thus that we can make sense of the fact that, in 1991, 72 per cent of French people questioned thought that France was a great power, more than twice as many as in the United States, and almost three times as many as in Britain.[4]

This informal meta-strategy and cultural tendency to seek single truths described in the Introduction have produced a certain type of popular writing about history that is almost universal, and that has implications for how formal strategy will develop in the future. At the most basic level, history books still have a preference for a view of history made by 'Great Men', and built around

4. *L'Express*, February 1991, cited by Tristan Doelnitz, *La France hantée par sa puissance*, Paris, Belfond, 1993, p. 14.

'Great Events'. Whilst nuances unknown to Lavisse or Michelet have now been introduced, children's history books still tend to adopt a linear approach, beginning with Vercingétorix and ending with de Gaulle. And for adults, there are any number of popular history series with titles like 'The Kings who made France'. Those who stay at school until eighteen (the majority), have a range of books to help them study for the all-important *bac* exam. The history syllabus at the moment covers France and the world since 1945, and thus, implicitly, much of the subject matter of this present study. As is common in French education generally, the presentation is highly schematic and didactic, with potted biographies of important figures, and frequent use of 'points to retain' and 'general orientations', in bold type. The consistent, if slightly diffuse, view of the world that emerges is by now familiar. Although not necessarily uncritical of de Gaulle or of Gaullism, they depict a world in which weakness after 1945 led to American domination, the Fourth Republic was a failure, and de Gaulle arrived to restore independence and unity, only to be brought down by the events of May 1968.

The high status of the public service in France has produced massive competition, not just to enter ENA, but to carry out the preparatory studies at the *Sciences-Po*. In turn, this has produced a rash of handbooks to help pass the entry examinations themselves. Those concerned with the history test (which covers the history of this century) adopt much the same approach: methodological advice is followed by a series of model mini-essays giving the approved wisdom on the events of the period. And it should be noted that those who have been through this selection process and graduated from ENA are not only to be found in the public sector. They have also come to dominate political life, a good part of the media and much of the higher echelons of industry, to the extent that complaints about their dominance have started to be heard.[5]

The same general tendency can be seen at a more popular level. For example, Editions Marabout publish a series of multiple-choice tests on French history from the earliest times to the present day, aimed at the general reader. The organisation of the books would probably seem odd to us, since it assumes, again, a single answer to all historical questions, whether they are questions of fact, or, as often, questions of interpretation (such as whether the

5. See, for example, Thierry Pfister, *La république des fonctionnaires*, Paris, Albin Michel, 1988.

Evian accords were favourable, unfavourable or acceptable for France),[6] which Anglo-Saxons would expect to be treated in a judicious, balanced fashion, and not as yes-no questions. With a little determination, such books could be made to yield a complete, authorised interpretation of French history, assembled from questions and answers. The questions themselves are often mini-essays, incorporating assumptions that we might find questionable, such as: 'Military independence is the necessary corollary of political independence, and can scarcely be conceived of outside the nuclear context.' Or again: 'March 1959 saw the first demonstration of the Head of State's wish for independence from the American "partner". What was this event?' The answer – the withdrawal of the French Mediterranean fleet from NATO – is characterised as the 'first act which marked the desire of General de Gaulle to free France from servitude ... he had no intention of pledging the allegiance of the French military machine to American command'.[7]

The point of these citations is to emphasise how mundane are the ways in which the 'Gaullist' myth has found its way into the popular imagination. The authors of the texts described above would not, of course, regard themselves as propagandists, nor even as putting forward one viewpoint among many. They are simply presenting, in a summary fashion, 'the essential' of the story as they understand it to be, and as, no doubt, it was told to them.

The effect of all this is greatly to strengthen, in the minds of politicians, journalists, opinion formers and the general public, the broad outlines of the myth of fall and redemption, of weakness followed by recovery, of servitude replaced by freedom – which is in any case a popular one, for reasons described in the last chapter. In addition, history itself will periodically furnish the raw material to renew the myth itself, and the myth is so powerful that it can accommodate almost anything to itself. Thus, anyone in Paris doubting the wisdom of de Gaulle's 1966 decision might have been persuaded by the so-called Soames affair three years later. The facts are not completely clear; but it seems that, in early 1969, de Gaulle and the British ambassador, Sir Christopher Soames, discussed the future of Franco-British relations, and de Gaulle spoke of political and defence co-operation between France, Britain, Germany and Italy, outside the context of the EEC, which Britain was

6. Favourable.
7. Both from *300 questions tests sur l'Histoire de France: La Ve République*, Alleur, Editions Marabout, 1992.

then trying to join. NATO would continue for a time, but eventually Europe would have to organise its own defence. Would the British like to discuss this further? There was no French record of the discussions, but the French informally confirmed the accuracy of the British one. Such was the distrust of the general, that London feared a trap, and decided to inform France's EEC partners, as well as the United States. De Gaulle was furious. In a response that Bernard Ledwidge, then minister at the embassy, describes as 'extraordinary', the Foreign Office then issued the full text of Soames's record to the media, claiming that it was an agreed record, and accompanied it with guidance suggesting that de Gaulle was trying to break up both NATO and the EEC.[8] What de Gaulle was after will never be known, and the incident simply confirmed yet again, in French eyes, the faithlessness of nominal allies.

The Soames affair, however mysterious, was at least a real event. By contrast, a much more recent example of the same thing never even happened. In May 1991, the NATO Defence Planning Committee agreed to the formation of the Allied Command Europe Rapid Reaction Force, under British command, and with a large British contingent. The French did not sit on the DPC, and were thus not involved. News of the decision was greeted with fury in Paris, where it was alleged, both privately and publicly, that the British, with their usual cynical ruthlessness, had masterminded a plot to sideline the French, ensure that reaction forces were under British leadership, and rule out French participation. It was also assumed to be a move in the political union negotiations then under way. There was no truth in any of these assertions, but the memory of past betrayals by the British, real or imaginary, was so strong, that the informal meta-strategy was able seamlessly to incorporate this non-existent incident into a pre-existing pattern. And of course the memory of *this* betrayal becomes a factor in judgements to be made in the future: history, in other words, becomes an ingredient of history, in an endlessly self-referential cycle.

In the light of all these factors, there is very little incentive for any future French government to give up 'Gaullist' orientations, in the sense in which I defined them in the previous chapter. It is worth pausing a moment, however, to appreciate the range of possibilities that are, nonetheless, available without compromising the basic policy. Improved relations with the United States and

8. Bernard Ledwidge, *De Gaulle*, London, Weidenfeld and Nicolson, 1982, pp. 363–7.

with the NATO integrated structure are not a betrayal of Gaullism: they are what every French government since de Gaulle has wanted. Closer bilateral co-operation with the United Kingdom has had the same status. The French would be prepared for much closer co-operation with NATO structures, and for their troops to come under American command as they did in the Gulf, provided this is a free decision and not a compelled one. No foreseeable French government will come back into the integrated military structure, since that would be to accept 'American command' once more; but the degree of flexibility available in Paris in future years will surprise those still wedded to 'Vulgar Gaullism' as an interpretation of French policy.

In any event, after decades of waiting, things may actually be going France's way. The degree to which the 'Gaullist' model, not only of France, but of Europe, has been convincing, has depended on how the future is seen, and this changes all the time. A decade or so ago, during the winter of the second Cold War, it was easy to write off de Gaulle's visions (and therefore traditional French concerns) as fantasies, and to take the rather cool view of his initiatives that Jean Lacouture did in his biography. Who, after all, could take 'Gaullist' notions seriously, when they included a reunited Germany, an Eastern Europe free from Soviet influence, an end to the Soviet Union itself, a United States less militarily influential and perhaps going home, an end to the system of *blocs*, and a Europe with a genuine security and defence identity, with armed forces not beholden to NATO, and thus to the United States? Of course, we are not there yet, and it might in time be shown that de Gaulle's analysis, as opposed to his assumptions, was quite wrong.

These postulates – some objectives, others not necessarily wished for – are not, of course, peculiar to de Gaulle, and many antedate his time in power. The 'Gaullist' model – to use that phrase for the last time – is perhaps, after many decades of wandering and hardship, about to come into its inheritance. Certainly, as the European integration process proceeds, and as Europe increasingly acquires a security and defence identity, France emerges, not as the natural leader, perhaps, but as the natural point of contact, especially for the United States. In the defence and security field, and as long as the Franco-German axis endures, France is able both to interpret European thinking and to lead it, in a way in which the British, the 'loyal courtiers', have never claimed to be able to do.

In any event, one can assume that the French will, in the future as in the past, combine tactical flexibility with a few simple, long-range objectives. They will continue to see their history as that of a nation with a high destiny, constantly betrayed by disunity and the jealousy of less fortunate nations; and they will continue to interpret unfolding events in the light of these assumptions. Many of their tactical shifts will appear far more significant to Anglo-Saxons than they really are, whilst their long-term goals will continue to seem irritatingly nebulous. Opportunities for mutual incomprehension are by no means exhausted yet.

BIBLIOGRAPHY

PRINTED PRIMARY SOURCES

French

Assemblée Nationale, Document No 2344 (1947), *Rapport ... sur les événements survenus en France de 1933 à 1945*, 8 vols, Paris, Imprimeries de l'Assemblée Nationale, 1951.

Imprimerie des Journaux Officiels, *Procès du Maréchal Pétain*, Paris, 1945.

Ministère des affaires étrangères, *Documents diplomatiques: Documents relatifs au négotiations conçernant les garanties de sécurité contre une aggression de l'Allemagne, 10 janvier 1919–7 décembre 1923*, Paris, Imprimerie nationale, 1924.

—— *Documents diplomatiques: Conférence de Washington, juillet 1921–février 1922*, Paris, Imprimerie nationale, 1923.

—— Commission de publication des documents relatifs aux origines de la guerre 1939–45, *Documents diplomatiqes français, 1932–1939*, Paris, Imprimerie nationale, 1964–1986.

—— Commission de publication des documents diplomatiques francais 1954–, *Documents diplomatiques français, 1954–*, Paris, Imprimerie nationale, 1987–.

British

Documents on British Policy Overseas, London, Her Majesty's Stationery Office, 1984–.

Documents on British Foreign Policy 1919–1939, London, Her Majesty's Stationery Office, 1964–1986.

U.S.

Department of State, *Papers Relating to the Foreign Relations of the United States, Washington, US Government Printing Office*, 1861–.

SECONDARY SOURCES

—— *L'Élection du Chef d'état en France de Hugues Capet à nos jours*, Paris, Beauchesne, 1988.

Adamthwaite, Anthony, *France and the Coming of the Second World War, 1936–1939*, London, Frank Cass, 1977.

—— *The Lost Peace: International Relations in Europe 1918–1939*, London, Edward Arnold, 1980.

Albrecht-Carrié, René, *France, Europe and the Two World Wars*, New York, Harper, 1961.

Alexander, Martin M., *The Republic in Danger: General Maurice Gamelin and the Politics of French Defence 1933–1940*, Cambridge, Cambridge University Press, 1992.

Allmand, Christopher, *The Hundred Years War: England and France at War c. 1300–c. 1450*, Cambridge, Cambridge University Press, 1989.

Azéma, Jean-Pierre, *From Munich to the Liberation, 1938–1944*, trans. Janet Lloyd, Cambridge, Cambridge University Press, 1984.

—— and Winock, Michel, *La Troisième République*, Paris, Calman-Levy, 1970.

Bankwitz, Philip Charles Farwell, *Maxim Weygand and Civil-Military Relations in Modern France*, Cambridge, Massachusets, Harvard University, Press, 1967.

Barbas, Jean-Claude, ed., *Philippe Pétain, Discours aux Français: 17 juin 1940–20 aout 1944*, Paris, Albin Michel, 1989.

Beaufre, General Andre, *1940: The Fall of France*, trans. D. Flower, London, Cassell, 1965.

—— *NATO and Europe*, trans. Joseph Green and R. H. Barry, London, Faber and Faber, 1967.

Behrens, C.B.A, *The Ancien Régime*, London, Thames and Hudson, 1967.

Bernard, Philippe and Dubief, Henri, *The Decline of the Third Republic 1914–1938*, trans. A. Foster, Cambridge, Cambridge University Press, 1988.

Bernier, Oliver, *Fireworks at Dusk: Paris in the Thirties*, London, Little, Brown and Company, 1993.

Best, Geoffrey, ed., *The Permanent Revolution: The French Revolution and its Legacy 1789–1989*, London, Fontana, 1988.

Bialer, Uri, *The Shadow of the Bomber: The Fear of Air Attack and British Politics 1932–1939*, London, Royal Historical Society, 1980.

Bloch, Mark, *L'Étrange défaite: Témoinage écrit en 1940*, new edn, Paris, Gallimard, 1990

Bluche, Francois *Louis XIV*, trans. Mark Greengrass, Oxford, Basil Blackwell, 1990.

Bonnet, George, *Quai d'Orsay*, Isle of Man, Times Press and Anthony Gibbs and Phillips, 1965.

Bond, Brian, *Britain, France and Belgium 1939–1940*, 2nd edn, London, Brassey's 1990.

Bozo, Frédéric, *La France et L'OTAN: De la guerre froide au nouvel ordre européen*, Paris, Masson, 1991.

Bullitt, Orville H., *For the President, Personal and Secret: Correspondence Between Franklin D. Roosevelt and William C. Bullitt*, London, Andre Deutsch, 1973.

Burke, Peter, *The Fabrication of Louis XIV*, London, Yale University Press, 1992.

Camus, Albert, *The Myth of Sisyphus*, trans. Justin O'Brien, London, Hamish Hamilton, 1955, Penguin edn, 1975.

—— *The Plague*, trans. Stuart Gilbert, London, Hamish Hamilton, 1948, Penguin edn, 1960.

—— *The Rebel*, trans. Anthony Bower, London, Hamish Hamilton, 1953, Penguin edn, 1971.

Cerny, Philip G., *The Politics of Grandeur: Ideological Aspects of de Gaulle's foreign policy*, Cambridge, Cambridge University Press, 1980.

Chantebout, Bernard, *L'Organisation générale de la défense nationale en France depuis la fin de la Seconde Guerre Mondiale*, Paris, Librairie Générale de droit et de jurisprudence, 1967.

Chebel D'Appollonia, Ariane, *L'extrême-droite en France: de Maurrass à Le Pen*, Brussels, Editions Complexe, 1988.

Chenais, François, and Serfait, Claude, *L'armement en France: genèse, coût et ampleur d'une industrie*, Paris, Nathan, 1992.

Citron, Suzanne, *Le Mythe nationale: L'histoire de France en question*, Paris, Les Editions Ouvrières/Études et Documentations internationales, 1991.

Cohen, Samy, *La Monarchie nucléaire: Les coulisse de la politique étrangère sous la Ve République*, Paris, Hachette, 1986.

—— *Le défaite des généraux: Le pouvoir politique et l'armée sous la Ve Republique*, Paris, Fayard, 1994.

Cohen-Solal, Annie, *Sartre: A Life*, London, Heinemann, 1987.

Cohn, Norman, *Warrant for Genocide: The Myth of the Jewish World-Conspiracy and the Protocols of the Elders of Zion*, London, Eyre and Spottiswoode, 1967, Penguin edn, 1970.

Colville, Sir John, *The Fringes of Power: Downing Street Diaries 1939–1955*, London, Hodder and Stoughton, 1985.

Coutau-Begarie, Hervé and Huan, Claude, *Darlan*, Paris, Fayard, 1989.

Crémieux-Brilhac, Jean-Louis, *Les Français de l'an 40*, 2 vols, Paris, Gallimard, 1990.

De Beauvoir, Simone, *The Prime of Life*, trans. Peter Green, London, Andre Deutsch and Weidenfeld and Nicolson, 1962, Penguin edn, 1965.

—— *Force of Circumstance*, trans. Richard Howard, London, Andre Deutsch and Weidenfeld and Nicolson, 1965, Penguin edn, 1968.

De Gaulle, Charles *The Army of the Future*, London, Hutchinson, 1940.

—— *War Memoirs Vol. 1: The Call to Honour 1940–42*, trans. Jonathan Griffin, London, Collins, 1955.

—— *War Memoirs Vol. 2: Unity 1942–1944*, trans. Richard Howard, London, Weidenfeld and Nicolson, 1959.

De La Gorce, Paul Marie, *The French Army: A Military-Political History*, trans. Kenneth Douglas, London, Weidenfeld and Nicolson, 1963.

—— *L'Après-guerre 1944–1952, Naissance de la France moderne*, Paris, Grosser, 1978.

De La Saussay, Francois, *L'Héritage institutionel français 1789–1958*, Paris, Hachette, 1992.

Debbasch, Charles and Pontier, Jean-Marie, *Les Constitutions de la France*, Paris, Dalloz, 1989.

Debray, Regis, *À Demain de Gaulle*, Paris, Gallimard, 1990.

Debré, Michel, *Trois Républiques pour une France: Mémoires*, Paris, Albin Michel, 1984.

—— *Agir*, Paris Albin Michel, 1988.

Destremau, Bernard, *Quai d'Orsay: derrière la façade*, Paris, Plon, 1994.

Doelnitz, Tristan, *La France hantée par sa puissance*, Paris, Belfond, 1993.

Doise, Jean, and Vaisse, Maurice, *Diplomatie et outil militaire*, Paris, Imprimerie Nationale, 1987.

Dumamel, Alain, *De Gaulle-Mitterand: La marque et la trace*, Paris, Flammarion, 1991.

Duroselle, Jean Baptiste, *Politique Etrangèere de la France: La Décadence 1932-1939*, Paris, Imprimerie Nationale, 1979

—— *Politique Etrangère de la France: L'Abîme 1939–44*, Paris, Imprimerie Nationale, 1986.

—— *Clemenceau*, Paris, Fayard, 1988.

Duval, Marcel and Le Baut, Yves, *L'arme nucléaire française: pourquoi et comment?*, Paris, SPM/Kronos, 1992.

Edwards, Jill, *The British Government and the Spanish Civil War, 1936–1939*, London, Macmillan, 1979.

Emerson, James Thomas, *The Rhineland Crisis, 7 March 1936: A Study in Multilateral Diplomacy*, London, Maurice Temple Smith, 1977.

Etzold, Thomas H and Gaddis, John Lewis, eds., *Containment: Documents on American Policy and Strategy 1945–1950*, New York, Columbia University Press, 1978.

Ferro, Marc, *Pétain*, Paris, Fayard, 1987.

Fonvielle-Alqmer, Francois, *The French and the Phoney War 1939–40*; trans. and with an introd. by Edward Ashcroft, London, Tom Stacey, 1971.

Foldscheid, Dominique, and Wunenburger, Jean-Jacques, *Méthodologie philosophique*, Paris, Presses Universitaires de France, 1992.

Foucault, Michel, *Discipline and Punish*, trans. Alan Sheridan, London, Allen Lane, 1977, Penguin edn, 1991.

Gamelin, General Maurice, *Servir*, 3 vols, Paris, Plon, 1946.

Gildea, Robert, *The Past in French History*, London, Yale University Press, 1994.

Gill, Rosemary H., *Political Thought in the Court of Charles V of France, 1346–80*, Unpublished Ph. D. thesis, University of London, 1987/88.

Girardet, Raoul, *Le nationalisme français, Anthologie 1871–1914*, Paris, Seuil, 1983.

—— *Mythes et mythologies politiques*, Paris, Seuil, 1986.

——, ed., *La Crise militaire française 1945–1962: Aspects sociologiques et idéologiques*, Paris, Armand Colin, 1964.

Gordon, Philip, *A Certain Idea of France: French Security Policy and the Gaullist Legacy*, Princeton, Princeton University Press, 1993.

Griffiths, Richard, *Marshal Pétain*, London, Constable, 1970.

Grosser, Alfred, *La IVe République et sa politique extérieure*, Paris, Armand Colin, 3rd edn, rev., 1972.

—— *Affaires exteriéures: La politique de la France 1944–1989*, Paris, Flammarion, 1989.

Harrison, Michael M., *The Reluctant Ally: France and Atlantic Security*, Baltimore, Maryland, Johns Hopkins Press, 1981.

Heuser, Beatrice, *Western 'Containment' Policies in the Cold War: The Yugoslav Case 1948–1953*, London, Routledge, 1989.

Horne, Alistair, *The French Army and Politics, 1870–1970*, London, Macmillian, 1982.

—— *To Lose a Battle: France 1940*, London, Macmillan, 1969, Penguin edn, 1979,

Howorth, Jolyon, and Chilton, Patricia, eds., *Defence and Dissent in Contemporary France*, London, Croom Helm, 1984.

Hughes, Judith, *To the Maginot Line: The Politics of French Military Preparation in the 1920s*, Cambridge, Massachuesets, Harvard University Press, 1971.

Hurstfield, Julian G., *America and the French Nation, 1939–1945*, London, University of North Carolina Press, 1986.

Jackson, Julian, *The Popular Front in France: Defending Democracy, 1934–1938*, Cambridge, Cambridge University Press, 1988.

Jonas, Raymond A., 'Constructing Moral Order: The Sacré Coeur as an Exercise in National Regeneration', in *Proceedings of the Annual Meeting of the Western Society for French History*, XIX, 1992, pp. 191–201.

Jordan, Robert S., *The NATO International Staff/Secretariat: A study in International Administration*, London, Oxford University Press, 1967.

Kedward, H.R., *The Dreyfus Affair: Catalyst for Tensions in French Society*, London, Longmans, 1965.

—— *Resistance in Vichy France: A Study of Ideas and Motivation in the Southern Zone 1940–1942*, Oxford, Oxford University Press, 1978.

—— and Austin, Roger, eds., *Vichy France and the Resistance: Culture and Ideology*, London, Croom Helm, 1975.

Lacouture, Jean, *Léon Blum*, Paris, Seuil, rev. edn, 1979.

—— *Pierre Mendès-France*, trans. George Holoch, London, Holmes and Meier, 1984.

—— *De Gaulle*, 3 vols, Paris, Seuil, 1984–86.

Lacroix-Riz, Annie, *Le Choix de Marianne: Les relations Franco-américains de la Libération aux debuts du plan Marshall (1944–1948)*, Paris, Messidor/Editions Sociales, 1985.

Ledwidge, Bernard, *De Gaulle*, London, Weidenfeld and Nicholson, 1982.

Leffler, Melvyn P., *The Elusive Quest: America's Pursuit of European Stability and French Security, 1919–1933*, Chapel Hill, University of North Carolina Press, 1979.

Lotman, Herbert R., *The People's Anger: Justice and Revenge in Post-Liberation France*, London, Hutchinson, 1986.

—— *The Left Bank: Writers, Artists and Politics from the Popular Front to the Cold War*, London, Heinemann, 1982.

Luckas, John, *The Last European War, September 1939–December 1941*, London, Routledge and Kegan Paul, 1976 (actually 1977).

Magraw, Roger, *France 1815–1914, The Bourgeois Century*, London, Fontana, 1983.

Martin, Marie-Madeline, *Histoire de l'Unité Française: L'idée de Patrie en France des origines à nos jours*, Paris, Presses Universitaires de la France, new edn, 1982.

Mayer, Arno J., *Politics and Diplomacy of Peacekeeping: Containment and Counterrevolution at Versailles, 1918–1919*, London, Weidenfeld and Nicolson, 1968.

Michel, Henri, *The Shadow War: Resistance in Europe 1939–1945*, trans. Richard Barry, London, André Deutsch, 1972.

—— and Mirkine-Guetzevitch, Boris, *Les Idées politiques et sociales de la Résistance: Documents clandestins, 1940–1944*, Paris, Presses Universitaires de la France, 1954.

Mitterand, Francois, *Le coup d'État permanent*, Paris, Plon, 1964.

—— *Réflexions sur la politique extérieure de la France: Introduction a vingt-cinq discours (1981–1985)*, Paris, Fayard, 1986.

Nere, J., *The Foreign Policy of France from 1914 to 1945*, London, Routledge and Kegan Paul, 1975.

Nobecourt, Jacques, *Une Histoire politique de l'Armée, 1919–1942: de Pétain à Pétain*, Paris, Seuil, 1967.

Novick, Peter, *The Resistance Versus Vichy: The Purge of Collaborators in Liberated France*, London, Chatto and Windus, 1968.

Ory, Pascal, *Les Collaborateurs 1940–1945*, Paris, Seuil, 1976.

Parker, R.A.C., *Chamberlain and Appeasement: British Policy and the Coming of the Second World War*, London, Macmillan, 1993.

Paxton, Robert O., *Parades and Politics at Vichy: The French Officer Corps under Marshall Pétain*, Princeton, Princeton University Press, 1966.

—— *Vichy France: Old Guard and New Order, 1940–1944*, London, Barrie and Jenkins, 1972.

Perrol, Gilbert, *La grandeur de la France*, Paris, Albin Michel, 1992.

Pfister, Thierry, *La république des fonctionnaires*, Paris, Albin Michel, 1988.

Planchais, Jean, *Une Histoire Politique de l'Armée, 1940–1967: de de Gaulle à de Gaulle*, Paris, Seuil, 1967.

Plessis, Alain, *The Rise and Fall of the Second Empire, 1952-1871*, trans. Jonathan Mandelbaum, Cambridge, Cambridge University Press, 1988.

Reid, Escott, *Time of Fear and Hope: The Making of the North Atlantic Treaty 1947–1949*, Toronto, Macmillan and Stewart, 1977.

Rémy, Dominique, ed., *Les lois de Vichy: Actes dits 'lois' de l'autorité de fait se prétendant 'gouvernement de l'État français'*, 2nd edn, Paris, Romillat, 1992.

Reynaud, Paul, *La France a sauvé l'Europe*, 2 vols, Paris, Flammarion, 1947.

Rioux, Jean-Pierre, *The Fourth Republic, 1944–1958*, Cambridge, Cambridge University Press, 1987.

Rossi-Landi, Guy, *La Drôle de Guerre, la vie politique en France 2 septembre 1939–10 mai 1940*, Paris, Armand Colin, 1971.

Rousseau, Jean-Jacques, *The Social Contract and Discourses*, trans. G.D.H. Cole, Dent, London, new edn, 1973.

Rousso, Henri, The *Vichy Syndrome: History and Memory in France since 1944*, trans. Arthur Goldhammer, London, Harvard University Press, 1991.

Rudé, George, *Robespiere: Portrait of a Revolutionary Democrat*, London, Collins, 1975.

Sartre, Jean-Paul *L'existentialisme est un humanisme*, Paris, Nagel, 1946.

——— *The Age of Reason*, trans. Eric Sutton, London, Hamish Hamilton 1947, Penguin edn, 1961.

——— *The Reprieve*, trans. Eric Sutton, London, Hamish Hamilton, 1947, rev (Penguin) trans., 1963.

——— *Iron in the Soul*, trans. Gerald Hopkins, London, Hamish Hamilton, 1950, Penguin edn, 1963.

——— *Altona and Other Plays*, various trans., London, Penguin 1962.

Sharp, Alan, *The Versailles Settlement: Peacemaking in Paris 1919*, London, Macmillan, 1991.

Shennan, Andrew, *Rethinking France: Plans for Renewal, 1940–1946*, Oxford, Clarendon Press, 1989.

Sieyes, Emmanuel, *Qu'est-ce que le Tiers état: édition critique avec une introduction et des notes par Roberto Zapperi*, Geneva, Droz, 1970.

Silverlight, John, *The Victors' Dilemma: Allied Intervention in the Russian Civil War*, London, Barrie and Jenkins, 1970.

Soutou, Georges-Henri, 'La politique nucléaire de Pierre Mendès-France', in *Relations internationales*, No. 59, Autumn 1989, pp. 317–30.

Talbot, John, *The War Without an Name: France in Algeria, 1954–1962*, London, Faber and Faber 1981.

Talmon, J.L., *The Origins of Totalitarian Democracy*, Penguin edn, London, 1986.

Temperley, H. W. V., ed., *A History of the Peace Conference of Paris*, 5 vols, London, Hodder and Stoughton, and Oxford, Oxford University Press, 1920.

Tessier, George, *Le Baptême de Clovis*, Paris, Gallimard, 1964.

Thomas, R. T., *Britain and Vichy: The Dilemma of Anglo-French Relations, 1940–1942*, London, Macmillan, 1979.

Tissier, Pierre, *The Riom Trial*, London, Harrap, 1942.

Todorov, Tristan, *Nous et les autres: La réflexion française sur la diversité humaine*, Paris, Seuil, 1989.

Tulard, Jean, *Napoleon: The Myth of the Saviour*, trans. Teresa Waugh, London, Weidenfeld and Nicolson, 1984.

Vaisse, Maurice, 'Aux origines du mémorandum de septembre 1958', in *Relations internationales*, No. 58, Summer 1989, pp. 253–68.

Wall, Irwin, *The United States and the Making of Postwar France 1945–1954*, Cambridge, Cambridge University Press, 1991.

Walworth, Arthur, *Wilson and his Peacemakers: American Diplomacy at the Paris Peace Conference, 1919*, London, W. W. Norton, 1983.

Warner, Geoffrey, *Pierre Laval and the Eclipse of France*, London, Eyre and Spottiswoode, 1968.

Warner, Marina, *Joan of Arc: The Image of Female Heroism*, London, Weidenfeld and Nicolson 1981, Penguin edn, 1983.

Watson, David Robin, *Georges Clemenceau: A Political Biography*, London, Eyre Methuen, 1974.

Watt, D.C., *How War Came: The Immediate Origins of the Second World War, 1938–1939*, London, Heinemann, 1989.

Weygand, General Maxime, *Recalled to Service: The Memoirs of Général Maxime Weygand of the Academie Française*, trans. E. W. Dickes, London, Heinemmann, 1952.

Williams, Philip M., *Crisis and Compromise: Politics in the Fourth Republic*, London, Longmans, 1964.

Winock, Michel, ed., *Histoire de l'extrème droite en France*, Paris, Seuil, 1993.

Woodward, Sir Llewellyn,*British Foreign Policy in the Second World War*, London, Her Majesty's Stationery Office, 5 vols 1970–76.

Yates, Frances A, *Astrea: The Imperial Theme in the Sixteenth Century*, London, Routledge and Kegan Paul, 1971.

Young, John W, *France, the Cold War and the Western Alliance, 1944–49: French Foreign Policy and Post-War Europe*, London, Leicester University Press, 1990.

Zeldin, Theodore, *France 1848–1945*, 2 vols, Oxford, Oxford University Press, 1973.

INDEX